I0817044

SCRIPTURE IN DOCTRINAL DISPUTE

DOCTRINE AND SCRIPTURE IN EARLY CHRISTIANITY

SCRIPTURE IN DOCTRINAL DISPUTE

FRANCES M. YOUNG

WILLIAM B. EERDMANS PUBLISHING COMPANY
GRAND RAPIDS, MICHIGAN

Wm. B. Eerdmans Publishing Co.
4035 Park East Court SE, Grand Rapids, Michigan 49546
www.eerdmans.com

Published 2024

Book design by Lydia Hall

Printed in the United States of America

30 29 28 27 26 25 24 1 2 3 4 5 6 7

ISBN 978-0-8028-8299-8

Library of Congress Cataloging-in-Publication Data

A catalog record for this book is available from the Library of Congress.

To all who along the way have opened my eyes

Contents

Foreword

It is a rare experience to be able to witness the creation of a *magnum opus* step by step. Beginning slowly before the Covid-19 pandemic, increasing in frequency during it, and now finally completed, I have been receiving from the author chapter after chapter of *Doctrine and Scripture in Early Christianity*. It has been a scholarly, historical, hermeneutical, theological, and spiritual feast. It has also been a culmination to Frances Young's *oeuvre*, whose range and depth were already astonishing, embracing biblical studies, early Christian history, literature and theology, ecumenical and interreligious engagement, theological method, contemporary Christian theology on all the main doctrines, theology and disability, spirituality, preaching, and poetry. Yet that is not all.

A Magisterial, Field-Encompassing Culmination

The originality and long-term importance of the present two volumes is in their core achievement: they bring to a critical and constructive culmination more than two centuries of modern scholarly and theological engagement with the early centuries of Christianity. Those early, identity-forming centuries are still of immense significance for more than two billion Christians in the twenty-first century—above all through giving them their core text, the Bible, but also through showing how earlier Christians worked out basic, long-lasting ways to understand the Bible and discern its essentials for Christian life and thought.

Yet recent centuries have also delivered one shock after another to mainstream, traditional Christian ways of reading the Bible and of receiving the history and theology of the early church. In volume 1 Frances Young gives some account of this radical shaking, and she is alert to it through both volumes. She describes the responses to it by such figures as John Henry Newman and Adolf von Harnack and acutely analyzes their inadequacies. She then sets herself the massive task of giving better answers to the fundamental questions:

> Is it possible to construct a new account of the arguments that produced dogmatic discourse, particularly of the ways in which appeals to scripture functioned as new questions were raised? Can we find another way of telling the story that acknowledges that, in the process of forming a distinct identity, there is inevitable tension between "acculturation" on the one hand, and, on the other, self-conscious challenge to the all-pervasive cultural milieu—this challenge, in the case of the early Christians, being grounded in certain key convictions ultimately deriving from scripture? These two volumes on *Doctrine and Scripture in Early Christianity* constitute a perhaps rash attempt to produce such an account. . . .
>
> Then, maybe, through the dynamic of an "ethical reading,"[1] which respects the text while acknowledging the tension between the reader's difference from and identification with the material in view, we may find insights that might affirm or challenge our own hermeneutics and our own use of scripture in doctrinal and ethical debate—after all, as Newman noted, Christians have always engaged in justifying their theological and ethical commitments from scripture. Can we clear a path through early Christian argument by recognizing how the definition of doctrine was a process of making sense of scripture in terms of the rationality of that time? And then, perhaps, make a parallel journey of sensemaking in our very different intellectual context . . . ? (12–13 in volume 1)

All her academic life Frances Young has wrestled with such questions, refusing to avoid their immense complexity and implications, not least for Christian living and thinking today. She has circled around them, approaching them from one angle after another, and she has discerned more and more clearly how to respond to them with both scholarly and theological integrity

1. For "ethical reading" see Frances Young, "The Pastoral Epistles and the Ethics of Reading," *JSNT* 45 (1992): 105–20; and "Allegory and the Ethics of Reading," in *The Open Text: New Directions for Biblical Studies?*, ed. Francis Watson (London: SCM, 1993). In her introduction to *God's Presence* (see below) she describes "ethical reading" as "being as true as possible to texts from the past, while also being true to ourselves" (1).

and wisdom. She has written articles and monographs that have opened fresh ways of engaging with them and has written textbooks and edited authoritative works of reference that helped to define and shape the field.[2] And the field to which she is contributing is far wider than that of the early church and its thinking: in particular, she has something vital to say to any Christian theology that wants to draw on the Bible in its thinking today and to practice faith seeking understanding.

Now, finally, these summative volumes give a rich, mature account of how in the twenty-first century we can both learn the many lessons and avoid the many pitfalls of recent centuries, in order to arrive at a retrieval of early Christianity that rings true with thorough scholarship, sophisticated hermeneutics, and theological wisdom.[3] Not only is the time right for her to distill her understanding from a lifetime in the field, which began as a classicist steeped in the history and culture of the early Christian centuries in the Hellenistic world. The time is also ripe for the field of early Christian life and thought, which has been much divided by different disciplinary approaches and by conflicts of many sorts, to be given a detailed yet coherent response to those key questions she identifies. There is probably no one else in the field so well equipped to do so, and this is probably also the first time in recent centuries

2. Specifically on scripture and doctrine, her main specialist books relating to early Christianity have been *Biblical Exegesis and the Formation of Christian Culture* (Cambridge: Cambridge University Press, 1997); *Exegesis and Theology in Early Christianity* (Farnham: Ashgate, 2012); and *Ways of Reading Scripture: Collected Papers* (Tübingen: Mohr Siebeck, 2018). Her principal textbooks and works of reference are *From Nicaea to Chalcedon* (London: SCM, 1983; 2nd ed. 2010); *The Making of the Creeds* (London: SCM, 1991); *The Cambridge History of Early Christian Literature*, coedited with Lewis Ayres and Andrew Louth (Cambridge: Cambridge University Press, 2004); and *The Cambridge History of Christianity*, vol. 1, coedited with Margaret M. Mitchell (Cambridge: Cambridge University Press, 2006).

3. A key event in my own theological formation was a five-year collaboration in teaching and writing about Paul's second letter to the Corinthians, which resulted in our coauthored work, Frances M. Young and David F. Ford, *Meaning and Truth in 2 Corinthians* (London: SPCK, 1987). That work's interweaving of scholarship, hermeneutics, theology, and spirituality, developed in conversation with Frances Young, has informed my thinking since then. During the final years of work on *The Gospel of John: A Theological Commentary* (Grand Rapids: Baker Academic, 2021), I was reading *Doctrine and Scripture in Early Christianity* as it was being written, and it is part of the hidden background of the commentary. One way of seeing the commentary is as an attempt to combine scholarship, hermeneutics, theology, and spirituality by interpreting the Gospel of John (which has probably been the single Christian biblical text that has most deeply shaped Christian thinking) in ways that have learned from Frances Young's *oeuvre*. As she says in the preface to her second volume, "this work would appear to endorse the recent turn to theological commentaries on biblical texts."

that there are the scholarly, hermeneutical, and theological resources available to let it be done convincingly.

The result is a magisterial achievement by one person that is also epochal in its significance for the field. Frances Young, who is not only steeped in the modern field of early Christian studies but also acutely aware of its inadequacies and its fragmentation, has produced a fresh, rigorous, and deep integration of it that can act as the paradigm best suited to understanding it today. It is to be hoped that these volumes will soon become a standard textbook for those studying early Christianity during the rest of this century.

An Earlier Culmination: God's Presence—a Contemporary Recapitulation of Early Christianity

Doctrine and Scripture in Early Christianity is not the first culminating work by Frances Young. A decade ago she published *God's Presence: A Contemporary Recapitulation of Early Christianity*.[4] That too is summative, but with a central concern for intelligent, imaginative, and wise Christian faith today, arising out of dialogue with the leading teachers of the early church.

God's Presence is essential reading if one is to understand the extensive twenty-first-century implications of the present two volumes. Rowan Williams says of it:

> No-one but Frances Young could have written a book like this. It combines an immense professional expertise in the literature of early Christianity with intense personal and pastoral reflection, an insightful perspective on contemporary theological concerns, and an interweaving of sermons and poetic meditations that remind us of Frances' stature as a spiritual guide. It is a book of exceptional human maturity as well as intellectual challenge. Frances Young has always combined these elements in a rare way, but this book is a summation of all that has been most fruitful and nourishing in both her academic and her pastoral ministry. It is a treasury of real wisdom, both authoritative and vulnerable.[5]

God's Presence is a lively, attractive account of how one can be alert simultaneously both to two millennia of Christian life and thought and also to such

4. Cambridge: Cambridge University Press, 2013.
5. From the cover.

recent factors as developments in the natural and human sciences; challenges of modern and postmodern hermeneutics of suspicion; new forms of interreligious engagement; feminism; racism; and big changes in politics, economics, technology, and warfare. The book is a rewritten and expanded version of Frances Young's acclaimed Bampton Lectures at Oxford University, and, like *Doctrine and Scripture in Early Christianity*, it is a search for integration with integrity in the course of a journey through modernity into whatever we might call the twenty-first century—"late modernity"? "post-modernity"? "chastened modernity"? The integration sought is not just intellectual but also embraces church life,[6] public life,[7] and personal life.[8] Seeking to do justice to these leads her into daring to communicate through ways less conventionally academic, such as poetry, storytelling, the visual arts, prayer, liturgy, sacramental spirituality, personal testimony, "snapshots" of everyday living, and preaching.

All of this is in line with what she draws on again and again: the history and theology of the early centuries of Christianity. She summarizes the recurrent motifs rooted there as "reading of the Bible as essentially a transformative text"; God's creativity and human creatureliness; "the wisdom of intellectual humility"; the transcendent God working "through particularities and the constraints of history, paradoxically exercising power through weakness"; "the sacramental perspective which seems to shape and unite the incarnation, the scriptures as Word of God, the eucharist, the church, enabling discernment of the Creator through the creation, of the Spirit in ordinary, physical dailiness, of God in God's human image and the human community of the Body of Christ"; the overarching narrative of fall and redemption with all its ambiguities, and its realism about how things go wrong; true love, modeled on God's love, as beyond power and possessiveness; "the significance of facing the 'other' for theological, ethical and spiritual transformation"; the "otherness" of God and "the paradox of God's concurrent absence and presence"; and "the mystery of

6. ". . . the search for an understanding of theology that can affirm and celebrate different histories, relationships and identities, including the ministry of women, within an ecumenical horizon" (*God's Presence*, 3).

7. ". . . the search for an understanding of Christian theology which is robust enough to discern the presence of God in a post-Christian, pluralist society, within a globalised world dominated by science and technology, and on a planet subject to humanly induced climate change" (*God's Presence*, 3).

8. ". . . from long, and sometimes desperate, searching for answers to the discovery that questions of theodicy cease to engage as over forty years of caring for a profoundly disabled son gives privileged access to the deepest truths of the Christian religion" (*God's Presence*, 3).

the Trinity as the all-embracing, overflowing wisdom of divine love."[9] There is one further motif on her list, intrinsic to that core mystery of the Trinity, which recurs in her daring, Augustinian postscript to the second volume of *Doctrine and Scripture in Early Christianity*: "the inseparability of truth, beauty, and goodness."

The importance of those motifs should be enough to convince anyone concerned with the meaning, truth, and practice of Christianity today that it is still vital to learn from those early centuries. Yet until *Doctrine and Scripture in Early Christianity* she had not brought together in one work her key insights and overall "sense-making" of the Bible and the early Christian centuries. It is fascinating to see how she has now gone about this.

Doctrine and Scripture in Early Christianity: Key Elements

The basic twofold approach is indicated in the titles of each volume.

Volume 1, *Scripture, the Genesis of Doctrine*, tells the story of the early Christian church as it worked out its identity amid the complexities of the pluralist Roman Empire, in which it did not fit any of the available categories.

The Christian communities would have seemed more like a network of schools than a religion:

> Teaching and learning were their business, and they were both like and unlike other schools. They were dissimilar from these schools in that all comers were welcome—the poor, slaves, women, outcasts, orphans, widows. But they were like other schools in other respects, in that their teachers advocated a particular lifestyle and grounded ethics in an account of the truth: truth about the way things are, about God, about human destiny. And sooner or later they would argue for distinctive positions with respect not just to ethics but to such topics as cosmology, physics, and metaphysics. Again, like other schools, this one distilled wisdom concerning these branches of philosophy from ancient written texts, albeit stylistically crude texts that came from a "barbarian" source rather than the classics. (41–42 in volume 1)

Those "crude," strange texts testified to the distinctive "good news" of Christianity, believing and trusting in which was at the heart of this commu-

9. *God's Presence*, 5–6.

nity's distinctiveness.[10] The rest of volume 1 narrates (with critical attention to alternative narratives) how the priority given to the Bible was the subject of much debate and conflict and resulted in the recognition that, while reading and interpreting scripture was the highest study in the community, it also required the guidance of teaching—dogma or doctrine ("teaching" in Greek is *dogma*, in Latin *doctrina*)—distilled over many years and embodied in the rule of faith (leading to the creeds) and in catechetical teaching. So scripture and doctrine belong together in a school-like environment.

The surrounding culture was one where education was based on a canon of ancient literary and philosophical texts in which were found indicators both to a right way of life and to the truth about the way things are. Christians adapted many of classical culture's methods of textual interpretation in learning from their own scriptural texts a way of life and an understanding of reality. There was both "acculturation" and a distinctive, scripture-centered identity that challenged the culture through believing and trusting in the one Creator God who is the Father of Jesus Christ. The debates were of course carried on with the modes of reasoning learned through their culture, and in response to the questions and events of their time, but the distinctiveness is irreducibly scriptural. Scripture was thus the genesis of doctrine, and the kind of "teaching" discerned was a response to current intellectual questions about life, the universe, and everything. This complex, culturally shaped yet culturally transformative coinherence of scripture and doctrine is the basic lesson of volume 1. Some of its detailed lessons for our century are worked out in *God's Presence: A Contemporary Recapitulation of Early Christianity.*

Volume 2, *Scripture in Doctrinal Dispute*, concentrates mainly on issues relating to the two core questions that dominated much theological discussion and controversy in the early church and are still utterly central to Christian life and thought: Who is Jesus Christ? and Who is God?

Christians today still read the Bible as their primary way of trying to answer them, and the answers affect all other key teachings. But the way the early church arrived at their answers and expressed the coinherence of scripture and doctrine has often been dismissed by modern biblical scholarship. As Frances

10. The work of a younger scholar, Teresa Morgan (who, like Frances Young, combines classics, scholarship on scripture and early Christianity, and theology), on *fides* and *pistis* in the Roman Empire, Hellenistic Judaism, the Septuagint, and the New Testament is a rich, corroborating accompaniment to *Scripture, the Genesis of Doctrine*. See especially Teresa Morgan, *Roman Faith and Christian Faith:* Pistis *and* Fides *in the Early Roman Empire and Early Churches* (Oxford: Oxford University Press, 2015), and *The New Testament and the Theology of Trust: 'This Rich Trust'* (Oxford: Oxford University Press, 2022).

Young says, "The basis of these doctrines in scripture was and remains far from self-evident: they emerged out of conflict and debate over the implications of the biblical material, and modern biblical scholarship has largely treated them as anachronistic models for interpreting the canonical texts."[11]

Faced with this challenge, one response is to ignore it and to reaffirm the early church approach and conclusions, or even to ignore both modern scholarship and the ways the early church wrestled with scripture and try to bypass both by going back to the "plain text" of the Bible. Another response is to take modern historical-critical scholarship as the primary guide, leading to the contemporary irrelevance of the early church engagement with scripture.

Frances Young argues strongly against both responses. She is a historical-critical scholar both of the Bible and of the early Christian centuries, but is also acutely aware of (and has written extensively about) the limitations of that modern method when it comes to the sort of questions being pursued by both early and contemporary Christians, above all concerning who Jesus Christ is and who God is. As she states in the prefaces to both volumes, "Ultimately we seek on this journey to move beyond the estrangement between doctrine and scripture brought about by modernity and the historico-critical method, so as to rediscover how scripture and doctrine have the kind of theological coinherence that the fathers of the church attributed to them" (xxiv in volume 1).

To move beyond this estrangement, while doing justice to both sides, is a complex task, with no simple affirmation or negation of one side or the other. It is, as she says, a journey, and it is one in which the experience along the way is essential to where one arrives at the end. It is tempting in any large book to jump to a summary of the conclusions. That would be especially unfortunate with these volumes. Immersion in the particularities of how scripture, historical and cultural context, and doctrine were shaped through their inseparable interaction over several centuries is the only way to appreciate both the significance of what happened during those centuries and their profound relevance today. Frances Young's achievement is not only to guide readers on that journey through the formative centuries of what is now the world's largest religion, but also, especially in *God's Presence: A Contemporary Recapitulation of Early Christianity*, to give an example of how learning from those centuries can inspire an analogous coinherence of scripture and doctrine for our century. But to be in a position to understand and assess her achievement it is essential to engage with the particularities of her work, in both its historical and

11. Page xxv below.

its contemporary aspects. The centuries covered in the current work deserve the hours of slow reading and reflection that the two volumes demand.

A Third Culmination: Augustine, the Future of the Text, and the Christian Future

Both volume 1 and volume 2 conclude with reflections on major texts of Augustine. In volume 1, *Teaching Christianity*, Augustine's summative discussion of the interpretation of scripture, is the theme; in volume 2 it is his *The Trinity*. Augustine emerges as a consummate practitioner and creative developer of the coinherence of doctrine and scripture, exemplifying Frances Young's decisive verdict:

> Surely the burden of these two volumes has been that the doctrinal articulation of scripture's overall meaning was both vital and valid, and the continuing identity of Christianity depends upon our capacity to embrace this coinherence. It is from this reading that the one God comes to be identified as Father, Son, and Holy Spirit, the three names into which every believer is baptized. At the end of *On the Trinity*, Augustine prays: "Directing my attention toward this rule of faith as best as I could, as far as you enabled me to, I have sought you and desired to see intellectually what I have believed." (p. 277 below)

Augustine prayed these words as his civilization faced collapse, and his "doctrinal articulation of scripture's overall meaning" was to prove formative and generative for many, not only during the coming traumas of his own civilization, but also during later centuries. One of Frances Young's hermeneutical concepts for such generativity is "the future of the text," and she argues for the wisdom and appropriateness of the ways in which the future of the biblical text was, through much debate, trial, and error, opened up during these centuries, not least by Augustine. Her detailed discussion of elements in his writing (such as his use of allegory, proof-texting, and christological reading of the Old Testament), which have in recent centuries been seen as most problematic, is integrated into a robust justification of his central concern with the overarching scriptural narrative. For him, and for Frances Young, the Bible rings truest when it is read in line with the conclusions of both volume 1, where the decisive interpretative guidelines in *Teaching Christianity* are love of God and love of neighbor, and volume 2, where the decisive guidelines in the *The Trinity* are the rule of faith; who Jesus Christ is—incarnate, crucified, resurrected; and who God is—Father, Son, and Holy Spirit. Doctrine and scripture are complementary ways of attending to the truth.

Frances Young, too, writes and prays in a century facing massive civilizational challenges, to several of which she has responded theologically and prophetically. In the midst of these challenges, Christian churches easily lose touch with the depths of scripture, as opened up through those guidelines. But Augustine by no means has the last word, and the future of the Bible needs to be opened up afresh—continually, critically, and creatively. In the final chapter of volume 2, her retrieval of Augustine leads into three further "words" that together offer a Christian wisdom for the twenty-first century.

The launchpad is the hypothesis that Augustine's "distinction between 'intellectual cognizance of eternal things' and 'rational cognizance of temporal things' might perhaps anticipate the kind of insight we need to both characterize and close the gap . . . between doctrine and scripture."

First, she gives a fascinating autobiographical account of three stages in the intellectual journey toward her present position on how to describe and how to close that gap. She begins in the 1970s with her strongly historical-critical contribution to *The Myth of God Incarnate.* Next, in the 1990s, comes her interrelation of the historical-critical approach with a more synthesizing, imaginative mindset, as in her inaugural lecture, "The Critic and the Visionary." Then, in the early twenty-first century, the neuroscientist, psychiatrist, and philosopher Iain McGilchrist helps to stimulate a fuller integration of analysis and synthesis, as seen in *God's Presence: A Contemporary Recapitulation of Early Christianity.* The gap is closed when rational knowledge both is affirmed and becomes wisdom.

The second "word" (the final one in the final chapter) is worship. There she finds the performance of the coinherence of doctrine and scripture and the lived reality of transcending any gap between them. The final subheading, "Worship: Where Scripture and Doctrine Truly Coinhere," brings her to the heart of her own tradition: "At this point my Methodist self cannot resist the temptation to demonstrate how deeply both scripture and the doctrines of incarnation and Trinity are embedded in the hymns of Charles Wesley."

Yet that is not all. The demonstration of her position through verses from some profound, little-known hymns of Charles Wesley overflows into three remarkable meditations, one "after Augustine," one "after Augustine with McGilchrist," and the last "after Augustine, with Gregory Nyssen." They are an invitation to readers to enter more and more deeply, wisely, and wholeheartedly into what the two volumes have opened up—that is, into who Jesus Christ is;

who God is; and the truth, goodness, and beauty in God and created by God. It is a daring, doxological culmination:

> *Father, we adore you, lay our lives before you, how we love you.*
> *Jesus, we adore you, lay our lives before you, how we love you.*
> *Spirit, we adore you, lay our lives before you, how we love you.*[12]

DAVID F. FORD

12. Terrye Coelho (1972).

Preface

This second volume on *Doctrine and Scripture in Early Christianity* focuses on the scriptural basis claimed for the core theological doctrines established by the mid-fifth century, namely, the doctrine of the Trinity and of the two natures of Christ. The story of the controversies through which these doctrines were finally formulated has been told often enough before. However, the role of hermeneutical argument and of appeal to scriptural proof needs deeper consideration. The basis of these doctrines in scripture was and remains far from self-evident: they emerged out of conflict and debate over the implications of the biblical material, and modern biblical scholarship has largely treated these doctrines as anachronistic models for interpreting the canonical texts. Volume 1 largely circumvented these central tenets; volume 2 will address that deficit.

The substantive chapters of this volume were drafted prior to the decision to divide into two what was conceived as a single work. That fact is an indication of how closely these volumes hang together: the first maps the overall context within which took place the disputes surveyed in the second, and the second takes up and develops the doctrinal conclusions reached in the first. Nevertheless, despite their dependence on one another, these volumes have been designed to stand alone as far as possible. The principal findings of volume 1 are carried forward in the opening chapter of volume 2 to facilitate the reader's grasp of the overall perspective of the entire project, and the interim conclusions of volume 1 are rehearsed and further developed in the final overall concluding chapter. At the same time cross-references will surely be better appreciated if the reader has access to both parts of this study.

As indicated in the preface to volume 1, this work on the relationship of doctrine and scripture in the early church has proved a fitting climax to my research contribution over the past decades. It has yielded some fresh insights while building on my previous engagement with early Christian interpretation of scripture. It has also enabled me to take account of shifts in scholarship over the last half century and more, and to consider the implications for reassessing the process whereby doctrine was formulated in the early centuries and the consequences for contemporary doctrinal theology. Indeed, this work would appear to endorse the recent turn to theological commentaries on biblical texts; for historico-critical reconstruction of some kind of evolutionary process was never enough, given that it was discourse and hermeneutical argument which generated doctrinal propositions. Doctrine and scripture were, for the fathers of the church, always coinherent. Their coinherence, however, has never been straightforwardly evident; it was and remains constantly under discussion, ever controversial. But as indicated in the preface to volume 1, "ultimately we seek on this journey to move beyond the estrangement between doctrine and scripture brought about by modernity and the historico-critical method, so as to rediscover how scripture and doctrine have the kind of theological coinherence which the fathers of the church attributed to them." It is my hope that this volume in particular will enrich the work of Systematic Theologians, not just specialists in early Christian studies.

The resource constraints under which this work has been produced remain as acknowledged in the preface to volume 1: the Covid-19 pandemic closed libraries and I had to rely on what I had assembled over the years, apart from a few subsequent visits to check references and some original Greek and Latin texts. The final preparation of volume 2 was further constrained by retiring from Birmingham to Sheffield and downsizing even my own resources. I apologize again if I have missed recent work of which I should have taken account. For the most part I have worked directly from primary rather than secondary material, and largely used texts available in translation, not just because of the difficult circumstances already acknowledged but for the sake of theologians in general—for the matters discussed go far beyond specialist interests, and are of particular significance for Christian ecumenism over time.

FRANCES M. YOUNG
Sheffield, UK

Abbreviations

The abbreviation of biblical books and patristic texts follow the conventions established in the *SBL Handbook of Style*, second edition.

PRIMARY SOURCES

Athanasius

C. Ar.	*Orations against the Arians*
Decr.	*Defense of the Nicene Definition*
Ep. Epict.	*Letter to Epictetus*
Ep. Serap.	*Letters to Serapion concerning the Holy Spirit*
Inc.	*On the Incarnation*
Tom.	*Tome to the People of Antioch*

Athenagoras

Leg.	*Embassy for the Christians*

Augustine

Conf.	*Confessions*
Doctr. chr.	*Teaching Christianity*
Trin.	*On the Trinity*

Barn.	**Epistle of Barnabas**

Basil

De Spir.	*On the Holy Spirit*

1 Clem. **1 Clement**

Cyril of Alexandria

Comm. Jo. *Commentary on John's Gospel*
Ep. *Letters*
Un. Chr. *On the Unity of Christ*

Didymus the Blind

Trin. *On the Trinity*

Ephrem

Eccl. *Hymns on the Church*
Fid. *Hymns on Faith*
Haer. *Against Heresies*
Nat. *Hymns on the Nativity*
Par. *Hymns of Paradise*
Res. *Hymns on the Resurrection*

Eusebius

Hist. eccl. *Ecclesiastical History*
Marc. *Against Marcellus*

Gregory of Nazianzus

Ep. *Letters*
Orat. *Orations*

Gregory of Nyssa

De hom. *On the Making of Humankind*
Eun. *Against Eunomius*
Hom. beat. *Homilies on the Beatitudes*
Hom. Cant. *Homilies on the Song of Songs*
Hom. Eccl. *Homilies on Ecclesiastes*
Inst. *On Christian Practice*
Or. cat. *Great Catechism*
Virg. *On Virginity*
Vit. Mos. *Life of Moses*

Hippolytus

Haer. *Refutation of All Heresies*
Noet. *Against Noetus*

Irenaeus

Epid.	*Demonstration of the Apostolic Preaching*

Jerome

Ep.	*Letters*

John Chrysostom

Hom. 1 Cor.	*Homilies on 1 Corinthians*
Hom. Heb.	*Homilies on Hebrews*
Hom. Jo.	*Homilies on John's Gospel*

Justin

1 Apol.	*First Apology*
2 Apol.	*Second Apology*
Dial.	*Dialogue with Trypho*

(Ps.-)Macarius

Hom.	*Homilies*

Novatian

Trin.	*The Trinity*

Origen

Cels.	*Against Celsus*
Comm. Jo.	*Commentary on John*
Princ.	*On First Principles*

Tertullian

Herm.	*Against Hermogenes*
Prax.	*Against Praxeas*

Theodore

Inc.	*On the Incarnation of the Lord*

Theodoret

Ep.	*Letters*
Eran.	*Eranistes*

Theophilus

Autol.	*To Autolycus*

Secondary Literature

ACO	*Acta Conciliorum Oecumenicorum*. Edited by Eduard Schwartz. Berlin: de Gruyter, 1914–1984
ACW	*Ancient Christian Writers*
ANF	*The Ante-Nicene Fathers*. Edited by Alexander Roberts and James Donaldson. 1885–1887. 10 vols. Repr., Peabody, MA: Hendrickson, 1994
CCSG	Corpus Christianorum: Series Graeca
CCSL	Corpus Christianorum: Series Latina
CSEL	Corpus Scriptorum Ecclesiasticorum Latinorum
CWS	Classics of Western Spirituality
FC	Fathers of the Church
GCS	Die griechischen christlichen Schriftsteller der ersten [drei] Jahrhunderte
GNO	*Gregorii Nysseni Opera*. Edited by W. Jaeger et al. Leiden: Brill, 1952–
HUT	Hermeneutische Untersuchungen zur Theologie
JEH	*Journal of Ecclesiastical History*
JTS	*Journal of Theological Studies*
LCL	Loeb Classical Library
LXX	Septuagint
NPNF	*A Select Library of Nicene and Post-Nicene Fathers of the Christian Church*. Edited by Philip Schaff and Henry Wave. 28 vols. in 2 series. 1886–1889. Repr., Peabody, MA: Hendrickson, 1994
OECS	Oxford Early Christian Studies
OECT	Oxford Early Christian Texts
PG	Migne, Patrologia Graeca
PTS	Patristische Texte und Studien
SC	Sources Chrétiennes
StPatr	Studia Patristica
VC	*Vigiliae Christianae*
VCSup	Vigiliae Christianae Supplements
WUNT	Wissenschaftliche Untersuchungen zum Neuen Testament

1

Setting the Scene

RETROSPECT AND PROSPECT

The focus of this second volume will be the period from Nicaea to Chalcedon in which the major doctrines of the Christian religion were formulated through controversy and refined through debate. To an extent doubtless surprising to many readers, the doctrines of the Trinity and of the two natures of Christ were somewhat marginal to our discussion in volume 1, despite being the key topics of a history of dogma. The interesting question as to why the issues did not sooner become problematic will hover in the background as we trace the trajectory of debate through the third-century monarchian controversies to their legacy in the disputes arising from so-called Arianism. The extent to which scripture was the court of appeal in that process is what we seek to uncover: how far was scripture the actual source and proof of doctrinal propositions?

First we need to pick up threads from the previous volume so as to be aware of the conditions and continuities within which the debates were conducted, and the implicit assumptions and precedents that shaped the language and concepts in play. The legacies of second-century disputes were crucial, and identifying the parameters established early on will be an important feature of this transitional chapter. But here we shall also prepare the ground for the substantial topics to follow by tracing the third-century monarchian reaction against Logos-theology, thus exploring the principal precursor to the disagreements that will concern us in this volume.

1. Divine Pedagogy and the School-Like Character of Early Christian *Ecclēsiai*

Readers of the previous volume will have noticed a recurring motif whereby I unveiled moments of illumination, particular books, or incidents that opened my eyes and allowed, or confirmed, significant insights. Let me likewise share an illuminating study that coheres with the approach adopted so far in our attempt to probe the relationship between doctrine and scripture in the early church.

The work I refer to is David Rylaarsdam's book *John Chrysostom on Divine Pedagogy*. Chrysostom, he suggests, regarded priests as

> God's agents, called to participate in the process of leading people to union with Christ by imitating divine pedagogy. . . . The church is a spiritual school where a teacher sits down and extemporaneously delivers oral discourses which apply an authoritative text. In this Christian *paideia*, the familiar ingredients are evident: a philosopher, literature, orations, pedagogical strategies, and the goal of forming a student's way of life. However, these elements are transformed. The key text is scripture. The philosophical orations are homilies in a worshipping community.[1]

Thus, as I argued in volume 1, so too for Chrysostom the church is a kind of school, gathered around authoritative books, forming souls, molding the character and lifestyle of those seeking wisdom.

Divine pedagogy, Rylaarsdam suggests, is the theme that gives theological and practical coherence to Chrysostom's vast extant corpus of largely homiletic material. Pedagogy requires "adaptability" to the diverse needs of pupils at different stages. The cultural grounding of pedagogy in the conventions of the rhetorical schools of antiquity is traced, but in Chrysostom's theological usage it is found to be Christianized. God is depicted as intensely pursuing "communion with human creatures, persuading them like a classical philosopher into dialogue about a fitting way of life."[2] This picture is filled out from scripture and above all from the incarnation: humility is already evident in God's speech in the Old Testament, but God's willingness to take on flesh, his "adaptation" to humanity through self-emptying (*kenōsis*), entails inconceivable divine humility. Such "accommodation" is explored theologically; it

1. David Rylaarsdam, *John Chrysostom on Divine Pedagogy: The Coherence of His Theology and Preaching*, OECS (Oxford: Oxford University Press, 2014), 226.

2. Rylaarsdam, *John Chrysostom*, 41.

is the prime characteristic of the incomprehensible God, who "adapts" self-revelation to our creaturely level out of *philanthrōpia*, an "adaptation" that implies "condescension" (*synkatabasis*) to human limitations yet acts through persuasion not compulsion.

> As Chrysostom preaches to a mixed audience, he points out that God can make philosophers of all people, not simply educated élites. Whereas Greek *paideia* distinguished "the well-born few from the common man," God is a teacher who makes his philosophy available even to uneducated rustics. The church is God's school and, unlike other schools, this one does not charge for its lessons. The fact that God's teachings, which are wiser than those of all humans, are received by ordinary church attendees testifies to the "greatest wisdom in the teacher."[3]

Chrysostom is shown to discern God adapting in various ways to the level of the human audience, and this then provides a model to imitate. Paul, the great exemplar, himself wrote: "Be imitators of me as I am of Christ" (1 Cor 11:1), and Chrysostom models on Paul his own adaptation to the various pastoral needs of congregations.[4] This, he suggests, is what all priests and bishops should be doing.

Introducing his study of Chrysostom, Rylaarsdam looks back briefly to Origen, whose whole approach, as we saw in the fifth chapter of volume 1, was pedagogical, and whose commitment to the church's provision of schooling for all people, not just elites, was likewise fundamental. Rylaarsdam then turns to the words of Athanasius in his *On the Incarnation*:

> Desiring to do good to human beings, as human he comes, taking to himself a body like the rest; and through his actions done in that body, as it were on their own level, he teaches those who would not learn by other means to know himself, the Word of God, and through him the Father. He deals with them as a good teacher with his pupils, coming down to their level and using simple means. (*Inc.* 14–16)[5]

3. Rylaarsdam, *John Chrysostom*, 35, quoting Richard Lim, *Public Disputation, Power, and Social Order in Late Antiquity* (Berkeley: University of California Press, 1995), 138, and Chrysostom, *Hom. 1 Cor.* 5.1.

4. See also my article, "John Chrysostom on 1 and 2 Corinthians," StPatr 18.1 (1986): 349–52. Cf. Margaret M. Mitchell, *The Heavenly Trumpet: John Chrysostom, and the Art of Pauline Interpetation* (Tübingen: Mohr Siebeck, 2000).

5. As quoted by Rylaarsdam, *John Chrysostom*, 28–29, though altered slightly.

Thus, Chrysostom's viewpoint is not idiosyncratic. His biblical and pastoral theology, Rylaarsdam reckons, "is more characteristic of the theology of the early church generally than the dogmatic theology which has preoccupied many historians of Christian thought."[6]

At first sight the above comment appears to have considerable cogency, although perhaps largely because of the narrowing of our understanding of "dogma." It is important to remember that the Greek word *dogma* simply means "teaching," as does the Latin word *doctrina*. Teaching and books belong to schools and other educational settings. The centrality of books, along with the very fact that converts were taught the truth through catechesis, is an indication of how school-like Christian assemblies would seem within the sociocultural world of the Roman Empire. Furthermore, there was no distinction between "biblical and pastoral theology" and "dogmatic theology," for it was in the process of trying to capture the essential teaching of scripture that "doctrinal" summaries and propositions came into play. What this study of Chrysostom exemplifies is that throughout the period covered in this second volume, in which the canon of scripture and doctrinal orthodoxy were classically defined, the school-like character of the church (for which volume 1 argued) remained evident, with its focus on interpreting biblical teaching and forming the character and lifestyle of persons from any level of society. The burden of that teaching was that the one God had reached out through his Word and Spirit to create, teach, and renew erring human beings. In other words, *the church was the locus of divine pedagogy.* So it is the school-like character of the early Christian *ecclēsiai* that explains the unusual importance of doctrine and scripture in the Christian tradition by comparison with other religions.[7]

Doctrines as such were generated in response to

- the need to make unitary sense of the collection of disparate books, written in a variety of genres, which were received as the word of the one God;
- the need to specify summarily and propositionally the meaning and implications of the scriptures—that is, their *dogma* (Greek) or *doctrina* (Latin)—within the intellectual assumptions and parameters of the then contemporary culture;
- the need to respond to questions and challenges arising from that intellectual context, both from within and beyond the network of school-like *ecclēsiai*.

6. Rylaarsdam, *John Chrysostom*, 7.

7. For fuller treatment of this point, see volume 1, chapter 2.

In volume 1 we found the overall outcome enunciated in the *Catechetical Homilies* of Cyril of Jerusalem, an overview of Christian teaching that enabled us to grasp his claims: (1) that the whole "edifice" was structurally integrated, one doctrine fitting another in a coherent way, so that all held together securely; and (2) that the creedal summary and the teaching of scripture were coinherent with one another.[8]

Such teaching was the product of interpretation and argument—indeed, doctrine was the outcome of a process of generating discourse true to the texts often through dispute about their meaning and their appropriate articulation. Inevitably, different, indeed rival, options (*haireseis*) were canvassed, which then necessitated the discovery of scriptural proofs for confirming the true reading. Thus doctrinal discourse was created by argument and counter-argument, not least about what scripture said or meant, and it would be more and more precisely enunciated, especially in the period with which we shall be concerned in this second volume. Conceptual models were produced in the fires of controversy and can only be understood through recognizing this dialectical process. Proposals were met by counterproposals, and rejected solutions became heresies to be excluded. This was no process of natural development, but of hard and sometimes intolerant and prejudiced wars of words, with armories of prooftexts as the word of God inscribed in scripture was deployed to deliver opposing accounts of the Word of God incarnate in Jesus Christ. The universal assumption was that the doctrinal outcome was to be proved from scripture and to be coherent with scriptural teaching.

Such in brief was the burden of volume 1. We began, however, with a perceived gap between scripture and doctrine in modern scholarship, with strong caveats concerning their coinherence. For some the gap was minimized by positing an evolutionary model—the natural development of what was already inherently present. For others the gap was exacerbated by historical criticism, which denied that doctrines such as that of the Trinity were to be found in the New Testament and attributed to Hellenization the doctrinal overlay that distorted the original simple gospel. The account in these volumes draws something from each of those long-standing positions yet remains critical of both. For neither position quite captures the way in which the doctrinal discourse characteristic of Christianity was formulated, both in interaction with scripture and in response to the then current "common sense" about the way reality was understood. Doctrine was constituted through teaching and learning, reading and interpreting, arguing and testifying—a process of

8. See volume 1, chapter 6.

inquiry, and often bitter debate, in and between school-like *ecclēsiai*. Of course, these "assemblies" had features that were recognizably religious, as did every household, every club and association, every interest group, and every school (philosophical or otherwise) in that society. Christian communities were gathered around books and teaching, as schools were, and dogmas or doctrines were simply what they taught, the truths they found in their books.

2. The Legacies of Second-Century Debate

Volume 1 provides treatment of early tensions over the constitution and implications of the canon of scripture, particularly in the struggles with Marcion and the gnostics. That volume also shows how the "canon of truth" (or "rule of faith") was deployed to settle some of the questions raised and argues that both canons emerged alongside each other during the second century. Not only were they regarded as coinherent but also as constituting the apostolic tradition, and this meant that the rule of faith was deployed as a yardstick for interpreting scripture's meaning. Some other key points we should recall, especially as found in the work of Irenaeus and later, with some shifts in understanding, in Cyril of Jerusalem:[9]

- the rule of faith provided the unitive *hypothesis* or summary of scripture—the overarching narrative that could make sense of God's providential plans from creation to eschaton via humankind's fall and redemption;
- the rule of faith was threefold because it corresponded to the three "names" into which converts were baptized;
- the rule of faith provided character sketches of the three "names" whose words and actions are played out in scripture's overarching narrative; for Irenaeus the three were held together by treating the Son and the Spirit as the two "hands" of the one Father God.

The rule of faith, then, was "essentially confessional, doxological testimony . . . implicitly drawing on the biblical narrative." But it became "the indispensable hermeneutical key" for dismissing what were perceived as false readings of scripture.[10] Indeed, in volume 1 we found Irenaeus, Origen and Augustine testing out readings of scripture against the rule of faith or its equivalent—it

9. For Irenaeus, see volume 1, chapter 4. For Cyril of Jerusalem, see volume 1, chapter 6.
10. Quotations from pp. 97 and 98 of volume 1.

provided criteria for proper hermeneutics. That perspective will remain cogent in this volume, as baptismal confessions turned into creeds, and creeds were adapted to convey what became essential doctrinal propositions, thus becoming "articles of belief." So one significant legacy was the assumption that creedal statements were coinherent with scripture, and that when it was not easy to agree exactly what scripture implied or meant, let alone how scripture's sense was to be expressed, the apostolic tradition enshrined in the rule of faith, and later in the creed, would provide the appropriate doctrinal framework within which to reach a conclusion.

The other significant legacy of those early struggles was the firm acceptance of the view that the Creator God of the scriptures was identical with the one supreme God, not with some lesser being.[11] This was captured in the word *monarchia*. Not only did this indicate God's sovereignty, but it also emphasized God as the single *archē* (first principle): no secondary first principle could be entertained, not even the eternal existence of infinite matter that might be organized into the cosmos—the one Creator God must therefore have created out of nothing. Clearly provoked by scripture's insistence on the one God who was the Creator of all things, this was a profoundly countercultural response to contemporary accounts of the way things are: a proverb stated that "nothing comes from nothing," and it was assumed that anything from nothing must be a sham. Yet in Christian argument *creatio ex nihilo* would come to signify a positive reevaluation of matter, for matter was not some negative reality from which to seek release, but rather God's good creation declared good by God's own word. Furthermore, it meant a radicalization of God's transcendence; in Irenaeus's terms God contained all things without being contained, that is, God was infinite, beyond limit, ungraspable, beyond knowledge. Platonism had never expressed such a radical position; God might be hard to trace but could be known through the soul's kinship with the divine and by the techniques of synthesis, analysis, and analogy. The roots of Christian apophaticism lay less in Platonic ideas and more in Hellenistic Judaism and its traditional way of eschewing the pronunciation of God's sacred name. It was also entailed by espousal of the doctrine of *creatio ex nihilo* for this meant utter otherness, a fundamental difference between Creator and creature. It would take time, however, for that consequence to become clear.

Meanwhile, however, the doctrine of God's *monarchia* began to seem in tension with the "three names" drawn from scripture into which converts were initiated.

11. See volume 1, chapter 3, 2.1–3.

3. The Monarchian Controversies

Maybe too quickly we suggested at the start of this chapter that the monarchian controversy of the third century was the precursor of the later disputes that will preoccupy us in this volume, for the argument in the succeeding century had somewhat shifted, as we shall see. Yet these earlier conflicts supplied the tags with which each side would tar the other, as first the struggle with Arianism was played out, then the conflict over Christology. That makes it important for us to backtrack enough to consider the scriptural input to these first arguments about the relationship between the Son of God and the supreme Father. Origen's *Against Celsus* can set the agenda for us.[12]

3.1. The Fundamental Question and Origen's Revealing Response

Origen, in his work against Celsus, quotes his opponent as saying:

> If these people worshipped no other god but one, perhaps they would have a valid argument against the others. But in fact they worship to an extravagant degree this man who appeared recently, and yet think it is not inconsistent with monotheism if they also worship God's servant. (*Cels.* 8.12)

As an outsider Celsus perhaps perceived earlier and more clearly than believers what the distinctive mark of Christianity was, and how logically absurd it was. The problem was undoubtedly exacerbated by the second-century insistence on the *monarchia* of the one God.[13] To underline again the full force of the term, the word *archē* in Greek is ambiguous, meaning both "sovereignty" and "beginning," and in philosophy it was the long-standing term used to express the "first principle" or "source" of all reality. This double thrust indicates the comprehensive way in which *monarchia* linked notions of monotheism and creation: the one source and ruler of all is the one true God, beside whom there is no other. How, then, did the Lord Jesus Christ, by now the object of Christian devotion, relate to this one and only Lord God?

Origen recognized there could be an issue. Celsus's above comment he introduces with the words, "Someone might think that there is some plausibility

12. Greek text of *Against Celsus* in P. Koetschau, ed., *Die Schrift vom Martyrium, Buch I–IV gegen Celsus* and *Buch V–VIII gegen Celsus, Die Schrift vom Gebet*, Origenes Werke 1–2, GCS 2–3 (Leipzig: Hinrichs, 1899). English translation by Henry Chadwick, *Against Celsus* (Cambridge: Cambridge University Press, 1965).

13. See volume 1, chapter 3, 2.1–3.

in his next criticism of us." His immediate response to Celsus was to quote the Gospel of John:

> I should say to this that if Celsus had considered the saying, "I and my Father are one," and the prayer uttered by the Son of God in the words, "As I and thou are one," he would not have imagined that we worship another besides the supreme God. "For the Father," he says, "is in me and I in the Father."[14]

Immediately, however, he has to qualify this:

> If, however, anyone is perturbed by these words lest we should be going over to the view of those who deny that there are two existences [*hypostaseis*], Father and Son, let him pay attention to the text "And all those who believed were of one heart and soul," that he may see the meaning of "I and my Father are one." . . . Therefore we worship the Father of the truth and the Son who is the truth; they are two distinct existences, but one in mental unity, in agreement, and in identity of will.[15]

Why should Origen be so anxious about seeming to deny two *hypostaseis*? He worries (though this might not have been the case at the time when Celsus was writing) that

> some of those among the multitude of believers take a divergent view, and because of their rashness suppose that the Saviour is the greatest and supreme God. But we at least do not take that view, since we believe him who said: "the Father who sent me is greater than I." (*Cels.* 8.14)[16]

These brief extracts from a somewhat rambling argument might suggest that Origen was basically grappling with the tension inherent in John's Gospel between statements concerning the unity of Father and Son, on the one hand, and statements of the Son's subordination to the Father, on the other; but there is more to it than that. By the mid-third century some Christians were merging Father and Son, and Origen's insistence on distinct existences (*hypostaseis*) betrays his awareness of the controversies. He had visited Rome during the time when Zephyrinus was the bishop there, and it was then and there that these issues were most obviously causing disagreement.

14. Quoting John 10:30; 17:21–22; 14:10–11; 17:21.
15. Quoting Acts 4:32 and John 10:30.
16. Quoting John 14:28.

3.2. Monarchians in Rome[17]

With respect to the so-called monarchian controversies it is not easy to untangle the events, personalities, and arguments, scriptural or otherwise. Eusebius makes little of what was going on in Rome and is mainly interested in anticipations of his arch-heretic Paul of Samosata (*Hist. eccl.* 5.28).[18] All he offers are some extracts from an unnamed writer who sought to resist the view, attributed to Artemon, that the Savior was merely human. The first extract reports that recent adherents to that point of view were claiming that all earlier generations, including the apostles, had "held the things they say themselves" (that is, that Jesus was just human) and perversion of this perspective occurred recently. However, Eusebius's informant asserted, a very different picture was presented in scripture and also in earlier writers such as Justin, Miltiades, Tatian, Clement, Irenaeus, and Melito, who all proclaim Christ as God and man. Furthermore, psalms and hymns "sing of Christ as the Word of God and address him as God." The extract then notes that Victor, the bishop of Rome, excommunicated Theodotus the shoemaker, who was the "prime mover and father of this God-denying apostasy," indeed, "the first to declare Christ was merely human." Further extracts indicate that under Victor's successor, Zephyrinus, people were led astray by a second Theodotus, a banker and disciple of the earlier Theodotus. The writer accuses their followers of corrupting the word of God, resorting to syllogisms and Euclidean geometry, falsifying the text, and claiming to have corrected scripture. (Note that previously we found Marcion and others making the same claim—it was well known in antiquity that manuscripts might get corrupted and so be in need of correction.)[19] Scripture was what remained in contention, and in principle all sides in debate treated these books as both the source and proof of true teaching.

But, pace Eusebius, the reduction of Christ to a mere man was not the only issue, as other evidence makes clear. There seem to have been two roughly contemporary attempts to protect God's *monarchia*—the prime platform of

17. An earlier version of the material in sections 3.2, 3.3.1, and 3.3.3 appeared in my chapter on "Monotheism and Christology" in the *Cambridge History of Early Christianity*, ed. Margaret M. Mitchell and Frances M. Young (Cambridge: Cambridge University Press, 2006), 1:452–69. Reproduced with permission of Cambridge University Press through PLSclear.

18. Greek text of Eusebius's *Ecclesiastical History* in Eduard Schwartz, ed., *Eusebius Werke: Die Kirchengeschichte*, 2 vols., GCS 9 (Leipzig: Hinrichs, 1908). English translation by G. A. Williamson, trans., *The History of the Church* (Harmondsworth: Penguin, 1965).

19. For second-century exegetical arguments see volume 1, chapter 3.

Christian argument established through the second-century debates. Novatian's work on the Trinity indicates that some noticed how it was written that there is only one God and concluded that Christ is a man, while others argued that if there is only one God and Christ is God, then the Father must be Christ—otherwise, contrary to the scripture, there are two gods (*Trin.* 30).[20] Taking up the hint, modern scholarship has posited two monarchianisms: "*dynamic* monarchians" suggested that Jesus was a "mere man" *empowered* by God; while "*modalist* monarchians" spoke of the one God appearing in different *modes*, now as Father, then as Son, then as Holy Spirit.[21] Sources other than Eusebius introduce us to this second approach, notably two works attributed to Hippolytus—the *Refutation of All Heresies* and the *Against Noetus*[22]—along with Tertullian's *Against Praxeas*.[23] These suggest that in the time of Zephyrinus and Callistus it was modalist monarchianism that was the more serious issue. For the author of the *Refutation of All Heresies* (hereafter "Hippolytus") the leading opponents seem to be followers of Noetus. It is common knowledge, he thinks, that Noetus claims that the Son and the Father are the same. The Father was pleased to undergo generation, and once begotten became his own Son. This was how Noetus intended to establish God's *monarchia*—Father and Son are one and the same substance, not one individual produced by another.

20. Latin text of *The Trinity* in W. Yorke Fausset, ed., *Novatiani Romanae urbis presbyteri De Trinitate liber*, Cambridge Patristic Texts (Cambridge: Cambridge University Press, 1909); more recently G. F. Diercks, ed., *Novatiani opera*, CCSL 4 (Turnholt: Brepols, 1972). English translation in *ANF* 5and FC 67.

21. Against this mainstream view, see R. M. Hübner with Markus Vinzent, *Der paradox Eine: Antignostischer Monarchianismus im zweiten Jahrhundert*, VCSup 50 (Leiden: Brill, 1999), who trace modalist views back to Melito of Sardis, regarding it as an Asian tradition opposed to Gnosticism, especially considering Gnosticism's divine plurality and its docetism, as already evident in Ignatius.

22. The identity of Hippolytus is contentious; for discussion, see e.g., R. E. Heine, "Hippolytus, Ps-Hippolytus and the Early Canons," in *Cambridge History of Early Christian Literature*, ed. Frances Young, Lewis Ayres, and Andrew Louth (Cambridge: Cambridge University Press, 2004), 142–51. Greek text of *Refutation of All Heresies* in Paul Wendland, ed., *Hippolytus Werke: Refutatio omnium haeresium*, GCS 26 (Leipzig: Hinrichs, 1916); English translation in *ANF* 5 and selections in Werner Foerster, *Gnosis: A Selection of Gnostic Texts*, vol. 1, *Patristic Evidence*, trans. R. McL. Wilson (Oxford: Oxford University Press, 1972). Greek text of *Against Noetus* in M. Simonetti, ed., *Contro Noeto*, Biblioteca Patristica 35 (Bologna: EDB, 2000); English translation by R. Butterworth, *Hippolytus of Rome: Contra Noetum*, Heythrop Monographs 2 (London: Heythrop College, 1977).

23. Text and translation of *Against Praxeas* in E. Evans, *Tertullian's Treatise against Praxeas* (London: SPCK, 1948).

However, the two approaches clearly addressed the same problem and appealed to many of the same scriptural texts, and they could be conflated (Hippolytus, *Noet.* 3.1). This is possibly implied by Tertullian's discussion (*Prax.* 27) as well as by the story of Beryllus of Bostra who, according to Eusebius, "tried to bring in ideas alien to the faith, actually asserting that our Saviour and Lord did not pre-exist in his own form of being before he made his home among men, and had no divinity of his own but only the Father's dwelling in him" (*Hist. eccl.* 6.33). Apparently Origen was summoned to sort out his unorthodox ideas, and Eusebius claimed to have to hand the full record of the synod at which Origen did so successfully. The association of the two ideas is noticeable: the Savior was a human being in whom the one God dwelt, a perspective already perhaps associating a "dynamic" view of the essentially human Savior with a "modalist" view of God. Furthermore, elusive as may be the precise teachings of Paul of Samosata, both projected monarchianisms were perhaps involved. The distinction between the two may be conceptually neat, but it might simply obscure the interconnections.

Even if Rome became their epicenter, the challenges, it seems, were widespread: Noetus came from Smyrna; Praxeas, Tertullian tells us, imported the heresy from Asia in the time of Victor; the places Bostra and Samosata indicate Syria and again Asia Minor. But the impact in Rome is clearest, for Hippolytus was there during the crucial episcopacies of Zephyrinus and Callistus.[24] He is highly critical of both for a variety of reasons, disciplinary and doctrinal, and it is not unlikely that there were underlying political tensions arising from attempts to bring together the "fractionated" church in Rome under a monepiscopate.[25] That both bishops are presented as sometimes siding with one side, sometimes the other, perhaps reflects attempts at diplomacy. Tertullian apparently uses a pseudonym for the object of his attack: the name "Praxeas," otherwise unknown and meaning "busybody," might be a cipher for one or another of those bishops, with the implicit suggestion of association with modalists such as Noetus, Epigonus, Cleomenes, or Sabellius, as Hippolytus also seems to suggest. Indeed the latter gives no credit for the fact that, after the death of Zephyrinus, Callistus excommunicated Sabellius—still he charges him with favoring Sabellianism and being an impostor.

24. See book 9 of *Refutation of All Heresies.*

25. A. Brent, *Hippolytus and the Roman Church in the Third Century: Communities in Tension before the Emergence of a Monarch-Bishop*, VCSup 31 (Leiden: Brill, 1995); and Brent, *The Imperial Cult and the Development of Church Order: Concepts and Image of Authority in Paganism and Early Christianity before the Age of Cyprian*, VCSup 45 (Leiden: Brill, 1999); see also volume 1, chapter 2, 4.1, for the "fractionated" Roman church.

Here the detail of personalities and events hardly concerns us directly, but the nub of the problem is reflected in two apparently contradictory statements attributed to Zephyrinus: (1) "I know that there is one God, Jesus Christ; and except for him I do not know any other that is begotten and amenable to suffering"; and (2) "The Father did not die, but the Son." By both Zephyrinus and Callistus, Hippolytus and his associates were designated ditheists: "worshippers of two gods." Callistus is said to teach that the Logos himself is both Son and Father, being one indivisible Spirit; the Father is not one person and the Son another, but they are one and the same, all things transcendent and immanent, being full of the divine Spirit. Indeed, the Spirit that became incarnate in the Virgin's womb was no different from the Father, a point substantiated by appeal to scripture, specifically John 14:11: "Do you believe that I am in the Father and the Father in me?" Callistus, it seems, did try to avoid saying that the Father suffered as such, claiming that the Father suffered alongside the Son, but that leads Hippolytus to mock his inconsistencies: his suggestion that Callistus is betrayed into the error of Sabellius one minute and that of Theodotus the next would again point to underlying connections between those monarchian positions.

Celsus's question, then, clearly anticipated issues that would exercise the church at Rome in the first part of the third century, and at the time there was more sympathy for monarchian views of one sort or another than later historians were comfortable to recount—hence, perhaps, the inadequacies of Eusebius's information.

3.3. *Divergent Traditions*

To understand the arguments and the prooftexts deployed against monarchian doctrines we need to trace the roots of their use in second-century exegesis and apologetics. The second century was largely preoccupied with other issues, not least cosmology and creation.[26] But these had an impact on Christology. The "docetic" notion that the spiritual being, Christ, was never truly enfleshed appeared very early, and Gnosticism reinforced the tendency, for associating Christ with the true transcendent Father alienated him from the material creation, which was the product of a lesser, fallen demiurge and challenged the reality of his birth, suffering, and death.[27] No different in its

26. See volume 1, chapter 3.

27. See my discussion in the prelude to *The Cambridge History of Christianity*, ed. Margaret M. Mitchell and Frances M. Young (Cambridge: Cambridge University Press, 2006), 1:33.

implications was the teaching of Marcion which, though perhaps not primarily cosmological, still contrasted the judgmental Creator of the scriptures with the loving Father of Jesus Christ. Defense of the material creation as the work of the one transcendent Creator God was the preoccupation of the second century. In mapping divergent traditions about the one affirmed as Son of God in scripture and tradition, it is that context we need to take into account.

3.3.1. Ditheism: Where Did This Charge Come From?

Logos-theology has generally been named as the doctrine against which monarchianisms were the reaction. The fact that both Justin and Origen could refer to the Logos as a "second god" seems to explain the charge of ditheism.[28] That this was accepted as a serious accusation would account for the defensive arguments developed against the monarchians.

The Logos-theologians had effectively produced what I once called "the first Christological teaching which could potentially deliver a conceptual model capable of explanatory power."[29] The roots of Logos-theology and the influences that contributed to it have been much discussed and need not preoccupy us here beyond indicating that, like the Stoics, they conceived the Logos as the divine immanent in the material cosmos, while also maintaining that the one, true, transcendent Father was the ultimate source of all. These notions they grounded in scripture, noting that God created "by his Word" (Ps 33:6) and reading Genesis in the light of Proverbs 8, so that it was God's Wisdom (i.e., Logos) who was the instrument whereby the transcendent God created everything, as well as the one with whom God conversed, saying, "Let us make humanity in our own image." The Word of the Lord came to the Hebrew prophets, according to Justin (*1 Apol.* 5; *2 Apol.* 10)—and also to Socrates—but was fully present in Jesus Christ; he restored God's image to humankind after its defacement through Adam's disobedience, this being

28. See Origen, *Cels.* 5.39; Justin, *1 Apol.* 13. Greek text for Justin's *1 Apology* in Miroslav Markovich, ed., *Iustini Martyris Apologiae pro Christianis*, PTS 38 (Berlin: de Gruyter, 1994); English translation in *ANF* 1. See also Denis Minns and Paul Parvis, eds. and trans., *Justin, Philosopher and Martyr: Apologies*, OECT (Oxford: Oxford University Press, 2009).

29. See F. Young, "Monotheism and Christology," 1:455. "Potentially," I suggested, "because sufficiently vague that interpreters with later concepts in their minds can reach opposing conclusions as to exactly what was envisaged." E.g., Theophilus's view is interpreted as monarchian by D. S. Wallace-Hadrill, *Christian Antioch. A Study of Early Christian Thought in the East* (Cambridge: Cambridge University Press, 1982), and, as "subordinationist," by J. N. D. Kelly, *Early Christian Doctrines* (London: Black, 1960).

God's providential plan as foretold by the Holy Spirit in the scriptures. Thus the Logos-theologians were able to affirm Christ as the visible form of the invisible God, God's own offspring yet also fully human, God's chosen instrument, the one generated by divine providence to effect creation, revelation, and redemption. The Prologue to John's Gospel, of course, would confirm this reading of scripture's teaching.

That summary, and its basis in scriptural texts, is exemplified by Theophilus of Antioch. After identifying the prophets as "inspired and instructed by God," he states:

> in complete harmony they taught that God made everything out of the non-existent. . . . Having his own Logos innate in his own bowels (Ps 109:3 LXX), God generated him together with his own Sophia, vomiting him forth (Ps 44:2 LXX) before everything else. God used this Logos as his servant in the things created by him, and through him God made all things (John 1:3). He is called Beginning because he leads and dominates everything fashioned through him. It was he, Spirit of God (Gen 1:2) and Beginning (Gen 1:1) and Sophia (Prov 8:22) and Power of the Most High (Luke 1:35), who came down into the prophets and spoke through them about the creation of the world and all the rest. (*Autol.* 2.10)[30]

Theophilus here hardly seems to make any clear distinction between the Logos and the Spirit, and it is no wonder that Logos-theology has so often been called "Binitarian." Yet elsewhere he speaks of a triad consisting of God, God's Logos, and God's Sophia (2.15) and seems to refer to the Logos and Sophia as God's own hands (2.18).

Later, struggling with how the supreme God could walk in paradise, Theophilus identifies the Logos as the one present there, whose voice Adam heard (*Autol.* 2.22). He adds that it was through this Logos that God made all things, that he is God's "Power and Wisdom" (1 Cor 1:24), and again states that he was "always innate [*endiathetos*] in the heart of God":

> For before anything came into existence God had this as Counsellor, God's own Mind and Intelligence. When God wished to make what God had planned to make, God generated this Logos, making him external [*prophorikos*], as the *firstborn of all creation* (Col 1:15). God did not deprive

30. Greek text and English translation of *To Autolycus* in R. M. Grant, ed. and trans., *Theophilus of Antioch: Ad Autolycum*, OECT (Oxford: Clarendon, 1970).

> himself of the Logos but generated the Logos and constantly converses with his Logos. Hence the holy scriptures and all those inspired by the Spirit teach us, and one of them, John, says, "In the beginning was the Logos, and the Logos was with God" (John 1:1). He shows that originally God was alone and the Logos was in him. Then he says, "And the Logos was God; everything was made through him, and apart from him nothing was made" (John 1:1–3). Since the Logos is God and derived his nature from God, whenever the Father of the universe wills to do so God sends him into some place where he is present and heard and seen.

It is worth noting that the terms *endiathetos* and *prophorikos* are borrowed from Stoic analysis, the first representing Logos as reason-in-the-mind, the second Logos as reason-spoken-out-in-a-word. But whatever its conceptual origin, clearly Theophilus found deeply embedded in scriptural prooftexts this idea of the "generation" of God's own innate Logos as a "servant" to deal with creation.

Chapters 61 and 62 of Justin's *Dialogue with Trypho* provide another instructive indication of the way this concept was forged out of the conflation of many scriptural passages. Here Proverbs 8:21–36 is quoted in full as a way of justifying the claim that before all creatures God begat a beginning, and this is named in scripture, now the Glory of the Lord, now the Son, now Wisdom, now an angel, then God, and then Lord and Logos. This is then confirmed by appeal to Genesis, "Let us make man in *our* own image," and "Behold Adam has become as *one of us*." The deduction is made that there were clearly two entities involved in the act of creation, and it was the one Solomon calls Wisdom, begotten as a beginning before all creatures, that God thus addressed.

So it is in the context of cosmological debate that Logos-theology should surely be assessed. Justin has often been charged with eclecticism, but the second-century apologists, by integrating with the legacy from Judaism ideas of transcendence and immanence from prevailing philosophies, actually achieved a remarkably coherent response to the cosmological questions at issue. The way had, of course, been pioneered to some extent by Hellenised Jews before them: the Wisdom of Solomon describes God's wisdom as immanent using language reminiscent of the Stoic Logos, and Philo the Jewish philosopher had already explored the concept of Logos as a complex intermediary between the multiplicity of creation and the unity of God. Some, if not all, of the apologists were aware of the Prologue to the Gospel of John, which provided a precedent for their use of Logos-language, even if the originator of that text was far from envisaging what it might lead to conceptually. That John's Gospel was a favorite text with gnostics—the gnostic Heracleon apparently wrote the first commentary on this Gospel—may have enhanced its appropriateness: a nongnostic reading was required.

Perhaps it was this clever but almost ditheistic concept that provoked Celsus's objection and turned him into the first person we can identify who effectively put his finger on the core theological problem for Christianity.[31] If the pagan Celsus had difficulty with it, so would some who saw themselves as believers within the Christian tradition. It was bound to be contested. Logos-theology, in hindsight identified as the "orthodox" tradition and further developed by Irenaeus, Tertullian, Clement, and Origen, meanwhile had to be defended against rival appeals to scripture and tradition. The so-called monarchian controversies explicitly raised such issues. Undoubtedly the way in which Logos-theology introduced confusion about the *monarchia* of the one and only Creator God was the principal factor behind the controversies.

3.3.2. *Three Names Rather Than Two?*

Maybe Theophilus failed to make a clear distinction between Logos and Spirit, but for all the "Binitarian" flavor of Logos-theology, Justin seems not to have made any similar conflation: the prophetic Spirit is clearly differentiated from "the Son who came forth from God" (*1 Apol.* 6),[32] and baptism is "in the name of God, the Father and Lord of the universe, and of our Saviour Christ, and of the Spirit" (*1 Apol.* 61).[33] Thus he anticipates Irenaeus, who made it clear that three names were to be confessed in the rule of faith, the three names into which the faithful had been baptized.[34]

Hidden in Irenaeus's *Demonstration of the Apostolic Preaching* among the great collection of prooftexts demonstrating the fulfillment of prophecy is a telling statement:

31. See A. J. Droge, "Self-Definition vis-à-vis the Graeco-Roman World," in Mitchell and Young, *Cambridge History of Christianity*, 1:237–40, where Droge argues that Celsus was responding to Justin.

32. Cf. *Dial.* 55, where "the Spirit of prophecy admits another God besides the Maker of all things." Greek text of the *Dialogue with Trypho* in Miroslav Markovich, ed., *Dialogue with Trypho*: *Iustini Martyris Dialogus cum Tryphone*, PTS 47 (Berlin: de Gruyter, 1997); English translation in *ANF* 1.

33. Cf. volume 1, chapter 4, 2.3.

34. Cf. volume 1, chapter 4, 2.4.

> it is necessary to affirm that it is not David or any one of the prophets who speaks for himself—for it is not man who utters prophecies—but the Spirit of God, conforming Himself to the person concerned, spoke in the prophets, producing words sometimes for Christ and at other times for the Father. (*Epid.* 49)[35]

This statement is worth closer examination, for it leads us into another illuminating discovery, prompted by Matthew Bates in his book *The Birth of the Trinity*.[36] This work shows how the early church discovered in the old scriptures conversations in which the three names discussed in advance events to take place in the incarnation, and it traces this back to a remarkably early date—indeed Bates's argument is that this is not merely to be found already in the New Testament but even on the lips of Jesus himself. Be that as it may, in the statement quoted above Irenaeus clearly identifies in scripture the rhetorical technique of *prosōpopoia*, thus presupposing the preexistence of three divine beings discussing not just the divine providential provisions for the incarnation but even creation itself.

Justin anticipated Irenaeus in this too; he assigns lists of prophetic words to each of the three names (*1 Apol.* 37–39) and prefaces those lists with the statement that prophecies delivered "as from a person" should not be regarded as "spoken by the inspired themselves, but by the divine Word who moves them," and while the Word sometimes "declares things that are to come to pass,"

> sometimes he speaks as from the person of God the Lord and Father of all; sometimes as from the person of Christ; sometimes as from the person of the people answering the Lord or his Father, just as you can see even in your own writers, one man being the writer of the whole, but introducing the persons who converse. (*1 Apol.* 36)

Thus Justin explains the literary device of *prosōpopoia*, before going on to give examples where a prophet speaks "from the person of the Father," where "the Spirit of prophecy speaks from the person of Christ," and "where the Spirit of prophecy speaks as predicting things that are to come to pass." The three names thus become integral to his prophetic exegesis.

35. English translation from J. Behr, trans., *On the Apostolic Preaching* (Crestwood, NY: St. Vladimir's Seminary Press, 1997).

36. Matthew W. Bates, *The Birth of the Trinity: Jesus, God, and Spirit in New Testament and Early Christian Interpretations of the Old Testament* (Oxford: Oxford University Press, 2015).

Our earlier citations from Theophilus included the statement that God "constantly converses with his Logos" (*Autol.* 2.22). By the time of Irenaeus some examples of divine conversation had become classic, having appeared in the New Testament and been repeated in other early Christian texts, while other accretions have appeared along the way. We may list a few noteworthy cases used by Irenaeus:

(1) *The Lord said to my Lord, "Sit at my right hand until I make your enemies your footstool"* (Irenaeus, *Epid.* 48).[37] Prior to Irenaeus, Psalm 110:1 was cited in 1 Clement 36, the Epistle of Barnabas 12, and Justin (*1 Apol.* 45; *Dial.* 32–33, 56, 83, 127), as well as in the Synoptic Gospels when Jesus was shown in dispute with the scribes and Pharisees (Mark 12:35–37; Matt 22:41–46; Luke 20:41–44). The text not only seems to imply that he was more than the Son of David but also appears to record a conversation that took place between the Lord God and the preexistent Lord. Further statements from this same psalm also suggest conversation between Father and Son conveyed through David by the prophetic Spirit, such as, "From the womb before the morning star have I begotten you," possibly alluded to by Theophilus (*Autol.* 2.10) as well as Justin and Irenaeus (*Epid.* 43, 48, 51), and also "The Lord has sworn and will not repent, 'You are a priest for ever after the order of Melchisedek,'" which was already cited in Hebrews 7:17 and found here in Irenaeus as well.

(2) *The Lord God says to my Anointed Lord, whose right hand I grasped, that the nations are obedient before him* (Irenaeus, *Epid.* 49).[38] The Epistle of Barnabas 12 couples this quotation from Isaiah with our previous example, and Irenaeus links it with the above quotes from the Psalms, adding Isaiah 49:5–6 and suggesting that first

> is that the Son of God preexisted, the Father spoke with Him, and caused Him to be revealed to people before His birth; and then, that it was necessary for Him to be begotten, a man amongst human beings, and that the same God Himself fashions Him from the womb, that is, He would be born of the Spirit of God.

(3) *Your throne, O God, is for ever and ever. . . . Therefore God has anointed you with the oil of gladness* (Irenaeus, *Epid.* 47).[39] This too was previously cited in Hebrews 1:8–9. Irenaeus comments:

37. Citing Ps 109:1 LXX.
38. Quoting Isa 45:1.
39. Citing Ps 44:7–8 LXX.

> More clearly still, David speaks about the Father and Son in this way, [inserting here the relevant quotation above], for the Son, as He is God, receives from the Father, that <is>, from God, the throne of the everlasting kingdom, and the oil of anointing above His fellows: and "the oil of anointing" is the Spirit by whom He is the Anointed, and His "fellows" are the prophets and righteous and apostles and all who receive participation in His kingdom, that is, His disciples.

(4) *The Lord said to me, "You are my Son; today have I begotten you: ask of me and I will give you the nations and the ends of the earth as a possession"* (Irenaeus, *Epid.* 49). Psalm 2:7–8 also appears in the New Testament, particularly at Jesus's baptism and transfiguration.[40] Like Irenaeus, Justin discusses this text more than once (*Dial.* 88, 103, 122). As Bates puts it:

> for the earliest Christians Psalm 2.7 was consistently regarded not merely as a direct speech made by the Father to the Son, but rather it was taken as *a speech within a speech that was originally spoken by the Son*, who was reporting the words the *Father had spoken to him at an earlier time*, all of which has critical implications for how Christology and Trinitarian dogma developed.[41]

It is hardly surprising that the recognition of these potential dialogues would develop into what Bates calls "prosopological exegesis." Justin, for example, traces through Psalm 22 a script spoken in advance by the preexistent Son, which is then inhabited as "the Son actualizes the words the Spirit had given David in ages past, as he spoke from the *prosōpon* (character) of the Christ as the Christ addresses the Father."[42] Nor is it so surprising, once the idea of conversation between the three names caught on, that the early Christians read this right back into the creation story.[43] "God said, 'Let us make humankind after the image and likeness' . . . to none other than God's own Logos and God's own Sophia," wrote Theophilus (*Autol.* 2.18). Justin wondered whether God said it to himself, as we do sometimes, or to the elements, the earth and other substances, but he concluded that "God conversed with someone who was numerically distinct from himself and also a rational being" (*Dial.* 62.1–3).

40. Mark 1:11; 9:7; Matt 3:17; 17:5; Luke 7:22; 9:35.
41. Bates, *Birth of Trinity*, 64.
42. Bates, *Birth of Trinity*, 129.
43. Bates, *Birth of Trinity*, 82.

Irenaeus is clear that "here the Father addresses the Son, the wonderful Counsellor of the Father" (*Epid.* 55). The notion of conversation implies distinct identities, as indeed does the insistence on the three names. As suggested in chapter 4 of volume 1, these are the characters active in the dramatic narrative of scripture; now we see them conversing in advance about what is to be as the plot unfolds according to the providential *oikonomia* of the Creator God.

Those committed to this by now traditional approach to reading the prophetic texts of scripture would surely not take kindly to a monarchianism that reduced Christ to a mere man or treated the names as mere designators or masks rather than as distinct identities. How to read scripture was bound to be a key element in the arguments.

3.3.3. Meeting Modalist Monarchianism: Arguments and Prooftexts

Both Tertullian and Hippolytus bear witness to the nature of these arguments and the use of key prooftexts, the former in his *Against Praxeas* and the latter in the work *Against Noetus*, which is described in the manuscript as a homily by Hippolytus, archbishop of Rome and martyr, but is probably not by the same author as the compiler of the *Refutation of All Heresies*,[44] from which we have previously drawn. Both seem to be earlier than the account in the *Refutation*, and it may be that Hippolytus was indebted to Tertullian's work.

These two works, then, unveil the arguments used by the opponents of the monarchians to refute their position. Several things are noticeable:

- recourse to tradition, or the rule of faith, against what is treated as a novelty, a strange doctrine taught by strangers (*Noet.* 1.1; *Prax.* 3);
- the centrality of scripture—for both sides, indeed—with exegesis and counterexegesis, and appeals to prooftexts from both Old and New Testaments;
- the exposition of Logos-theology as a means of holding together God's oneness and the requirement to acknowledge the "economy."

Tertullian's use of the word "dispensation" (*dispensatio* as the Latin equivalent the Greek *oikonomia*) captures a sense of God's providential "arrangements," whereby unity is disposed into Trinity, and a plurality produced without divi-

44. The critical arguments surrounding this work are discussed by Butterworth in the introduction to his English translation of *Contra Noetum*. The author of *Against Noetus* is not considered by scholars to be the same as the author of the *Refutation*. If Brent is right, both works come from someone in Hippolytus's school rather than Hippolytus himself.

sion (*Prax.* 2–3). He uses as an analogy the one empire, for the one emperor may choose to share sovereignty with a son as agent without dividing the sovereignty—in fact, the single monarchy is not threatened by the delegation of power to many provincial governors. So too God's *monarchia* is not divided by the fact that his agents are the Son and the Holy Spirit, and the angels are his ministers. Next, Tertullian develops the idea that the lone God was not alone given that his "Reason" (Logos) was always within and became "Discourse" (Logos) when God spoke (*Prax.* 5–8). Thus there was the Word, the Son, another beside God, never separated from God but of the same "substance" as a shoot is "son of the root," a river "son of the spring," a beam "son of the sun." The monarchy is not undermined by the Trinity, for the Son is not other than the Father by diversity but by distribution, not by division but by distinction, while the Holy Spirit is a third constituting this relationship. This "economy" must be affirmed alongside the oneness of God.

In the course of this exposition, scripture is often cited as witness. First Corinthians 15:27–28 speaks of the Son reigning until God has put all his enemies under his feet, and then being subjected himself so that God may be all in all—meanwhile two obviously share the monarchy. Proverbs 8:22–31 and Genesis 1 are woven into the description of God's internal conversation and the agency of creation, as had become traditional. Tertullian's treatise will eventually exploit John's Gospel to show the "dispensation" whereby there are two, yet "I and the Father are one" (John 10:30).

Clear then is the imperative to counter the opposition's appeal to scripture: "You shall have no other gods but me" (Exod 20:3) and "I am the first and the last, and besides me there is no other" (Isa 44:6). These and other such scriptural affirmations lay at the heart of their argument, as is even clearer in Hippolytus's *Against Noetus*. Most of these prooftexts were drawn from what Christians were already calling the Old Testament.[45] Baruch 3:35–37 seems to have been particularly important to the monarchians: "This is our God. No other will be compared to him. He found out the whole way of knowledge and gave it to Jacob his son and to Israel who is his beloved. Afterwards he was seen on earth and conversed with men." According to Hippolytus, Noetus deduced from this that the God who is the one alone was subsequently seen and talked with human beings (*Noet.* 2.5). This, Hippolytus suggests, was the reason why Noetus felt himself bound to "submit to suffering" the single God that exists, while Rom 9:5, which seems to describe Christ as God over all, clinched the argument.

45. See volume 1, the opening of chapter 1, for the use of the same prooftexts by Oneness Pentecostals in our time.

Neither Hippolytus nor Tertullian was prepared to scrap the "economy," even though they both accepted that there was only one God revealed in scripture. Hippolytus in particular resorts to appealing to context and indications in each passage that point to Christ Jesus, quoting other texts to confirm his readings (*Noet.* 4.1–7.7). The notion that the transcendent Father comes into being, suffers, and dies is treated as blasphemous. Tertullian's rhetoric articulates his sense that Praxeas managed two pieces of the devil's business—driving out prophecy through opposition to the Montanists as well as introducing the patripassian heresy: "he put to flight the Paraclete and crucified the Father" (*Prax.* 1). It is through the "economy" that the invisible and impassible God could become visible and passible in the Son, both authors using John's Gospel extensively to demonstrate this "economy."

The climax of the *Against Noetus* is a scripturally informed celebration of the Word who is at the Father's side and whom the Father sent for the salvation of humanity. As the one proclaimed through the Law and Prophets, the Word became the "new man" from the Virgin and the Holy Spirit, never disowning his human being—hungry, exhausted, weary, thirsty, troubled when he prays, sleeping on a pillow, sweating in agony and wanting release from suffering, betrayed, flogged, mocked, bowing his head and breathing his last, he took upon himself our infirmities, as Isaiah said. Yet he was raised from the dead, and is himself the resurrection and the life. Caroled by angels and gazed on by shepherds, at his baptism he received God's witness, "This is my beloved Son," changed water into wine, reproved the sea, raised Lazarus, and forgave sins.

> This is God who became human on our behalf—he to whom the Father subjected all things. To him be glory and power as well as to the Father and the Holy Spirit in the Holy Church, both now and always and from age to age. Amen.

Thus the arguments were all about articulating the true teaching of scripture and conceptualizing the liturgical confession of the church.

Deductions from scripture were vital for determining the being of God's Word. However, it is also evident that scriptural prooftexts could not resolve the questions—different citations are employed against each other. Traditions enshrined in liturgy and the rule of faith prove to be what makes the difference, and arguments tending away from these traditions are treated as "strange doctrine taught by strangers" (*Noet.* 1.1). Hermeneutics grounded in the appeal to long-standing prooftexts from prophecy counterbalance the commitment to the one Creator God whose *monarchia* is absolute, and the tension is not really resolved. Origen's revealing response to Celsus shows up the tension: on the one hand, Father and Son are one, but on the other, there are two *hypostases*, two existences individual enough to hold a conversation.

4. Prospect: The Nub of the Question Shifts[46]

For the monarchians God's oneness was the primary concern: two divine beings could not be entertained—it would be the slippery slope to pagan polytheism and definitely nonbiblical. The *monarchia* of God was absolute. Undoubtedly this remained an underlying concern, but the focus shifted. *Creatio ex nihilo*—that other second-century *dogma*—began to play into the picture: if everything but God was created out of nothing, what about the so-called second God, the Logos or Son of God? Was he a creature, created out of nothing? This was a new and disturbing question for those committed to the apostolic tradition. It will concern us as we make explicit what was implicit in the arguments and appeals to scripture that emerged when the Arian controversies rocked the church for half a century. It is worth asking, though, why the question had not surfaced earlier.

Let us hazard an answer. From this distance, and painting with a very broad brush, we might portray as much the same the structure of the universe assumed by Celsus and Origen (even though details varied) as well as by Valentinian Gnosticism, various philosophical systems, and even by the Judaism of the time. All alike had hierarchical presuppositions: at the top one supreme God with other beings on a ladder of descent, whether divine or angelic, spiritual or earthly. Two questions were contested among these different groups: (1) how material or corporeal reality was to be evaluated and (2) where sat the proper object of worship. Celsus and later Neoplatonists like Porphyry, on the one hand, would argue that through traditional rituals, offered to many lesser but more accessible gods or daemons, worship is offered, if somewhat indirectly, to the supreme transcendent God. Origen, on the other hand, would follow the Jewish tradition that only the one true God is to be worshipped, despite the existence of angels aplenty; for God's mere servants, worship is not appropriate. Regarding the other issue of materiality, gnostics would claim

46. The following discussion was partially anticipated by my paper "Christology and Creation: Towards an Hermeneutic of Patristic Christology," in *The Myriad Christ: Plurality and the Quest for Unity in Contemporary Christology*, ed. T. Merigan and J. Haers (Leuven: Leuven University Press, 2000), 191–205. Used with permission.

to belong already to the spiritual world and to be awaiting redemption from the flesh, while for Irenaeus God's material creation was fundamentally good; Origen perhaps tried to have it both ways.

So how was it that these various systems had such a family likeness? Surely it bespeaks a common fuzziness about distinguishing between God and other orders of being. The well-known Euhemeran theory of religion, whereby gods were formed by the apotheosis of kings or heroes, was exploited against each other by both Celsus and Origen. It was usual to assume souls were immortal, if not divine (though on occasion Christians demurred, insisting on their creation by God). Even in Judaism the angels mediated God's presence and had names deriving from divine attributes, while human prophets and righteous human beings could be regarded as God's sons, embodying God's word, wisdom, or spirit; indeed, the assumption of Enoch to heaven paralleled the apotheosis of other "divine men." As a result of these common hierarchical assumptions, there was not merely a general blurring of any line between the one supreme God and other beings, between the divine and the human, but rather a common failure to realize that such a line should be drawn.

So, where Christ, or the Logos, was important, he naturally took his place within a hierarchy. It could be a matter of contention where exactly in that hierarchy he sat: if the monarchians conflated him with the ultimate one Creator God, most Christians preferred to place him within the hierarchy in the key mediatorial place. Indeed, Origen perhaps thought in terms of the Logos as the One-Many, the link between the ultimate One and the multiplicity of creation envisaged in some contemporary Platonic philosophy—he certainly suggests that in wisdom, which he identifies with the Word, there was implicit every capacity and form of the creation that was to be (*Princ.* 1.2.2). Be that as it may, my general point is that it was assumed that the Logos was the key mediator in the presumed hierarchy of beings, a point undoubtedly reinforced by the attribution to him in scripture of the title "Son of God."

As hinted earlier in section 2 of this chapter, the line between the divine and the human was potentially, but not yet actually, clarified by the doctrine of *creatio ex nihilo*. The denial of the existence of eternal matter was an explicit rejection of Platonist assumptions, and its grounds lay in the need to affirm the absolute priority of God as the sole first principle.[47] But the full consequences of the adoption of the formula *creatio ex nihilo* would take a long time to work out. Theophilus was instrumental in arguing for God's capacity to create from nothing, and he also seems to have been the first to refer to the "Triad," yet

47. See volume 1, chapter 3, 2.3.

even he blurred the distinction between Creator and created, writing in one place, "in the fourth place is man . . . ; so that there might be God, Logos, Sophia, Man" (*Autol.* 2.15). Origen certainly accepted the *ex nihilo* doctrine, but he also blurred the issue by arguing that, if God was Creator and God was unchangeable, God must always have been Creator, and therefore creation must be as eternal as the one who created it. He used the same argument, of course, to establish the eternal generation of the Son from the Father, conceiving an eternal hierarchy in which there was no clear dividing line between the Father, Son, Spirit, angels, and other rational beings. For Origen it was just the material creation that came into being out of nothing with time, and that was God's answer to the problem of disobedience in the eternal spiritual creation.

Thus far the challenge offered to prevailing assumptions about matter by the notion of God's power to create out of nothing had as its principal outcome the establishment of the goodness of the material creation, for creation was grounded in God's providential goodwill, as observed in Genesis 1. It would take time for further consequences to be explicitly identified, such as the radical difference between the Creator and every mode of creaturely existence, whether spiritual or material, angelic or human; if perhaps implicit in the monarchian challenge, it certainly was not yet explicit. Pre-Nicene Logos-theology worked precisely by avoiding such a distinction. The question where to draw the line between Creator and created was never put, as creation was delegated to the Logos, a point confirmed by such scripture texts as Proverbs 8:22–31 and Colossians 1:15–20. It was the very role of the Logos to be a mediator between different levels in a continuous ladder of existence with no breakpoint, a universe in which there was the kind of blurring between the divine and the creaturely that we have observed. No clear distinction was envisaged, no line drawn.

Historians may argue about whether the issue of drawing such a line was raised by Arius's challenge or Athanasius's reply, but my observation is more hermeneutic than historical. The fundamental issue between Athanasius and the Arians was whether the Logos incarnate in Jesus belonged to the divine or created order, a question that was bound to shatter the traditional Logos-theology and create what we know as the christological problem. The gulf between God and the created order became fundamental, and the person and work of Christ had to be reconceived within such a framework. It was this tension that came to a head in the fourth century: the tension between the tendency to think in hierarchical terms and the radical distinction implied by God's *monarchia*—a concept fundamental to Christianity from the beginning and, as we saw earlier, ultimately derived from scripture.

The shift necessitated some kind of reconceptualization, and this would mean offering a challenge not only to contemporary cultural and philosophical norms, but also to traditional assumptions about the meaning and indeed the consistency of the scriptures and the rule of faith. This volume will explore these issues, focusing on the deployment of scripture in Christianity's defining doctrinal controversies.

2

Three Names, One God?

PART 1, MAKING SENSE OF SCRIPTURE

The doctrine of the Trinity will concern us for the next two chapters as we tease out the role of scripture in its specification as well as in the subsequent theological exploration of the concept and its biblical roots. We shall observe how the church struggled to deal with what seemed a perverse doctrinal deduction—it simply did not fit with long-held assumptions about the preexistent Logos of God and devotion to Christ yet was apparently the logical outcome of those key second-century doctrines concerning God's *monarchia* and *creatio ex nihilo*. Nor could the issues be settled by straightforward appeal to scripture, whose ambiguity offered no clear guidance on what was an essentially new question.

It is striking how the fourth-century debates were as much about scripture and its implications as they were about the nature of the Logos or the Spirit. In volume 1 we found that doctrinal frameworks, such as the rule of faith, time and again provided the key to correct scriptural interpretation; yet that doctrine was itself distilled from scripture in the process of making sense of it. Exploring the relationship between doctrine and scripture in Origen's work, we traced the movement from one to the other in each direction. In this chapter we shall find the same double movement as Athanasius seeks to counteract the Arian claim to teach scriptural doctrine, and as Basil endeavors to ground in scripture the true doctrine of the Holy Spirit.

1. The Arian Controversies

1.1. Setting the Scene

The so-called Arian controversies present us with complex interactions between politics and personalities, positions and parties; it is impossible within the compass of this chapter to reexamine all relevant sources or to reconstruct what is a very complicated story. There are in any case many other scholarly narratives available, particularly as the past half-century has seen a flowering of research in this area and a radical reappraisal of what was going on.[1] Suffice it, then, to make a few initial statements of the position that will be assumed in the following discussion.

1. The "historical Arius" together with his antecedents, intentions, and specific teaching is a fascinating and much discussed subject, but in the end he was a minor player. Many accused of being Arian refused the label, not least those who stated at the Council of Antioch in 341: "We are not followers of Arius, for how could we who are bishops follow a presbyter?" He was the mere catalyst of a wider and more significant struggle toward a clearer articulation of core Christian doctrines.
2. It is no longer possible to regard the story as a binary conflict between "Nicenes" and "Arians," nor to deploy other labels, such as "Semi-Arians," "Homoians," "Homoiousians," or "Homoousians" in a way that sheds much clear light on the matters at stake. On each side of the supposed binary there were significant differences between key players; there were various stages of the struggle, shifting alliances, and differing aspects of the issues that were brought into play, not to mention the changing political scene.
3. Certainly, over the fifty plus years between the Councils of Nicaea (325) and Constantinople (381), different theological traditions and emphases came into conflict. Some reached eventual compromise, but tracing those trajectories, given the shifts and overlaps, may not give the truest access to the questions at stake.

1. E.g., Robert Gregg and Dennis Groh, *Early Arianism: A View of Salvation* (Philadelphia: Fortress, 1977); Rowan Williams, *Arius: Heresy and Tradition* (London: Darton, Longman and Todd, 1987); R. P. C. Hanson, *The Search for the Christian Doctrine of God: The Arian Controversy, 318–381* (Edinburgh: T&T Clark, 1988); Michel R. Barnes and Daniel H. Williams, *Arianism after Arius: Essays on the Development of the Fourth Century Trinitarian Conflicts* (Edinburgh: T&T Clark, 1993); Lewis Ayres, *Nicaea and Its Legacy: An Approach to Fourth-Century Trinitarian Theology* (Oxford: Oxford University Press, 2004).

4. The same may be the case with the key terminology, particularly given the way in which nonscriptural terms—such as the "substance-language" of *ousia* and *hypostasis*—though introduced to be quite specific, in fact proved too elastic or too easily misunderstood immediately to advance conceptual clarity.
5. More significant were sensitivities about inherited understandings of certain key passages of scripture, not to mention the faith into which one had been baptized (the rule of faith by now being encapsulated in local baptismal creeds). These constituted fundamental drivers toward particular docrinal outcomes in the minds of participants in the struggle. All wanted to do justice to the faith of their fathers, all claimed precedents, and all identified heresies to be avoided, usually charging their immediate opponents with being representatives of those previously banned expressions of the faith.

Given that our objective is to explore the relationship between doctrine and scripture, we will now take some soundings in the literature produced during the course of the controversies, beginning with Athanasius's three *Orations against the Arians*. Inevitably we will hear the voices of the winners more clearly than those of the losers, but our aim is to discern something of the two-way traffic between scripture and doctrine evident on both sides: how were doctrinal deductions made from scripture? And conversely, how was scripture deployed to substantiate doctrinal frameworks or propositions?

1.2. Doctrinal Frameworks

It is now generally accepted that Athanasius's *Orations against the Arians*, written in the 340s, effectively constructed "Arianism"—sharpening up the issues at stake in the complex debates of the time by turning current tensions into a binary conflict, tracing its roots back to the pre-Nicene dissension between Arius and his bishop, refuting its basic principles, and challenging "Arian" exegesis of key texts.[2] Treating the first three *Orations against the Arians* as authentic, we find evident throughout them the two-way traffic that interests us.[3] On the

2. Greek text in *Athanasius Werke*, vol. 1.2, *Orationes I et II contra Arianos*, ed. K. Metzler, D. U. Hansen, and K. Savvidis (Berlin: de Gruyter, 1998), and *Athanasius Werke*, vol. 1.3, *Oratio III contra Arianos*, ed. K. Savvidis and K. Metzler (Berlin: de Gruyter, 2000); English translation, unless otherwise noted, in *NPNF*[2] 4.

3. The authenticity of book 3 was challenged by C. Kannengiesser, "Athanasius of Alexandria and the Foundation of Traditional Christology," *Theological Studies* 34.1 (1973): 103–13; Kannengiesser, "Athanasius of Alexandria, Three Orations against the Arians: A Re-

one hand, apart from the opening half of the first book, these orations almost entirely engage with the scriptural texts that emerged in the controversies as susceptible to opposing interpretations. However, on the other hand, prior to embarking on text-by-text exegetical discussion, Athanasius first sets out the basic shape of Arian doctrine, then summarizes his own overall approach, and contrasts the two. These frameworks, he seems to recognize, are fundamental to the way scripture is read on either side, yet scripture itself, along with traditional readings of it, has undoubtedly contributed to those frameworks.

At the very start, then, Athanasius treats the Arian heresy as crafty and cunning, dressing herself in scriptural language, but "denying the Son and reckoning him among the creatures" (*C. Ar.* 1.1, 4). Their fundamental propositions he sets out as:[4]

- God was not always Father; once God was alone, not yet Father, but afterward he became Father;
- the Son was not always;
- all things are made from nothing;
- the Word of God was made out of nothing and once was not;
- God, wishing to form us, made a certain one and named him Word and Wisdom and Son, that God might form us by means of him;
- this Wisdom participates in God's wisdom (but is therefore other than the true wisdom of God), and so is named Word and Son according to grace;
- by nature the Word is alterable, remaining good by free will, but able to change, as we can;
- the Word is called God, but is not true God, but rather God by participation and grace, so God only in name, with neither understanding nor exact knowledge of the Father;
- the essences of the Father, the Son, and the Holy Spirit are separate and estranged, disconnected and alien, utterly unlike each other.

For Athanasius all this is blasphemy, however much it could be dressed up in scriptural language (1.8). For us, it is surely evidence that the old traditional, and essentially biblically based, doctrines of God's *monarchia* and *creatio ex*

appraisal," StPatr 18 (1982): 981–95; both reproduced in Kannengiesser, *Arius and Athanasius* (Aldershot: Variorum, 1991). Whether authentic or not, for our purposes, book 3 of *C. Ar.* represents a key text which, received as Athanasian, would have considerable influence on subsequent christological debates.

4. *C. Ar.* 1.5–6; cf. 1.9 for a somewhat parallel account.

nihilo have been brought into association to challenge longstanding assumptions about the hierarchy of being and the nature of the Logos.

Athanasius next claims to take scripture and from it set out the faith "as a light on its lampstand":

> He is by nature the true and authentic Son of the Father, proper to his being, only-begotten Wisdom, true and only Word of God. He is not a creature or a made thing, but proper offspring of the Father's being. Wherefore he is true God, being of one substance with the true Father. But the others, to whom he said, "I have said, you are gods," have this grace from the Father only by participation in the Word through the Spirit. For he is the imprint of the Father's substance, and light from light, and power, and true image of the Father's being. For again, the Lord said this: "the one who has seen me has seen the Father." He always was, and is, and never was not. For since the Father is eternal, so also would his Word and Wisdom be eternal. (*C. Ar.* 1.9)[5]

In subsequent sections Athanasius builds up a dossier of texts and arguments to substantiate this. Already that statement contains echoes of scripture, but nonbiblical expressions are also evident: this is the only place in the *Orations* where the Nicene *homoousios* is used, whereas the phrase "proper offspring [*gennēma*] of the Father's being [*ousia*]" (1.9) will prove a repeated refrain all through these discourses, summing up what is the import of scriptural testimonies, such as John 10:30, 14:9, and 10; 1 Corinthians 1:24; Colossians 1:15; and Hebrews 1:3.[6] The overall point, of course, is that the scriptures declare the Son's eternity, and items in this dossier will become "touchstone texts" repeatedly reiterated in the ongoing argument.[7] Time and again some or all of Word, Wisdom, Power, and Radiance are run together as a composite title for the Son with frequent unpacking of the underlying biblical images.[8] Just as the sun can never be separated from its radiance, so the Son is the "radiance of God's glory"; the fountain of wisdom and life generates a stream of living water.[9] So too the Word is the expression of God's own thought (1.20), so he is the "imprint of the Father's substance" (Heb 1:3). We can recognize these

5. . English translation of Athanasius here from James Ernest, *The Bible in Athanasius of Alexandria* (Leiden: Brill, 2004), 134.

6. See *C. Ar.* 1.16, 20, 24, 28, 39.

7. I borrow the phrase from James Ernest; see the useful Table of Touchstone Texts in *Bible in Athanasius*, 154–55.

8. E.g., *C. Ar.* 1.6, 20, 46, 49, 58, 60; 2.34, 41; 3.6, 29. Scriptural allusions include Ps 36:9; Jer 2:13; 17:12–13; Bar 3:12; John 1:1; Heb 1:3.

9. For the radiance of God's glory, see *C. Ar.* 1.13–14, 16, 24–25, 43; 2.2, 31–33, 42; 3.1,

images from previous use by Tertullian: they purport to express inseparable distinction.

But then there are undoubtedly scriptural proofs that would point to the Arian doctrinal framework, and it is these with which Athanasius has to deal in the rest of these orations. The rival frameworks determine the selection of texts and the reading of those texts, yet the frameworks themselves seek to do justice to the overall thrust of scripture considered. God's *monarchia* and the mediatorial function of the Logos clearly shape the Arian viewpoint, and it was these inherited perspectives that gave traction to their claims, despite articulating certain novel deductions. What is it that drives Athanasius's contrary views? We may discern this by exploring his handling of texts where *prima facie* the Arians had the advantage.

1.3. Traditional Texts, Disputed Meanings

It is noticeable that those texts we considered in the previous chapter as potentially implying conversations between the "three names" are significantly represented among those now in contention, for example:

- Psalm 45:6–7: Therefore God, your God has anointed you with the oil of gladness beyond your companions.
- Isaiah 45:1: Thus says the Lord to his anointed (i.e., Christ).
- Psalm 110:1: The Lord says to my lord: "Sit at my right hand, till I make your enemies your footstool."
- Psalm 2:7 (in the form found In Matthew's narrative of Jesus's baptism): He said to me, "You are my son, with whom I am well pleased."

To these others were added, particularly from the New Testament, texts that include:

- Isaiah 61:1: The Lord has anointed me.
- Acts 2:36: God has made him both Lord and Messiah.
- Philippians 2:9: Therefore God exalted him.
- Colossians 1:15: . . . the firstborn of all creation.
- Hebrews 1:4: He was made better than the angels.
- Hebrews 3:2: . . . faithful to him that made him.
- Hebrews 7:22: Jesus has become . . .

3–4, 11, 13, 15, 67. The fountain and living water imagery can be found in *C. Ar.* 1.14, 19, 27; 2.2, 42; 3.3.

The trouble was that most of these texts suggested that the Father would or had anointed, appointed, exalted, made, adopted, or created the Logos or Son, which implied that he was a "work" or that he had been promoted or advanced from a subordinate state. Thus they encouraged the Arian deduction that the sole first principle, the only truly eternal being that never came into being (*agenētos*), could only be the one supreme God. Even though the Logos was the first and greatest of the creatures—indeed, had been brought into being to create everything else—he was not truly God in the same sense as God was God: "I, even I, am he: there is no other God beside me" (Deut 32:39). Clearly the Arians thought this was always what scripture meant: the *monarchia* of the one God and the mediatorial function of the Logos, who was the firstborn of all creation, created as a "medium," since things brought into being could not endure the "absolute hand of the One who never came into being" (*C. Ar.* 2.24; cf. *Decr.* 8). Surely the reason for the long-drawn-out struggle was exactly this: that common unquestioned assumptions about the plain meaning of the scriptures—and not least classic prooftexts—had combined with key doctrinal propositions to shape a particular overall understanding of the Creator's relationship with the creation and the role of the mediating "second God." In many ways you could say that Athanasius was the one out on a limb, while the so-called Arians were the traditionally minded bishops.

How then does Athanasius deal with these contentious texts?

(1) In some cases all he has to do is to point to the immediate wider context of the verse in question. Philippians 2:9–11, for example, may refer to the Son's exaltation but only after insisting on his self-emptying: "existing as God, he took the form of a servant, and in taking it, was not promoted but humbled himself" (*C. Ar.* 1.40), and the anointing in Psalm 45:7 is almost immediately preceded in verse 6 by "Your throne, O God, endures for ever and ever."

(2) Athanasius's more frequent tactic is to find countertexts. For example, John 17:5, which reads "Glorify me with the glory I had with you before the world was," counteracts the idea that Philippians 2:9–10 implies promotion (*C. Ar.* 1.38), while in Hebrews the apostle's quotation of Psalm 45:6 shows he was always superior to the angels, as does his reference to Psalm 102:25–27: "You, Lord, did found the earth in the beginning" (*C. Ar.* 1.57–58). Needless to say, the "touchstone texts" appear time and again.

(3) Sometimes he points to terminological issues. For example, "faithful," attributed to Jesus in Hebrews 3:1, might be taken "as if he exercises faith and so receives the reward of faith," but God is also called "faithful." This indicates "two senses of the word" in scripture, either "believing" or "trustworthy," the first applying to Abraham and the second to God (*C. Ar.* 2.6). Often, however,

he avoids getting into spats at such a terminological level by moving to larger considerations. "Terms are not prior to essences, but essences first and terms second" (2.3; cf. 2.11), he says, introducing a long disquisition on the ambiguities of scriptural usage of "make," showing how it can mean "beget" in certain contexts. Elsewhere, of course, he wants to document exactly the difference between "make" or "create" and "beget," between a "work" external to its maker and a "son" proper to its parent's being (2.57).

(4) He appeals to the need to identify the time or occasion, the speaker's person, and the subject to show how the text should really be taken (*C. Ar.* 1.55). So the words "having become so much better than the angels" in Hebrews 1:4 cannot be taken to suggest the Son "became" absolutely—thereby being a "work" or "creature"—for it is followed by "better" (*C. Ar.* 1.56). Nor should comparison be taken to imply the Word and angels are of the same kind. The apostle was not comparing the "essence" of the Word to things that have become, for they are incommensurable (1.59). This text is all about the incarnation and the superiority of the Son who brought the new covenant over the ministry through angels, mere servants.

(5) This brings us to his most repeated strategy—to distinguish texts referring to the divine nature of the Word from those referring to the time when "the Word became flesh" (John 1:14). Sometimes this strategy is effective.[10] We can easily agree that his being "faithful to the one who made him" (Heb 3:1) is about the time when "he was in all things made like his brothers" (Heb 2:14–18). But, as we shall see later, for some key texts to which he keeps returning, such as Proverbs 8:22, it is less obvious. Still, with respect to all those terms which are proper to human beings, there is arguably no difficulty, as long as the incarnation is the reference (*C. Ar.* 2.11). This principle is applied to Acts 2:36, then Psalm 110:1 is satisfactorily related to the resurrection and ascension along with Psalm 16:10: he is not promoted as Word or Son but as the climax of the story of incarnation.

(6) Often these tactics are used to show how it was all "for our sake." Being "anointed beyond your companions" in Psalm 45:7 points ultimately to his baptism, which was not about promotion for the Word but about our sanctification, that "we might share in his anointing." John 17:19, which reads "for their sakes, I sanctify myself," enables this deduction (*C. Ar.* 1.46–47). Indeed

10. This strategy is particularly heavily drawn upon in book 3 of *Orations against the Arians*, where there is treatment of texts, especially but not solely from the Synoptic Gospels, which the Arians took to show weakness, ignorance, and so on. Discussion will necessarily be more substantial in chapter 4 below.

the words of that very psalm needed further elucidation along these lines, for clearly the suggestion had been made that loving righteousness and hating iniquity implied changeability. For Athanasius it implies the exact opposite: human beings needed the immutability of the righteousness of the Word as an image and type for virtue (*C. Ar.* 1.51).

(7) The really important point for Athanasius, however, is that every text of scripture should be brought before the bar of what James Ernest has called his "metanarrative." Essentially this is his understanding of creation, fall, redemption, and union with the divine by participation in the truly divine Son (*theopoiēsis* or *huiopoiēsis*)—the fundamental story into which we are drawn by scripture and which only makes overall sense if the Redeemer embodies absolutely that divine nature into which we may be adopted. This overall narrative is set out in Athanasius's earlier work, *Against the Pagans/On the Incarnation*, and it is implicit as the backdrop to his discussion of the problem texts.[11]

This last point is interesting in that the metanarrative does not come in any recognizable creedal form, nor is appeal made to a "canon of truth" or "rule of faith." In fact, such baptismal confessions are apparently superseded by this overarching sense of the whole biblical narrative in a spirit more reminiscent of Irenaeus's comprehensive tracing of the biblical narrative in his *Demonstration of the Apostolic Preaching*, though here tightly compressed to make a point.[12] As James Ernest notes: "Athanasius can . . . on occasion compose texts of his own by weaving language from all parts of the canon into concise summaries of the overall shape of the biblical metanarrative."[13] Note the example Ernest provides at this point:

> For the Son of God, being himself the Word, is Lord of all, while we who were from the beginning subject to the enslavement to corruption and the curse of the law then little by little fashioning non-existent things for ourselves, began to serve, as the blessed apostle says, things that are by nature not gods. And we were ignorant of the true God, while we esteemed non-existent things more highly than the truth. But later, just as the former people, being burdened down in Egypt, groaned, so also when we, having the implanted law, and imploring according to the unutterable groanings

11. Athanasius, *Contra Gentes and De Incarnatione*, ed. and trans. Robert W. Thomson, OECT (Oxford: Clarendon, 1971).

12. See volume 1, chapter 4.

13. Ernest, *Bible in Athanasius*, 132.

> of the spirit, said, "Lord, our God, possess us," just as he became a house of refuge and a God of defense, so also he became our Lord. (*C. Ar.* 2.14)[14]

By book 3 of *Orations against the Arians* we find the phrases "the scope of scripture," "the scope of the Christian faith," and "the ecclesiastical scope." This scope is to be used as a rule for reading scripture. What it consists of is:

> a double account of the Savior; that he was always God, and is the Son, being the Father's Word and Radiance and Wisdom; and that afterwards for us he took flesh of a Virgin, Mary Bearer of God,[15] and was made man. And this scope is to be found throughout inspired scripture. (*C. Ar.* 3.28)[16]

Athanasius calls this *skopos* a rule or canon, and it might appear to allude to some traditional phrases of the creed or rule of faith; but it hardly identifies the "names" of the baptismal confession in the way that we found the old canon of faith did, nor does it seem to designate something like the *hypothesis* of scripture, its "plot" or "summary"; the previous quotation was nearer to suggesting that. Rather it picks out the intention or goal of scripture with respect to the specific christological issues at stake.

Interestingly, however, it refrains from using any of the "technical terms" of the dispute, the slogans used as repeated councils tried to draw up an agreed confession of faith. It is as though Athanasius is determined in the *Orations against the Arians* to focus on scripture, indeed on the metanarrative he has distilled from scripture as a whole, and to use its basic shape to develop a framework for his exegesis of particular texts. So is Athanasius's doctrine in his *Orations against the Arians* necessarily biblical, possessing a kind of mutual coinherence of scripture and framework? The answer must be both yes and no: it does constitute, maybe, the sense of scripture, but it is reexpressed in other terms, which implies a certain transmutation to accommodate the demands of new questions.

For, first, Athanasius accepts typical nonbiblical philosophical assumptions—God is simple and without body, parts, or passions; the Son is not part of God, rather God is impassibly and indivisibly Father of the Son (*C. Ar.* 1.28).

14. English translation from Ernest, *Bible in Athanasius*, 133.

15. That is, *Theotokos*. That Athanasius was thought to have used this term will become significant in chapter 5.

16. Translation from Ernest, *Bible in Athanasius*, 144.

If God's creativity is different from that of human beings in that God needs no material from which to make things, how much more will God's begetting or generation be utterly different from that of humankind (1.23)! God is assumed to be unalterable (1.35), though it is true that arguments about the unchangeability of God, Father and Son, are often couched in biblical terms. For example, Psalm 102:26–28 contrasts heaven and earth with the Creator who endures, is eternal, and remains the same, while the point is proved by Malachi 3:6, "For I, the Lord, do not change," and Hebrews 13:8, "Jesus Christ, the same yesterday, today and for ever." Scripture, then,

> signifying under the name of heaven and earth that the nature of all things originate and created is alterable and changeable, yet excepting the Son from them, shews us thereby that He is in no wise a thing originate, nay teaches that He changes everything else and is Himself not changed. (*C. Ar.* 1.36)

Elsewhere the faithfulness of God is understood to signify God's immutability (2.10). But sooner or later the biblical repertoire of terms for God's nature was bound to prove inadequate—indeed Athanasius found himself drawing on analogies and admitting the inadequacy of any human language to speak of God, let alone the nature of the relationship between Father and Son (1.23). The paradox of eternal generation stretched the possibilities of prooftexts.

Then, second, the way in which Athanasius's framework was shaped, particularly his understanding of scripture's *skopos* (though not so much his overarching metanarrative), was evidently influenced by the specific doctrinal questions at issue. Once it was pointed out that this long-standing doctrine of creation out of nothing—with its inseparable corollary, God's *monarchia*—must mean that God alone was *agenētos* (unbegotten), it was inevitable that at some point the nature and status of the "only-begotten" Son or Logos would come into question and the presumed hierarchy would become problematic. In *Orations against the Arians* Athanasius seems to be trying as far as possible to deal with the issues from the basis of scripture alone, seeking to specify the nature, character, and relationships of the key player(s) in the biblical drama through scriptural terminology and prooftexts. By his *Defense of the Nicene Definition*, however, he would have to concede the necessity of using nonscriptural terms to refine the definition of what scripture was all about. Meanwhile, in book 2 of *Orations against the Arians*, after repeated reference to Proverbs 8:22, he eventually could no longer put off extended treatment of the key problem text that literally seemed to endorse the deductions of his opponents.

1.4. Proverbs 8:22–31

No one in the fourth century challenged the fundamental approach to Proverbs 8 that we can already trace in the work of the second-century apologists. The christological reference of personified wisdom was assumed. Before we turn to Athanasius's novel reading of Proverbs 8:22–31, it is worth retracing its prior usage.[17]

Logos-theology was the context in which the apologists exploited Proverbs 8:22–31; Athenagoras can provide an example:

> If in your great wisdom you would like to know what "Son" means, I will tell you in a few brief words: it means that he is the first begotten of the Father. The term is used not because he came into existence (for God, who is eternal mind, had in Godself God's Word or Reason from the beginning, since God was eternally rational) but because the Son came forth to serve as Ideal Form and Energizing Power for everything material. . . . The prophetic Spirit also agrees with this account. "For the Lord," it says, "made me the beginning of his ways for his works" (Proverbs 8:22). (*Leg.* 10.3–4)[18]

Thus the Son of God, who is the eternal Logos or Mind of the Father, is also the first-begotten one, who is identified with Wisdom, personified here in Proverbs and presented as the one through whom God created the world.[19] This example could be reinforced by many others, such as Theophilus and Justin, who are followed by Origen and Tertullian.

Three aspects of this exegesis would become significant in the future:

- As we already noted in the previous chapter, this whole approach produced collages of scriptural texts, assembled to paint a picture of this preexistent

17. See chapter 1 of M. Simonetti, *Studi sull' Arianismo* (Rome: Editrice Studium, 1965). Simonetti undertook the initial research into how this passage was exploited by the Arians and the defensive reactions to it. I have considered the question more than once in past publications, such as "Exegetical Method and Scriptural Proof: The Bible in Doctrinal Debate," StPatr 24 (1989): 291–304, republished in Young, *Exegesis and Theology*. See also chapter 2 of my *Biblical Exegesis* and F. Young, "Proverbs 8 in Interpretation (2): Wisdom Personified," in *Reading Texts, Seeking Wisdom*, ed. David F. Ford and Graham Stanton (London: SCM, 2003), 102–15. This section is a later version of this last publication. Used with permission.

18. Greek text and English translation (here altered) in Athenagoras, *Legatio and De Resurrectione*, ed. and trans. W. R. Schoedel, OECT (Oxford: Clarendon, 1972).

19. This general approach to Proverbs 8 can be further documented by turning back to Theophilus of Antioch, *Autol.* 2.10; cf. chapter 1 above.

Logos through whom God created, and with whom God conversed when he said, "Let *us* make . . ." (Gen 1:26).[20]

- The actual sentence in Proverbs 8:22 was exploited to solve the exegetical problems of Genesis 1:1 "in the beginning." Beginning was treated as one of the titles of the Logos or Son of God—"he created me a Beginning"—construing the syntax as a double object.[21]
- Already in Tertullian's *Against Praxeas*, this exegetical tradition has acquired doctrinal significance: against the modalist monarchians, Proverbs 8 is quoted at length to demonstrate a real distinction between the Logos and the Father, the Logos being found in the scriptures also under the name of Wisdom (*Prax.* 6).

By the fourth century, then, a consistent approach to the reference of this text had been established. The Arian controversy made no difference to this consensus concerning the reference of Proverbs 8:22–31. Despite shared as-

20. For the link with Genesis see Justin, *Dial.* 61–62, where he quotes Proverbs 8 at length and then argues for a correlation with Genesis, raising the question who was God addressing when he said, "Let us make . . ." and "Behold, Adam has become as one of us." For Justin it is clear that God is addressing his offspring, who is to be identified as the one Solomon calls Wisdom.

21. When exercised about the correct construal of the word "beginning" in Genesis 1:1, Origen and Tertullian both appeal to Proverbs 8 to settle the issue. See Origen, *Comm. Jo.* 1.17. Text in E. Preuschen, ed., *Der Johanneskommentar*, Origenes Werke 4, GCS 10 (Leipzig: Hinrichs, 1904); English translation in *ANF* 9 and R. Heine, trans., *Commentary on the Gospel according to Saint John*, 2 vols., FC 80, 89 (Washington, DC: Catholic University of America Press, 1989, 1993). Origen here takes it that "Beginning" is a title for Christ, confirming this on the basis of Proverbs 8:22, where he construes *ektisen* (he created) as having a double object, as a verb of appointment would have: thus, "the Lord made me Beginning of his ways." Tertullian is arguing against Hermogenes, who stated that the Genesis text supported the idea that God created out of preexistent matter. The word "Beginning" Hermogenes interpreted as something substantial (i.e., matter). See Tertullian, *Herm.* 19. Latin text in Frédéric Chapot, ed., *Contre Hermogène*, SC 439 (Paris: Cerf, 1999); English translation in J. H. Waszink, trans., *Treatise against Hermogenes*, ACW (New York: Paulist, 1956). Here, Tertullian argues that "in the beginning" is comparable to "at last" and is about order not origin, simply referring to the inception of the activity. Appealing to the Greek *archē* (beginning), he adds that the sense is not only priority of order but of power as well, and he goes on to argue that the word must refer to the initial one, that is, the one who says, "The Lord established me as the beginning of his ways for the creation of his works"—in other words, Wisdom in Proverbs 8. For him Proverbs makes clear that the beginning of God's ways or works was Wisdom. And Wisdom is the Lord's right hand, the energy that produced creation (cf. *Herm.* 45, which also quotes Proverbs 8).

sumptions, however, one key word in the text provoked different conclusions about the nature of the Logos.

The Arians seized on the Greek verb *ektisen* (he created) found in verse 22, although in verse 25 the verb *genna* (he begets) is used. Prior to the controversy, these verbs were assumed to be synonyms, both of them indicating the generation of the Logos from the Father. Athanasius reports that Dionysius of Rome considered it improper to call the Son a *poiēma* (a creature), for scripture speaks of his *gennesis* (begottenness). Faced with Proverbs 8:22, however, he had argued that *ktizein* (to create) has various senses: there is usually a difference between *ktizein* and *poiein* (to make); and through cross-references he had established that in Proverbs 8, the *ektisen* of verse 22 must be the equivalent of the *genna* of verse 25, so making explicit what had been assumed all along (*Decr.* 26). But now for Athanasius's opponents, Proverbs 8:22 became a key prooftext, the implication being that they took the opposite view; namely, that *genna* was to be understood in terms of *ektisen*. Which of the two terms determined the meaning of the other? That was the question.

During the fourth-century controversies only Eusebius of Caesarea managed to maintain the traditional reading. As Simonetti noted, prior to the Arian controversy he had been considering the point that the generation or creation of the Logos in Proverbs 8 could indicate neither separation from the Father nor diminution or division. On the other hand it could not mean that the Logos, like other created beings, was created out of nothing. Eusebius could describe the Son as "the fragrance and splendour of the light of the Father," but regarded the mystery of the Son's generation of the Son as hidden. Later, in *Against Marcellus*, Eusebius treads the same tightrope, refraining from the Arian reading but also avoiding the novel suggestions made by Athanasius and others. Eusebius keeps the context intact with its picture of preexisting Wisdom as God's assistant in the creation of everything else and correlating with her the preexistent cosmic Christ. This text, he insists, is not an account of how the Logos came into being; rather it asserts his precedence over the creation of the whole world and his sovereignty over everything because he was set over them by the Lord, his Father, thus reasserting the traditional exegetical consensus. To do this he turns to philology, raising the question concerning the meaning of *ektisen*.

Eusebius maintains that *ktizein* does not here to mean "create" in the sense "bring into existence out of nothing," but rather the sense is "order" or "unite." The Hebrew and variant translations of Proverbs 8 are deployed to show that the sense is something like *ektēsato*: "he possessed." The Father established the Logos as the foundation of all things, "to sum up things in Christ, whether the things of heaven or the things of earth" (Eph 1:10). Rather than being about the origin of the Logos, Proverbs 8 is about God's providential activities; indeed, the origin of the Logos is a mystery beyond understanding or expression. So, by rendering the word *ektisen* differently, it was possible to retain the natural sequence of thought, unlike those opposed to Arius. Their somewhat dubious ploy was to claim that *ektisen* referred to the incarnation. Marcellus probably originated this approach. Accepting that the meaning of *ktizein* was "to create what did not previously exist," he asserted that the human flesh assumed by the Redeemer by means of the Virgin Mary was the creature here signified.

According to Simonetti, the novelty of this interpretation was masked by recourse to traditional typology, though whether that is the best term for conveying the exegetical techniques in question is another matter. Still, an apparently consistent interpretation of Proverbs 8:22–25 was produced by treating it as a prophecy of the new dispensation, indeed of the renewal brought about by the Savior, who said "I am the Way," and so "in the beginning of his ways" was made the Way of piety for us. Moves of this kind rendered the passage coherent as a whole. To give one other example: in light of the text, "No other foundation can anyone lay except that which is laid, which is Jesus Christ" (1 Cor 3:11), it was proposed that "before the ages he founded me" referred to God's providential foreordaining. So, phrase by phrase, the passage was given a more or less coherent exegesis as a reference to the incarnation rather than the generation of the Son from the Father. However, in the end there was resort to allegory, for in verse 24 there are statements referring to a time before the earth or the depths or springs existed—what has this to do with the incarnation? Well, the "earth" could be taken to refer to the flesh, for flesh was made from the dust of the earth according to Genesis 2:7 and will return to dust according to Genesis 3:19 but is restored through participation in the Logos. Then "the depths" could refer to the hearts of the saints, "which in their depths have the gift of the Spirit," and the "springs" could refer to the apostles, as the reference to the twelve springs of Elim in Exodus 15:27 was traditionally associated with the Twelve. So went on the allegorizing, but eventually the focus on the incarnation gets blurred, as the continuation of the passage in verses 27–30 refers to the Wisdom or Logos of God immanent in creation. Eusebius must surely be commended for challenging these arbitrary expedients in his reply to this piecemeal approach to the text.[22]

The high profile given to exegesis of this text in the anti-Arian works of Athanasius proves that it lay at the very heart of the Arian controversy. Indeed,

22. For Augustine's way of following the pro-Nicene reading in terms of the incarnation, see chapter 6 below.

Athanasius devotes about one third of book 2 of his *Orations against the Arians* to this text, exploiting various exegetical techniques to modify its embarrassing literal sense. He identifies the genre as proverb, so the sayings are expressed in the way of proverbs. Each proverb demands inquiry as to its reference and religious sense, which must be unfolded and sought as having hidden meaning. Scriptural usage and intertextuality enable this unfolding. Citing other texts he shows that the term *ektisen* usually relates to creatures and is not found where scripture speaks of the Son's generation. Furthermore, there are two scriptural senses of the word—it may concern origin but also renewal as in the plea, "Create in me a new heart." This proverb, in its hidden meaning, is thus taken to be about renewal rather than about the generation of the Word, and so not about the essence of the Logos but rather his humanity.

Turning to the syntax, Athanasius follows the old tradition arguing for the verb having a double object, so that "The Lord created me a beginning of his ways" parallels "My Father prepared for me a body." The proverb, then, designates the Son a "beginning of his ways" and this can be compared with "The Word became flesh and dwelt among us." These texts are not about an absolute becoming or creation, but about one relative to "us" or to "his works." Athanasius now notes a distinction between *ektisen* (he created) in Proverbs 8:22 and *genna* (he begets) in 8:25: the former is modified by an expression of purpose, "for his works," while the latter has no similar modifier. So the "begetting" in verse 25, as elsewhere in scripture, is stated absolutely, whereas the word "created" is relative, that is, relative to the *oikonomia*, and so to the incarnation as the expression of God's providential plan of salvation.

Fundamental to Athanasius's discernment of the mind of scripture is the distinction just made between speaking absolutely of the Son's Being and speaking of him relative to the created order (or the "Economy"). Intertextual references, gathered under such an overarching perspective, here enable interpretation of the text in terms of renewal or re-creation: "We are his workmanship, created in Jesus Christ," writes Athanasius, using Ephesians 2:10 among many other passages. It all leads up to his classic distinction, which, in his view, is fundamental to scripture: God's offspring (*gennēma*) was *begotten but then made*, that is, made flesh for our salvation in the Economy, whereas creatures (*poiēmata*) were *made and then begotten* through Christ, becoming sons by grace. So he is "the firstborn of all creation" as the origin of the new creation; he could not be firstborn of God, since he is the only-begotten of God.

Now, however, the problem of context raises its head. How can the resultant reading of Proverbs 8:22 be satisfactory? For in verse 23, we find: "before the world, he founded me in the beginning." The proverbial character of the material is again the first recourse; then the text from 1 Corinthians 3:11 "No other foundation can anyone lay . . ." is used to indicate that Proverbs is speaking of the providential preparation of this grace for us before the foundation of the world—a ploy, it seems, which Marcellus had already used. So the essence of Wisdom was not created, despite the Arian exploitation of this text; the impress of Wisdom in the works of God as a copy of the divine image was what was created, and thus will the whole world be filled with the knowledge of God.

We are now in a position to consider the strategies used to circumvent the Arian use of this text. Deductive argument is key, but this depended on using intertextuality to determine the overarching "mind" of scripture, and applied insensitively this could twist the sense of a particular passage to an implausible outcome—Proverbs 8:22 was surely not about the incarnation! Athanasius would perhaps have done better to pursue the tactic noted earlier whereby he highlighted the ambiguities of the scriptural usage of "make," showing it could mean "beget" in certain contexts.[23] After all, the reference to Proverbs 8:25 three verses later could have clinched it. Here, however, his scriptural parallels are designed to do the opposite: to establish that "created" refers to creatures in normal scriptural usage, so the text must refer to the created nature assumed by the Logos. The deductive process, then, involves attention to the meaning of words, establishing any particular biblical sense, then to the syntax and context of the text in question. Yet the way Athanasius approaches the questions posed by Arian exploitation of this passage primarily raises issues about genre, explicitly about the genre of the text in question, which clearly he properly identifies, but also about the "reading genre"—the text is not, as it were, autonomous, but must be read as scripture. So Athanasius can shape its sense to be coherent with what he discerns as the mind of scripture. The framework or metanarrative is all important not only in finding a solution to the problem posed by the particular text but even for posing the problem in the first place, for if wisdom in Proverbs 8 had not long been taken as a reference to the preexistent Christ, the issue would never have arisen.

1.5. Athanasius on Scripture and Doctrine

It is in the *Defense of the Nicene Definition* that we find indication of how Athanasius himself understood the relationship between scripture and doctrine. The issue of using nonscriptural language was already raised in the *Orations against the Arians*, Athanasius endeavoring to turn the tables on the Arians.

23. Cf. p. 35 above, and reference to *C. Ar.* 2.3.

Blaming the Nicene bishops for use of phrases not in scripture, the Arians were themselves tarred with the same brush—they borrowed the problematic term *agenētos* from the Greeks (*C. Ar.* 1.30). Written probably ten or fifteen years later than *Orations against the Arians*, *Defense of the Nicene Definition* expresses a more explicit commitment to the *homoousion* as the doctrinal way forward.

The *Defense of the Nicene Definition* responds to the question, "Why did the fathers at Nicaea use terms not in scripture, 'Of the essence' and 'One in essence'?" (*Decr.* 1). We eventually reach a straight answer: with nods and winks the Arians could interpret every scriptural phrase according to their own way of thinking (*Decr.* 19–20). It was because every phrase suggested could be twisted in this way that "the bishops were compelled on their part to collect the sense of the scriptures" and state it "more distinctly." The simple "of God" or "from God" is applicable to us, and the only way to signify that the Word was other than a creature like us was to specify "of the Father's *ousia*." The Arians could even cite specific scripture texts to show that "true power" or "exact image" could apply to us, Athanasius explains.

So now we can see why up to this point in his treatise Athanasius has expended huge effort to establish the double sense of "son" in scripture—essential and adoptive. Deuteronomy 13:18 and John 1:12 show that we may indeed become "children of God" or "sons of God" by grace or moral improvement (*Decr.* 6), and that is, of course, the sense in which the Arians wished to read the sonship of Christ—indeed the sonship of the preexistent Logos through whom God created. Athanasius has by now recognized that simply to cite "This is my beloved Son" from scripture does little to deal with the issue. In *Defense of the Nicene Definition* he pleads for the other sense of "son"—naturally begotten as Isaac was son of Abraham (*Decr.* 10). He insists on the need to study scripture and discriminate according to the subject in hand, to avoid confusion of sense, so as not to conceive of the things of God in a human way or ascribe human things to God. He asserts that God's begetting cannot involve passion or partition, and that the Son's generation exceeds and transcends human thought, the uncompounded Father having just one Son, the only-begotten in the Father's bosom (*Decr.* 11–12). He again tackles Proverbs 8:22 (*Decr.* 13), appealing to verse 25, along with the "touchstone texts" such as Psalm 110:3, Psalm 2:7, and John 1:18. He again appeals to the biblical images of God as fountain of wisdom (*Decr.* 12 and 15) and of the Son as the radiance of the divine light and the expression of God's being.[24] He even finds a scriptural basis for the fact that the Word or Wisdom is the very hand of God

24. *Decr.* 12, 23, 24, alluding to Heb 1:3.

that laid the foundation of the earth,[25] so challenging the Arian focus on the Logos as the mediating hand, bearable to things made from nothing, whereas the direct hand of God was not (*Decr.* 8; cf. *C. Ar.* 2.14). As Hanson puts it, "Arian theology tended to see the Son as a safeguard against God the Father coming into dangerous contact with the world."[26] Athanasius thus replays much of the argumentation and scriptural proof we have already surveyed, but now he clearly sees that nonscriptural terminology can alone provide the necessary specification and that, "even if the expressions are not in so many words in the scriptures, yet, as was said before, they contain the sense of the scriptures" (*Decr.* 21).

We also find in the *Defense of the Nicene Definition* a greater engagement with nonscriptural argument. Athanasius is now aware that a principal objection to the *homoousion* lies in its susceptibility to interpretation not just in modalist but also in materialist terms. Divine incorporeality becomes more of an issue along with indivisibility and impassibility. The fact that God is not as a human being, nor human beings as God, is underlined with new emphasis on the fact that divine generation cannot be material and passible (*Decr.* 10). Later on Athanasius more specifically challenges the idea that God is compound, or finite, insisting that God's being is invisible and incomprehensible (*Decr.* 22): "I am that I am" and "I am the Lord God" (Exod 3:14–15) indicate the "incomprehensible essence" of God. To say the Son is from God's essence is no different from saying he is from God "as a son, genuine and natural, from a father." It is not to make God corporeal. The radiance, unlike "fire kindled from the heart of the sun" and "external" to it, is intended to "signify his being from the essence, proper and indivisible, and his oneness with the Father" and to "secure his true unchangeableness and immutability" (*Decr.* 23). *Homoousios* therefore expresses this identity with his own Father. Every corporeal influence is therefore to be banished (*Decr.* 24). We must apprehend the genuine relationship of Father and Son by "transcending every imagination of sense" and "with pure understanding and with the mind alone."

> As the words "Offspring" [*gennēma*] and "Son" bear, and are meant to bear, no human sense, but one suitable to God, so when we hear the phrase "one in essence," let us not fall upon human senses and imagine partitions and divisions of the Godhead, but as having our thoughts directed to things immaterial, let us preserve undivided the oneness of nature and the identity

25. Isa 48:13; 51:16; Ps 104:14; Prov 3:19; John 1:1–3; 1 Cor 8:6 in *Decr.* 17.
26. Hanson, *Search*, 426.

> of light; for this is proper to a son as regards a father, and in this is shewn that God is truly Father of the Word. (*Decr.* 24)

This, Athanasius insists, is what those who met at Nicaea meant and, he claims, they were in line with precedent.

It would seem, then, that in the *Defense of the Nicene Definition* Athanasius has come to acknowledge that the implications of scripture have to be doctrinally conceptualized: otherwise false deductions can so easily be made and false doctrinal constructions justified. Right reading depends on right doctrinal concepts, even though the nature of God is humanly inconceivable. Even in the *Orations against the Arians*, suggests Ayres, "He is increasingly clear that beyond stating the logical distinction of Father from Son, charges of modalism and materialism are most appropriately resisted by focusing attention on the character of the divine existence as unique and beyond comprehension."[27]

The final paragraphs of the *Defense of the Nicene Definition* (28–30) return to the Arian term *agenētos*, which was borrowed from the Greeks, used ignorantly given its range of senses, and unscriptural—all points made earlier in the *Orations against the Arians* (1.30). Athanasius insists that it is more accurate to denote God as Father from the Son than to call God "unoriginated" by contrast with the works of creation. Baptism is "not into the name of Unoriginate and originate, not into the name of Uncreate and creature, but into the name of Father, Son and Holy Spirit" (cf. *C. Ar.* 1.34; 2.42). *Agenētos* has an appropriate religious use, he concedes, but not as a means of dishonouring the Savior. He ends with a doxology: "to God and the Father is due the glory, honour and worship with the coexistent Son and Word, together with the All-holy and Life-giving Spirit, now and unto endless ages of ages. Amen." The three "names" are back in play.[28]

The next generation, with new stages in the debate, would move toward a full doctrine of Trinity; but Athanasius had already mapped the groundwork, not least by explicitly making a clear differentiation between creature and Creator, dismantling those older conceptions of mediation through a hierarchical ladder of being and ensuring that the one Creator God must be the divine Triad. He had moved heaven and earth to ground this conclusion in scripture, constantly seeking to establish the "mind" or "sense" of scripture as a whole. Yet ultimately he had to admit that it was necessary to enshrine conclusions about that overall sense in doctrinal concepts, which could then become a

27. Ayres, *Nicaea and Its Legacy*, 117.
28. See volume 1, chapter 4.

guide to scriptural interpretation, even at times overriding the obvious sense of the words—for realities, he said, are prior to terms.

2. The Holy Spirit

We have been observing how problem texts exploited by the opposition, such as Proverbs 8:22, necessitated efforts to work at bringing them into conformity with a doctrinal framework understood to be more representative of the "mind" or basic *skopos* of scripture—a move from doctrine to scripture. But when it came to the Spirit the move was the other way. In volume 1 we found that Origen thought that the Holy Spirit needed particular investigation, as it appeared to be unique to Christianity and only known "by means of those scriptures that were inspired by the Holy Spirit." Here it was clearly a case of working from scripture to doctrine through a process of deduction from gathered scriptural texts, which notably showed baptism not to be complete without naming the Father, the Son, and the Holy Spirit. The baptismal liturgy and scripture remained the principal courts of appeal as controversy moved from the Son to the Spirit.

Yet scripture was by no means straightforward. There was no clear-cut statement that the Spirit was God, and it was all too easy to associate the Spirit with other spirits such as angels—the "ministering spirits" of Hebrews 1:14. The controversy threw up its own problem texts: 1 Timothy 5:21 spoke of God, Christ Jesus, and the elect angels with exactly the implication just mentioned, while Amos 4:13 LXX suggested that the Spirit was created. Exegetical moves were again crucial for establishing true doctrine.

2.1. *Athanasius*

For most of Athanasius's career the debates he had to focus on concerned the Father-Son relationship, but occasionally in the *Orations against the Arians* and elsewhere he mentions the Triad.[29] If the Arian account of the Son were right, he wrote, the Triad would not be everlasting—there would be a Monad at first and afterward a Triad by addition. Furthermore, the Triad would be "unlike itself, consisting of strange and alien natures and essences." He spoke

29. *C. Ar.* 1.17–18; cf. 2.41; 3.15. Triad and Monad also appear, e.g., in his quotations from the two Dionysii in *On the Opinion of Dionysius.*

of "an eternal and one Godhead in a Triad," of "one glory of the Holy Triad," of the Triad as Creator, and of a "doctrine of God perfect in a Triad."

That might sound like a bit of abstract doctrinal terminology, and his objection to bringing together "strange and alien natures and essences" certainly betrays his fundamental concern to maintain the utter difference in nature between creature and Creator.[30] However, baptism in the "three names," as enjoined by scripture (Matt 28:19), surely lies at the base of the argument, as it had since Irenaeus; this is evident from the above lampooning of the baptismal consequences of adopting the Arian position—baptism is not into the Unoriginate and Originate, the Uncreated and the creature, but into the name of the Father, the Son, and the Holy Spirit.[31] And yet it is that very distinction between the Uncreated and the creature, which should put both Son and Spirit on God's side of the line, that disrupted the old hierarchical way of conceiving things.

Athanasius would need to develop his arguments further to meet criticism of the idea that the Spirit shared divine being with Father and Son. Already, however, Athanasius had specifically targeted that additional question, for the Arians had provoked his response by claiming that Christ's anointing with God's Spirit suggested promotion or adoption, appealing particularly to Psalm 44:7–8 as quoted in Hebrews 1:8–9 (*C. Ar.* 1.46–50). It was as man that the very one who supplies the Spirit is said to be anointed with the Spirit, claimed Athanasius; this was for our sake—after all in John's Gospel (17:18–19) Jesus said of the disciples that it was "for their sakes" that he sanctified himself. Further scriptural references are gathered to support Christ's reception of the Spirit on our behalf, while Christ gives the Spirit to sanctify the saints.[32] The implication that the Spirit is of God is perhaps reinforced by reference to the text about blasphemy against the Holy Spirit (Mark 3:29), though explicitly Athanasius's discussion is again focused on the fact that it was as man that Jesus cast out demons through God's Spirit. As ever he is primarily anxious to ensure that the Arian deduction could not fly—namely, that the Logos was a creature in need of the Spirit.

Elsewhere in the *Orations against the Arians* Athanasius explores the fact that Christ poured the Spirit on us, explaining that creatures are sanctified by the Holy Spirit, which is the gift of God and not something a creature could

30. For extended treatment of Athanasius's commitment to this fundamental distinction, see Khaled Anatolios, *Athanasius: The Coherence of His Thought* (London: Routledge, 1998).

31. Cf. above p. 47, quoting *C. Ar.*1.34; 2.42.

32. 1 Cor 3:16; Isa 61:1; Acts 10:38; John 16:7, 14; 20:22; 1 John 2:20; Eph 1:13.

impart (2.18). Again the nub of Athanasius's argument concerns the nature of the Son's "everlasting Godhead," but implicitly he associates the Spirit in its sanctifying activity with the Father and Son. This discussion is perhaps further elucidated by a passage in *Orations against the Arians* where "we come to be in him and he in us" through the grace of the Spirit, and "since it is the Spirit of God, we are considered to be in God and God in us" (3.24). Athanasius explains that our participation in God is not the same as the Son's participation in the Father—for "we, apart from the Spirit, are foreign and distinct from God," but by participation of the Spirit, we are "knit into the Godhead." Previously, in *Orations against the Arians*, we find Athanasius quoting John's Gospel (14:23 and 17:21), as well as Paul's invariable "Grace and peace . . . ," to show how Father and Son come to be one in us; then he again appeals to baptism, citing the Matthaean text and thus including the Spirit (*C. Ar.* 2.42).

All this was to be sharpened up by controversy. In his *Letters to Serapion concerning the Holy Spirit*, addressed to a bishop troubled by some people treating the Holy Spirit as if it was just an angelic spirit, Athanasius again makes it clear that the Holy Spirit is not a creature and that the Holy Trinity is one.[33] The Tropici, so named probably because of their erroneous exegesis (*tropos*), were placing the Spirit among the "ministering spirits" and exploiting the problem texts noted earlier.[34] Athanasius's basic ploy was to dismiss them as latter-day Arians—even more stupid, indeed, for despite not wishing "the Son of God to be a creature," yet "content to countenance that the Spirit of the Son is a creature" (*Ep. Serap.*1.2).

Addressing the issue of Amos 4:13 (noted above), Athanasius focuses on scripture's linguistic usages, distinguishing at length, with catalogs of examples and instances, between "spirit" without qualification and the Holy Spirit, showing how the latter is always qualified by the designations "of God," "of the Father," "from me" (i.e. from God), "my," "his," "of Christ," "of the Son," or with the definite article or by being called "Paraclete" or "of Truth," if not "the Holy Spirit" in full (*Ep. Serap.* 1.3–10). The "spirit" said to be "created" in that Amos text is not thus qualified, and further prooftexts show that "spirit" may refer to the human spirit, or even to the wind. Athanasius rereads the Amos text (surely correctly) in terms of the latter, then in response to objections turns to the former. Other words in Amos 4:13 refer to the incarnation, so it is "our

33. E.g., *Ep. Serap.* 1.17; Greek text in *Athanasius Werke*, vol. 1.4, *Epistulae I–IV ad Serapionem*, ed. Dietmar Wyrwa (Berlin: de Gruyter, 2010); English translation in *Works on the Spirit: Athanasius the Great and Didymus the Blind*, ed. and trans. Mark DelCogliano, Andrew Radde-Gallwitz, and Lewis Ayres (Yonkers, NY: St. Vladimir's Seminary Press, 2011).

34. See the introduction to DelCogliano, Radde-Gallwitz, and Ayers, *Works on the Spirit*, 21.

spirit" which is renewed in him.[35] Then another collage of texts is produced in support (including Ezek 36:26–27, Pss 104:29–30; 51:12; Eph 2:12; 4:24). As in the case of Proverbs 8:22, Athanasius's exegesis is surely determined by what he sees as the overall *skopos* of scripture.

Next he turns to another problem text, Zechariah 4:5: "The angel who spoke within me" must be the Spirit, they say. Athanasius first appeals to the context of Zechariah's vision: the angel, speaking *for* "the Lord Almighty," refers to "my Spirit" and thus God's Spirit is clearly other than the angel who is speaking. Scripture's differentiation between the angels and the Spirit is now documented, with the problem of 1 Timothy 5:21 in view. The multiplicity of angels (Dan 7:10) cannot all be ranked with the Trinity, and the Holy Spirit is specified as the one who descended when the heavens opened (Luke 3:22). Gospel references to the angels serving Christ give way to three key texts: (1) John 20:22, "when he gave the Spirit to the disciples"; (2) the baptismal injunction of Matthew 28:19, on which Athanasius comments, "he did not rank an angel with the divinity, nor was it through a creature that he joined us to himself and to the Father, but through the Holy Spirit" (*Ep. Serap.* 1.11); and (3) John 15:26, where Jesus promises not to "send an angel, but the Spirit of Truth which proceeds from the Father." Even Moses made the same differentiation: Exodus 33 shows him refusing an angel as guide to lead the people from Egypt, begging God's self to do this, while Isaiah (63:11) states that the Holy Spirit came down and did so, and other texts confirm that the Lord led them through the wilderness (e.g., Lev 11:45; Deut 1:30; Pss 76:21; 77:53; 135:16). Athanasius thus concludes, "And so, the Spirit of God cannot be an angel, nor a creature, but proper to the divinity" (*Ep. Serap.* 1.12).

The reason for the omission of the Holy Spirit from 1 Timothy 5:21 still rankles, however, not to mention the actual inclusion of "the elect angels" where the Spirit might be expected. Athanasius's appeal to texts that omit one or another member of the Trinity may seem unconvincing from our perspective, especially when they are texts from the Old Testament. Still more unconvincing are his parallels to the inclusion of a man, Moses, or an angel along with the Lord. However, his position is soon explicit:

> The holy and blessed Trinity is indivisible and united in itself. When the Father is mentioned, with him are both his Word and the Spirit who is in the Son. If the Son is named, the Father is in the Son and the Spirit is not external to the Word. (*Ep. Serap.* 1.14)

35. LXX reading includes the mistranslation, "announcing his Christ to humans."

First Timothy 5:21 reflects the fact that "Paul . . . knew that the Spirit had not been divided from the Son, but was in Christ, as the Son is in the Father" (1.14). The "apostolic faith" determines exegesis, so the discussion proceeds to justify the oddity of including the angels here.

The exegetical battle now gives way to answering absurdities, such as the idea that if the Holy Spirit is not a creature he must be a second Son or even a grandson. Athanasius reduces this to asking inappropriate "human questions about God" when God is not like a human being (*Ep. Serap.* 1.15; cf. Num 23:19). Old arguments about the inapplicability to God of the sexual or material connotations of father and son, of begottenness, or division into parts are replayed. But Athanasius's principal concern remains the distinction between creature and Creator, the absolute necessity of ranking the Holy Spirit with the Trinity, "for the whole Trinity is one God . . . nothing foreign to the Trinity is mixed with it, but it is indivisible and self-consistent" (*Ep. Serap.* 1.17). Human knowledge should rest content at that and not speculate further. Tropici and Arians are equally at fault for raising contentious questions.

Before long Athanasius is back appealing to scripture, again rehearsing anti-Arian testimonies: God as fountain and light, the Son as radiance and river; the true Son through whom we are adopted as sons if we receive the Spirit; the Son as life, the life we are given in the Spirit (*Ep. Serap.* 1.19). He deduces both order and unity in the Trinity—the three are inseparable, and "it is incorrect for the Spirit, who is in the Son and the Son in him, to be ranked with creatures or be separated from the Word, thereby destroying the perfection of the Trinity" (1.20–21). The Tropici "have falsified the meaning of the sayings of both the Prophet and the Apostle." In Athanasius's mind there is no doubt that it is scripture that teaches true doctrine. Things come into being through the Word, and therefore it is correct to think of him as not a creature; so, in the course of the letter, we find Athanasius asking or proposing the following:

> Is it not blasphemy for you to say that the Spirit is a creature, in whom the Father, through the Word, perfects and renews all things? (*Ep. Serap.* 1.9)

> It is enough to know that the Spirit is not a creature, nor is he numbered with the things that are made. For nothing foreign is mixed with the Triad; it is indivisible and consistent. (1.17)

> But finally let us look, one by one, at the references to the Holy Spirit in the divine scriptures, and, like good bankers, let us judge whether he has anything in common with the creatures, or whether he pertains to God; that

> we may call him either a creature or else other than the creatures, pertaining to and one with the Godhead which is the unoriginated Triad. (1.21)[36]

Scripture is thus the court of appeal, yet the doctrinal principle whereby the creating Triad is distinguished from creatures brought into being from nothing is clear. For "that which joins creation to the Lord cannot belong to the creatures; and that which bestows sonship upon the creation could not be alien from the Son" (1.25). We become partakers of God through the Spirit's anointing; if the Spirit were a creature, "we should be strangers to the divine nature" (1.24). Sonship is bestowed by Spirit, so the Spirit cannot be alien from the Son: "the Spirit, therefore, does not belong to things originated; he pertains to the Godhead of the Father, and in him the Word makes things originated divine" (1.25). Athanasius's doctrine of *theopoiēsis* depends upon the true divinity of the Spirit with whose seal we are anointed in baptism.

Athanasius is constantly applying the logic whereby the "three names" belong together as Creator—indeed, twice in these epistles to Serapion we even find the *homoousion* applied to the Spirit (*Ep. Serap.* 1.27; 2.6)—and creature and Creator do not share the same nature. From the three names at baptism, from doxologies with scriptural roots, from scriptural usage whereby the Spirit is always associated with God or with the Father and the Son, and not least from the way scripture attributed sanctification to the Spirit, the doctrine was built up that the Spirit is God, even if not directly named as such. Thus Athanasius anticipated the thrust of the first great treatise on the Spirit: Basil's *On the Holy Spirit*.[37]

2.2. Basil of Caesarea, On the Holy Spirit

For his friend, Gregory of Nazianzus, Basil was far too circumspect and much too reserved in his language when it came to the Holy Spirit, never directly calling the Spirit God or using the *homoousion* of the Spirit. Gregory half admits it was politic at the time, and he perhaps appreciated this better after his own failure to get such direct statements accepted at the Council of Constantinople in 381. Still he reckoned highly Basil's treatise on the Holy Spirit,

36. Here Athanasius uses a "common aphorism" that good bankers would distinguish between genuine and counterfeit coinage. See DelCogliano, Radde-Gallwitz, and Ayers, *Works on the Spirit*, 86 n. 55.

37. Greek text in B. Pruche, ed., *Liber de Spiritu Sancto*, SC 17 (Paris: Cerf, 1947); English translation in *NPNF*² 8 and David Anderson, trans., *On the Holy Spirit* (Crestwood, NY: St. Vladimir's Seminary Press, 1980).

acknowledging that "by the use of other terms, and by statements which unmistakeably had the same meaning, and by argument necessarily leading to this conclusion," he left his opponents "without reply." He asserted that Basil did acknowledge that the Spirit is God, even "publicly preached this truth whenever opportunity offered, and eagerly confirmed it when questioned in private" (*Orat.* 43.68–69).

Basil's treatise was occasioned by protests over the form of doxology he had used in the liturgy. Instead of giving glory to the Father through the Son and in the Holy Spirit he had used "with" (*meta*) the Son and "together with" (*syn*) the Holy Spirit. He embarks on a long and rather pedantic discussion of the prepositions. For all that, he clearly perceived where the objection lay: people were unhappy with coordination of the three rather than subordination (*De Spir.* 13)—they were wedded to the old hierarchy, we might say. So what arguments does Basil use to counter this?

The preliminary tack is to replay the old arguments against Arianism, so as to remove the notion that the Son is "after" the Father or "in a lower place," in the process stacking up scriptural proofs: "for scripture puts before us the magnificence of the dignity of the Son by the use of dignified language indicating the seat of honour" (*De Spir.* 15). Thus he cites certain texts to counter the suggestion that sitting at God's right hand implies inferiority of rank, and other texts, of which the opposition takes no account, that indicate the "equal dignity of His glory with the Father."[38] More testimonies from scripture enjoin the same worship and glorification for Father and Son, who "in nature, in glory and in dignity is conjoined with him" (16). Basil's application of all this to the form of doxology is of particular interest: "with whom" is proper to "the ascription of glory," while "through whom" is "specially appropriate in giving thanks" because "grace is effected for us through him and in him." To demonstrate this he continues to pile up examples of scriptural usage of each term. The proper conception of the Father-Son relationship is, of course, apposite to the issue of the doxology, but more importantly it has to be firmly in place before discussion of the Spirit, and it is scripture which, for Basil, is the court of appeal.

Eventually, however, Basil is ready to turn specifically to the Holy Spirit (*De Spir.* 22). Now, alongside scripture he appeals to "the unwritten tradition of the Fathers," listing the titles given to the Spirit that imply lifting one's "conception to the supreme nature," namely, "Spirit of God" (Matt 12:28 et al.), "Spirit

38. For the former, see John 6:27; 1 Cor 1:24; Col 1:15; Heb 1:3. For the latter, see Mark 8:38; John 1:14, 18; 5:23; 14:9.

of truth which proceeds from the Father" (John 15:26), and above all "Holy Spirit." This, Basil comments, "is a name specially appropriate to everything that is incorporeal, purely immaterial, and indivisible," adding reference to the words of Jesus to the Samaritan woman, "God is spirit" (John 4:24). He deduces that with reference to spirit "it is impossible to form an idea of a nature circumscribed, subject to change and variation, or at all like a creature," and spells out conceptions advanced "to the highest"—that is, "an intelligent essence, in power infinite, in magnitude unlimited, unmeasured by times or ages, generous of its good gifts"—adding words that indicate how sanctification, virtue, inspiration, life, illumination, energy, and light are found when the Spirit is brought into "intimate association with the soul." The very word, "spirit," thus confirms what is found on the lips of Jesus in scripture, while the Spirit's role in cleansing souls, making them spiritual, and restoring the "Royal Image"—indeed in *theopoiēsis* (divinization)—shows the greatness, dignity, and works to be attributed to the Spirit, as indicated by the Spirit's own *logia* (*De Spir.* 23).[39]

Scripture, then, is the fundamental basis of Basil's argument, and now he turns to the baptismal command (Matt 28:19), using it to confute those who would not rank the Spirit with the Father and Son (*De Spir.* 24). Still, however, his opponents clamor for "written proof"—in other words, the issue is that scripture makes no clear, unequivocal statement on the matter. For a second time Basil mentions the "unwritten tradition of the Fathers," treating it as the "apostolic tradition" (25). What he means by this may perhaps emerge toward the end of the treatise.

Meanwhile the baptismal formula guarantees regeneration if the faith is kept secure, namely by keeping "the Spirit undivided from the Father and the Son, preserving both in the confession of faith and in the doxology the doctrine taught them at their baptism" (26). Indeed, renouncing the devil and his angels, the objectors had confessed belief in the Father and in the Son and in the Holy Spirit, and now they are violating the covenant of their salvation "for he who does not believe in the Spirit does not believe in the Son, and he who has not believed in the Son does not believe in the Father," a statement proved by quoting 1 Cor 12:3 and John 1:18. "It is impossible to worship the Son but by the Holy Spirit," Basil states, "impossible to call on the Father but by the Spirit of adoption."

The objection to that, however, is found in the way that scripture frequently mentions Christ alone in relation to baptism, as in Gal 3:27 or Rom 6:3

39. Presumably *logia*, which may mean "oracles," refers to the inspired words of scripture.

(*De Spir.* 28). Basil picks up texts to show that naming Christ means "confession of the whole," noting also frequent references to anointing with, or baptizing with, the Spirit (e.g., Luke 3:16; Acts 1:5; 1 Cor 12:13). The three names are vital for both confession of faith and for baptism, he insists.

Still it remains all too easy to make other deductions from scripture: the angels are often associated with the Father and Son (*De Spir.* 29; cf. 1 Tim 5:21), and some were baptized into Moses (*De Spir.* 31–32; cf. Exod 14:31 LXX)—Basil is drawn into exegetical explanations and the workings of typology. More to the point he faces reduction of baptism to a mere dip in the water, a literalizing that generates an exposition of the overarching story of fall and redemption (*De Spir.* 34–35) and of baptism as a kind of burial and rebirth, the latter being the work of the Holy Spirit—so "it follows that if there is any grace in the water, it is not of the nature of the water, but of the presence of the Spirit." The climax is our restoration to paradise, our adoption as sons of the Father, and our participation in Christ through baptism by the Holy Spirit (36).

Basil thus hopes to convince that the Holy Spirit is inseparable from the Father and Son. He briefly brings in prophecy and the distribution of the gifts of the Holy Spirit (1 Cor 12:4–6; 14:24–25), but it is creation that clinches it (*De Spir.* 37). The Father he names as the "original cause," the Son as the "creative cause," and the Spirit as the "perfecting cause" of all things, visible and invisible, including the angels. Citing Psalm 36:6, he denies that the Word is a mere impression in the air or the Spirit some kind of vapor; rather the psalm shows that the heavens were made by the Word of the Lord, and all the host of them by the Spirit of the Lord's mouth, thus indicating how the Lord gives the order, the Word creates, and the Spirit perfects in holiness. His ensuing discussion contrasts angels, as creatures needing sanctification, with the Spirit who does the sanctifying, constantly appealing to scripture proofs.

From creation Basil moves to God's dispensations with respect to humankind: the blessing of the patriarchs, the law, the types, the prophecies, the signs, the incarnation—it is all "through the Spirit." In greater detail he focuses on the incarnation: the Spirit's descent and presence with "our Lord in the flesh," everything done through cooperation with the Spirit, from the temptation through the mighty works to the resurrection, not to mention the breathing of the Spirit over the disciples and the ordering of the church through the Spirit's gifts. Nor will the Spirit be without function at the last judgement (*De Spir.* 39–40).

Now Basil has to face the objections to all this. Somewhat philosophical points about the implications of numbering "with" or "under" (41) reveal the continuing attraction of hierarchical models while appeals to God's *monarchia* remain potent (44). Basil endeavors to use scripture as well as logical argument to confirm the inappropriateness of applying number or division to the divine nature—there is a fundamental unity and communion. Still there are objections to glorifying the Spirit: Basil's answers repeat much that has gone before with plenty of scriptural prooftexts. Eventually he returns to those prepositions and their use in scripture, examples piled up to prove his points.

It is in the course of this discussion that Basil finally addresses the issue of written and unwritten authority. Basil's form of doxology lacked written endorsement according to the objectors. Basil appeals to many written precedents from Irenaeus to Dionysius of Alexandria (71–74); with all that previous authority, how can he be an innovator? Clearly, however, at the root of the problem is the lack of explicit scriptural authority for coordinating the Spirit with the Father and the Son in this way. So first he draws attention to various "mysteries" that lack written authority, declaring it "apostolic" to keep to "unwritten traditions" and referring to a distinction between *kerygma,* open public proclamation, and *dogma*, silence: "the Apostles and Fathers who laid down laws for the church from the beginning thus guarded the awful dignity of the mysteries in secrecy and silence" (66). His examples of such unwritten and silent traditions include the sign of the cross, turning to the East to pray, the words of the prayers over the eucharistic elements, the blessing of the baptismal water and the oil of the chrism, the threefold baptism, plus standing for prayer on the first day of the week—liturgical actions with no written authority but replete with meaning, as he shows.

Perhaps it is not surprising that Basil's appeal to unwritten "mysteries" generated some scholarly discussion about exactly what he implied—did he think in terms of some kind of advanced secret teaching for an elite?[40] Surely it is evident, however, both from the context and from the examples Basil offers, that what he is referring to is what initiates understood through their catechetical training and subsequent participation in the liturgy, which was, of course, reserved for the baptized. During this period, they would be a select group; crowds flocked to the church now endorsed by imperial authority, but baptism was not infrequently delayed till one's deathbed for fear of postbaptismal sin, unless one was being dedicated to a religious life. The context of the whole

40. E.g., R. P. C. Hanson, *Tradition in the Early Church* (Philadelphia: Westminster, 1962), and Hanson, "Basil's Doctrine of Tradition in Relation to the Holy Spirit," *VC* 22 (1968): 241–55; E. Amand de Mendietta, "The Pair *Kerygma* and *Dogma* in the Thought of Basil of Caesarea," *JTS* 16 (1965): 129–42; and Mendietta, *The 'Unwritten' and the 'Secret' Apostolic Traditions in the Theological Thought of St. Basil of Caesarea*, Scottish Journal of Theology Occasional Papers 13 (London: Oliver and Boyd, 1965).

discussion is the meaning of the doxology in the worship of the church and its import for understanding the nature and work of the Holy Spirit. Beside scripture, which was not unproblematic on the issue of the Spirit's divinity, stood the church's liturgical life and the regenerative work on the Spirit within that context.

3. The Need for a New Conceptuality

The doctrinal legacy of the second century had been twofold:

- The *monarchia* of the one Creator God;
- The creation as brought into being out of nothing: neither out of Godself nor out of preexisting matter, for that would mean a second eternal principle beside God.

The underlying problem in the fourth century lay in the tension between the implied radical distinction between Creator and creature, on the one hand, and the instinctively hierarchical mode of thinking that allowed the three names to map onto a ladder of existence reaching from the ultimate God through mediators and angels to human creatures and lesser beings, with no obvious cutoff points. In a sense these controversies might be seen as a replay with respect to the Son and the Spirit of that second-century debate about creation: was each out of God or, like creatures, out of nothing? Put like that one must surely agree that the thrust of the New Testament would endorse "out of God." Somehow the texts require a recognition that it really was God present in Jesus and at work in the Spirit's inspiring and sanctifying activities. The exegetical arguments to that effect prevailed, but the puzzle remained: how could there be "three names" (*hypostaseis* or persons) representing the one and only eternal Creator God? How could the "only-begotten Son" be "unbegotten" or "unoriginated"—as must be the eternal God who has never come into being but has always been? The old Monarchian solutions had proved off beam—a new conceptuality was surely required.

3

Three Names, One God?

PART 2, CONCEPTUAL THOUGHT AND BIBLICAL HERMENEUTICS

So, the old monarchian solutions had proved off beam—a new conceptuality was needed. That necessary fresh conception would be honed into shape as the nub of the issue shifted once more. Stimulated by Eunomian attempts to define God as essentially *agenetos* (unoriginated), the Cappadocians would find themselves obliged to tackle issues concerning the language and concepts appropriate to the mystery of the divine Triad. As in the case of the Arian controversy, so in this area too there has been a flowering of research, to which readers are again referred, for it is entirely unrealistic to undertake at this point a comprehensive study of this stage of the debate, whether historical, biographical, or theological.[1] We will attempt again to keep the focus on the relationship between doctrinal argument and the interpretation of scripture.

1. The Concept of the Trinity

First we will explore the work of the Gregory known as "the theologian," with some asides to Basil and his brother Gregory of Nyssa.[2] As we go along, we shall see:

1. Cf. books listed in chapter 2, note 1 (p. 29 above), especially Hanson, *Search*; Barnes and Williams, *Arianism after Arius*; and Ayres, *Nicaea and Its Legacy*. See also Richard Paul Vaggione, *Eunomius of Cyzicus and the Nicene Revolution*, OECS (Oxford: Oxford University Press, 2000).

2. See John A. McGuckin, *Gregory of Nazianzus: An Intellectual Biography* (Crestwood, NY: St. Vladimir's Seminary Press, 2001); Christopher A. Beeley, *Gregory of Nazianzus on the Trinity and Knowledge of God* (Oxford: Oxford University Press, 2007).

- how seemingly abstract conceptual work was grounded in a profound response to the God of the scriptures;
- how the three "names" of the Rule of Faith, and the potency of the Triad in the baptismal liturgy, provided the conceptual structure for a God worth worshipping;
- how the long-standing and fundamentally biblical issue of God's *monarchia* was given fresh and imaginative cogency in the context of a fully Trinitarian understanding of the Godhead;
- how the doctrine of the Trinity was not an attempt to define the being of God; rather, "*theologia* is knowledge of the Trinity as it is revealed in the divine economy"[3] (recalling that, as Beeley puts it, the "economy" represents "God's purposeful governance, administration and arrangement of the affairs of the created order . . . from creation to the final consummation, as it is definitively represented in the biblical revelation")[4];
- how the hope of *theopoiēsis*, of sanctification by the Spirit and participation in the divine sonship of Christ, shaped an overarching sense of the doctrine of the Trinity as the appropriate articulation of scripture's meaning.

1.1. Scripture and the Formulation of Trinitarian Doctrine

Scripture is deeply embedded in the rhetoric of Gregory's *Orations*.[5] As I have demonstrated elsewhere, he deploys biblical quotations, allusions, and narratives in the same way as classical literature had long been deployed by rhetoricians.[6] This was not a matter of stylistic ornamentation, but a means of reinforcing the subject matter by suggesting precedent, aligning persons with characters from well-known narratives, and giving the content a veneer of authority. A case in point is the opening of Gregory's farewell address, *Oration* 42, which in its present form is probably an expanded version of Gregory's valedictory to the assembled bishops in Constantinople in 381 later edited to create an apologia for his career:

> What do you make of our plight, dear shepherds and colleagues—you whose "feet are beautiful," as you "proclaim peace" and the "good news" with which

3. Beeley, *Gregory*, 197.
4. Beeley, *Gregory*, 195.
5. Greek text in PG 37–38; Greek text of Orations 1–12 and 20–43 can be found in *SC*; English translation of select orations from *NPNF*² 7, unless otherwise noted. See also Brian E. Daley, *Gregory of Nazianzus* (London: Routledge, 2006).
6. See chapter 5 of F. Young, *Biblical Exegesis*.

> you have come? Your feet are beautiful also in our eyes, since you have come just in time for us: not to rescue a wandering sheep, but to care for a shepherd who is, like you, a wanderer far from home. (*Orat.* 42.1 [Daley])

Recognizably Gregory here plays with scriptural motifs from Isaiah 52:7 and Matthew 18:10–14, and then scripture shapes his account of the struggles to establish in Constantinople a flock true to faith in the Trinity, "with a dazzling array of biblical allusions and quotations."[7] At first the shepherd-flock image is maintained, then a picture is built up of a tiny field with precious little harvest, incorporating into that gospel motif phrases from the prophets, until Gregory rejoices in the God "who makes poor and makes rich . . . who brings death and gives life," paralleling recent events with the exodus so that this flock is now "flourishing and spreading" (*Orat.* 42.2–6).[8] I could go on, but my point about Gregory's profound earthing in scripture is surely made.

Later in this same oration Gregory sets out his teaching and then offers some comments on the debates (*Orat.* 42.18). Busybodying about "the begetting of God and his ineffable origin," he dismisses as just producing "dialectical, mischievous arguments." He claims to follow scripture: the way to "hold onto salvation" is by "breaking up the stumbling blocks that lie in [scripture] to trip up the blind." However, he eschews on this occasion any discussion of prooftexts—there has been quite enough of that, he reckons, including his own efforts. In fact now is not the moment "to solve or rearrange the problems of interpretation in scripture." Like Athanasius, he seems to have reached the point where he recognizes that appeal to scripture alone cannot sort the problems. Nor, after half a century of battles since Nicaea to agree on a creedal confession or find a nonscriptural term that could be unequivocally adopted without ambiguous interpretations, would any one of those paths alone lead to a conclusion.

The inadequacy of exegetical argument Gregory had long since recognized in his arguments over the divinity of the Holy Spirit.[9] It would appear that Basil thought it possible to deduce the divinity of the Holy Spirit from certain prooftexts but, as Beeley points out, Gregory differed from Basil not only in being more explicit about the Spirit's divinity but also in regarding "such biblical

7. Daley, *Gregory*, footnote on 237.

8. Daley's notes to these opening paragraphs collect thirty-two scriptural allusions or quotations.

9. Cf. chapter 2, 2.2.

argumentation both polemically improbable and dogmatically impossible."[10] It is worth sidestepping to observe how devious Basil's comments could be. For example, he quotes from 2 Thessalonians 3:5, "May the Lord direct your hearts to the love of God and to the patient waiting of Christ" (*De Spir.* 52). Who, he then asks, is the Lord who does this directing? If it is God the Father, then it would read, "May the Lord direct you into his own love," or if it is the Son, it would have added "into his own patience." So one needs to seek for what other person there is who is worthy to be honoured with the title "Lord." Basil then quotes from 1 Thessalonians 3:12–13, "And may the Lord make you to increase and abound in love for one another and for all . . . so that he may establish your hearts unblamable in holiness before God, even our Father, at the coming of our Lord Jesus with all his saints," and again asks "What Lord?" The Lord is identified as the Spirit by cross-referencing 2 Corinthians 3:17–18. Deductions of this kind were barely convincing to the opposition, and Gregory discerned that.

The opening of *Oration* 31 on the Holy Spirit (the last of his theological *Orations*) indicates that Gregory felt accused of having introduced "a strange and unscriptural God." He quickly acknowledges that in scripture the Spirit is never straightforwardly called God (*Orat.* 31.21), but it is necessary to go beneath the letter and look for the inner meaning. Those contentious terms *agenētos* and *agennētos* are not in scripture (*Orat.* 31.7)—one has to go beyond terms to things, to read according to the spirit and not the letter, and understand according to the whole record of the *oikonomia*. "The Old Testament proclaimed the Father openly and the Son more obscurely, while the New Testament manifested the Son and suggested the deity of the Spirit, and now the Spirit dwells among us," he said (31.26). This statement neither delineated some kind of anachronistic development of doctrine nor referred to some sort of charismatic experience; rather it was fundamentally dispensational, while providing a specific affirmation of the New Testament witness to new creation in Christ and new birth through anointing with the Spirit (31.28). This is further indicated by Gregory's subsequent listing, first, of the role of the Spirit in the gospel narratives, second, of the names accorded the Spirit in scripture, and third, his demonstration of the Spirit's involvement in guiding, sending, illuminating, dividing gifts, and making apostles, prophets, evangelists, pastors, and teachers (31.29).

It was not the letter of scripture that testified to the deity of the Holy Spirit; nor did the letter of scripture establish the Trinitarian nature of God. Rather both were grounded in the biblical witness to the "economy": God's

10. Beeley, *Gregory*, 299.

engagement with creatures, enabling salvation, sanctification, and divinization. Gregory could play the prooftext game, as *Oration* 30 proves. There in the fourth of his theological *Orations* he had indeed sought to remove those stumbling blocks in scripture—the problems of Proverbs 8:22, Philippians 2:9, Hebrews 5:8, and John 5:19 and 20:17 along with other awkward texts through which he works. But just like Athanasius, he knew that prooftexting did not yield true doctrine on its own.

1.2. The Conceptualization of the Godhead

This is no place for a comprehensive study of Gregory's Trinitarianism, particularly as the conceptual discussion often seems remote from scripture, but some attention to certain features can sharpen the sense of Gregory's commitment to a concept of the Trinity that captures the nature of the God disclosed in scripture's narrative.

The emerging formula, one *ousia* and three *hypostaseis* or persons, Gregory was identified with, but we have already observed a certain impatience with the endless arguments over terminology (*Orat.* 31.29). Gregory's preferred usage is instructive; for the unity of the Trinity he may use *ousia*, but favors the biblical terms "God," "Divinity," and "nature," while his emphasis on the three unique beings each with their own characteristics (*idiotētes*) he found best represented by the "three names" of the baptismal rite—Father, Son and Holy Spirit—which ultimately come, of course, from scripture.[11] Preaching on the Holy Lights at Epiphany, Gregory said:

> When I speak of God, let yourselves be surrounded with a flash of that light which is both one and three: three in properties, or indeed in hypostases, if one wants to call them that, or indeed in "persons"—for we will not become involved in a battle over names as long as the syllables point towards the same notion—and one with regard to the concept of substance, or indeed divinity. It is divided without division if I may put it that way, and is joined together in the midst of distinction. The divinity is one in three and the three are one—those three in whom the divinity exists, or to put it more accurately, who are the divinity. (*Orat.* 39.11 [Daley])

The passage confirms Gregory's reluctance to reduce reality to a fixed linguistic formula, yet it remains a highly abstract statement. Immediately,

11. Beeley, *Gregory*, 221, citing Col 2:9 for "Divinity," and Rom 1:26 and 2 Pet 1:4 for "nature."

however, Gregory turns to scripture, quoting 1 Corinthians 8:6: "For us there is one God, the Father, for whom are all things, and one Lord Jesus Christ, through whom are all things," adding "one Holy Spirit in whom are all things." The prepositions, he says, do not divide natures but rather express the peculiar characteristics of one unconfused nature, a point confirmed by "from him and through him and to him are all things; to him be glory for the ages. Amen" (Rom 11:36). Abstract though it may seem, the passage under consideration is preceded by a call to worship and opens, we recall, with the image of light.

It is worth digressing a bit to observe that elsewhere light captures Gregory's very conception of the Trinity, as scriptural allusion shapes his thinking:

> "There was the true light, which enlightens everyone who comes into the world" (John 1:9)—the Father. "There was the true light which enlightens everyone who comes into the world"—the Son. "There was the true light which enlightens everyone who comes into the world"—the other Paraclete (John 14:16, 26). "Was" and "was" and "was," but one thing was; "light" and "light" and "light," but one light and one God. This is what David imagined long ago when he said, "In your light we shall see light" (Ps 36[35]:9). And now we have both seen and proclaimed the concise and simple theology of the Trinity: out of light (the Father) we comprehend light (the Son) in light (the Spirit). (*Orat.* 31.3 [Beeley])

As Beeley comments, Gregory "moves . . . easily between simple doxology and fine conceptual work."[12] McGuckin draws attention to Gregory's "synthetic ingenuity."[13] He is not tied to fixed formulae, but comes up with new and old ways of capturing the reality. One of his summary outlines identifies Father, Son, and Holy Spirit as the Cause, the Creator, and the Perfecter respectively (*Orat.* 34.8), thus capturing characteristics that ultimately go back to scripture: the Father being the ultimate cause of all things, while creation is attributed to the Logos/Wisdom/Son (John 1:1–3; Col 1:15–17), and the Spirit is the one who sanctifies.

Meanwhile, let us return to the Epiphany oration, where Gregory next details the peculiar characteristics of the three, drawing out the relationships enshrined in formulae he is willing to develop further:

12. Beeley, *Gregory*, 188.
13. McGuckin, *Gregory*, 58.

> The Father is Father and without beginning, for he is from no one. The Son is Son and not without beginning, for he is from the Father. If you understand "beginning" in the sense of time, however, he too is without beginning; for he is the maker of all time, not subject to time. The Holy Spirit is truly spirit, coming forth from the Father, but not in the manner of a son or by generation but by procession (if one must create new terminology for the sake of clarity). (*Orat.* 39.12 [Daley])

Not only does he find from scripture (John 15:26) a distinct term for the way the Spirit issues from the Father, but he has switched away from the nonscriptural and problematic term *agenētos* to more biblical terms. This switch is arresting, recalling as it does the early apologists who, conflating biblical texts and titles, identified the Logos with the "beginning" in Genesis 1:1 and John 1:1 (e.g., Justin, *Dial.* 61.2).[14] This terminology appears again in Gregory's outline of his teaching in his farewell address: "the One without beginning and the Beginning and the one who is with the Beginning are one God" (*Orat.* 42.15 [Daley]). Thus the earthing of Gregory's Trinitarian thinking in scripture is paralleled by the way he integrates into current articulations of doctrine older insights deeply rooted in earlier ways of reading scripture doctrinally.

But the switch also enables a clearer statement of the key Cappadocian reply to Eunomian claims: the negative *agenētos* cannot be treated as a definition of God's being. Gregory explains that

> Being without beginning is not the nature of the One without beginning, nor is being unbegotten; for nature is never a designation for what something is not, but for what something is. The affirmation of what is is not the denial of what is not. Nor is the Beginning kept separate from that which is without beginning by the fact that it is a Beginning: for being the Beginning is not his nature, any more than being One without beginning is the nature of the other. And the one who is with the one without beginning and with the Beginning is not something else than what they are. The name of the one without beginning is "Father," of the Beginning "Son," of the one with the Beginning is "Holy Spirit." There is one nature for all three: God. (*Orat.* 42.15 [Daley])

Gregory again prefers to focus on "nature" rather than "essence," and on relationship rather than distinction.

14. See chapter 1, p. 16; and chapter 2, p. 40, especially notes 20 and 21.

Furthermore, he here places the unity of the three in the Father, "from whom and towards whom everything else is referred, not so as to be mixed together in confusion, but so as to be contained, without time or will or power intervening to divide them." This is an example of how Gregory often speaks of the Father as the ultimate first principle. There are two reasons why Beeley's study of Gregory's Trinitarianism is important for us. The first is because he identifies as distinctive Gregory's conception of the Father's *monarchia* as the source and cause of the Trinity:

> It is the special property of the Father to be both the source of himself—in the sense that he is self-existent divinity, being unbegotten, uncaused and without source—and the source of the Son and the Holy Spirit, and thus the source of the Trinity as a whole.[15]

Two quotations from Gregory himself bear this out:

> So, according to my argument, the unity of God would be preserved, and the Son and the Spirit would be referred back to one original cause, but not compounded or blended with each other; their unity would be based on the single, self-identical movement and will of divine being, if I may put it that way, and on identity of substance. But the three hypostases would also be preserved with no amalgamation or reduction or confusion conceived in our thought. (*Orat.* 20.7 [Daley])

> To us there is one God, for the Godhead is one, and all that proceeds from him is referred to one, though we believe in three persons. . . . When we look at the Godhead, or the First Cause, or the *Monarchia*, that which we conceive is one, but when we look at the persons in whom the Godhead dwells, and at those who timelessly and with equal glory have their being from the First Cause—there are three whom we worship. (31.14)

By constantly referring to the Father as the source and cause of the Trinity, Gregory avoids positing some kind of "divine essence" in which the three participate, some other source beyond the actual "existences," while upholding the obvious pattern in the scriptures, whereby the Father is God, and the Son and Holy Spirit in one way or another issue from God, so that it really is God with whom we are in touch through the incarnation and the gift of the Spirit.

15. Beeley, *Gregory*, 205.

My way of putting that brings out its correspondence with Beeley's second important contribution, namely, his critique of the usual reading of Gregory's thought in terms of the distinction between *theologia* and *oikonomia*. *Theologia* is indeed articulation of the concept of the Trinity but, as Beeley shows, it is

> the knowledge of the Trinity as it is revealed within the divine economy. When one comes to know God, one enters into God's own triune life, knowing the Divinity that comes from the Father in the face of Jesus Christ by the power of the Holy Spirit, who fully share that Divinity, as God come from God in God. In this regard, theology is for Gregory virtually synonymous with contemplation, illumination, and the vision of God, being the knowledge of God in the most comprehensive sense.[16]

So Gregory earths his concept of the Trinity in the scriptural narrative and revives the old deep-seated commitment to God's *monarchia*. By assigning *monarchia* to the Father, in a way surely more in line with earlier second-century doctrinal instincts arising from scripture, he is able to reaffirm the commitment to one first principle while repudiating Sabellianism and avoiding any setting of the Father apart from the Son and the Holy Spirit, the source of both being the Father. As he puts it:

> In effect, common to Father, Son, and Holy Spirit is the fact that they were not created, as well as their Divinity. Common to the Son and Holy Spirit is the fact that they come from the Father. Uniquely characteristic of the Father is unbegottenness [*agennēsia*], of the Son begottenness [*gennēsis*]; and of the Spirit being sent [*ekpempsis*]. (*Orat.* 25.16)[17]

We are back to the terminology that dogged the controversies, but Gregory's variations on it have illuminated the issues and offered some kind of resolution.

Gregory is, of course, very aware of the controversial context in which he delivers his account of the Trinity. In passage after passage he describes his teaching as a middle way. A little earlier in the oration just quoted, we find him stating, "we do not believe in three first principles, lest we espouse the polytheism of the Greeks; nor in a solitary principle, Jewish in its narrowness." In the third theological *Oration*, he contrasts *anarchia*, *polyarchia*, and *monarchia*, attributing the first two to the Greeks and offering a *monarchia* that is not con-

16. Beeley, *Gregory*, 197.

17. English translation from Beeley, *Gregory*, 204 (without transliteration of the Greek).

fined to one person but rather issues in Trinity (29.2). In one of his earliest orations (2.37), long before he was struggling with opposition in Constantinople, he identifies three weaknesses in theology, atheism, Judaism, and polytheism, and asks if he can avoid what is noxious in each. Sabellius is effectively atheist in asserting not so much that all are one as that each is nothing—producing something that is always ceasing to be what it is as it becomes something else or a composite mythical figment of the imagination. Arius is associated with Judaism, while others introduce gentile plurality by setting three principles alongside each other. Generally, however, Gregory plays with two opposing errors, that of Sabellius and that of Arius, seeking a middle way.

> So we adore the Father and the Son and the Holy Spirit, dividing their individualities but uniting their godhead; and we neither blend the three into one thing, lest we be sick with Sabellius's disease, nor do we divide them into three alien and unrelated things, lest we share Arius's madness. Why should we act like those who try to straighten a plant bent over completely in one direction by forcibly training it the opposite way, correcting one deviation by another? Rather, we should straighten it midway between the two. . . . When I speak of such a middle position, I mean the truth. (*Orat.* 20.5–6 [Daley])

We could multiply references, but one more may suffice:[18]

> Let Sabellius's aggregation and Arius's alienation be equally far from us—diametrically opposed evils equal in their impiety. For why should we either make God coalesce into an unholy mass, or cut him into unequal pieces? (*Orat.* 39.11 [Daley])

The important thing is to recognize that this tactic is not simply about navigating between extremes—rather it draws attention to the inadequacy of accounts that do not measure up to the God discerned through the "economy" to which the scriptures testify. Gregory offers a brilliant combination of thinking in biblical pictures while articulating a conceptual account of reality in accordance with the rule of faith. For him it is only through identifying the "three names" into which we are baptized and glimpsing their relationship as three persons in one God that we can do justice to the scriptural narrative, receive participation in the divine, and offer worship to a Divinity beyond our limited grasp.

18. Cf. *Orat.* 18.16; 21.13, 35; 31.9; 34.8; 38.8, 15; 42.16.

1.3. Beyond Definition Yet Not Unknown

It is, of course, to the five theological *Orations* (*Orations* 27–31) that most have turned to find Gregory's Trinitarianism. Beeley has described them as "chiefly defensive," and attributes "the typically narrow reading of Gregory in modern scholarship" to "over-reliance" on them.[19] They do indeed attend argumentatively to the issues that dominated the controversies, and Beeley is surely right to point beyond them, but he does admit that they are "key witnesses to Gregory's thought on many points."[20] So far we have only made odd cross-references to them, but for assessing the relationship between doctrine and scripture it is worth paying them a little more attention. After all, Gregory here tackles directly that new nub of the issue—whether God's being can be defined.

The implied starting point is the Eunomian claim that God is simple and knowable, indeed definable as *agenētos*, but at first Gregory eschews the kind of logical argument we found him using in his later farewell address, namely that you do not define a being by saying what it is not.[21] Instead, *Oration* 27 attacks his opponents' whole approach to doing theology, and then in *Oration* 28 we are invited to accompany Gregory up Mount Sinai with Moses, longing yet fearful to enter the cloud of God's presence (*Orat.* 28.2–3). Without sufficient purification it is simply impossible to go all the way—one can just wait below and hear the voice and the trumpet and see the mountain smoking and the lightning flashing. Gregory speaks of "running to comprehend God" and "drawing aside the curtain of the cloud," but "when he looked up, he scarce saw the back parts of God," yet he was "sheltered by the Rock, the Word that was made flesh for us." Looking more closely it is not the Trinity that he sees, but the traces and tokens of God like shadows and reflections of the sun on water. These are God's back parts. Even Moses and Paul could not reach complete comprehension of God, any more than we can look directly at the sun. God is simply too vast to be grasped. This graphic depiction is, of course, an amalgam of motifs from the book of Exodus, notably Exodus 33:19–23 where Moses is told that he cannot see God's face, but God shields him in a cleft in the rock, covering him with his hand while his glory passes by.

19. Beeley, *Gregory*, 190.

20. Cf. McGuckin's account of Gregory matching Eunomian syllogistic argument in *Gregory*, 282; see also the commentary and translation in F. W. Norris, with F. Williams and L. Wickham, *Faith Gives Fullness to Reasoning: The Five Theological Orations of St. Gregory Nazianzen*, VCSup 13 (Leiden: Brill, 1991).

21. See above, p. 65.

Gregory now embarks on an apophatic account of God's being.[22] Alluding first to that classic sentence of Plato concerning the difficulty of knowing and the impossibility of speaking of God, he continues:

> It is altogether impossible and impracticable mentally to encompass so great a subject, not merely for the indolent with lowly inclination, but even for those who aim high and love God. . . . It is not just the peace of God which passes understanding and knowledge . . . but God's very nature which is beyond our grasp and comprehension. (*Orat.* 28.4–5)

In his ensuing discussion, the classic apophatic terminology is deployed: the divine is incorporeal, infinite, unlimited, without form, untouchable, invisible, unbegotten, without beginning, unchangeable, and imperishable. God is the One who is "incomposite and incomparable by nature." In using these negative terms Gregory was of course drawing upon a tradition of Christian theology reaching right back to the early apologists.[23] But then Gregory does make the logical point that we saw him make elsewhere: not one of those negations can tell us what God is, what is God's being and *hypostasis*. Opposite predicates—such as corporeal, mortal, begotten—may be used of a man, a horse, or a cow, but to present such objects clearly to the mind, you need to know what each actually is (28.9). Eunomius's claim to know God's being on the basis of defining God as *agenētos* is therefore false. God's being is beyond our grasp and comprehension.

Three further approaches then rub home the fact that God cannot be circumscribed, even in thought:

- all the terms we use of God—like Spirit, Fire, Light, Love, Wisdom, Righteousness, Mind, and Reason—come clothed in associations from our corporeal existence;
- not even Enoch, Noah, Abraham, Jacob, Elijah, Isaiah, Ezekiel, Peter or Paul ever discovered what God is in nature and essence, despite each receiving theophanies;

22. An earlier version of some of the following discussion can be found in my article, "The God of the Greeks and the Nature of Religious Language," first published in *Early Christian Literature and the Classical Intellectual Tradition: In Honorem Robert M. Grant*, ed. W. R. Schoedel and R. L. Wilken, Théologie Historique 53 (Paris: Beauchesne, 1979); republished in Young, *Exegesis and Theology*.

23. See volume 1, chapter 3, 2.2.

- we do not even understand our own being, nor that of the various creatures of the natural world, geographical features, the weather, or astronomy.

In expansive rhetoric Gregory draws both on scripture and contemporary natural philosophy to generate wonder at God's creation and prove that even "secondary causes exceed the power of our intellect; much more, then, the first and only Nature."[24]

Beeley suggests that what Gregory means by God's incomprehensibility is "this creaturely inability to know the full magnitude or the entirety of God."[25] There are, however, indications that Gregory's conception grew beyond that. In *Oration* 28, Gregory certainly indicates that God's incomprehensibility to us is the result of the impurities and incapacities of the human mind, especially in its embodied state. But, he continues, whereas we can infer God's existence from "the heavens, the work of your fingers, the moon and the stars" (Ps 8:3), when it comes to the essence of "that nature which is above them and out of which they spring" it is another matter: "it is one thing to be persuaded of the existence of a thing, and quite another to know what it is." He now directly links incomprehensibility with infinity. Gregory wonders how, if circumscribed, God might be an object of worship. Thus he establishes God's incorporeality and transcendence.

All this is taken much further in *Oration* 38. In God's self all Being is summed up and contained, "like some great sea of Being, limitless and unbounded, transcending all conception of time and nature. . . . The Divine, then, is boundless and difficult to contemplate: the only thing completely comprehensible about it is its boundlessness" (*Orat.* 38.7 [Daley]). He goes on to speak of the mind having no resting place as it seeks to contemplate the "abyss above us," affirming again that God is infinite and it is impossible to get to the end of God. So Gregory seems to suggest that God's incomprehensibility is the inevitable corollary of infinity; it is not simply a matter of the incapacities and impurities of the creaturely mind, for it belongs to the Being of God.

It is likely that this is a sign of the influence of Gregory of Nyssa. Let us take a diversion to pursue this for a moment. Gregory of Nyssa, claimed Mühlenberg, was the first philosopher-theologian to utilize the concept of infinity in a positive sense, and it was debate with Eunomius that generated this.[26] It may

24. The final words of *Orat.* 28.

25. Beeley, *Gregory*, 96.

26. E. Mühlenberg, *Die Unendlichkeit Gottes bei Gregor von Nyssa* (Göttingen: Vandenhoeck & Ruprecht, 1966).

be that Mühlenberg underestimated earlier hints in Philo and Clement, yet undoubtedly it is in Gregory of Nyssa's works that we find God's incomprehensibility more closely associated with divine infinity than previously and more strikingly deployed as a core concept. His *Against Eunomius* affirms the complete dissimilarity between creatures and the infinite Creator, thus denying the long philosophical assumption that one's kinship with the divine enabled intuition of God's being. Insisting on the traditional apophatic terms, the work suggests that analysis or definition of an infinite being is simply impossible, so that rational discourse cannot provide any appropriate account of God—indeed, God is inconceivable, for without limit or boundary, God cannot be compared with anything else and there is no ordinary language adequate to describe the infinite. This impasse cannot be attributed solely to the incapacities of human reasoning, for it belongs to the very Being of God.

> The simplicity of true faith assumes God to be what God is, namely, incapable of being grasped by any term or any idea or any other device of our apprehension, remaining beyond the reach not only of the human, but of the angelic and of all supramundane intelligence, unthinkable, unutterable, above all expression in words, having but one name that can represent God's proper nature, the single name being "above every name." (Phil 2:9) (Gregory of Nyssa, *Eun.* 1.683 [*GNO* 1:222])[27]

What might seem purely philosophical turns out to have a religious dimension: it is not just that the scripture quote from Philippians provides confirmation, but also that a God worthy of worship is beyond comparison with anything derivative from God. We observed Gregory of Nazianzus recognizing the latter point in his *Oration* 28 when he asks how God can be an object of worship if he is circumscribable. God, if God is truly God, can never be pinned down.

So God is beyond definition. Yet both Gregories were sure that God is not absolutely unknown. Gregory of Nazianzus speaks of hints and traces which give us an inkling:

> God extends beyond all our notions of time and nature, and is sketchily grasped by the mind alone, but only very dimly and in a limited way; he

27. Greek text of Gregory's works against Eunomius in *GNO* 1 and 2; English translation in *NPNF*² 5, which I use unless otherwise noted. The *GNO* edition modifies the order and enumeration of the treatises and their subdivisions compared with older editions, including that behind the *NPNF* translation, hence the double references.

> is known not directly but indirectly as one image is derived from another to form a single representation of truth: fleeing before it is grasped, escaping before it is fully known, shining on our guiding reason—provided we have been purified—as a swift, fleeting flash of lightning shines in our eyes. (*Orat.* 38.7)

Oration 28 allows us to discern some such hints and traces—the "back parts," which, like Moses, Gregory scarcely saw. The first clue is the way Gregory identifies the rock that provided shelter as the Word made flesh. And when he looked closer, what he saw was not the ultimate Being, but "that nature which at last even reaches to us"—the majesty, the glory manifested among creatures, to which creation and scripture bear witness.

> For these are the back parts of God, which God leaves behind him as tokens of Godself, like the shadows and reflections of the sun in the water, which show the sun to our weak eyes, because we cannot look at the sun itself. (*Orat.* 28.3)

He goes on to hint, despite his overall theme being our lack of knowledge, that we know God by his benefits through his supply of our needs and through the abundant feast provided by nature (28.26).

It is when he reaches the fourth theological *Oration* that Gregory gives the subject more explicit consideration.

> The divine cannot be named. . . . For no one has ever breathed the whole air, nor has mind located or language contained the being of God completely. But sketching his inward self from his outward characteristics, we may assemble an inadequate partial picture. And the one who makes the best theologian is not the one who knows the whole truth, for the chain [of the flesh] is incapable of receiving the whole truth, but the one who creates the best picture, who assembles more of truth's image or shadow or whatever we should call it. (30.17)

On this basis Gregory then lists names of the Godhead and of each Person within it, making a distinction between names that are of God's essence and names that are "relative" to his creatures, just as Origen had done before him. The names are all drawn from scripture, but the only one that refers absolutely to God's essence is "the One who Is"—the name Moses received at the burning bush (Exod 3:14).

Gregory of Nyssa, however, was the one who addressed most systematically the problem of how language can refer to the infinite, incomprehensible source of all being. Interestingly he moves from a relativistic theory of language to confidence in God's will to make God's self known through creation and scripture, if indirectly and symbolically. Reason may supply us only with "a dim and imperfect comprehension of the divine nature," yet "sufficient for our limited capacity" is "the knowledge that we can gather from the names which piety allows us to apply to it" (*Eun.* 2.130 [*GNO* 1:263]).

Language is a human invention; Gregory is quite clear about that. The multiplicity of different languages arises from the freedom God granted to devise linguistic expression, and not even Hebrew is God-given! Nor was he the only one to say this kind of thing—in volume 1 we found Augustine making the same point.[28] Gregory is not afraid to state that even the names of God come from human conception, and their multiplicity is all to the good, for "no one suitable word has been found to express the divine nature" and by addressing God with many names, "each by some distinctive touch adding something fresh to our notions of God," we can manage "to gain some glimmerings for the comprehension of what we seek" (2.145 [*GNO* 1:267]). Of course Gregory is resisting Eunomius's attempt to capture God's essence in a single defining term, and he needs to underline the point that "we do not say that the nature of things was of human invention but only the names" (2.283 [*GNO* 1:310]). The gulf between Creator and creature, infinite and finite, is so huge that different attributes or names have to be associated together in order to correct one another. Thus certain peculiar and appropriate names are derived and Gregory makes space for a rich theological vocabulary drawn from what humans perceive of God's operations through scripture and contemplation of God's works (2.149–154 [*GNO* 1:268–270]).

What this implies is that God condescended to accommodate the divine self to the limitations of human perception and language, and that has consequences. On the one hand it means that, however inadequately, the language used is not utterly divorced from the reality to which it refers—God cannot be a party to deception (2.325 [*GNO* 1:321]). On the other hand the language is inadequate to the divine subject, so it is important to be ever conscious of difference, as well as similarity, in the applicability of such humanly contrived names to the divine. Difference is exemplified by the already familiar issue of what "son" might mean when applied to the divine: "We think of human generation one way; we surmise of the divine generation in another." For in the

28. Volume 1, chapter 7, p. 235.

case of divine generation, the mind has to reject notions of sex and passion, of time and place, and think simply of the Son as being eternally derived from the Father. Similarity comes into play as Gregory argues to the assertion that the Only-begotten shares the dignity and honor of God the Father from the fact that scripture honors him with the same names as the Father, and then from the fact that the incarnate Word named God Father to the unchangeability of that Fatherhood and the eternity of the Son's generation (2.15 [*GNO* 1:231]). Thus Trinitarian relationships are deduced from scriptural comments and the names have sufficient grounding in reality to form a basis for theological argument.

Creation and scripture, then, are expressive of God's will and God is truth. The names offer a limited yet adequate means of divine communication, similar to the signs and gestures used to communicate with those who are deaf (2.417–421 [*GNO* 1:348–349]). "There is a similarity of names between things human and things divine, revealing nevertheless underneath this sameness a wide difference in meanings" (1.622).[29] Yet, even though "the infinity of God exceeds all the significance and comprehension that names can furnish" (3.110 [*GNO* 2:41]) if such names are truly predicable of God, they should be understood in their most natural and obvious sense, though with a heightened and more glorious meaning (*Eun.* 3.87ff., 135ff. [*GNO* 2:33ff., 48ff.]).

That truer, though still shadowy, level of meaning could be identified by doing as Gregory of Nazianzus did, that is, by picking up Origen's distinction between absolute and relative reference.[30] As Gregory of Nyssa puts it:

> God is called Father and King and other names innumerable in scripture. Of these names, some can be pronounced absolutely . . . like immortal, etc.; others express God's service towards something, like Helper, Champion, Rescuer. . . . Some are both absolute and relative, like God or good. (*Eun.* 1.570–571 [*GNO* 1:190])[31]

Fatherhood is an absolute not a relative term, so Son of the Father must be distinguished from Shepherd, Light, Resurrection, and so on. Here Gregory of Nyssa has in his sights Eunomius's suggestion that all the names given to the Logos, including Son of God, are to be taken as metaphorical (2.294ff. [*GNO* 1:313ff.]). Such a suggestion made it the more urgent to clarify the status, and thus the doctrinal potency, of each name. The kind of thing both Gregories

29. The discussion ranges over *Eun.* 1.620–633 (*GNO* 1:205–208); cf. 3.76–77 (*GNO* 2:30–31).
30. See above, p. 73.
31. Cf. *Eun.* 2.130; 3.131ff. (*GNO* 1:263–264; 2:47ff.).

wished to say was that God is absolutely Father of the Son, but not absolutely our Father. Their aim was to distinguish degrees of symbolism in theological language—from the purely metaphorical to that closer approximation to truth. But in the end the most crucial point against Eunomius was that the names were all attributes—none could provide a definitive expression of God's Being (1.587ff. [*GNO* 1:195ff.]); while deploying many names was essential for gathering up different features of the incomprehensible infinite:

> while the divine nature is simple . . . and cannot be viewed under any form of complex formation, the human mind . . . in its inability to behold clearly the object of its search, feels after the unutterable Being in diverse and many-sided ways, and never chases the mystery in the light of one idea alone. (*Eun.* 2.475 [*GNO* 1:364–367])

and

> because in such cases there is no appropriate term to be found to mark the subject adequately, we are compelled by many and differing names . . . to divulge our surmises as they arise within us with regard to the deity. (*Eun.* 2.577 [*GNO* 1:394–395])

So faced with the Eunomian challenge, the two Gregories adapted earlier approaches to forge a viable theological language while refusing to allow the possibility of any simple or single definition. To clarify the applicability of any human language to the divine, endless qualifications and multiple terms and symbols were necessary. Yet it was God's will through creation and scripture to reveal appropriate attributes and names. As I previously have put it:

> The biblical narratives, treated imaginatively rather than literally, can become luminous of the divine reality beyond human expression; and the complete incarnation of one who was by nature totally transcendent was the crown of God's loving accommodation to human beings and the triumph of sheer grace which made possible human assimilation to God. The possibility of theological language was no longer located in any kind of natural kinship to the divine, but in God's will to create and redeem; and the symbolic character of theological language was no longer confined to allegorical exegesis but was fully recognized in formal theology.[32]

32. F. Young, "God of the Greeks," 70.

The concept of the Trinity may not be articulated as such in scripture itself, but what this discussion has shown is (1) that it is a mistake to treat the doctrine as a definition of God; and (2) that it was the dynamics of scripture itself that necessitated its formulation.

2. Biblical Hermeneutics and the Trinitarian Settlement

The following sentences, introducing the symbolic theology of Ephrem the Syrian, exactly capture what I hope to argue in this section:

> Doctrine is not meant to monopolize or manipulate the believer's intelligence and imagination by means of a system of abstract notions. . . . It is meant to facilitate and guide a personal and communal heuristic process, the outcome of which is always a gift of God that transcends whatever form of human control, either personal or ecclesial.[33]

Some discussion of Ephrem is a good place to start, but my intention is to explore a wider range of material, hoping to show how what we might call the Trinitarian settlement was actually liberating for worship, for the ascetic journey, but most of all for renewed engagement with the biblical narrative, its "types" and symbols, parables and analogies, in a way that enabled incorporation into it through Christ and the Spirit. The doctrine actually facilitated biblical hermeneutics.

2.1. Ephrem the Syrian

A challenge from Sebastian Brock was the gift of another illuminating discovery—he suggested that I should include consideration of Ephrem's work in my study of early Christian exegesis and gave me a copy of his book *The Luminous Eye*.[34] Subsequently I have not ceased drawing upon Ephrem's remarkable theological poetry, though largely dependent on the burgeoning scholarship of others given my smattering of beginner's Syriac. It is certainly not possible to do justice to Ephrem's theological vision here, but let me share just enough

33. Kees den Biesen, *Simple and Bold: Ephrem's Art of Symbolic Thought* (Piscataway, NJ: Gorgias, 2006), 26.

34. Sebastian Brock, *The Luminous Eye: The Spiritual Vision of Saint Ephrem the Syrian*, rev. ed. (Kalamazoo, MI: Cistercian, 1992); given to me when delivering the lectures on which my book *Biblical Exegesis and the Formation of Christian Culture* is based.

to show how he exemplifies my point that the doctrine of the Trinity became key to a heuristic process of symbolic association that draws participants into the biblical story and into richer depths of contemplation and worship.

Ephrem died in 373—in other words, prior to the political triumph of pro-Nicene theology in 381. Nevertheless, his work provides evidence of resistance to various heresies, including the Anomoean version of Arianism promulgated by Eunomius. As Brock puts it: "To Ephrem, theological definitions [Greek *horoi*, or boundaries] are not only potentially dangerous, but they can be blasphemous. . . . For by trying to define God one is in effect attempting to contain the Uncontainable, to limit the Limitless."[35] Like Athanasius, Ephrem affirmed the ontological gap—the chasm—between Creator and created, and for him that meant acknowledgement of what I might call a fundamental intellectual humility:

> Whoever is capable of investigating
> becomes the container of what he investigates;
> a knowledge which is capable of containing the Omniscient
> is greater than Him,
> for it has proved capable of measuring the whole of Him.
> A person who investigates the Father and Son
> is thus greater than them!
> Far be it, then, and something anathema,
> that the Father and Son should be investigated,
> while dust and ashes exalts itself! (*Fid.* 9.16)[36]

So God is hidden, yet God has revealed the divine self through the types and symbols to be found in scripture and in nature:

> In his book Moses
> described the creation of the natural world,
> so that both Nature and Scripture
> might bear witness to the Creator:
> Nature, through man's use of it,
> Scripture, through his reading of it.
> These are the witnesses

35. Brock, *Luminous Eye*, 23.
36. Translation from Brock, *Luminous Eye*, 26–27.

which reach everywhere,
they are to be found at all times,
present at every hour,
confuting the unbeliever
who defames the Creator. (*Par.* 5.2)[37]

Such metaphors and symbols are generative:

Even though Your symbol may be small,
yet it is a fountain of further mysteries. (*Fid.* 4.10)[38]

Ephrem celebrates the language of scripture as God's accommodation to our levels of need and understanding. Particularly striking is Ephrem's treatment of the garment of "names":

Let us give thanks to God who clothed Himself in the names of the body's various parts:
Scripture refers to His "ears," to teach us that He listens to us:
it speaks of His "eyes," to show that He sees us;
it was just the names of such things that He put on,
and, although in His true Being there is not wrath or regret,
yet He put on these names too because of our weakness.

Refrain: Blessed is He who has appeared to our human race under so many metaphors.

We should realize that had He not put on the names
of such things, it would not have been possible for Him
to speak with us humans. By means of what belongs to us did He draw close to us:
He clothed Himself in our language, so that He might clothe us
in His mode of life. He asked for our form and put this on,
and then, as a father with His children, He spoke with our childish state.

37. English translation from S. Brock, trans., *Hymns on Paradise* (Crestwood, NY: St. Vladimir's Seminary Press, 1990).

38. Translation from Brock, *Luminous Eye*, 56.

It is our metaphors that He put on—though He did not literally
do so;
He then took them off—without actually doing so: when
wearing them,
He was at the same time stripped of them.
He puts one on when it is beneficial, then strips it off in exchange
for another;
the fact that He strips off and puts on all sorts of metaphors
tells us that the metaphor does not apply to his true Being:
because that Being is hidden, He has depicted it by means of what
is visible.

Ephrem adds an amusing parable: someone teaching a parrot to speak hides behind a mirror so that the parrot sees itself and imagines it is conversing with another parrot.

The Divine Being that in all things is exalted above all things
in His love bent down from on high and acquired from us our
own habits:
He laboured by every means so as to turn all to Himself.
(*Fid.* 31.1–7)[39]

In other words God has taken the initiative to cross the chasm.

Somewhat like Origen and the Cappadocians, Ephrem in his own way distinguishes between names of God that are "perfect and exact" (parallel perhaps to "absolute") and those that are "borrowed" (perhaps "relative"). But maybe the contrast is subtly different, enhancing the gap between the divine nature and the gracious assumption of lowly language, even flesh, from us. The "perfect names" are "a revelation of God's hiddenness."[40]

Father, Son and Holy Spirit can be reached only by Their names;
do not look further, to Their Persons,
just meditate on Their names.
If you investigate the person of God, you will perish,
but if you believe in the name, you will live.
Let the name of the Father be a boundary to you,

39. Translation from Brock, *Luminous Eye*, 60–62.
40. Translation from Brock, *Luminous Eye*, 63.

do not cross it and investigate His nature;
let the name of the Son be a wall to you,
do not cross it and investigate His birth from the Father;
let the name of the Spirit be a fence to you,
do not enter inside for the purpose of prying into Him.
(*Fid.* 4.129–140)

The being of the Trinity is hidden, beyond understanding, but acceptance of that allows meditation on the "borrowed names" without misunderstanding:

God has made small His majesty
by means of these borrowed names . . .
what we perceive as His majesty is but a tiny part,
for He has shown us a single spark from it;
He has accorded to us only what our eyes can take
of the multitude of His powerful rays. (*Haer.* 30.4)[41]

This acceptance of limitation enables a fresh kind of mentality, one that appreciates the language of paradox, redolent of the condescension of God to our level, especially in the incarnation:

You, Who magnify all by being born, magnify my weak mind
that I may tell about Your birth, not to investigate Your majesty,
but to proclaim Your grace. Blessed is He Who is [both] hidden
and revealed in His actions! . . .
Who is sufficient to say that although He dwelt entirely in
the body,
still He dwelt entirely in the universe? Blessed is the Unlimited
Who was limited! (*Nat.* 23.1–2)[42]

It is a mentality that also revels not only in scriptural allusions but also in the imaginative interconnectedness of biblical "types," enabling extraordinary insights into the incarnation, as select verses from the first of Ephrem's *Hymns on the Resurrection* may demonstrate:

41. Translation from Brock, *Luminous Eye*, 65.

42. English translation of *Hymns on the Nativity* from Kathleen E. McVey, *Ephrem the Syrian: Hymns*, CWS (New York: Paulist, 1989), 187–88.

The Shepherd of all flew down
In search of Adam, the sheep that strayed;
On His shoulders He carried him, taking him up:
He was an offering for the Lord of the flock.
Blessed is His descent!

He sprinkled dew and life-giving rain
On Mary, the thirsty earth.
Like a seed of wheat He fell again to Sheol
To spring up as a sheaf, as the new Bread.
Blessed is His offering! . . .

From on high He flowed like a river,
From Mary He [stemmed] as from a root,
From the Cross He descended as fruit,
As the first-fruit He ascended to heaven.
Blessed is His will!

The Word came forth from the Father's womb,
He put on the body in another womb;
From one womb to another did He proceed,
And chaste wombs are filled with Him.
Blessed is He who has resided in us!

From on high He came down as Lord,
From within the womb He came forth as a servant;
Death knelt before Him in Sheol,
And Life worshipped Him at His resurrection.
Blessed is His victory! (*Res.* 1.2–3, 6–8)[43]

Luke 15:4–5 has been spotted in the first verse quoted; Isaiah 53:2, John 12:24, Leviticus 23:11, and John 6:36 in the second; Isaiah 11:1; Luke 3:32, Romans 15:12, and Colossians 1:18 in the third; John 1:18 and 14 in the fourth. But it is the extraordinary capacity to link Mary's womb with the womb/bosom of the Father which shows how doctrine freed the imagination. Elsewhere Ephrem plays with the parallels between Mary's womb and baptism in the Jordan:

43. Syriac text and English translation in *Ephrem the Syrian: Select Poems*, ed. and trans. Sebastian P. Brock and George A. Kiraz (Provo: Brigham Young University Press, 2006).

The river in which Christ was baptized
Conceived Him again symbolically;
The moist womb of the water
Conceived Him in purity,
Bore Him in chastity,
made Him go up in glory.

In the pure womb of the river
you should recognize Mary, the daughter of humanity,
who conceived having known no man,
who gave birth without intercourse,
who brought up, through a gift,
The Lord of that gift. (*Eccl.* 36.3–6)[44]

But more than anything else Ephrem's typology enables everyone to be drawn into the overarching biblical narrative. In the *Hymns on Paradise* we find biblical stories fused so as to constitute the story of "everyman":

The king of Babylon resembled
Adam king of the universe:
Both rose up against the one Lord
And were brought low. (*Par.* 13.4)

So did King David, who wept for Adam and his fall, but "In that king / Did God depict Adam" (*Par.* 13.6). The following verse declares that, "because it was not easy for us to see our fallen state," he depicted it in that king, "portraying our fall in his fall, and portraying our return in his repentant return" (13.7). The hymn draws similar points from Samson, Jonah, and Joseph. Thus, time and persons are fused into exemplars of a single human narrative of fall and redemption. Indeed, through Mary and Christ restoration to paradise has in principle been effected, and the church is a foretaste of that:

The assembly of saints
bears resemblance to Paradise:
in it each day is plucked
the fruit of Him who gives life to all . . .
The serpent is crippled and bound

44. Translation from Brock, *Luminous Eye*, 91.

By the curse . . .
Among the saints none is naked,
for they have put on glory . . .
for they have found, through our Lord,
the robe that belongs to Adam and Eve. (*Par.* 6.8–9)

For Ephrem, Adam and Christ, Eve and Mary, are universal "types," representing two kinds of truth about humanity; each human being may be drawn into this overarching narrative and find themselves reflected in it. And the patterns of interconnection allow the renewal of humanity in Christ to be discerned and received.

We could go on, exploring how Ephrem teases out the "recapitulation" theme noted in Irenaeus and long since explored in volume 1, as well as other symbols that run through his poetic works and imaginatively draw us into the story: oil, olive, pearl, water, wine, bread, lamb, light, fire, tree, rock, clothing, the robe of glory, the wedding garment, bridegroom and bride.[45] But hopefully these examples are enough to illustrate the point: the presupposition of pro-Nicene doctrine enabled this process of imaginative entry into scripture's overarching narrative of God's providential and redemptive activity, and so facilitated worship appropriate to the extraordinary—indeed paradoxical—grace, whereby human lives may be touched not by some semi-divine agent or servant of God, but by one who is truly God's offspring. The Arian logic excluded this paradox, but "paradox . . . triggers a process of re-shuffling the conceptual pack."[46] The issues concerned the very possibility of theological language, but Ephrem shows that "when we think in images, either in art or in religion, we are genuinely thinking."[47] Without the specification of doctrine, however, the amorphous potential of images may just confuse the truth, whereas with it, as Ephrem himself said, scripture is like a fountain, with a "multiplicity of inner meanings":

> Who is capable of comprehending the extent of what is to be discovered in a single utterance of Yours? For we leave behind in it far more than we take from it, like thirsty people drinking from a fountain. . . . Anyone who encounters Scripture should not suppose that the single one of its riches

45. Cf. volume 1, chapter 4.

46. Rowan Williams, *The Edge of Words: God and the Habits of Language* (London: Bloomsbury, 2014), 128.

47. Williams, *Edge of Words*, 194.

> that he has found is the only one to exist; rather, he should realize that he himself is only capable of discovering that one out of the many riches which exist in it. Nor, because Scripture has enriched him should the reader impoverish it. . . . Let the fountain vanquish your thirst, your thirst should not vanquish the fountain! . . . Give thanks for what you have taken away, and do not complain about the superfluity that is left over.[48]

2.2. *The Pseudo-Macarian* Homilies

If Ephrem's poetic celebration of incarnation through scriptural symbolism was securely rooted in Trinitarian doctrine, so too was the ascetic spirituality of the so-called Macarian *Homilies*. In neither case is the language or concept of Trinity as such particularly prominent, yet it is implicit and indispensable. The divine activity of creation and new creation through Christ and the Holy Spirit is clearly the basis of the life of prayer and action described in these homilies.

A particularly illuminating discovery for me was the pride of place given to these homilies in the multivolume *Christian Library* published by John Wesley for his preachers in eighteenth-century England. I have in the past argued that Wesley "democratized" the call to Christian perfection that he found set out here in texts whose reading of scripture paralleled his own.[49] I have also suggested that Wesley and "Macarius" have a common practical theology, a common stress on the love of God, and a common emphasis on the incarnation and the Holy Spirit as the generators of perfection.[50] Of course, their historical, social, and ecclesial contexts were very different, and Wesley mistakenly assumed, with tradition, that these homilies were composed by the "great Macarius of Egypt," yet their distillation of the way of holiness from the same scriptural texts is strikingly parallel, both presupposing and illuminating a robust Trinitarian doctrine as the basis of a dynamic theology of overflowing divine energies.

It is this which leads me to include the Pseudo-Macarian *Homilies* as another example of what I have called the liberating effect of the Trinitarian settlement.

48. Brock, *Luminous Eye*, 50–51, citing Ephrem's *Commentary on the Diatesseron* 1.18–19.

49. F. Young, "Inner Struggle: Some Parallels between the Spirituality of John Wesley and the Greek Fathers," in *Orthodox and Wesleyan Spirituality*, ed. S. T. Kimbrough Jr. (Crestwood, NY: St. Vladimir's Seminary Press, 2002), 157–72.

50. F. Young, "Essence and Energies: Classical Trinitarianism and 'Enthusiasm,'" in *Trinity, Community and Power: Mapping Trajectories in Wesleyan Theology*, ed. M. Douglas Meeks (Nashville: Abingdon, 2000), 127–41.

Modern scholarship has linked these texts with the Messalians, a group of enthusiastic ascetics hailing from the borderlands of Syria and Asia Minor (their Greek name seems to be a corruption of the Syriac for "those who pray"); their views came in for repeated condemnation in the late fourth century. Such dubious provenance of the homilies, however, was overridden by their erroneous attribution to Macarius, and they subsequently have had long-lasting ecumenical influence not just on Eastern Orthodox monasticism but even on Protestant pietism.[51]

"Macarius" is a theologian of the Holy Spirit and of transformation or transfiguration. "If anyone is in Christ, he is a new creature," he says, quoting 2 Corinthians 5:17, "for our Lord Jesus Christ came for this reason, to change and transform and renew human nature, and to re-create this soul that had been overturned by passions through the transgression." Christ came to "mingle human nature with his own Spirit of the Godhead," to effect in those who believe "a new mind and a new soul and new eyes, a new spiritual tongue, and, in a word, new humans," to "pour into them new wine which is his Spirit" (*Hom.* 44.1).[52] The Spirit is "the Lord himself shining in their hearts," and the one who possesses the Spirit fulfils "all the commands justly and practices all the virtues without blame, purely without forcing and with a certain ease" (18.1–2). To reach this state, hearers are encouraged to force themselves to observe the commandments, begging God to grant the gift of the heavenly grace of the Spirit (19.7). There is a practical recognition of synergism: the cooperation of divine grace and human will.

Striving for perfection in Christ lies at the heart of Pseudo-Macarian teaching. There are frequent references to "a 'mixing' of the Holy Spirit with the human soul," "to becoming 'one spirit' with the Lord, to being changed into a 'divine nature,'" and "to other ways of describing full communion with God." God comes to dwell in the soul, and then obedience to the commandments becomes "natural and easy." The "mature" Christian is the one who has grown up through the ascetical struggle and been "completed" by the gift of the Spirit. Hence "the emphasis on growth and progress."[53] Many passages develop Ephe-

51. See further my discussion of critical and other issues in *From Nicaea to Chalcedon*, 2nd ed. (Grand Rapids: Baker Academic, 2010), 116–27. The section on Macarius in *From Nicaea to Chalcedon* brought together my previous studies, and the following discussion is a reworked version of that section, used with permission.

52. Greek text in PG 34; English translation in George A. Maloney, SJ, trans., *Pseudo-Macarius: The Fifty Spiritual Homilies and the Great Letter*, CWS (New York: Paulist, 1992). All citations of Pseudo-Macarius's *Homilies* derive from the Collection 2 manuscript tradition.

53. Quotations in the last few sentences from Columba Stewart, *'Working the Earth of*

sians 4:13, which speaks of advancing "to maturity, to the measure of the full stature of Christ" (cf. Col 1:28), or Hebrews' reference to progressing from children's milk to the solid food of the mature (Heb 5:12–14). There is a profound oscillation between the need for constant struggle and the promise of reaching the goal, which is a return to paradise and restoration of the image of God; "sin is uprooted" and "the first creation of the pure Adam" received. However, renewal goes further than that: "by the power of the Spirit and the spiritual regeneration," one "not only comes to the measure of the first Adam, but also reaches a greater state than he possessed. For man is divinized" (*Hom.* 26.2).

All this is rooted in scripture. The *Homilies* are riddled with biblical quotations and allusions. Sometimes great collages are created:

> We have not yet been immersed in the leaven of sincerity (1 Cor 5:8), but we are still in the leaven of evil. . . . "We have not yet put on the new man who has been created after God in holiness" (Eph 4:24), because we have not yet put off "the old man that is corrupt according to the sinful lusts" (Eph 4:22). We have not yet "given birth to the image of the heavenly" (1 Cor 15:49) nor have we been made "conformed to his glory" (Phil 3:21). We have not yet adored "God in spirit and in truth" (John 4:24), since "sin reigns in our mortal body" (Rom 6:12). . . . We have not yet been "transformed by a renewal of the mind," since we are still "conformed to this world" (Rom 12:2) "in the vanity of the mind" (Eph 4:17). We are not yet "glorified with Christ" because we have not yet "suffered with him" (Rom 8:17). (*Hom.* 25.3–5)

And so it goes on, citing mainly but not exclusively Pauline texts.

Another habit is reference to biblical stories and models. Perseverance in the face of temptation is graphically illustrated by reference to one biblical hero after another: Joseph, David, Moses, Abraham, Noah. "We have offered these examples from Holy Scripture to show that the power of divine grace is in man and the gift of the Holy Spirit which is given to the faithful soul comes forth with much contention, with much endurance, patience, trials and testings" (9.2–7). Accounts of Elijah withholding and then commanding rain, Moses turning the rod into a serpent and back, David overcoming Goliath, Joshua impotently besieging Jericho till God commanded the walls to tumble down—all these and more are taken to be a "figure and shadow" of true realities to be applied to the spiritual journey. Like Jericho's walls, for example, the walls

---

the Heart': The Messalian Controversy in History, Texts and Language to AD 431 (Oxford: Clarendon, 1991), 78–82.

of evil "that obstruct your mind" will fall by God's power (1.1–3). Traditional "types" interiorize the law, circumcision becoming circumcision of the heart, baptism of the flesh becoming baptism with the Holy Spirit and fire, the sacrifices under the old covenant signifying Christ's sacrifice, while spiritual laws are written on the "fleshy tablets of the heart" rather than on tablets of stone (47.1–3). The Passover and exodus are all about human slavery to the Egyptians (i.e., the demons) and the deliverance accomplished in Christ; he leads the soul out of Egypt, away from darkness, and God patiently

> tests it to see whether it remains faithful, whether it has love for him. For God has planned such a road, leading to life (Matt 7:14), to be fraught with affliction and narrow escapes, in much testing and extremely bitter trials so that from there the soul may afterward reach the true land of the glory of the children of God. (*Hom.* 47.13)

Many of the images and metaphors used in these homilies are developments from biblical usage: themes like light and fire, water and oil, wind and trees, seed and fruit, bread and wine, mirrors and garments, pearls and treasure. The author refers to biblical parables and invents his own. Take the example of a rich woman with no protection, he says—she searches for a powerful husband and after much struggle finds a "strong wall" in the same way that the soul searches for its bridegroom (45.5). This is not the only time he uses this kind of parable; the idea of the heavenly bridegroom of the soul recurs time and again.[54] The scriptural basis of the "Macarian" teaching is clear on page after page, but it is scripture read in order to discern what is true for the heart on its spiritual journey to union with God, picking up typological traditions that parallel in many ways the symbolism of Ephrem.

This account of the scriptural element in Macarian teaching has already alerted us to its pervasive interiority. The focus is on experience, assurance, sensation, and communion, and this is found in prayer:[55]

> One kneels down in prayer and at once his heart is filled with the power of God. And his soul exults in the Lord as a bride with the bridegroom. . . . It happens that he is the whole day occupied by his work and can give himself

54. E.g., *Hom.* 4.6–7; 10.1, 4; 15.2; 25.8; 27.1; 28.5.

55. Stewart, *Working the Earth*, explores the distinctive Greek vocabulary used for this range of responses.

> to prayer for only an hour. The interior man is caught up in prayer and plunged into the infinite depths of that other world with great sweetness. . . .
>
> At times the fire flares out and burns with more vehement flames. At other times it burns more gently and slowly. . . . It is always burning and giving off light, but when it is especially trimmed, it burns more brilliantly, as though intoxicated by the love of God. (*Hom.* 8.1–2)

This experience, however, is grounded not only in the presence of the Holy Spirit in the heart but in the saving work of Christ. The most important designations of Christ in these homilies are "light" and "image," since transformation or transfiguration is the ultimate goal of the ascetic's life. At one point Macarius describes Christ as a portrait painter, endeavoring to reproduce his own image in the believer. The soul needs to have Christ stamped on it if it is to be coin in the treasuries of the kingdom (30.4–5). The bodies of the saints are like lamps lit from the fire of Christ:

> For as the body of the Lord was glorified when he climbed the mount and was transfigured into the divine glory and into infinite light, so also the bodies of the saints are glorified and shine like lightning. (*Hom.* 15.38)

Their transfiguration takes place by "putting on Christ," the "garment of salvation," the "ineffable light." Once clothed in Christ, the garment

> will never be put off for all eternity. But in the resurrection of their bodies also will be glorified by the glory of the Light with which the faithful and noble persons are even now clothed. (*Hom.* 20.1–3)

So Christ lies at the core of the Macarian transformative reading of the Bible. Christians become his friends, his brothers, his fellow heirs, participators of the divine nature, conformed to his glory.[56]

One passage exemplifying the re-creative role of Christ is the particularly fascinating *Homily* 1. It is a reflection on Ezekiel's vision of the chariot-throne of God (*merkabah*), a passage that figured large in Jewish mystical speculations and so was treated with great caution by the rabbis. Macarius starts off by saying that the prophet "described it in human terms but in a way full of mysteries that completely surpass the powers of the human mind." He insists that what the prophet saw, whether in ecstasy or in a trance, was true and certain. He

56. E.g., *Hom.* 25.4–5, quoting multiple New Testament texts; see also 27.1; 48.2.

thinks, however, that the "mystery hidden for generations" (Col 1:26) has been revealed "in our time, at the end of the ages" (1 Pet 1:20) when Christ appeared. What Ezekiel's vision is about is the "mystery of the human soul that would receive its Lord and would become his throne of glory."

The soul "is covered with the beauty of ineffable glory of the Spirit . . . with the beauty of the ineffable glory of the light of Christ, who mounts and rides upon the soul." It is "Christ who drives, guides, carries and supports the soul about and adorns and decorates the soul with his spiritual beauty." The animals that bore the chariot represent the will, the conscience, the mind, and the power of loving. The Rider—the authentic Charioteer—is mounted on the soul and guides it with the reins of the Spirit. What we seem to have here is an astonishing adaptation of the Platonic notion of the tripartite soul in which reason controls the soul's passions. Christ takes control and he knows the way—elsewhere Macarius speaks of Christ as the pilot of the soul. With Christ in the driving seat, the whole soul becomes the eye: "all light, all face, all eye . . . all glory, all spirit." This happens while in the body and anticipates the resurrection. So, as Golitzin has suggested, Macarius is affirming that it is no longer necessary to go up to heaven, as in apocalyptic visions, to see God on the glorious throne.[57] The ascetic teaching is an interiorization of the cosmic struggle of apocalyptic, and the soul becomes the locus of theophany—the pure in heart shall see God.

Be that as it may, what we find here is a "mystical union" which only makes sense through an implicit and visionary doctrine of the Trinity, as is surely demonstrated by the following extract from the *Great Letter* also attributed to Macarius:

> For such a soul, wounded by love for Christ, dies to any other desire in order, I speak boldly, to possess that most beautiful intellectual and mystical communion with Christ according to the immortal quality of divinizing fellowship. Truly, such a soul is blessed and happy when, conquered by spiritual passion, it has worthily become espoused to God the Word. Let her say, "My soul will exalt in the Lord, who has clothed me in the garments of salvation and has wrapt me in the cloak of integrity like a bridegroom

57. A. Golitzin, "A Testimony to Christianity as Transfiguration: The Macarian Homilies and Orthodox Spirituality," in Kimbrough, *Orthodox and Wesleyan Spirituality*, 129–56; see also Golitzin, "Temple and Throne of Divine Glory: 'Pseudo-Macarius' and Purity of Heart, Together with Some Remarks on the Limitations and Usefulness of Scholarship," in *Purity of Heart in Early Ascetic and Monastic Literature*, ed. Harriet A. Luchman and Linda Kulzer (Collegeville, MN: Liturgical, 1999).

> wearing his crown, like a bride adorned in her jewels" (Isa 61:10). For the King of Glory, ardently desiring her beauty, has deigned to regard her, not only as the temple of God, but also as the daughter of the king and also the queen. Indeed, she is the temple of God, since she is inhabited by the Holy Spirit. She is also the daughter of the king since she has been adopted by the Father of lights. She is also queen as endowed with the divinity of the glory of the Only-Begotten Son.[58]

Trinitarian doctrine has enabled this transformative reading of the new creation in Christ that the New Testament proclaims.

2.3. *Back to Gregory of Nyssa*

There is an intriguing overlap between the Macarian *Great Letter* and the work known as *On Christian Practice* (*De instituto christiano*) attributed to Gregory of Nyssa. Jaeger thought Gregory's treatise had been paraphrased by the *Great Letter*, whereas more recent scholarship has concluded the dependence was the other way around.[59] Here the connection provides a prompt to return to Gregory's thought, for the above quotation from the *Great Letter* not only expresses their common drive toward perfection (unattainable though both thought it to be) but also captures themes central to Gregory's "mystical" exegesis.

Since the mid-twentieth century there has been great flowering of scholarship on Gregory of Nyssa, but sometimes there almost seem to be several different Gregories in play: the doctrinal controversialist conceptualizing the Trinity, the continuator of his brother Basil's work on creation and anthropology, the "Neoplatonic" mystical exegete—one could go on. *Re-Thinking Gregory of Nyssa*, a collection of essays published in 2003, proposed responding to the challenge of integrating Gregory's thought overall, a potentially huge discussion.[60] Here we shall restrict ourselves to the way in which inherited doctrines modified Neoplatonic influence in crucial respects (remarkably, besides his positive view of infinity, Gregory has a positive view of mutability as well as materiality) and how fresh doctrinal outcomes shaped both Gregory's

58. English translation from Maloney, *Pseudo-Macarius*, 257.

59. Werner Jaeger, *Two Rediscovered Works of Ancient Christian Literature: Gregory of Nyssa and Macarius* (Leiden: Brill, 1954); R. Staats, *Gregor von Nyssa und die Messalianer: Die Frage der Priorität zweier altkirchlicher Schriften*, PTS 8 (Berlin: de Gruyter, 1968); Staats, *Makarios-Symeon: Epistola Magna. Eine messalianische Mönchs-regel und ihre Umschrift in Gregors von Nyssa 'De Instituto Christiano'* (Göttingen: Vandenhoeck & Ruprecht, 1984).

60. Sarah Coakley, ed., *Re-Thinking Gregory of Nyssa* (Oxford: Blackwell, 2003).

exegesis of scripture and his pedagogical and "mystical" understanding of the spiritual journey into union with God.

Initially several features found time and again in Gregory's works, whether doctrinal or exegetical, may be briefly identified, though each demands more adequate articulation than is possible here:

- his embrace of the utter difference between Creator and creatures as fundamental both to the church's teaching and the journey of the soul: while some divine attributes may be inferred from the Creator's activities, the gulf can only be bridged by divine grace;
- his positive evaluation of the utter unknowability of the infinite God, not just as an epistemological point in doctrinal argumentation, but as the prior condition for the created mind to lose itself, entering into darkness and its own incapacity, so as to become receptive of God in faith and love;[61]
- his affirmation that beyond discursive reasoning there is knowledge of God, not (given the radical difference between Creator and creatures) through some kind of kinship with the divine, but rather through the indwelling Word in the soul which, when purified, becomes a mirror reflecting the divine image;
- his positive evaluation (despite accepting God's immutability and the goal of *apatheia*) of change and desire, of the potential for transformation from glory to glory, summed up in the soul's eternal *epektasis* (straining toward what is ahead; Phil 3:12–13), of never-ending progress because the infinite God can never be completely grasped;
- his positive evaluation of embodiment as essential to humankind as created by God and capable of transformation through purification and ultimately renewal in the resurrection;
- his confidence in the possibility of participation in or union with God, who becomes present in the soul when it is receptive of the Word and the Spirit;[62]

61. That this was an epistemological point rather than some kind of mystical experience has been emphasized by myself in the article "God of the Greeks," as well as by Ron E. Heine, *Perfection in the Virtuous Life: A Study in the Relationship between Edification and Polemical Theology in Gregory of Nyssa*, Patristic Monograph Series 2 (Cambridge, MA: The Philadelphia Patristic Foundation, 1975); Martin Laird, *Gregory of Nyssa and the Grasp of Faith: Union, Knowledge, and Divine Presence*, OECS (Oxford: Oxford University Press, 2004).

62. Whereas Gregory of Nazianzus often speaks of *theōsis*, Gregory of Nyssa generally prefers the language of participation rather than that of deification; see Norman Russell, *The Doctrine of Deification in the Greek Patristic Tradition* (Oxford: Oxford University Press, 2004), 214–32.

- his underlying assumptions, occasionally made explicit, whereby, through the loving engagement of Father, Son, and Holy Spirit the overarching biblical narrative of creation, fall, and redemption becomes the narrative context of the soul's journey, which is enabled by the incarnation and the sacraments of the church.

Each of the above surely derives from doctrinal argumentation, while their particular articulation is often couched in language drawn from the scriptural texts upon which Gregory is commenting.

In other words, doctrine informed exegesis, but scripture provided the often paradoxical and imaginative language in which the journey of the soul was delineated. Furthermore, all of those features hang together as vital threads in Gregory's overall theological thinking. So doctrine facilitated "a personal and communal heuristic process, the outcome of which is always a gift of God."[63] To get the flavor of this, we need to sample some classic passages and themes from Gregory's work.

2.3.1. Endless Journeying toward God

Gregory's *Life of Moses*, probably a late work, was his response to an inquiry about the perfect life.[64] His prologue sketches his approach: perfection in sense objects means boundaries and limits, a beginning and an end, but not so perfection in life. He cites "the Apostle"—he never ceased "straining towards those things that are still to come" (Phil 3:13). Perfection is unattainable, he states, a point he then explains: the divine being is unlimited and infinite; true virtue is participation in nothing other than God, who is absolute virtue. This good has no limit, so there is no "stopping-place" on the way to attaining perfection. "The perfection of human nature consists perhaps in its very growth in goodness" (*Vit. Mos.* 1.5–10). As emerges later, this involves both doctrine and discipline: "religious virtue is divided into two parts, into that which pertains to the divine and that which pertains to right conduct" (2.167; cf. 2.192).

With this the prologue turns to scripture for guidance, briefly mentioning Abraham before settling on Moses. Book 1 is then a précis of Moses's life of

63. Quoted above, p. 77, from den Biesen, *Simple and Bold*, 26.

64. Greek text in *GNO* 7; also in J. Daniélou, ed., *Grégoire de Nyssa: La vie de Moïse*, 3rd ed., SC 1 (Paris: Cerf, 1968); English translation in Abraham J. Malherbe and Everett Ferguson, *Gregory of Nyssa: The Life of Moses*, CWS (New York: Paulist, 1978); see also translated extracts from Gregory of Nyssa's mystical writings in Herbert Musurillo, SJ, *From Glory to Glory* (New York: Scribner's Sons, 1961).

journeying, ever moving on, the doctrine of God's infinity thus captured in scriptural narrative with occasional anticipations of the fruits of contemplation that will be delivered in book 2. Thus, at Sinai Moses "boldly approached the very darkness itself" and entering "the inner sanctuary of the divine mystical doctrine" was present "with the Invisible." So Moses teaches that for one "to associate intimately with God" it is necessary to "go beyond all that is visible and (lifting up his own mind, as to a mountain top, to the invisible and incomprehensible) believe that the divine is there where understanding does not reach." There it was that Moses received "teachings concerning virtue, the chief of which is reverence and having the proper notions of the divine nature, inasmuch as it transcends all cognitive thought and representation and cannot be likened to anything which is known." Trying to examine the Divine with respect to quality, quantity, origin, or mode of being is out of bounds as "it is unattainable"—all we need to know is its existence (*Vit. Mos.* 1.46–47). We recognize the shadow of doctrines spelled out against Eunomius and remember Gregory of Nazianzus's *Oration* 28 where Moses's ascent was utilized for doctrinal argument.[65] Here it facilitates the amplification of the exodus narrative to provide a typological exposition of scripture, which could inspire the spiritual life.

Book 2 aspires to "lay bear the hidden meaning of the history" (*Vit. Mos.* 2.5). Thus the burning bush signifies the Virgin—the radiance shining through "the thorny flesh" that the gospel tells us is the true light (2.19–26). Other signs also signify the Lord's incarnation: Moses's hand transformed and the rod turned into a snake and back (*Vit. Mos.* 2.27–36; Exod 4:1–7; John 3:14). The crossing of the Red Sea indicates that "those who pass through the mystical water in baptism must put to death in the water the whole phalanx of evil" and the subsequent narrative yields "spiritual contemplation" as "he who left the Egyptian behind dead in the water, was sweetened by the wood [already identified with the cross], was delighted in the apostolic springs, and was refreshed by the shade of the palm-tress, is already capable of receiving God" (*Vit. Mos.* 2.125). For of course, according to the apostle, the rock is Christ, who becomes drink for the thirsty (2.136). The manna signifies the incarnate Word, and "whatever marvels the history enumerates . . . are teachings for the virtuous life" (2.141).

So on to Sinai and the elaboration of the reading already outlined in book 1. Knowledge of God is a mountain steep and difficult to climb. Only the purified can attempt the ascent, and the people had to rely on Moses, although some

65. See above, pp. 69–70.

were "stoned by their own reasonings," the stones being heretical opinions (2.157–161). Setting the illumination of the burning bush alongside the darkness of Sinai, Gregory suggests that scripture teaches by this that knowledge comes at first as light, as escape from darkness through participation in light. But "as the mind progresses" and "keeps penetrating deeper" it "gains access to the invisible and incomprehensible, and there it sees God." This is "true knowledge," the "seeing that consists in not seeing, because that which is sought transcends all knowledge, being separated on all sides by incomprehensibility as a kind of darkness." Gregory points to John "who penetrated the luminous darkness" and said, "no one has ever seen God" (John 1:18) Moses approached the dark cloud where God was (Exod 20:21)—the God who "made darkness his hiding place" (Ps 18:11) (*Vit. Mos.* 2.162–164).

So in the dark Moses enters the tabernacle not made with hands, the archetype of the sanctuary to be built below with its holy of holies within. How, asks Gregory is this to be understood?

> Taking a hint from what has been said by Paul, who partially uncovered the mystery of these things, we say that Moses was earlier instructed by a type in the mystery of the tabernacle which encompasses the universe. This tabernacle would be Christ who is the power and the wisdom of God, who in his own nature was not made with hands, yet capable of being made when it became necessary for this tabernacle to be erected among us. Thus, the same tabernacle is in a way both fashioned and unfashioned, uncreated in preexistence but created having received this material composition. . . . This one is the Only-Begotten God, who encompasses everything in himself but who also pitched his own tabernacle among us (cf. John 1:14). (*Vit. Mos.* 2.174–175)

Gregory then justifies applying the name "tabernacle" to Christ, clearly drawing on that doctrinal discussion of names as applied to God or Christ reviewed earlier in this chapter.[66] Like scriptural names such as physician, shepherd, bread, vine, way, door, or water, so tabernacle can be predicated of Christ "in accord with a signification fitting to God." Hebrews 10:20 allows him to suggest that the veil of the tabernacle is Christ's flesh (*Vit. Mos.* 2.176–178). Thus doctrinal debates have facilitated a spiritual reading of scripture. From the heavenly tabernacle Gregory moves to the earthly tabernacle, identifying it with the church; its pillars and lamps become the apostles, the pillars of the church and

66. See section 1.3, above.

the light of the world, as scripture indicates. The priestly vestments shown to Moses are related to being clothed in purity and becoming a living sacrifice; while the tablets of the law are inscribed by the Holy Spirit, God's "finger." The law's intention lay "in turning us away from evil and in honoring the divine," so anticipating the Spirit coming upon the Virgin (2.184, 190–201).

Gregory soon wonders why it is that Moses asks God to appear to him when scripture indicates that God had already spoken with him face to face. So again we are drawn into the notion of eternal progress: Moses never "stopped in his ascent, nor did he set a limit for himself in his upward course" (2.227). He remained unsatisfied. The Divine is by nature infinite, so "this truly is the vision of God never to be satisfied in the desire to see him" (2.230–239). Gregory ponders the cleft in the rock where God's hand covered Moses as God passed by: the rock is Christ, and Moses seeing God's back means following behind wherever God leads—that is what it means to behold God (2.240, 244, 252).

Now much of this we would regard as allegory; much of it Daniélou treats in terms of mystical experience.[67] But more convincing is the view that Gregory had doctrinal concerns. The speculations of Origen had become controversial, not least the idea that preexistent souls fell because they became satiated by the sweetness of contemplating God. But, Gregory implies, that is impossible given God's infinity—there are always never-ending possibilities, new ridges of the mountain to climb. And that concern coalesced with the issues provoked by Eunomius.[68] As I have shown elsewhere, in Gregory's *Great Catechesis* as well as his works against Eunomius we find close parallels to Moses's ascent.[69] Doctrinal and epistemological concerns shape the reading of scripture's journey narratives into models of the spiritual life. So, for example, Abraham

> went out by Divine command from his own land and kindred on a journey worthy of a prophet eager for the knowledge of God. . . . For going out from himself and from his country, by which I understand his earthly and carnal mind, and raising his thoughts as far as possible above the common boundaries of nature, and forsaking the soul's kinship with the senses,—so that untroubled by any of the objects of sense his eyes might be open to the

67. Jean Daniélou, *Platonisme et théologie mystique: Essai sur la doctrine spirituelle de saint Grégoire de Nysse*, 2nd ed. (Paris: Aubier. 1954); introduction to Musurillo, *From Glory to Glory*.

68. Heine, *Virtuous Life*.

69. F. Young, "*Paideia* and the Myth of Static Dogma," in *The Making and Remaking of Christian Doctrine: Essays in Honour of Maurice Wiles*, ed. S. Coakley and D. A. Pailin (Oxford: Oxford University Press, 1993), 265–83; republished in F. Young, *Exegesis and Theology*.

> things which are invisible, there being neither sight nor sound to distract the mind in its work,—so "walking," as saith the Apostle, "by faith, not by sight," he was raised so high by the sublimity of his knowledge that he came to be regarded as the acme of human perfection, knowing as much of God as it was possible for finite human capacity at full stretch to attain. (*Eun.* 2.84 [*GNO* 1.251])

God's power, goodness, being without beginning, infinity, or whatever could be stepping-stones for the upward course, yet all fell short of what he was seeking. Yet, in the end, he had to admit that God is greater and more sublime than any known signification (*Eun.* 2.89 [*GNO* 1.252]). Gregory is clear how widely the divine nature differs from our own and urges us quietly to remain within our proper limits. Dogmatic formulations issue from heretics who offer the figments of their own imagination. Anyone who searches the whole of scripture will find there no doctrine of the divine nature, he affirms (2.106).

Thus, insights arising from doctrinal argument enabled a biblical hermeneutic that could profoundly shape not just the intellectual journey but also the soul's spiritual ascent, and Gregory's theological thought is of a piece: "a common logic informs Gregory's works on disputed theological matters and on 'spirituality.'"[70] It is this emphasis on the ascent into unknowing that has led to the view that he was an early exponent of a mysticism of darkness.[71] But its roots in the doctrinal argument with Eunomius have led more recent scholarship to treat it as an epistemological issue.[72] Furthermore, attention has been drawn to his focus on not just darkness but light: as Laird puts it, in the twelfth *Homily on the Song of Songs* "Moses becomes like the sun and is unable to be approached by those drawing near because of the light beaming from his face."[73] We should also observe that, even if the nature of God is beyond discursive reasoning, some knowledge of God is received through the Word and the Spirit.[74] If not always entirely explicit, Trinitarian doctrine is fundamental to Gregory's so-called mystical exegesis of scripture. Sooner or later

70. Andrew Radde-Gallwitz, *Basil of Caesarea, Gregory of Nyssa, and the Tranformation of Divine Simplicity*, OECS (Oxford: Oxford University Press, 2009), 176.

71. Notably Daniélou, *Platonisme et théologie mystique*; and Hans Urs von Balthasar, *Presence and Thought: An Essay on the Religious Philosophy of Gregory of Nyssa*, trans. Mark Sebanc (San Fancisco: Ignatius, 1995).

72. See above, note 61.

73. Laird, *Gregory of Nyssa*, 204. Greek text of the *Homilies on the Song of Songs* in *GNO* 6. The veiling of Moses's face occurs in Exod 34:29–35.

74. Laird, *Gregory of Nyssa*, especially chapters 5 and 6.

we discover that the grasp of faith means that the darkness is luminous and in the darkness there is union with Christ. Indeed, as we saw, Moses entered the heavenly tabernacle to discover that the tabernacle is Christ, and that union with Christ is realized in the sacraments and worship of Christ's body, the church. Besides, Moses is not a solitary adept but a mediator (*Vit. Mos.* 2.45) and "the graces of sanctification which [the soul] receives she receives not for herself but that she may sanctify others; . . . the soul becomes a source of grace for others."[75]

> Theology is a steep and hardly accessible mountain. The great majority of people reach only the foot of it and that scarcely. But if anyone is a Moses, it will happen that in climbing the mountain he will become capable of hearing the sound of trumpets, a sound which, so the story goes, becomes louder and louder as one rises higher. . . . And if the multitude cannot stand its voice from on high but prefer to commit to Moses the personal knowledge of ineffable things, so that the people may be taught afterward what he has learned in his education on the mountain, this happens all the time in the Church: it is not everyone's business to press onward toward the comprehension of mysteries. (*Vit. Mos.* 1.373–376)[76]

This is exactly the point Gregory of Nazianzus makes in *Oration* 27: without the right purification and appropriate intellectual humility no one should dare to approach the mountain, but they may be taught true doctrine by those who have. "God is contemplated through orthodox concepts . . . correctness in doctrine and life, moreover, go hand in hand in the spiritual life depicted in the *Life of Moses.*"[77]

2.3.2. *Made in God's Image*

According to Hans Boersma, "[Gregory] rightly reminds us that it is through embodied lives of virtue that we are led upward in continuous participation in the eternal life of God."[78] In view of his evident interest in the soul's ascent this emphasis on embodiment might seem surprising—certainly it is one aspect of

75. Daniélou, *Platonisme et théologie mystique*, 310; as quoted by Andrew Louth, *The Origins of the Christian Mystical Tradition*, 2nd ed. (Oxford: Oxford University Press, 2007), 196.

76. As quoted by Balthasar, *Presence and Thought*, 172.

77. Heine, *Virtuous Life*, 195.

78. Hans Boersma, *Embodiment and Virtue in Gregory of Nyssa: An Anagogical Approach*, OECS (Oxford: Oxford University Press, 2013), 250.

Gregory's thought that runs counter to much emphasis on Neoplatonic parallels. It shows how Gregory's thinking is rooted in long-standing Christian teaching about creation and resurrection, in his own scriptural sense of humanity's place as a creature within the created order, and above all in the inseparability of "faith toward the divine and conscience toward life" (*Vit. Mos.* 2.192).[79] His understanding of humankind as made in God's image lies at the heart of his anthropology.

Gregory was Basil's continuator, writing the work known as *On the Making of Humankind* to complete his brother's *Hexaemeron*.[80] Here, to produce a coherent account, he played out the program Basil initiated of bringing the Bible together with contemporary philosophy—natural philosophy in the case of creation in general, medical philosophy for exploration of human nature.[81] Inevitably Gregory adopts the then current soul-body dualism, but he actually emphasizes psycho-somatic unity and, in line with previous Christian discussion, states that humankind was made as an embodied creature and would indeed be raised as such.[82] In his dialogue *On the Soul and Resurrection* it becomes abundantly clear that resurrection means reembodiment, even if in a purified and spiritualized form.[83]

So how is this embodied creature made in God's image? In *On the Making of Humankind*, Gregory explores the unique nature of humankind within the created order (e.g., upright stance, dexterous hands, naked vulnerability to cold and predators). Then, on the basis of Genesis 1:26, he establishes that the autonomous soul can exercise sovereignty within the created order because it is the image of the Sovereign of all (*De hom.* 4.1). God is mind, word, and love, all-seeing and all-hearing, and in humankind these divine characteristics are imitated (5.2). Gregory emphasizes the human power of self-determination: freewill, as well as rationality, are capabilities that imitate the divine. The image finds its resemblance to the archetype in being filled with all good, he suggests, so

> there is in us the principle of all excellence, all virtue and wisdom, and every higher thing we can conceive; but pre-eminent among all is the fact that we are free from necessity . . . [and] have decision in our power as we please, for

79. See above, p. 93.

80. Greek text of *On the Making of Humankind* in PG 44; English translation in *NPNF*^{2} 5.

81. See my article "Adam and Anthropos: A Study of the Interaction of Science and the Bible in Two Anthropological Treatises of the Fourth Century," *VC* 37 (1983): 110–40.

82. See volume 1, chapter 6, 2.8.1.

83. Cf. my account in *God's Presence*, 94–102.

virtue is a voluntary thing, subject to no dominion: that which is the result of compulsion and force cannot be virtue. (*De hom.* 16.11)

Gregory has a strong sense of human solidarity: in Genesis 1 "the whole race was spoken of as one man," and "our whole nature . . . extending from the first to the last, is, so to say, one image of Him who is" (16.16–18).[84] Elsewhere in defending himself against tritheism he affirms that strictly speaking humankind is one nature, as is the Godhead; image and archetype reflect one another.[85] It is surely not unlikely that this sense of solidarity comes not so much from Platonism as from the "corporate personalities" of Adam and Christ in the over-arching biblical narrative of fall and redemption. Elsewhere, strikingly, Gregory insists on the basis of human solidarity that the poor, destitute, and ill are "human beings in no way distinct from the common nature," "made in the image of God, entrusted with the governance of the earth and rule over all creatures," and therefore to be aided and supported, not only in imitation of Christ and of the Creator's goodness to all, but also because "we are all brothers."[86] His discussion here seems to reflect what Gregory of Nazianzus said in his oration on loving the poor (*Orat.* 14.8): echoing Galatians 3:28, he remarked that "we are all one in the Lord, whether rich or poor, whether slave or free, whether in good health of body or in bad and there is one head of all, from whom all things proceed: Christ."[87] Ministering to the poor, then, is ministering to Christ, as the parable of the sheep and the goats in Matthew 25:31–46 makes clear. Virtue is indeed practical and embodied,[88] but also rooted in human solidarity.

Gregory also develops the notion of "mirror." The mind, being in the image of what is the most beautiful and supreme good, "remains in beauty and goodness so long as it partakes as far as possible in its likeness to the archetype, . . . being formed as though it were a mirror" (*De hom.* 12.9). In his classic study of Gregory's work, Balthasar notes that it is characteristic of Gregory that when

84. Cf. David Bentley Hart, "The Mirror of the Infinite: Gregory of Nyssa on the *Vestigia Trinitatis*," in Coakley, *Re-Thinking Gregory of Nyssa*, 118–19. See further J. Zachhüber, *Human Nature in Gregory of Nyssa: Philosophical Background and Theological Significance* (Leiden: Brill, 2000).

85. See his *To Ablabius: On Not Three Gods*; Greek text in *GNO* 3.1; English translation in *NPNF*² 5.

86. See Gregory of Nyssa, *On Loving the Poor*; English translation in the appendix in Susan Holman, *The Hungry Are Dying: Beggars and Bishops in Roman Cappadocia* (Oxford: Oxford University Press, 2001), quotations from pp. 203, 201, 197, 195, 196, 199–200.

87. English translation is from Brian E. Daley, *Gregory of Nazianzus* (London: Routledge, 2006), 79.

88. See further Boersma, *Embodiment*, ch. 5.

he speaks of "image," he immediately substitutes "mirror," the soul contemplating the archetype in her own beauty as in a mirror and an image.[89] The theme becomes particularly prominent in the *Homilies on the Beatitudes*:

> If a [person's] heart has been purified . . . , he will see the Image of the Divine Nature in his own beauty. . . . When [the inner man] has scraped off the rustlike dirt which dank decay has caused to appear on his form, he will once more recover the likeness of the archetype . . . and thus he becomes blessed, because when he looks at his own purity, he sees the archetype in the image. (*Hom. beat.* 6)[90]

The archetype is, as Balthasar notes, the perfect eschatological image that is the total Christ, which is reached by "the elevation of the created image to the plane of the uncreated Image and its integration into it. . . . But what integrates us into this Image is love."[91] So the church, the body of Christ, becomes potentially the "truth" of the image in Gregory's thought, as Balthasar makes clear, quoting words which suggest that "contemplating the Church" is a way of seeing "the Invisible One in a more penetrating way."[92]

It is hardly surprising, then, that in his *Great Catechism* Gregory can use the human experience of having within both *logos* and breath as an analogy to parallel the differentiation without separation of the Word and Spirit within the Godhead (*Or. cat.* 1–2), thus allowing the scriptural notion of God's image in humanity to commend a Trinitarian doctrine of God.[93] In *On the Making of Humankind* he even suggests that since the nature of our own mind evades our knowledge it accurately reflects the incomprehensible nature of the Creator (*De hom.* 11.4).[94] There is profound interaction between doctrine and scripture in Gregory's thinking.

2.3.3. *The Way of Wisdom*

Commenting on the time for silence in Ecclesiastes 3:7, Gregory states that "human speech finds it impossible to express that reality which transcends

89. Balthasar, *Presence and Thought*, 115, 121–22, quoting from Gregory's *Homilies on the Song of Songs* and *On the Soul and the Resurrection*, among other works.

90. *The Lord's Prayer, The Beatitudes*, trans. Hilda C. Graef, ACW (New York: Paulist, 1954), 148–49.

91. Balthasar, *Presence and Thought*, 168–69.

92. Balthasar, *Presence and Thought*, 152, quoting *Hom. Cant.* 8.

93. See further chapter 6 below on the comparable insight of Augustine.

94. See further Hart, "Mirror of the Infinite," 113.

all thought and every concept" and "he who obstinately tries to express it in words unconsciously offends God." The gulf between creatures and the Creator means "our mind" cannot "comprehend a nature that has no dimension," and simply experiences vertigo:

> Though the mind in its restlessness ranges through all that is knowable, it has never yet discovered a way of comprehending eternity. . . . It is like someone who finds himself on a mountain ridge. Imagine a sheer, steep crag, . . . extending into eternity; on top there is this ridge which looks down over a projecting rim into a bottomless chasm. Now imagine what a person would probably experience if he put his foot on the edge of this ridge which overlooks the chasm and found no solid footing nor anything to hold on to. This is what I think the soul experiences when it goes beyond its footing in material things, in its quest for that which has no dimension and which exists from all eternity. For here there is nothing it can take hold of, neither place nor time, nor measure nor anything else; it does not allow our minds to approach. And thus the soul, slipping at every point from what cannot be grasped, becomes dizzy and perplexed and returns once again to what is connatural to it, content now to know merely this about the Transcendent, that it is completely different from the nature of the things that the soul knows. (*Hom. Eccl.* 7)[95]

This is the time for silence and wonder, since "of the magnificence of the glory of His holiness there is no end" (here Psalm 144:3 and 5 are conflated).

There is a time to speak, however, when it is a question of God's wonders and deeds, and what we can do to make progress in virtue. Here, spirituality and biblical hermeneutics reflect three fundamental outcomes of the doctrinal debates: (1) the gap between Creator and creatures; (2) the indefinability of God; and (3) the being of God as unknown, yet God known through the divine activities or operations.

Yet this is only part of the journey. Like Origen before him, Gregory treats the three Wisdom books—Proverbs, Ecclesiastes and the Song of Songs—as three stages, or perhaps moments, in the soul's approach to God, and whereas Origen sees the stages as moving through purification to contemplation, Gregory moves beyond contemplation—the Song of Songs is the way of union

95. Quotation of Gregory's *Homilies on Ecclesiastes* from Musurillo, *From Glory to Glory*, 127–28.

through love.[96] For Gregory the goal is not to suppress passion but redirect it to the appropriate object:

> When the [soul] has torn herself from her attachment to sin, and by that mystic kiss she yearns to bring her mouth close to the fountain of light, then does she become beautiful, radiant with the light of truth, having washed away the dark stain of ignorance. (*Hom. Cant.* 11)[97]

It is tempting now to engage with recent explorations of the imaginative ways in which Gregory exploits the language of this love song to articulate the soul's relationship with the Bridegroom, generating the paradoxical language of "sober inebriation," "watchful sleep," and even "passionless passion" for that paradoxical ecstasy of "luminous darkness" that was entered by Moses. The knowledge that comes through unknowing is played out again, recalling also the journeying of Abraham. Suffice it now, however, to consider the importance of the receptivity of the soul that has gone beyond contemplation.

There is a passage in Gregory's exegesis of the Song that not only picks up from Origen the idea of accommodation to different levels and advancement in the divine pedagogy but even points to the presence of Jesus maturing in the human soul:

> Now Jesus, who is born as a child in us, advances in wisdom and age and grace, in different ways in the hearts of those who receive Him. He is not the same in everyone, but only according to the measure of those in whom He dwells, adapting Himself to the capacity of each one who receives Him. To some he comes as a babe, to others as one advancing, to others in full maturity. (*Hom. Cant.* 3)[98]

This remarkable passage is further illuminated by Verna Harrison who, on the basis of Gregory's early work *On Virginity*, points out that Mary is an important model for Gregory:

> Notice that an essential feature of Mary's virginity and also that of the Christian soul is receptivity to God. Her purity and integrity open a place

96. See Louth, *Origins of Christian Mystical Tradition*, 80.

97. Greek text of *Homilies on the Song of Songs* in *GNO* 6; English translation here in Musurillo, *From Glory to Glory*, 246–48.

98. English translation from Musurillo, *From Glory to Glory*, 168.

> within her where God can enter, where Christ can be formed, and from which he can come forth. In the language of the Song of Songs, God is the bridegroom as well as the offspring. Mary's receptivity is intrinsic to her creaturehood: like all human persons, as Gregory understands them, she lives by participation in God and is not the source of her own life. . . . For Gregory the virginal soul, like Mary, receives the entrance of God and brings forth Christ, though spiritually, not physically.[99]

Gregory himself had suggested this parallel:

> what happened in the stainless Mary when the fullness of the Godhead which was in Christ shone out from her, that happens in every soul which leads by rule the virgin life. (*Virg.* 2)[100]

For Gregory, Harrison writes, Proverbs represents the immature soul, receiving instruction from its parents like a youth entranced with Wisdom's beauty or conversely tempted by the harlot, namely, foolishness. Proverbs 31 depicts the soul's marriage with one whom Gregory describes as a "manly woman"—Wisdom as Christ. This leads to Ecclesiastes, which teaches the soul to abandon external things that are transitory and vain and prepares the way for the Song of Songs. Now, Harrison suggests, the roles are reversed—the soul becomes the bride, the woman, by "typical patristic gender bending." The soul is the "receptacle" of God, the Bridegroom, experiencing always an insatiable longing for the Infinite; as Harrison puts it, "The soul seeking God must reach outward beyond the boundary of her own capacity into the incomprehensible. In this situation, the young man's quest for acquisition, possession and control of Wisdom can only be abandoned." Instead there can only be grateful reception of grace.

It is the wound of love which is our salvation. Gregory believes there is a correspondence between the motions and movements of the soul and the sense organs of the body, so our earthly response to beauty gives us a taste of what it would mean to transcend surface appearance and discern the Lord as the object of beauty *par excellence*. The implicit figure of Eros shooting darts of love finds authorization in explicit biblical texts and is startlingly couched in Trinitarian terms:

99. Verna Harrison, "Gender, Generation, and Virginity in Cappadocian Theology," *JTS* 47 (1996): 38–68.

100. Greek text in *GNO* 8; English translation in *NPNF*[2] 5.

> The bride says: "Because I am wounded with love." Here she explains the dart that has gone right through her heart, and the Bowman is love. From the scriptures we learn that God is love and also that he sends forth his only-begotten Son as his "chosen arrow" (Isa 49:20) to the elect, dipping the triple point at its tip in the Spirit of life. . . . It is a good wound and a sweet point by which life penetrates the soul; for by the tearing of the arrow she opens a kind of door, an entrance into herself. For no sooner does she receive the dart of love, than the image of archery is transformed into a scene of nuptial joy. (*Hom. Cant.* 4)[101]

For Gregory then the love of God requires receptivity, the abandonment of the desire to possess and control, and the acceptance of an eternal longing that can never be satisfied, a wounding with love's arrow that brings not just frustration but also fulfillment.

In such graphic images, Gregory expresses the apophatic, the anagogic, and the katabatic moves involved in knowledge and love of God. One has to hold together (1) the denial of likeness to anything created and so the confession of God's absolute transcendence; (2) the movement upwards from created things to a mind-blowing perception of higher reality; and (3) the reception of truth from the downward act of God's revelatory accommodation to the human level in the language of scripture and the life of Christ. Here it is that the doctrine of the Trinity, together with the conceptual moves made in the process of arguing for it, significantly shapes both Gregory's articulation of the spiritual life and his reading of scripture.

2.3.4. *The Grasp of Faith*

In his sixth *Homily on the Song of Songs*, Gregory writes:

> Having let go of all manner of comprehension, I found the Beloved by faith and never will I let go once found by the grasp of faith. (*Hom. Cant.* 6)[102]

Earlier we observed Abraham's journey to faith but without highlighting its Pauline cast: "as the Apostle says, Abraham walked by faith and not by sight" (2 Cor 5:7) and he "went out, not knowing whither he went" (Heb 11:8).[103] He

101. English translation from Daniélou and Musurillo, *From Glory to Glory*, 178–79.
102. Translation by Laird, *Gregory of Nyssa*, 64.
103. Gregory would have assumed the Pauline authorship of Hebrews.

"stretched himself forth to the things that were before" (Phil 3:13) and then abandoning "the curiosity of the mind," "he believed God and it was reputed to him unto justice" (Rom 4:3; cf. Gen 15:6). Gregory states that this "was written not for Abraham but for us, for it is by faith and not knowledge that men are accounted just before God," adding references to Hebrews 11:1 and Romans 8:4: Christian faith is "the substance of things to be hoped for," and "we do not hope for what we already possess." "Faith is therefore a guarantee for what is invisible" (Heb 11:27); faith "takes the place of that which escapes our knowledge" (*Eun.* 2.90–93).

So what is the relationship between faith and knowledge? Martin Laird's book throws illuminating light on the role of faith in Gregory's thought. The grasp of faith is "the faculty of apophatic union with God" and "a form of knowledge that resolves the *coincidentia oppositorum* of knowing and unknowing." It is not cognitive or conceptual, but a union beyond images and concepts, beyond knowledge, bridging the gap between the mind and God, a gap that safeguards the distinction between creature and Creator.[104] Developing the discussions of earlier scholarship and exploring the imagery of the *Homilies on the Song of Songs*, Laird traces how faith, having reached beyond concepts, is then able to communicate to the mind what it has grasped, translating intuitions into concepts—there is discontinuity between knowledge and faith but also continuity.

> The grasp of faith, therefore, mediates in two directions. Along a fairly rigorously maintained apophatic trajectory, faith mediates union with God beyond all concepts. However, this union with the Word initiates another trajectory; the tendency of the Word to fill the mouth of the bride with words, to express itself in the words and deeds of those who attain union with the Word. Put another way, the words and actions of Paul, John, and the bride manifest the Word and bear witness to their adherence to the Word by faith.[105]

The apophatic, Laird suggests, is balanced by the *logophatic*, as "the Word fills the mouth of the bride 'with words of eternal life,'" and "expresses itself through the deeds and discourse of the one whom the Word indwells."[106] So in the *Homilies on the Song of Songs* Paul becomes a prime example of the one who, having attained union with God, bears witness to the indwelling Word

104. Laird, *Gregory of Nyssa*, 102.
105. Laird, *Gregory of Nyssa*, 211.
106. Laird, *Gregory of Nyssa*, 155.

through his words and actions, and surely the same can be said of Moses, as we observed earlier.[107]

This, I suggest, enables us to see how profoundly interconnected are the underpinnings of Gregory's doctrinal arguments and his imaginative exegetical and mystical reflections. Earlier we explored his discussion of the language of scripture and the validity of theological discourse.[108] We found a subtle awareness that "names" applied to God are always inadequate yet neither arbitrary nor totally misleading as long as the similarities and differences between their applicability to human beings and to the divine are properly considered. Indeed, they ultimately derive from God's will to make the divine self known, through creation and through scripture. The classic treatments of Gregory's mysticism by Balthasar and Daniélou presumed its basis was Trinitarian, despite the relative paucity of explicit texts to that effect. Yet fundamentally they were right, for it bespeaks a reading of scripture that discerns divine revelation and true teaching through the Word of God and, through the Spirit, progressive purification, transformation, and union with the divine. This discernment is facilitated by doctrinal frameworks inherited from the past and refined through current debates.

So we have indeed shown that

> Doctrine is not meant to monopolize or manipulate the believer's intelligence and imagination by means of a system of abstract notions. . . . It is meant to facilitate and guide a personal and communal heuristic process, the outcome of which is always a gift of God that transcends whatever form of human control, either personal or ecclesial.[109]

Let us now allow Gregory of Nyssa to have the last word:

> let faith sound forth pure and loud in the preaching of the holy Trinity and let life imitate the nature of the pomegranate's fruit. . . . The philosophical life, although outwardly austere and unpleasant, is yet full of good hopes when it ripens. (*Vit. Mos.* 2.192–193)

***

107. See above, p. 98.
108. See above, p. 108.
109. See den Biesen, *Simple and Bold*, 26; cf. p. 77 above, and note 33.

These last two chapters have entered into the debates that generated the doctrine of the Trinity. They confirm that the articulation of this doctrine was a process of argument and that that argument was not least about the fundamental meaning of scripture. So what are the most significant insights to emerge for our question about the relationship between doctrine and scripture?

- The recognition that scripture could not simply be treated as a series of prooftexts from which, lifted out of context, deductions could straighforwardly be made.
- The instinct that the appropriate context for true interpretation is the overarching narrative of God's creative and providential dealings with the whole *oikonomia*.
- The correlation of God's Word in scripture spoken by the Holy Spirit, and God's Word embodied in humankind in the incarnation, both Word and Spirit issuing from the one God at work in the *oikonomia*, whose operations provide fragmentary insights into God but no definition of God's ultimate being nor any comprehensive or discursive knowledge of God's nature.
- The affirmation that sanctification by the Spirit and new creation in Christ (often described as *theopoiēsis*), require doctrinal articulation of an apparently paradoxical Triune concept of God, which then becomes a heuristic tool for prizing out of scripture truths hidden in symbols, "types," and images that fire ethical and devotional commitments.

The Trinitarian settlement, however, only raised more questions for understanding the incarnation. How could one *homoousios* with the Father, truly God in every sense so as to be utterly transcendent and not a creature, accept change, become a creature, be incarnate, be born, suffer, and die? The seeds of the question were already implicit in Athanasius and the Cappadocians. Further debate was inevitable, and as ever it would be about how to make sense of scripture.

4

Two Nations, One Christ?

PART 1, DIVERGING EXEGESES

In the aftermath of the Nicene settlement, from the late fourth century through to the Council of Chalcedon and beyond, disputes arose concerning the person of the incarnate Christ. By the early fifth century two parties had emerged, usually designated "Antiochene" and "Alexandrian." Each party was not entirely homogeneous, and indeed the two sides had much in common, but still both had reasonable grounds for challenging the other's approach to understanding the incarnation. There had been other responses, too, notably that of the Cappadocians, which does not fit neatly into either of the two Christologies that came into conflict, though all alike shared in reaction against the teaching of Apollinaris. Each side clearly had soteriological interests that would shape their approach to the distinct roles of divine and human in the saving drama of incarnation. Making sense of scripture certainly lay at the heart of the debate—indeed, specific texts were argued over, including many already in dispute between Athanasius and the Arians. The "Antiochenes" also mounted a critical attack on "Alexandrian" allegory, a fact sometimes linked to their supposed interest in history and the real humanity of Jesus Christ. However, this correlation, to my mind, is dubious: both sides were in their own way anxious to make sense of the overarching biblical narrative, both sides sought spiritual and doctrinal meanings, and, when it comes to their approach to proving christological doctrine from scripture, we shall observe little methodological difference between them.

In this chapter we will engage in a preliminary exploration of post-Nicene biblical exegesis, endeavoring to discern emerging trends that anticipate those subsequently competing Christologies. Key texts, along with significant exegetical strategies, had figured previously in response to Arianism, and these recur as new questions present themselves. We will first seek continuities and divergencies in their deployment. We will then sample exegetical homilies and commentaries produced prior to the outbreak of controversy by key figures from each incipient "party." The focus will be on the Epistle to the Hebrews and the Gospel of John, verses from both of which would subsequently become crucial in the controversy. This will not only enable us to see how little there is to choose between their hermeneutics, despite the fact that working out the consequences of the Nicene settlement would eventually produce divergent christological emphases, but also how crucial it had become to ground in the text of scripture doctrinal propositions honed through bitter debate.

1. Same Key Texts, Shifting Perspectives

Maurice Wiles, in his study of the interpretation of John's Gospel in the early church, *The Spiritual Gospel*, notes that "in large measure" Arian exegesis "built upon the foundation of the anti-monarchian writers of the previous century. Tertullian had appealed to those texts which spoke of the Father's giving of authority to the Son as evidence of the Son's distinct existence; these same texts were used by the Arians to illustrate his inferiority to the Father."[1] Similarly, he notes, Arians exploited texts speaking of the Son "being sent from the Father." These remarks are a sharp reminder of how appeal to the same texts keeps recurring as debate shifts from one set of questions to another. In this section we look at the continuities in the use of scripture from Athanasius's anti-Arian polemic to each of what would become the opposing Christologies.

1.1. From Athanasius to Miaphysite Formulae

In the discussion to which reference has just been made, Maurice Wiles goes on to sketch the reply given in the third book of *Orations against the Arians* to those Arian quibbles. Appealing to John 5:26, "as the Father has life in himself, so has he given to the Son also to have life in himself," Athanasius asserted that

> the Gospel itself requires us to understand such texts in a way which does not involve any inferiority but rather absolute equality between Father and

1. Maurice F. Wiles, *The Spiritual Gospel* (Cambridge: Cambridge University Press, 1960), 121, citing Tertullian, *Prax.* 21; then Athanasius, *C. Ar.* 3.7, 26 on John 3:25; 5:19, 22–23; 6:37–38.

> Son. . . . If the "as" and "so" are given their proper force, they rule out any idea of inferiority or difference of essence. The language of "receiving," however, is not altogether without purpose.[2]

Not only is it a safeguard against any Sabellian interpretation of Father and Son (Athanasius, *C. Ar.* 3.35–36), but

> it is congruent with the whole redemptive purpose of the incarnation that Christ should be said to receive God's gifts not as needing them himself, or for his own sake, but for the sake of mankind.[3]

The authenticity of book 3 of *Orations against the Arians* has been questioned in more recent scholarship.[4] However, we may presume that this third book was known as the work of Athanasius, and so it is likely it would have been treated as authoritative by those struggling with its potential implications in the christological controversy. We will therefore treat it as Athanasian as we review its content. The work presents itself as a continuation of the response begun in book 2 to texts apparently favouring the Arian reading of scripture. To begin with, the Arians are said to disparage John 14:10: "I in the Father and the Father in me." In response to Arian misreading, materialist assumptions are repudiated, and the text associated with "I and the Father are one" (John 10:30). How they are one but yet two—one in nature, one God, yet two in that the Word is the offspring of the Father's essence—is now explained, the old arguments reappearing: he is not a creature but Creator, and the oneness is not to be taken in the same sense as the oneness in which, according to Christ's prayer in John 17, we may share—the distinction between "sons" and "the Son" is paramount: "the Word, then, has real and true identity of nature with the Father, but to us it is given to imitate it" (*C. Ar.* 3.22). Before treating turn by turn a catalog of problematic gospel texts, which we will consider in the next section below, book 3 of *Orations against the Arians* provides an overview of the framework within which their meaning should be sought.

First, it is important to reject the Jewish perspective of the Arians, which questions why, being a man, he made himself equal to God (an allusion, of course, to John 5:18). Then, as previously noted, one must accept that the

2. Wiles, *Spiritual Gospel*, 121–22.

3. Wiles, *Spiritual Gospel*, 122, discussing Athanasius, *C. Ar.* 3.37–40.

4. Cf. chapter 2, note 3 (p. 30 above).

"scope" of scripture is "a double account of the Savior."[5] "He was ever God, and is the Son," and "afterwards for us he took flesh." This is borne out by John 1:14 along with Philippians 2:6–8, with support from the divine conversation of Genesis 1 and Matthew 1:23—the name Emmanuel being interpreted as "God with us." All these texts will recur in the literature of the christological controversy. Meanwhile, however, the ensuing account of this double scope has a distinctly unitary feel about it.

A key distinction is enunciated: the Lord "became man" but he "did not come into man" (*C. Ar.* 3.30). The Word had previously come to saints and prophets, but this is about "the Word of God, by whom all things came to be," becoming also "the Son of Man" and humbling himself by "taking a servant's form." So "to the Jews the cross of Christ is a scandal, but to us Christ is 'God's power' and 'God's wisdom'" (1 Cor 1:24). "The Word," as John says, "became flesh." Joel 2:28 is cross-referenced to show that "flesh" in scripture refers to "humankind." The argument is then pursued further: when he came to the saints and they suffered it was never suggested that the Word suffered, but when the Son was sent by the Father, then "it is said that he took flesh and became man, and in flesh he suffered for us" (1 Pet 4:1). The Godhead dwelt in flesh "bodily" (Col 2:9). The apostle implies "Being God, he had his own body, and using this as an instrument, he became man for our sakes." So

> the properties of the flesh are said to be His, since he was in it, such as to hunger, to thirst, to suffer, to [be] weary, and the like, of which the flesh is capable; while on the other hand the works proper to the Word Himself, such as to raise the dead, to restore sight to the blind, and to cure the woman with an issue of blood, He did through his own body. (*C. Ar.* 3.31)

Thus he "carried" our infirmities (Isa 53:4) and bears our sins, and "the body in which he bore them, was his own body." The Word himself was not harmed "by bearing our sins in his body on the tree" (1 Pet 2:24), but we were redeemed and "filled with the Word's righteousness."

The flesh suffered, then, but the Word was not external to it (*C. Ar.* 3.32). So the passion is said to be his, and when divinely he did his Father's works, the flesh was not external to him—it was "in the body itself" that the Lord did them (John 10:37–38 is quoted). Healing Peter's wife's mother, "he stretched forth his hand humanly, but stopped the illness divinely," and ditto the healing of the blind man (human spittle but divine healing) as well as the raising of

5. See above, chapter 2, p. 35; *C. Ar.* 3.29.

Lazarus (human voice and divine raising). It all happened because the Lord had a body, not in appearance but in truth, and it was his own. The "passibilities of the body" are proper to him and are ascribed to the one whose flesh it is, even though "they did not touch him according to his Godhead." Cyril's notorious paradox, *apathōs epathen*, might seem to be anticipated in this attribution of suffering and death to the impassible Word.[6] In one place, Athanasius dares to suggest that Christ *ta hēmōn emimēsato*, literally, "he imitated our condition" (*C. Ar.* 3.57), though a docetic interpretation can hardly have been intended and probably the translation, "he was conformed to our condition," better conveys what was meant.[7]

So we are not worshipping an ordinary man but the "true Son of God who has become man, yet is no less Lord and God and Saviour." Furthermore, all this is about our transformation (*C. Ar.* 3.33). Without the works of the Word's Godhead taking place through the body, and without the properties of the flesh being ascribed to the Word, neither deliverance nor deification could have happened. Sin and death are destroyed and, having risen according to the Word's power, human beings remain immortal and incorruptible. Christ is said not only to have suffered "for us in the flesh" (1 Pet 4:1) but also to have been hungry, thirsty, tired, ignorant, asleep, asking, fleeing, born, and so on (*C. Ar.* 3.34). It was all "for us in the flesh," not in his Godhead, and all of it "may be acknowledged as not proper to the Word itself by nature, but proper by nature to the flesh itself." Indeed this indicates "a more exact knowledge of the Word's impassibility." Yet, because of "the flesh which he put on" things proper to the flesh are ascribed to him, though in nature he remains impassible and is not harmed, but rather "obliterates and destroys" the flesh's corruption and mortality.

This account of the incarnation

- clearly engages with what is to be found in the New Testament, as the frequent quotations and allusions show;
- is based, however, on a particular reading of scripture in accordance with the metanarrative of Athanasius's *Against the Pagan* and *On the Incarnation*; that is, it focuses on the divine initiative to restore the Logos to humanity—the gift of grace given to Adam but lost in the fall;[8]
- is fundamentally unitary because it is the story of one and the same Son

6. Though see the excursus below, pp. 155–57.

7. This latter translation is found in *NPNF*[2].

8. See chapter 2 and especially Anatolios, *Athanasius*.

of God coming to earth: so, despite the fact that God's Son is truly divine and not subject to change or suffering, he becomes the subject of all the incarnate actions and experiences, and the properties of Word and body become interchangeable (*communicatio idiomatum* is the conventional term for this);
- purports to unite Creator and creature, mediation being located in the one person of the Savior bridging two realities: "The humanity was deified by the divinity, and the Lord was in the body when the body suffered."[9]

Read as christological analysis this rapidly becomes open to the standard critique of Athanasius's approach to the person of Christ. As Weinandy puts it:

> Does Athanasius understand the incarnation as the Son taking on the whole of our human nature or merely 'the body'? . . . Does the more common usage of *sōma* imply that, ultimately, Athanasius conceives the incarnation as the Son assuming merely a body devoid of a human soul, and thus does his conception fall under what is commonly termed a Logos/Sarx Christology? Could Athanasius, then, even be an Apollinarian before Apollinarius?[10]

Indeed, Athanasius's account of the incarnation seems not implausibly characterized in Grillmeier's terms as patterned according to a Logos-Sarx model.[11] It also seems to risk Hanson's unfortunate and anachronistic description "space-suit Christology."[12] In fact, in book 2 of *Orations against the Arians*, donning the high priest's robe so as to offer sacrifice for the people is one telling "type" of the Word's assumption of the body—the flesh does indeed seem like an outer garment (2.7). For all the protestations about "body" or "flesh" meaning "man," and all the assertions that the Word is not separated from the experiences of the body, the body largely appears as a "tool" whereby, or "temple" wherein, the Logos could subject himself to the human condition so as to overcome with divine power what has gone wrong with it.

Contesting Grillmeier's Logos-Sarx model, however, Anatolios has insisted that Athanasius was not interested in "the internal constitution of Christ's

9. David M. Gwynn, *Athanasius of Alexandria: Bishop, Theologian, Ascetic, Father* (Oxford: Oxford University Press, 2012), 103.

10. Thomas G. Weinandy, *Athanasius: A Theological Introduction* (Aldershot: Ashgate, 2007), 46.

11. Aloys Grillmeier, SJ, *Christ in Christian Tradition: From the Apostolic Age to Chalcedon (AD 451)*, trans. J. S. Bowden (London: Mowbray, 1965).

12. Hanson, *Search*, 448.

person," but rather in "the new relation between God and creation given in Christ."[13] For Athanasius, "the unity of Christ is explicated in terms primarily of the 'structure' of the act which joins humanity to God, rather than in terms of how the 'parts' of Christ intrinsically cohere."[14] The body is "a privileged locus wherein the invisible God becomes knowable and visible."[15] The incarnation is to do with mediation between God and the world: "the focus is not so much on how the divine-human being of Christ is internally constituted, but rather on the fact that Christ unites the extremes of God and world."[16] It is also the means whereby the Word had a body to offer in redemptive sacrifice. Anatolios's critique of Grillmeier has been generally accepted in more recent scholarship; the issue of unconscious Apollinarianism, however, persists. Was the body "devoid of human soul"? Once the question of "the internal constitution of Christ's person" had been raised, it could look as if Athanasius was Apollinarian before Apollinaris, and it is hardly surprising to find Apollinarian works were circulating with Athanasian attribution, works to whose authority Cyril would appeal for his miaphysite (one nature) formulae.[17]

Notoriously Apollinaris is said to have denied the presence of a human soul in the Christ, the soul being replaced by the Logos, which provided the body's intelligence and vitality. Thus he produced a hybrid or mixture, "one nature of the God-Word enfleshed." As ever, interpreting the stance of a condemned heretic is problematic, much of the evidence coming from opponents. A long-standing problem is whether Apollinaris had a dichotomist or trichotomist view of human nature: soul-flesh or mind-soul-flesh. The intriguing possibility for our discussion is that Pauline texts may have inspired his somewhat confusing categories. According to Paul, Apollinaris claimed, humanity is mind in flesh, and the last Adam is life-giving spirit, so "the Christ having God as spirit, that is, mind, together with soul and body, is reasonably called the 'man from heaven.'"[18] Perhaps this explains how it was that Apollinaris's ancient critics accused him not only of suggesting a truncated humanity but also of claiming that the flesh preexisted in heaven. However, it certainly seems that

13. Anatolios, *Athanasius*, 146.

14. Anatolios, *Athanasius*, 147, substantiated with a quote from *C. Ar.* 2.70.

15. Anatolios, *Athanasius*, 72.

16. Anatolios, *Athanasius*, 73.

17. See further my discussion in *From Nicaea to Chalcedon*, 316, referencing P. Galtier, "Saint Cyrille et Apollinaire," *Gregorianum* 37 (1956): 584–609.

18. For points in this paragraph, see frags. 29, 25, 69, 72, 89, 150–151 in H. Lietzmann, *Apollinaris von Laodicea und seine Schüle* (Tübingen: Mohr, 1904). For further discussion see my *From Nicaea to Chalcedon*.

he was opposed to attaching a man to God and wanted to differentiate between "God enfleshed" and "man inspired." Here, as in much else, he inherited Athanasius's emphases. His central concern may not have been the soul so much as the mind—every mind, he assumed, was *autokrator*, a self-moving, self-governing will, and how could two such entities exist in one person?[19] Surely it was inconceivable that Christ could be in two, potentially contrary, minds about anything! As a human being is "mind [*nous*] in flesh," so Christ is "Logos (reason/word) in flesh."

The overriding concern of Apollinaris's opponents, however, was that in his scheme the human mind or soul was not assumed by the Logos and was therefore not healed.[20] Human weaknesses, passions, and failings were not simply fleshly but lodged in the soul, so to focus on the flesh or body alone, as Athanasius largely had done, could not accomplish full salvation. After Apollinaris, universally, on both sides of the christological controversy, we find a reiterated refrain: the body assumed by the Logos was not without soul and mind. Athanasius himself joined in this theological debate in his late *Epistle to Epictetus*, and as these new questions gained traction, he was quick to see the problems:

> Truly our salvation . . . does not extend to the body only, but the whole man, body and soul alike, has truly obtained salvation in the Word himself. (*Ep. Epict.* 7)[21]

There is then a trajectory from Athanasius and his anti-Arian exegesis to the one-nature Christology of Cyril and the so-called Alexandrians. But it is not straightforward continuity. New questions were posed as the focus shifted from proving the Godhead of the Son to considering how the divine Logos could "become" human. New ways of reading biblical texts, and new formulae for capturing scripture's meaning, had to be devised. It is through hindsight that critics identify as inadequate the Christology of Athanasius; for the most part he was not consciously dealing with questions that would emerge later as the implications of the Nicene *homoousion* began to be addressed. The question is whether Cyril, in the aftermath of Apollinaris's condemnation in

19. Frags. 150–151 in Lietzmann, *Apollinaris*.

20. Notably argued by Gregory of Nazianzus, *Ep.* 101.

21. Translation of the *Letter to Epictetus* from *NPNF*² 4. Cf. *Tom.* 7: "the Saviour had not a body without a soul, nor without sense and intelligence; for it was not possible, when the Lord had become man for us, that his body should be without intelligence; nor was the salvation offered in the Word himself a salvation of body only but of soul also."

381, could move on from Athanasius's anti-Arian exegesis to provide a more satisfactory account of how the unchangeable divine Logos could "become" incarnate. Still, it was Athanasius's insistence on somehow holding together the story of the same one who is truly one with the Father also becoming truly human that would drive Cyril's miaphysite one-nature Christology.

1.2. From Athanasius to "Partitive Exegesis"

The other side in the controversy could also claim an Athanasian legacy. It was the christological controversy that generated the practice of citing in evidence not just biblical texts but also patristic testimonies (florilegia or collections of quotations from earlier authoritative "fathers" of the church), and Theodoret's dialogues are a case in point. All the dossiers Theodoret appended to the dialogues that make up his *Eranistes* feature extensive quotations from Athanasius.[22]

We have already had occasion to notice (1) how Athanasius found it necessary "to distinguish texts referring to the divine nature of the Word and those referring to the time when 'the Word became flesh'";[23] and (2) how book 3 of his *Orations against the Arians* introduces as "the scope of scripture"

> a double account of the Savior; that he was always God, and is the Son, being the Father's Word and Radiance and Wisdom; and that afterwards for us he took flesh of a Virgin, Mary Bearer of God, and was made man. And this scope is to be found throughout inspired scripture. (*C. Ar.* 3.29)[24]

This necessity to provide a double account produces what I have called "partitive exegesis"—assigning texts or parts of texts either to the "human" or to the "divine" nature of the Savior. Most of the rest of book 3 of the *Orations against the Arians* applies this double "scope" to texts from the gospels so as to answer the Arians. For when "they hear and see the Saviour's human attributes in the Gospels," they ask, "with arrogant and audacious tongue" how the Son can be "from the Father by nature" and "like him in essence," given that he receives authority, judgment, power, glory, and so on from the Father, and also given that his soul is troubled, that he increased in wisdom and stature, that he cried out, "My God, my God, why hast Thou forsaken me?," that he prayed that God

22. See further chapter 5, 2.2, for the *Eranistes*.
23. See chapter 2, pp. 35 and 37 above.
24. Translation here from Ernest, *Bible in Athanasius*, 144.

would glorify his name, that he was ignorant of "that day and that hour," and other such things inappropriate to the divine (*C. Ar.* 3.26). To create this list there is allusion or citation of a whole raft of gospel material, especially key Johannine texts.[25] But "what they interpret ill has a right interpretation" (3.35) and so these problem texts are worked through one after another.

Thus, when the Jesus of the gospels asks where Lazarus is laid (John 11:34) or "Who do you say that I am?" (Matt 16:13; Mark 8:29), this does not necessarily mean he is ignorant. After all, according to John 6:6 he already knew what he was going to do when he asked about where they should buy bread, and that can apply to the other examples. But if that response is disallowed, then those bad interpreters must be told that there is no ignorance in the Godhead, but ignorance is proper to the flesh. In the case of Lazarus, after all, he had already said, "Lazarus is dead" when a great way off, and according to John 2:25 he was aware of what was in each person's heart (*C. Ar.* 3.37).

> Therefore this is plain to everyone, that the flesh indeed is ignorant, but the Word himself, considered as the Word, knows all things even before they come to be. (*C. Ar.* 3.38)

The same line of argument Athanasius later develops at length with respect to Jesus's ignorance of the day and the hour (3.42–50).

As for his supposed promotion, Christ received power, glory, and so on *humanly*—the flesh received, so that the gift would be secured for us (*C. Ar.* 3.38–40). Likewise, "he advanced in wisdom and stature" (Luke 2:52). Of course we cannot deduce from this that he was imperfect to start with—how did Wisdom advance in wisdom? It is human creatures that are capable of advancing in wisdom, like Enoch, Moses, Isaac (Gen 26:13) and Paul (Phil 3:13). The Son of God humbled himself and is humanly said to advance—the body advanced and the Godhead was more and more revealed (*C. Ar.* 3.52). He suffered in the flesh, hungered in the flesh, was fatigued in the flesh, and also advanced in the flesh (3.53). Here the distinction is glossed by emphasis on the fact that the Word was not external to the flesh—the body was God's temple and the flesh became the body of Wisdom, so that this kind of advance was secured for us. However, the advance was not the Word's:

25. Quoting, in order, Matt 28:18; John 5:22; 3:35–36; Matt 11:27; John 6:37; 12:27–28; Matt 26:39; John 13:21; Luke 2:52; Matt 26:46; John 12:28; 17:5; Matt 26:41; Mark 13:32.

> not Wisdom, as Wisdom, advanced in respect of itself; but the manhood advanced in wisdom, transcending by degrees human nature, and being deified, and becoming and appearing to all as the organ of Wisdom for the operation and the shining forth of the Godhead. (*C. Ar.* 3.53)

Now we turn to his weeping, his troubled soul, and his God-forsakenness on the cross (John 11:35; 12:27; Matt 26:39; Mark 15:34). If he were "mere man," of course he would weep and fear death, but as he is himself life and the source of a string of scriptural injunctions not to fear death, how could that be (*C. Ar.* 3.54)?[26] These feelings were not, of course, "proper to the nature of the Word, as far as he was Word," but the Word was "in the flesh which was thus affected." To make his human attributes a ground for low thoughts about the Son of God is to ignore the fact that he also raised Lazarus, gave sight to the blind, and said, "I and the Father are one" (John 10:30; also quoted are John 10:38; 14:10). "Though God impassible, he had taken passible flesh" (*C. Ar.* 3.55). The Evangelists declare that

> the words, "Why hast thou forsaken me?" are his . . . (though he suffered nothing, for the Word was impassible), . . . since the Lord became man, and these things are done and said as from a man, that he might himself lighten these very sufferings of the flesh, and free it from them. (*C. Ar.* 3.56)

He "combined his own will with human weakness," so that he might make humankind "undaunted in the face of death." All these problematic words are therefore spoken "humanly," and "he let his own body suffer" (*C. Ar.* 3.57–58).

In his late *Epistle to Epictetus* Athanasius is exercised by various new questions consequent upon anti-Arian arguments and exegesis: the status of the body vis à vis the Word, indeed vis à vis the Trinity, has become problematic, and he has to insist that the body is not coessential with the Word's Godhead, nor does the Triad become a Tetrad. Rather, the body is from Mary, and Jesus was made like his brethren in all things (Heb 2:16–17). It was the body that was circumcised, ate and drank, was weary, was nailed to a tree, suffered, and was laid in the tomb, but "the impassible and incorporeal Word of God" was in it. The Word was not "changed into bones and flesh," and "the Body was not the Word, but the Body of the Word."

26. Quoting Luke 12:4; Gen 15:1; 26:24; Exod 4:12; Josh 1:6; Ps 118:6.

> It was this that Thomas handled when it had risen from the dead, and saw in it the print of the nails. . . . And verily it is strange that He it was who suffered and yet suffered not. Suffered, because His own body suffered, and He was in it, which thus suffered; suffered not, because the Word, being by nature God, is impassible. And while He, the incorporeal, was in the passible body, the Body had in it the impassible Word, which was destroying the infirmities inherent in the Body. (*Ep. Epict.* 5)

Here, then, Athanasius surely does anticipate Cyril's *apathōs epathen*.[27] And yet, differentiation remains fundamental. Despite attempting to articulate the union, and despite insisting on the *communicatio idiomatum* in this very passage, conflation of Word and flesh will not do, and the paradoxes have to be maintained.

This very passage is one that the Antiochene Theodoret would quote in the florilegium appended to his third dialogue of the *Eranistes* along with other extracts from the same epistle.[28] In fact, all three of the florilegia quote from that letter, which is Athanasius's late and most explicit treatment of christological issues. Other Athanasian texts from which Theodoret draws include *On the Incarnation*, book 2 of *Orations against the Arians*, *On the Opinion of Dionysius*, the work known as *On the Incarnation and against the Arians* and the *Greater Sermon on Faith*.[29] The authenticity of the last of these is no longer accepted, and that of the previous title has been questioned—more evidence that the authority of Athanasius was erroneously being given to works that seemed to support one side or the other in the controversy. What Theodoret was doing was appealing to apparently Athanasian material, which distinguished the body that died and the Word that gave it back its life, instancing John 2:19: "Destroy this temple, and in three days I will raise it up" (*Eran.* 3.28).[30]

> Living he cannot die but on the contrary quickens the dead. He is therefore, by the Godhead derived from the Father, a fount of light; but he that died, or rather rose from the dead, our intercessor, who was born of the

27. See the excursus below, pp. 155–57.

28. See further chapter 5, 2.2, below, for discussion of this work and full references to Greek text and English translation.

29. For a comprehensive list and discussion of the patristic testimonies provided by Theodoret see the introduction to the critical text edited by Gerard H. Ettlinger, *Theodoret of Cyrus, Eranistes* (Oxford: Oxford University Press, 1975), 9–35. The bracketed references here are to the florilegia, indicating to which book they are appended and where in the numbered order in Ettlinger's text. English translation in *NPNF.*

30. Quoting Pseudo-Athanasius's *Greater Sermon on Faith* 236.

> Virgin Mary, whom the Godhead of the Word assumed for our sake, is man. (*Eran.* 3.29)[31]

The sharp differentiation characteristic of Antiochene Christology is given Athanasian sanction.

All of this tends to confirm the view expressed initially—it was the struggle to work out the christological consequences of the Nicene formulation that generated two different approaches, both claiming the legacy of Athanasius's anti-Arian exegesis.

2. Christological Exegesis after 381

So to what extent does exegesis of key New Testament writings prior to the controversy reveal these two different approaches? We will first explore John Chrysostom's set of *Homilies on Hebrews*, preached in Constantinople around 403 or 404. Then we will turn to Cyril's *Commentary on John's Gospel*, which certainly dates from before the outbreak of controversy, probably in the late 420s. We shall, of course, concentrate on the christological ramifications of the exegesis of Hebrews and John's Gospel, and in each case we will endeavor to assemble comparative material. Expecting contrasts between representatives of the two parties, we shall be surprised by how much they have in common. First, however, it is worth noting the pedagogical character of the principal works to which we shall give attention, recalling how the principal pedagogical activity in schools was in fact reading and interpreting texts.

Many have observed how Cyril announces in the preface to his *Commentary on John's Gospel* his intention to provide "more doctrinal [*dogmatikōtera*] exegesis." But what does he mean? As we shall see, there are plenty of good reasons for jumping to the conclusion that his principal object was to discern correct doctrine in the Johannine Gospel and to equip his readers with correct antiheretical readings. However, *dogma* basically means teaching. In the introduction to his translation of Cyril's commentary, David Maxwell opens up the question for whom the commentary was written and suggests on the basis of a "good deal of evidence" that Cyril's intended readers are "charged with teaching the faith, especially to catechumens."[32] Examples could be multipied, but here are just a couple:

31. Quoting Pseudo-Athanasius's *Greater Sermon on Faith* 236. English translation in *NPNF.*

32. David Maxwell, trans., *Cyril of Alexandria: Commentary on John*, ed. Joel C. Elowsky,

- It is not "in vain" that the Baptist repeats "Behold the Lamb of God" in John 1:36; "it is a mark of excellence in teaching to implant a message . . . from repetition," a point reinforced in the next paragraph, "let whoever is entrusted with the task of teaching learn from this [repetition]." (*Comm. Jo.* 2.1 [1:86])
- "An excellent teacher can deal with the mind of the hearers in various ways and go through many ideas, heaping up demonstrations for those things whose explanation seems difficult." Thus, Jesus provides "wind" as an example in John 3:7–8. Indeed, "we who have the authority to teach should learn from this that . . . faith in simple arguments is better than a deep discourse and a very complicated exposition." (*Comm. Jo.* 2.1 [1:98])

Indeed, Cyril presents Jesus's discourse with Nicodemus, and also with the woman at the well, as models for teaching the faith to the catechumenate, and in much of the commentary, Maxwell says, he seems to anticipate questions from the audience to which such teachers would need to be equipped to respond.

Maxwell also draws attention to the curious arrangement whereby "chapter headings" indicate a doctrinal topic rather than representing the overall exegetical content of the ensuing section. Listed at the head of each book, these are later inserted into the text at the appropriate point. To take one example: in book 1 of the commentary, which covers John 1:1–26, Cyril sets out at the start ten "chapters," all of which except one specify christological propositions (the odd one out, number 9, having Origen in his sights). In each case the statement in the gospel that triggered the proposition is indicated, so a couple of examples from the ten appear thus:

9. The human soul does not exist before the body, nor is embodiment the result of former sins, as some say; on the words, "He was the true light which enlightens everyone coming into the world. He was in the world."
10. The Only-begotten alone is by nature the Son of the Father because he is from him and in him; on the words "No one has ever seen God."

What this surely suggests is not "headings" at all, but rather the highlighting of doctrinal *theses* that will emerge as the line-by-line exegesis proceeds.

---

2 vols., Ancient Christian Texts (Downers Grove, IL: IVP Academic, 2013, 2015), 1:xviii–xix. English translation, unless otherwise noted, from Maxwell. Greek text in P. E. Pusey, *S. Cyrilli Archiepiscopi Alexandriae in S. Joannii Evangelium*, 3 vols. (Oxford: Clarendon, 1872). The Maxwell translation pages, which also include the Pusey edition page numbers, will be cited in brackets alongside the citations of Cyril's *Commentary on John's Gospel.*

Indeed, there are occasions when the *thesis* seems to come after the text that gives rise to the proposition rather than acting as an advance heading. For example, it is *after* John 5:21 (concerning the Son giving life as the Father raises the dead) that we find the summing up thesis, "No God-befitting dignity or superiority is in the Son by participation or addition from outside" (*Comm. Jo.* 2.7 [1:149]). Of course, this is also followed by words concerning the "God-befitting" action of judging (John 5:22).

Across the twelve books of the commentary, out of the fifty-four theses enumerated, all but around eight have a christological or Trinitarian focus, thus betraying the anti-Arian intent of the commentary. Maxwell notes Cyril's own statement as to their purpose—he has added numbers so as to enable readers to find "very quickly" what they are looking for. In other words, his commentary is meant to provide a reference book for teachers, and his exegesis is a kind of systematic distillation of theses enshrining the truth to be derived from scripture. It is "more dogmatic" not simply in being doctrinal but in being pedagogical.

As for Chrysostom, already we have had occasion to explore the pedagogical cast of Chrysostom's theology as a whole.[33] In his *Homilies on Hebrews* we can see the teacher at work, deploying school methods as he reads, explains, and expands upon the meaning and intention of the author (in his view, Paul), and derives practical and doctrinal lessons for the congregation.[34] Those methods include:

- The constant deployment of questions to the "class": "What does he say?" "How . . . ?" "Why . . . ?" "Who . . . ?" "What . . . ?" "Do you see . . . ?" Chrysostom is actually addressing a mass congregation, of course, and answers his own questions; but his style comes from the *quaestiones* tradition that we explored earlier.[35]
- The repeated reference to the aim of the author: a basic element in rhetorical schooling was specifying the intent or subject-matter as distinct from the style or wording—what was it the author wished his hearers or readers to be persuaded of? Chrysostom, himself both pastor and preacher, constantly

33. See chapter 1 and the important work referenced there, namely Rylaarsdam, *John Chrysostom.*

34. Greek text of Chrysostom's *Homilies on Hebrews* in PG 63; English translation in *NPNF*[1] 14. See further my paper "Teasing Out Meaning: Some Techniques and Procedures in Early Christian Exegesis," StPatr 100 (2020): 3–18; the listed points are essentially derived from that paper. Used by permission.

35. See volume 1, chapter 3, 1.1 (pp. 49–52).

recognized the pastor and preacher in Paul and constantly read between the lines to bring out Paul's tone of voice and rhetorical tactics.[36]

- The use of paraphrase, synonyms, and explanatory enlargement of the sense: rhetorical training was about finding the appropriate wording and style for any given content, and that implied the possibility of saying the same thing in different ways. So paraphrase along with other ways of representing the same sense were natural exegetical techniques to explore in class, and Chrysostom adopts all of them, even inventing parables to help the congregation to grasp what the author intended.
- Proper attention to the sequence (*akolouthia*), the line of argument, and the coherence of the text: Chrysostom attends to Hebrews as the school teacher would to any classical text. He constantly alerts his audience to what is going on, to the way the apostle leads them step by step: "See . . . ," "Note . . . ," "Observe . . . ," "Consider. . . ."
- Attention to figures of speech, metaphors, and hyperbole: this aspect of "grammar" (*to grammmatikon*), as well as some comments on construal of sentences, Chrysostom obviously shares with the schools.
- Explanatory background notes: in the schools *to historikon* provided material to explain allusions to stories, myths, events, persons, natural history, geography, and so on. Chrysostom supplies the necessary information to explain Hebrews's allusions to the exodus, the law and covenant, the sacrifices, and other biblical material.
- Cross-reference: just as a schoolteacher would discuss distinct Homeric usage and meanings, so Chrysostom uses biblical cross-references to establish the "scriptural" meanings of words, Paul's characteristic usage, and other such points to establish the sense of particular sentences and the overall meaning of passages in the text.

But, of course, the moral and doctrinal implications of the text were also part of Chrysostom's pedagogy, as they were for any rhetorician or philosopher interpreting literary texts in antiquity. Cyril and Chrysostom shared the view that the scriptural text, rightly interpreted, teaches truth and excludes false teaching. In the post-Arian situation they were looking for the truth about the Lord Jesus Christ, Son of God and Savior.

36. See further my paper, "John Chrysostom on First and Second Corinthians," StPatr 18 (1986): 349–52; republished in F. Young, *Exegesis and Theology*. See also Mitchell, *Heavenly Trumpet*.

2.1. Interpreting the Epistle to the Hebrews

2.1.1. John Chrysostom, Homilies on Hebrews

In Hebrews 1:3 we find the words: "He is the reflection of God's glory and the exact imprint of God's very being" (*apaugasma tēs doxēs kai charactēr tēs hypostaseōs autou*). It is surely no surprise that in anti-Arian argument these striking phrases about the nature of the Son had figured alongside all those other key texts establishing the Godhead of the Only-begotten.[37] However, Hebrews had also provided many problem texts suggesting inferiority and creatureliness. The quotations from the Psalms in chapter 1 were clearly among those exploited by the Arians to suggest the Son had been anointed and promoted, while the later description of the Only-begotten as "apostle and high priest . . . faithful to the one who made him" (Heb 3:1–2) could suggest his creatureliness. Athanasius had already set such claims in the context of the incarnation, in the latter case quoting Hebrews 2:14–3:2 as a whole to establish the point (*C. Ar.* 1.46–51, 58–64; 2.7–9). That Chrysostom should make such doctrinal points in his opening homilies on Hebrews is surely to be expected—this, despite his sensitive appreciation that Paul is primarily concerned to exhort his readers to remain steady in the face of persecution, a point that proves the more significant as he takes his audience deeper into the text.

In his first homily, then, Chrysostom

- distinguishes between prophets and the Son, noting that it was by him that God created the worlds (Heb 1:2), so, picking up the classic Arian claim, he asks, "Where are those who say, there was [a time] when he was not?" (*Hom. Heb.* 1.1, 3);
- asserts that his appointment as heir was "of the flesh" (1.2) as was his being "made better than the angels" (1.3), which represent typical anti-Arian points;
- insists on the wisdom of Paul in oscillating between the humble and the exalted as, on the one hand, he speaks of "the reflection of God's glory and the express image of God's very being" and, on the other, of his incarnation, the latter through the language of appointment, inheritance, being made better, and, after purging sins, sitting at God's right hand—all of which is spoken of the flesh, since God the Word had it all already. Paul wishes "both to establish the 'economy' and also to teach about the incorruptible nature" (1.3).

37. These texts include John 1:1–3, 18; 8:58; 10:30; 14:10, 20; Matt 11:27.

The second homily picks up that last point, now explicitly stating that Paul "goes on two paths, by the one leading us away from Sabellius, by the other from Arius." The homily begins with contemplation of God's incomprehensibility—if the peace of God passes understanding, how much more "the God of peace and the Creator of all things." Chrysostom instances as things we know but do not understand the notions that God is everywhere, that there is an incorporeal cause of good things, and that God is without beginning, climaxing the list with the idea that "he begat from himself." Hebrews 1:3 must be approached with similar deference: he is of him, neither greater nor lesser, and yet a distinct being. Chrysostom asks his hearers to note "how he applies to the Son that which is proper to the Father" (*Hom. Heb.* 2.1). Points made in homily 1 are repeated and developed explicitly against the know-it-all heretics, and then Hebrews 1:3 is expounded with cross-references to demonstrate:[38]

- how one essence (light) indicates two subsistences (light of light), by which we are enlightened;
- how an "express image" is other than its prototype yet similar in all respects (Chrysostom makes sure to distinguish this imaging from the way humankind is in God's image);
- how everything is upheld by the creative Word.

Now, "having spoken concerning those marvellous and great matters," Paul turns to his "care for humans." Anyone who has ever read any of John's Chrysostom's work will have noticed the frequency of his use of the word *philanthrōpia*. The reference to his purging of sins and sitting at the right hand (Heb 1:3b) suggests crucifixion, resurrection, and ascension, but the "throne" points to equal dignity with the Father, and the name "Son" points to true relationship—not "by grace," otherwise he would be less than the angels. The quotations of Psalms in Hebrews 1:5, however, are to be taken as referring to "the flesh": "the flesh partakes of the high things, just as the Godhead of the lowly." Being God and Lord and Son of God, he did not refuse to take the form of a slave, cross-referencing Philippians 2:5–11 (*Hom. Heb.* 2.2). Thus, Chrysostom's approach to exegesis of Hebrews 1 has been shaped by anti-Arian exegesis: partitive, indeed, yet also stressing the Son's initiative and the mutual participation of the divine and the fleshly in Christ.

38. These cross-references include John 8:12; 1 Cor 2:10–12; Phil 2:6–7; Gen 1:3; John 1:1, 3–4; Ps 110:2.

So too in homily 3 the distinction between Creator and creature becomes paramount as the angels are contrasted with the Son, and the old Arian proof-texts, such as Proverbs 8:22 and Acts 2:36, are dragged in alongside Hebrews's quotes from scripture, all alike being referred to the flesh. The citation of Psalm 45 in Hebrews 1:9 is an example, its reference to the flesh (implicit in "being anointed with joy") being contrasted with the words quoted in the previous verse from the same Psalm (45:6: "Your throne, O God, will last for ever and ever"). Constant qualification hits against various heresies, states Chrysostom, and "with the doctrine concerning his uncreated nature he always joins also that of the 'economy'" (*Hom. Heb.* 3.1–2). Hebrews 1:10–12 applies to the Son things that relate to the Father, striking blows against Paul of Samosata and Arius (*Hom. Heb.* 3.3), while the Father's treatment of the Son's enemies is no indication of any supposed weakness on the Son's part but rather of his sovereignty, equal dignity, and honor. That the angels minister to our salvation indicates that they are servants of the Son of God, fellow servants and creatures with us (3.4). Chrysostom sets these post-Nicene emphases within the framework of old and new covenants, thus tying it into Hebrews's principal point of argument as the text moves into chapter 2.

The fourth homily turns to the subjection of all things to humankind (Heb 2:5–8, quoting Ps 8:3–6), embracing Hebrews's suggestion that the Psalm applies "more properly to Christ according to the flesh" (*Hom. Heb.* 4.2). The preacher waxes lyrical about the cross, his tasting death for everyone by the grace of God (4.3). Significantly Hebrews 2:10 is referred to the Father: the Father is the one bringing many sons to glory. Thus Chrysostom does not anticipate the way the text was used by Antiochenes in the subsequent christological controversy, namely, to distinguish between the divine Son, who brings many sons to glory, and "the man assumed," who was the "pioneer of our salvation." Chrysostom does already emphasize that the "pioneer" is set forth "as an example to others, like some noble wrestler that surpasses the rest": "he is Son and we are sons; but he saves and we are saved"—and later on in Hebrews 2:11, "he sanctifies, we are sanctified" (*Hom. Heb.* 4.5)—so, he notes, the text "brings us together and yet separates us" (4.4).

Needless to say, the idea of the Savior "being made perfect through suffering" (Heb 2:10) could have been treated as highly problematic, but Chrysostom makes it evidence of God's love for humankind (*philanthrōpia*): his "taking flesh to suffer" he describes as a "far greater thing" than creation out of nothing. Now, however, he shifts back to the focus on bringing "many sons to glory": "for Christ was glorified then when he suffered," and so too the faithful, for whom all this is a comfort. However, with half an eye on the Arian controversy, he glosses it with:

> when I say, he was glorified, do not suppose that there was an accession of glory to him: for that which is of nature he always had, and received nothing in addition. (*Hom. Heb.* 4.4)

"He was not ashamed to call them brothers" (Heb 2:11b): this demonstrates his superiority and humility, Chrysostom states, for it is not a statement about his nature but about the loving affection of the one "not ashamed." There is a great difference: the one who sanctifies is "of the Father, as a true Son, that is, of his substance," whereas we are "created, that is, brought out of nothing." But now Chrysostom underlines the reality of his flesh and blood against the heretics: he did not come in appearance only—his "brotherhood" was complete (*Hom. Heb.* 4.5) and the cause of the "economy" was that "through death he might destroy the one who has the power of death" (Heb 2:14). Freedom from fear of death then becomes the theme of this homily's long concluding exhortation (*Hom. Heb.* 4.6–8).

The fifth homily dwells on the kindness and love for humankind that led to Christ taking on "the seed of Abraham" (Heb 2:16). So he was made "like his brothers in every respect" (2:17): what this means is that he was "brought up, grew, suffered all things necessary, at last he died." Paul is said by Chrysostom to have shifted from discussion of his "glory on high" to the "dispensation": he was eager to be made like us, to destroy death and "become our high priest"—he took flesh for love of humankind "that he might have mercy on us" and "make reconciliation for the sins of the people" (*Hom. Heb.* 5.1–2). He was a faithful high priest, and he became human to "offer a sacrifice to purify us." Following Hebrews's emphasis on his capacity to help those tempted as having been tempted himself, Chrysostom suggests this is "low and mean and unworthy of God," but such is nevertheless said of the one made flesh for the encouragement of the hearers, for

> "now" he is not ignorant of our sufferings; not only does he know them as God, but as man also he has known them, by the trial wherewith he was tried; he suffered much, he knows how to sympathize. Yet God is incapable of suffering: but he describes here what belongs to the incarnation, as if he had said, Even the very flesh of Christ suffered many terrible things. He knows what tribulation is: he knows what temptation is, not less than we who have suffered, for he himself also suffered. (*Hom. Heb.* 5.2)

Chrysostom is clearly adopting the "partitive exegesis" that had become the way to circumvent the Arian position. As he moves to Hebrews 3, this becomes all the clearer with his comments on when God "made him" apostle and high priest (Heb 3:1–2): "he is not speaking at all in this place of his essence, nor of his Godhead; but so far concerning human dignities" (*Hom. Heb.* 5.4).

But what really engages Chrysostom is the encouragement to those going through struggle; as many consider "experience the most reliable means of knowledge, he wishes to show that he that has suffered knows what human nature suffers" (5.5). In the next few homilies he will distil for his congregation not just the scriptural background in the exodus but also the enduring importance of the Epistle's exhortation to keep going forward in hope, for "a rest remains for the people of God" and "we have been made partakers of Christ" (Heb 3:14), a phrase he expounds with cross-reference to Paul's image of Christ being the head and us the body (*Hom. Heb.* 6.4).[39] So, by the time he reaches the next passage about the high priest (Heb 4:14; *Hom. Heb.* 7.5), Chrysostom is ready to reinforce again the fact that "our high priest" is not ignorant but has had experience, has endured all things, and was "in all points tempted as we are yet without sin"—"he was persecuted, was spit upon, was accused, was mocked at, was falsely informed against, was driven out, at last was crucified." Thus Hebrews suggests that "it is possible even for one in afflictions to go through them without sin." The "likeness of flesh" means real flesh—"likeness" is used because he was speaking of "sinful flesh," same flesh yet "in sin no longer the same." Chrysostom here draws Romans 8:3 into his discussion of Hebrews 4:15. Now we can "come boldly" because "we have a sinless high priest" and we approach a throne of grace and not one of judgment; mercy is available "now" if not "then"—that is, at the end (*Hom. Heb.* 7.6).

But next the need for partitive exegesis recurs. To sit on the throne, whether granting pardon or judgement, is of God, but a high priest does not sit but stand. So for him "to be made high priest is not of nature, but of grace and condescension and humiliation." The Son's *synkatabasis* was one of Chrysostom's most characteristic themes,[40] just as *kenōsis* would be for Cyril, as we shall see later. In the next homily Chrysostom tackles the heretics directly. Hebrews 5:7–8 cannot be attributed to God with its references to "prayer" and "tears," to "fear," to "learning obedience" and "suffering" (*Hom. Heb.* 8.3). "This is spoken concerning the incarnation." With multiple cross-references Chrysostom teases out the fact that he did it all "for those who believed in him" and that "it is in reference to the flesh that lowly things are spoken concerning himself." In fact it was all exemplary: his "success" came from "himself rather

39. Citing Eph 3:6; 5:30; cf. Rom 12:4–5 and 1 Cor 12:12–27.

40. Cf. chapter 1 above.

than God's favor," and if he, being the Son, gained obedience from his sufferings, much more shall we. This is the way we too must arrive at perfection. Picking out verses from Hebrews 4:14–5:12, Chrysostom underlines the fact that the author means the human nature of Christ, excluding "the suspicion that these things relate to the divine nature" (*Hom. Heb.* 8.5). The preacher seems to require for exemplary and pedagogical reasons that the human nature of Christ achieves its own victory over temptation and suffering, so receiving response to his prayers and reaching the goal of perfection.

This quick survey of the eight opening homilies anticipates most of the christological discussion in the collection. Hebrews 7:1–3 will, of course, be used to reinforce the fact that the Son has no beginning or earthly genealogy, so underlining his eternity (*Hom. Heb.* 12.3). It is, however, that tension between standing as priest or minister and sitting as judge or king that will keep reappearing. For example, commenting on Hebrews 10:11, Chrysostom specifies that to stand "is a sign of ministering" while to sit "is a sign of being ministered to" (18.3). In *Homily on Hebrews* 13, with reference to his intercession in Hebrews 7:25, Chrysostom insists that it is when he appears as priest that he intercedes, and so it is said "according to the flesh" (13.6). Again, in the following homily, Paul is said to mix "lowly things and the lofty," and Christ's condescension in being "a minister in the sanctuary" is set alongside his sitting at the right hand (Heb 8:1–2):

> His sitting belongs to the dignity of the Godhead, but [his priesthood] to his great lovingkindness and tender care for us. (*Hom. Heb.* 14.2)

It is stated by Hebrews itself, and followed by Chrysostom as he comments on Hebrews 7:25, that he "ever lives to make intercession for us" (*Hom. Heb.* 13.6), so we potentially have the uncomfortable notion that within the very person of Christ the human nature stands before the seated Godhead—the two natures divided indeed![41]

Yet, as we shall see, Cyril will be caught in much the same paradox, and Chrysostom himself repeatedly tries to avoid dividing the Christ. For example, back in the thirteenth Homily, while Chrysostom first notes how Hebrews 7:26 describes our high priest as "holy, blameless, undefiled, separate from sinners"—all of which must be said with reference to the "manhood," for no one could say such things about God—he then continues:

41. As suggested in my article "Christological Ideas in Greek Christian Commentaries on the Epistle to the Hebrews," *JTS* 20 (1969): 150–63; reprinted in *Christology, Hermeneutics, and Hebrews*, ed. Jon C. Laansma and Daniel J. Treier (London: T&T Clark, 2012), 33–47.

> But when I say the "manhood," I mean [the manhood] having Godhead; not dividing [one from the other]. (*Hom. Heb.* 13.7)

In a later homily, commenting on Hebrews 9:11, he takes "the greater and more perfect tent (not made with hands)" as a reference to the flesh, which is "greater and more perfect" because "God the Word and all the power of the Spirit dwells there" (*Hom. Heb.* 15.4). Thus Chrysostom endeavors to hold together the natures separated by his partitive exegesis.

He also at times consigns specifically to the time of incarnation the acts done humanly. The thirteenth homily, following the Epistle's text, insists that his sacrifice, and therefore his priesthood, was once for all, and then "he sat down."

> Lest thou suppose that he is standing on high, and is a minister, he shows that the matter is [part] of a dispensation [or economy]. For as he became a servant, so also [he became] a priest and minister. But as after becoming a servant, he did not continue a servant, so also having become a minister, he did not continue a minister. For it belongs not to a minister to sit but to stand. (*Hom. Heb.* 13.8)

Thus Chrysostom now seems to consign his priesthood and sacrificial offering to the cross. So too his mediation of the new covenant (or testament). Like the Epistle itself, Chrysostom plays on the ambiguity of covenant/will/testament as he describes Christ returning the inheritance to the dispossessed:

> The Son became Mediator between the Father and us. The Father willed not to leave us this inheritance, but was wroth against us, and was displeased [with us] as being estranged [from him]; he accordingly became Mediator between us and him, and prevailed with him. . . . How did he become Mediator? . . . We had offended: we ought to have died: he died for us and made us worthy of the Testament. (*Hom. Heb.* 16.2)

Again in the seventeenth homily, as he dwells on the condescension of one who was victim and priest and sacrifice—just once for all, not repeatedly—Chrysostom states that he offered "a sacrifice which had power to propitiate the Father" (17.2). At the same time, however, struggling to maintain that salvation comes from God's love of humanity, he suggests that he bore our sins by taking them from humans and bearing them to the Father for forgiveness (17.4).

This tendency to focus on the accomplishment of the saving act perhaps modifies the implied image of humanity standing before seated divinity within the very person of Christ—though his continual intercession might surely keep that unfortunate picture in play. What Chrysostom's homilies on Hebrews reveal is that the strategy of partitive exegesis, adopted against the Arian interpretation of scripture, could lead to awkward deductions and would do so even more once questions about the nature (or natures) of the incarnate Logos became paramount. Nevertheless, there is little here deserving the charge of teaching "two Sons"—he has specifically indicated that "the flesh partakes of the high things, just as the Godhead of the lowly."[42] Furthermore, at the heart of Chrysostom's theology, even in these homilies, are God's *philanthrōpia* and the pedagogical *synkatabasis* of the divine Logos. Indeed, his taking flesh to suffer Chrysostom calls "a far greater thing" than creation out of nothing, implicitly, therefore, to be classed among those incomprehensible realities noted in his second homily. No matter how conceptually difficult, Chrysostom is affirming that in the incarnation the Creator himself lived, and paradoxically died, as a human creature. No wonder Rylaarsdam reached the surprising conclusion that his Christology "sounds more Alexandrian than Antiochene."[43]

2.1.2. Other Post-Nicene Exegetical Material on Hebrews

In the early 1960s my research career began as a project to explore patristic exegesis of Hebrews. Back then, attention to exegesis was undermined by distracting interests in doctrine: my doctoral thesis came to focus on sacrifice and atonement, while one of my earliest articles was on "Christological Ideas in the Greek Commentaries on the Epistle to the Hebrews."[44] This was able to draw on my identification of extant exegetical material on Hebrews from the period, including the commentary by Theodoret and fragments from the commentaries by Theodore of Mopsuestia and Cyril of Alexandria.[45] Access to this material may enable us to put Chrysostom's work more appropriately in the context of those emerging christological traditions.

Theodoret tells us that the Arians regarded this epistle as inauthentic and rejected it from the canon because of Hebrews 1:3 (PG 82:681c). However, as

42. See above, p. 126, citing *Hom. Heb.* 2.2.

43. Rylaarsdam, *John Chrysostom*, 139–40.

44. Cited above, note 41.

45. For the text of Theodoret's commentary, see PG 82. The fragments of Theodore of Mopsuestia are collected in K. Staab, *Pauluskommentare aus griechischen Kirche, aus Katenenhandschriften gesammelt* (Münster: Aschendorff, 1933). For the fragments of Cyril of Alexandria, see PG 74 and the edition in Pusey, *Cyrilli Archiepiscopi Alexandriae*, 3:362–440, 461–68. Citations of Pusey will appear in brackets alongside those of PG 74. Other passages Pusey assigns to *On the Right Faith.*

we have seen, they certainly exploited texts cited in Hebrews to suggest that the Son was promoted from an inferior position. All of our commentators presuppose the Nicene faith, appeal to Hebrews 1:3, and use chapter 1 to argue against the Arians that Christ is greater than the angels and is *homoousios* with the Father. All alike also draw a distinction between the essential nature of the Son of God and things said about the flesh, his humanity, or the incarnation. Cyril states that at the same time he acts as priest humanly, in that he became man, and sits in authority divinely, in that he remains Logos (PG 74:972b [3:468]). Theodoret explains that he is apostle and high priest as man—it was in the incarnation he was sent, using the verb from which "apostle" is derived (PG 82:697b). In contrast, Cyril in his commentary attacks those claiming Christ cannot be *homoousios* on grounds of this text (Heb 3:1), explaining it is only said about the incarnation (PG 74:969b [3:466]). In other words, they have much in common because all share the anti-Arian "partitive exegesis," but perhaps they meant something slightly different.

Anyone turning to the *apparatus criticus* of a Greek New Testament will find a relatively rare alternative reading in the manuscript tradition of Hebrews 2:9. Instead of "by the grace of God [χάριτι Θεοῦ (*chariti theou*)] he tasted death," it reads "apart from God" (χωρίς Θεοῦ [*chōris theou*]). Discussing this textual problem, Theodore of Mopsuestia, Chrysostom's fellow student in Antioch, had suggested that the former reading was introduced by copyists who could not imagine how Paul (as ever the assumed author) could have suggested "apart from God." However, Christ's suffering was not proper to his Godhead, so when used in relation to his death, it ensures that the Godhead of Christ is not compromised. What was proper to the Logos was his action in displaying as perfected through suffering the pioneer of everyone's salvation, the man that he took.[46] This is a particularly graphic instance of Antiochene separation of the natures and might well deserve the "two Sons" caricature. Perhaps it also reveals what would become a prime Antiochene concern in the controversy—namely, the need to defend the true "Godness" of the Son against any kind of compromise through change, suffering, or death. Theodore was certainly not followed by Chrysostom: for the latter it was by God's grace that he suffered, for God "spared not his own Son" (Rom 8:32). It was not "owed" but was done "of grace," and he tasted death "for the whole world," not just believers (*Hom. Heb.* 4.3).

Cyril does not, of course, emphasize the sharp differentiation in his commentary, yet he does insist that he is priest and God *at the same time*. Does he really differ all that much from Chrysostom, then? Rather than distinguishing

46. Staab, *Pauluskommentare*, 204.

the divine Logos from assumed human nature, Cyril makes a distinction between the preincarnate and the incarnate Logos. On Hebrews 1:9 he insists that the anointing only applies to the incarnation situation, but explains, "though he remained as he was when he became man, by the anointing of manhood with Godhead he united creation to himself and made both one thing [*hen*]" (PG 74:961b [3:462; cf. 3:401]). On Hebrews 2:6–18, all commentators both ancient and modern agree that the quote from Psalm 8 is applied to Christ, although the psalmist intended ordinary human nature, but whereas Chrysostom had elaborated on Christ's genuine experience of our condition, for Cyril the passage is all about the *kenōsis* of the Logos by which he took a body liable to death and suffered so as to destroy death and raise humanity to immortality (PG 74:964a–69a [3:463–66]). The Son remained God when he took the body, and his unity of person can be understood by analogy with the unity of body and soul: though the flesh assumed by the Logos, he keeps reaffirming, was a man with a soul and a mind. It was in order to overcome sin and death that he took our flesh and blood, so the Logos made expiation for our sins *according to the power of his divinity*. Only the power of God could bring about salvation. So on Hebrews 7:27 Cyril explicitly states that as God he was stronger than sin—hence the superiority of his priesthood and sacrifice to that of the Jews.[47] Time and again Cyril insists that the Logos was not changed by the incarnation but united humanity to his divinity, so healing it and raising it to heaven to be presented purified to the Father as a sweet-smelling offering.[48]

So Cyril makes little of Chrysostom's point about Christ undergoing temptation and therefore being able to help the tempted from his own experience. His temptation is simply identified with the cross and the whole saving action whereby human nature was perfected, and all that was enacted through divine power. He did not "become" merciful or compassionate from experience—he was always merciful. Cyril is sure the incarnation did not change or improve the Logos in any way: even if the Logos had not become man, he would have known human weakness as creator, for he knows our formation. This contrasts with what we have seen in Chrysostom's exegesis of the same Hebrews passages. Both Cyril and Chrysostom attribute salvation to the love and goodness of God, but one concentrates on the invisible activity of divine power and

47. PG 74:976b–c; Pusey attributes the passage to *On the Right Faith*; see *Cyrilli Archiepiscopi Alexandriae*, 3:402 and the note on 406.

48. PG 74:977a–b; 985c–d; 988c–d; Pusey attributes these passages to *On the Right Faith*; see *Cyrilli Archiepiscopi Alexandriae*, 3:396.

the injection of divinity into humanity, while the other concentrates on the exemplary power of human suffering and the achievement of human victory over sin. Remember that, in Chrysostom's view, Christ's "success" came from "himself" rather than God's favor, and the importance of his demonstration was the possibility of human enduring without sin, for in nature his flesh was the same as ours, though in sin no longer the same.[49]

On Hebrews 2:17–18, Theodoret, like Chrysostom, emphasizes Christ's learning from experience, underlining the point that this is said about his human nature (PG 82:696c). He was high priest as man and not as God. Nor did he suffer as God but as man; nor as God did he learn our condition by experience, for as God and Creator he already knows everything. On Hebrews 4:14 he is clear that distinguishing what pertains to the *theologia* and what to the *oikonomia* is necessary, and on 4:15 he notes how the author encourages believers subject to persecution—Christ can offer suitable help, for our high priest not only knows of our weakness as God but has also experienced our sufferings as man, remaining uninitiated only in sin (PG 82:708c–d). Such distinctions Chrysostom had already made, but for Theodoret in the context of the christological controversy they were yet more important. He even applies partitive exegesis to Hebrews 13:8: "Jesus Christ is the same yesterday and today and for ever": "yesterday and today" are attributed to the humanity and eternity to the divinity (PG 82:733c).[50]

Theodoret also explicitly states that as man he offered the sacrifice in which he was both priest and victim, while as God he received it (PG 82:733b). As we noticed earlier, Chrysostom had found it challenging to avoid assigning to the very person of Christ the tension between offering and receiving sacrifice, between judgement and forgiveness. Clearly, engaging with the Epistle to the Hebrews, the Antiochenes implicitly place both the tensions and their reconciliation not only within the Trinity but even within the person and saving action of Christ. By comparison Cyril underlines the union: "with flesh the only-begotten Logos of God rules everything, not apart from the Father." He sits as God and serves as man at the same time. As already observed, the sacrifice is an act performed by the power of divinity to heal humankind: the

49. See above, pp. 129–30, quoting *Hom. Heb.* 8.3 on Heb 5:7 and following.

50. This point is noted by Paul B. Clayton Jr., *The Christology of Theodoret of Cyrus: Antiochene Christology from the Council of Ephesus (431) to the Council of Chalcedon (451)*, OECT (Oxford: Oxford University Press, 2007), 206; see further his review of Theodoret's exegesis of Hebrews on 202–7.

same person receives and gives and is the sacrifice whereby humankind is purified, raised to heaven, and offered to the Father.

In the process of teasing out the doctrine of the Epistle to the Hebrews in the post-Nicene situation, different readings have emerged with rather different consequences for articulating the nature of Christ's person. Of course the epistle itself evidences unresolved christological tensions, yet these exegetical outcomes were largely generated by the way in which anti-Arian exegesis had been formulated. The results also reflect different approaches to what is necessary for salvation: Cyril saw the power of divinity as the essential ingredient for healing, renewal, and restoration to life—that is, for *theopoiēsis*—whereas Chrysostom, with an eye to exhorting his congregation, wanted to show that by following the way pioneered by Christ, a human being can be made perfect through suffering, and he was followed by other Antiochenes. Yet all post-Nicene exegetes, faced with the actual text of scripture, have much in common, their approach being shaped by anti-Arian argument. For all of them, the subjection to suffering and death of one identified as fully God is a paradox to be resolved or embraced: embraced through the notion of the *kenōsis* or *synkatabasis* of the Logos, or resolved through keeping apart, at least notionally, divine and human agency.

2.2. *Interpreting the Gospel of John*

2.2.1. *Cyril of Alexandria,* Commentary on John's Gospel

It will hardly be possible to do justice here to the twelve books Cyril wrote commenting verse by verse on John's Gospel (extant in full apart from books 7 and 8, of which we have fragments). We will take a look at the first book, which dwells upon the divine nature of the Word—hardly surprising given both the focus of the Johannine Prologue and the post-Arian context. We will then take some further soundings from across the commentary to trace how Cyril's initial christological position shapes his subsequent exegesis.

2.2.1.1. Interpreting the Prologue to the Gospel

The Johannine Prologue starts with the iconic statement, "In the beginning was the Word, and the Word was with God, and the Word was God. He was in the beginning with God." Unlike the other Evangelists, John does not "provide a precise account of our Saviour's genealogy according to the flesh," Cyril notes. Rather he "reaches for subjects that are beyond human comprehension."

To avoid leaving the road "wide open for false teachers," John "gets right to the point, to the chief of all divine doctrines" (*Comm. Jo.* 1.1 [1:5]). Cyril assumes, then, that heretics were already around sowing confusion, and the words were directed against recognizably Arian propositions. With cross-references and arguments he defends his first thesis: *the Only Begotten is eternal and before the ages.*[51] "He is before all time," Cyril writes, directing the reader to a horizon beyond the temporal. The Word is the Father's "wisdom, power, imprint, radiance and image," existing in and from the Father and indeed, "in the substance of the Father; he radiates out from that substance like beams from the sun or heat from a fire." The Son cannot be "alien or foreign" or "in second place after the Father." He was not "first called into existence when he took the temple from the holy virgin and became human for us." The Evangelist "positively pounces on those who teach wrongly" by suggesting that the Son "is one of the creatures created in time" (*Comm. Jo.* 1.1 [1:6–9]).

Cyril's second thesis is: *the Son, who is both God and of the same substance as the Father, exists in his own hypostasis, just as the Father does.* Having "closed every loophole for those who claim that the Son is from nothing," the Evangelist excludes those who "in colossal ignorance say that the Father and the Son are one and the same," indicating with the words, "the Word was *with* God," that "the Son is one thing and subsists in himself, while God the Father, '*with*' whom 'the Word was,' is another" (1.2 [1:9–10], emphasis added). Cyril has named neither the Arians nor the Sabellians here, but we can easily discern whom he had in mind, and he now assembles a considerable series of proofs and cross-references to back up this thesis (1.2 [1:10–12]).

In similar vein and with similar documentation he draws from the text further theses, for example:

Number 3. *The Son is God by nature and is in no way less than or unlike the Father; on the words "and the Word was God."*

Number 5. *The Son is by nature creator with God the Father because he is from the Father's substance and not taken on as a subordinate; on the words "all things came to be through him."*

That the Son is by nature life and light—indeed, alone true light, whereas the creation participates in light—are further theses stated and elaborated as the exegesis proceeds (numbers 6–8). Overall, a full catalog of anti-Arian argumentation is found to be rooted in the Johannine text. In elaborating these

51. See above, pp. 122–23, for explanation of his theses in this commentary.

theses, the Arian opponents are occasionally named—indeed, the opinion that "the Word in the mind of God the Father" is to be differentiated from "the one called 'Son' in the holy Scriptures" is attributed to "the followers of Eunomius" (number 4). However, Cyril is less interested in name-dropping than in stating falsities to be contested and truths to be taught:

> The Theologian has to introduce the Only Begotten to us as the creator and craftsman by nature. . . . By the same words through which he says the creation has been made, he teaches clearly that the one who calls things into being is different from that creation. By his ineffable power, he brought all things into existence from nonexistence. Thus, it is possible from the beauty of the creatures to see proportionately the creator and to recognize the one who is truly God, through whom all things have come to be and are now preserved. (*Comm. Jo.* 1.5 [1:29])

Cyril here comments that the author "deftly deploys the passage from the Gospel against the false worship of the Greeks" but also, he adds, against the heretics. He elaborates this point further: the Son is not some "underling or servant" who receives "the power to create from someone else." Nor are there two creators. All this triggers statements about the divine nature of the Trinity as a whole—the Father, Son and Holy Spirit should be understood individually though not as separate or different (1.5 [1:30]).

It is tempting to go on, but something of Cyril's procedure and principal concerns should by now be evident. After a lengthy discussion of the difference between being life and light and participating in them, he offers a summary:

> no argument will permit us to think that the Son of God is originate or created; rather, he surpasses our condition in every way, and he transcends the nature of created beings. He is completely other. (*Comm. Jo.* 1.7 [1:39])

So far so good, but what, if anything, has Cyril to say about the incarnation in this first book? "Little by little," he writes on John 1:11, "he comes down from sheer theology to an explanation of the *oikonomia* with the flesh which the Son accomplished for us" (1.9 [1:59]). Yet not a single one of Cyril's theses relates to the Word becoming flesh. It is as though referenced dogmatic formulations are required for the divine nature of the Word, given the Arian controversy and its definitive outcome, but not yet for "the *oikonomia* with the flesh," statements that remain at the level of confession.

For yes, of course, Cyril does make such statements as he provides exegesis for John 1:11–14. His first interest is in the consequences for us, and John 1:12 gives him the opportunity to contrast "the earthly man" with "the heavenly man," affirming that

> We became participants in him through the Spirit. We were sealed into his likeness, and we ascend to the archetypal form of the image according to which Holy Scripture says we were also made. (*Comm. Jo.* 1.9 [1:60])

This recovery of "the ancient beauty of our nature" is even surpassed by our refashioning "in relation to the divine nature"; though

> we will not be sons of God unchangeably like he is, but we will be sons of God in relation to him by the grace of imitation. He is the true Son existing from the Father, but we are adopted because of his love for humanity. . . . Being something by nature is different from being something by adoption, and being something truly is different from being something by imitation. . . . We enjoy the good that comes by grace rather than the honors that come by nature. (1.9 [1:60])

Reinforcing this distinction as he comments on verse 13, Cyril goes on to say:

> Those who rise to divine sonship through faith in Christ are baptized not into anything originate but into the Holy Trinity itself through the Word who is the mediator. He joins what is human to himself through the flesh that was united to him, and he is joined by nature to the Father since he is by nature God. (1.9 [1.61])

Mediation is thus located in the very person of Christ—the conjoining of divine and human in union is crucial to this. It is by "participation in the true Son" that "we who received new birth through the Spirit of faith are called born of God" (1.9 [1:61]). Cyril is tempted "to go into a long discourse about these matters," but says he has already done so in his book on the Holy Trinity (1.9 [1:62]). Still his primary focus is clear: the incarnation was about our assimilation to the divine through the union of the truly divine with what is human.

So concerning the classic text, John 1:14—"the Word became flesh and dwelt in us"—Cyril makes a series of points (*Comm. Jo.* 1.9 [1:60–65]):

- "The Only Begotten has become and is called the Son of Man"—which means, Cyril explains, that he "became a human being," and he uses cross-references to show how "flesh" in scripture means "the whole creature."
- The text "does not say that the Word came into flesh but that the Word became flesh"—to prevent anyone assuming that "he came to it temporarily the way he came to the prophets or the other saints."
- Rather, "God is both in and with the flesh by nature, on the grounds that he has it as his own"—indeed, "he is worshipped in and with it." Isaiah 45:14 is quoted: "they will worship you and pray to you since God is in you, and there is no God besides you." That last clause indicates that there should be no "separating the flesh from the Word," but rather "uniting the Word to that which he carries as his very own, that is, the temple of the virgin. For there is one Christ of both."
- "Became" does not signify "change," as the Evangelist indicates by adding "and dwelt in us." You should not suppose that "the Word departed from his own nature and was changed into flesh and suffered—which is impossible because the divine, by its mode of being, is far removed from all alteration and from changing into something else." Paul is quoted: "for in him the whole fullness of the deity dwelt bodily" (Col 2:9).
- "Dwelt in us" signifies that "we were all in Christ, and the shared properties of our human nature were taken up into his person." Hence "he is called the last Adam." Cyril spells out the overarching story of fall and redemption with various biblical cross-references. It is because the one "who is by nature Son and God" dwelt in "all people" that "we cry out Abba! Father!"
- "And we saw his glory . . ." For Cyril this means he "preserves his divine dignity intact" and remains "full of the Father's attributes" despite his descent to kinship with "slaves and creatures": "he did not fall away from his primaeval power and glory when he clothed himself with our weak and most inglorious body."
- Again he emphasizes the difference between Christ and the saints: they "borrowed power from above," whereas the works of Christ showed him "as great in power as the Father." So also "the one who is God by nature exceeds humanity and the true Son exceeds those who are sons by adoption."
- Furthermore, Luke's comment that "Jesus advanced in wisdom and grace" (Luke 2:52) must be understood, not as an advance "insofar as he is the Word and God, but because his works kept showing him ever more marvellous and gracious." The spectre of Arian counterexegesis hovers ever in the background.

Reviewing that catalog overall, we can see not only Cyril's anti-Arian and Trinitarian focus but also, in anticipation, what will be Cyril's primary concerns when he subsequently engages in debate about the incarnation. The Savior is the Son/Word of God who, fully divine in every sense, retains the divine identity and power throughout. This enables him to mediate divine life and light to the human nature, which was "his own" and to which he was united, precisely in order that we might all be adopted and raised up as children of God. Thus, Christ is to be clearly differentiated from those who are "sons" by adoption, participation, or imitation, including prophets and saints. Prompted by the propositions he discerns in the Johannine Prologue, Cyril reads the gospel story as one of divine descent and ascent out of sheer love for humanity, indeed, of the assimilation and regeneration of human nature through the divine initiative—mediation, indeed, but not through finding a mean or creating a mixture, for in Christ it is genuinely our human nature that is really endowed with the very Word of God.

2.2.1.2. Tracing the Prologue's Perspectives in Narrative and Discourse

So how does this work out as Cyril moves through the narratives and discourses of the Gospel of John?

Before answering that question we should acknowledge the capacity of Cyril's commentary to draw readers into the gospel story, fostering a life of true worship and virtuous living that avoids wickedness and blasphemy alike. We should observe how rich it is in terms of communicating both the story itself and its place in the overarching scriptural narrative of fall and redemption, along with its constant use of cross-references, types, prophecies, and symbols. We should attest its grasp of how the new covenant fulfils and surpasses the old, and how old Adam is recapitulated in the second Adam—indeed, it is a strikingly Pauline reading of John's Gospel. As we abstract comments relevant to Cyril's christological teaching, it is important to be aware of this overall hermeneutic, a perspective already to be found across his exegetical works on the Pentateuch.[52] Also evident is bias against the Jews, though that clearly has some basis in the gospel text itself. Less obviously Johannine is his constant

52. I refer to the works known as *Of Adoration in Spirit and Truth*, and the *Glaphyra*; cf. my article "Theotokos: Mary and the Pattern of Fall and Redemption in the Theology of Cyril of Alexandria," in *The Theology of Cyril of Alexandria: A Critical Appreciation*, ed. Thomas G. Weinandy and Daniel A. Keating (London: T&T Clark, 2003).

detection of signs in the narrative pointing to the coming shift to the gentiles. Still, much of the commentary does, in fact, facilitate impressive insights into the dynamics of John's Gospel. The truth is here but veiled in flesh; and Cyril renders what the gospel writer presents, with all its paradoxes, as the descent and ascent of the Word of God, which becomes the core and climax of the entire biblical story of divine engagement with creaturely humankind.

How, then, does that core motif play out? Consistently striking is the presentation of the one speaking and acting as the Word/Son of God, though unrecognized given his human fleshly presence. Nicodemus calls him "a teacher from God," even a "co-worker with God"; but, Cyril states,

> he does not yet know that he is God by nature, and he clearly does not understand the message of the *oikonomia* with the flesh. He approaches him thinking he is a mere man and has little understanding of him. (*Comm. Jo.* 2.1 [1:97])

This kind of perspective is notably the case where Cyril is interpreting dialogues with the Jews, for example, the debate in John 5 concerning the authority with which Jesus has healed the man at the pool on a Sabbath (2.5–6 [1:140–61]). This Cyril senses is all at cross purposes because "the Jews are ignorant and do not know who the Only Begotten is by nature." They see him "being a man" yet saying "that God was 'his own father'" for they "concentrate only on the flesh without recognizing that God dwells in the flesh." Similarly commenting on those further debates in John 8:

> The Pharisee goes astray because of the flesh. . . . [W]hen he sees the Lord making statements that far surpass humanity and hears words that are most appropriate for God, he still thinks of a common man. (*Comm. Jo.* 5.2 [1:319])

Returning to John 5, we note how Cyril's commentary takes Jesus's affirmation that he only does what he sees the Father doing as testimony "to the identity of substance with him." For "things of the same nature as each other will act in the same way." Soon, however, Cyril is again drawing on anti-Arian argumentation, defending the Son from being inferior to and receiving from the Father. The thesis introduced here is: *The Son is not less than the Father either in potentiality or actuality when it comes to any work, but he is of equal might and of the same substance since he is from him by nature.* By "the exact identity of their works, he shows himself to be like the Father in all things." And so he "must incontrovertibly be understood to be God by nature." Indeed, no one should be "scandalized" when he says he cannot do anything on his own but only what he sees the Father doing—it is all to do with the *oikonomia*: "he was now clothed in the form of a slave and had become human by being united to flesh," so in stating that "on his own he could do nothing" he did not "fully let his language loose to the point of God-befitting boldness." Sometimes he "used speech which because of the *oikonomia* was fitting both for God and for man. He was, after all, really both in the same." So Christ shames the Jews who are trying to persecute him "by showing that God the Father is merciful on the sabbath day." The Father has the Son as the "operative power for everything," so the Son "reveals his will and activity in any matter." Proof of their equality comes with the delegating of resurrection and judgement, authority which "in that he is Word and God he inherently has, but, in that he has become human . . . he confesses that it was fitting for him to receive that authority." On this basis another thesis is now introduced: *no God-befitting dignity or superiority is in the Son by participation or addition from the outside* (2.7 [1:149]). Receiving authority to judge "perfectly fits the *oikonomia* with the flesh when he was called a slave and when he humbled himself, being made in our likeness."

Cyril now builds a new thesis upon John 5:23: *Since the Son is God and from God by nature and is the exact image of the one who begat him, he has equal honor and glory with him* (*Comm. Jo.* 2.8 [1:150]). He then engages in a long disquisition on the relationship of Father and Son, the Only-begotten being:

> the image of God the Father with respect to identity of wills; with respect to dignity, glory and God-befitting power; with respect to the activity of creating and performing miracles; with respect to reigning and ruling over everything; with respect to judging and being worshipped, by angels, humans and all creation in general. Through all these things, as he shows us the Father in himself, he says not that he is of his hypostasis, but is the "imprint of his hypostasis" (Heb 1.3). (*Comm. Jo.* 2.8 [1:153])

Cyril thus renders the import of Jesus's claims in the Gospel of John in terms of the then current anti-Arian propositions concerning his true identity. That his views are not entirely untrue to the Johannine text is surely borne out by Käsemann's reading of the gospel in terms of a naïve docetism, claiming it presents a "picture of Jesus as God walking on the face on the earth."[53]

53. Ernst Käsemann, *The Testament of Jesus: A Study of the Gospel of John in the Light of Chapter 17*, trans. Gerhard Krodel (London: SCM, 1968), 73, cf. 4–26.

This attention to the true, yet concealed, identity of Jesus occurs across the commentary. In narratives of the miraculous signs, the giver of light and life is revealed but not recognized. On the healing of the blind man in John 9, for example, Cyril comments:

> Just as we believe that the body of Christ is life-giving, since it is the temple and dwelling place of the living Word of God and possesses all his energy, so also we say that it supplies illumination, since it is the body of the one who is the true light by nature. . . . [H]ere he smears saliva on the man, teaching that his body is the supplier of illumination even with a mere touch. That is because it is the body of the true light, as we have said. (*Comm. Jo.* 6.1 [2:32])

But none of the characters in the story recognize this. Indeed, on John 9:31, Cyril comments:

> The man who had been blind has too earthly a conception of Christ. Since he has not yet accurately learned that he is God by nature, he thinks and speaks as if Christ were a prophet to whom he might blamelessly ascribe reverence toward God. But this does not fit Christ at all. He is God by nature, and so he receives worship as their spiritual sacrifice from those who are reverent. (6.1 [2:48])

Again, in discourses with the disciples their ignorance shows how they have not yet understood fully who Jesus is. Commenting on Thomas's question and Jesus's response in John 14:5–6, Cyril insists that, as the way and the truth, he is "the rule and plumb line of an unerring understanding of God," and "true faith" is belief "in the true Son, that is, begotten of the substance of God the Father, not a bastard or a so-called son or a creature or handiwork," and he enlarges on this theme at length. But, he notes, all this Jesus says "enigmatically": he is "telling the truth" but "in shadows and enigmas" because "the divine nature is completely inaccessible." Jesus has seemed "to rebuke the disciples for their ignorance" but "he heals them by saying "from now on you do know him and have seen him" (John 14:7).

Thus Cyril finds repeated occasions to discuss the presence here of true divinity and the errors of heretical deductions concerning his secondary or inferior nature on the basis of his assumption of flesh. For him the author of the gospel anticipates these falsities. Cyril's lengthy essays repeat time and again the implicitly anti-Arian propositions of the Gospel's prologue—indeed, the majority of the theses in the subsequent books are concerned with this truth—the real presence of God the Word in flesh. These propositions we will sample further, indicating the occasion which generates each one. As we do so it will become noticeable how they principally concentrate on the fullness of the divine nature yet also from time to time induce some comment both on the fullness of the human nature and on the oneness of the person of Christ.

(1) *The Only-begotten is the imprint of God the Father's hypostasis, and there is no other imprint besides him that either exists or is conceived of* (*Comm. Jo.* 3.5). This is occasioned by John 6:27: the food "which the Son of Man will give you" is food which remains for eternal life, "for on him God the Father has set his seal." According to Cyril, Jesus is here anticipating charges against him arising from Jewish ignorance. His immediate concern is the point that the Son of Man "will supply God-befitting blessings." This is possible because "he has been sealed to the image of God the Father." The Son's being "of the substance of the Father" will soon be defended at length, but first Cyril states:

> he permits no division that cuts off the temple of the virgin from the true sonship; instead, he defines himself and wants to be understood as one. Christ is in fact truly one for our sake, wearing a royal purple robe, as it were, as his own clothing (I mean the human body) or a temple that is of course composed of body and soul since Christ is one from both. (3.5 [1:197])

(2) *The Son is not a participant in the life of someone else but he is life by nature; on the words "Just as the living Father sent me, and I bore witness to the Father, so whoever eats me will live because of me"* (*Comm. Jo.* 4.3). Occasioned by the words quoted from John 6:57, this passage may seem unclear, Cyril surmises, though it is not impenetrable "to those who choose to think rightly" (4.3 [1:239]). The Son's reference to his being sent refers to "nothing else but becoming flesh. When we say 'becoming flesh', however, we mean that he became a complete human being." Cyril proceeds to put words into the mouth of Jesus:

> The Father . . . has made me human. . . . And because I, God the Word, was begotten as life from that which is life by nature, I have filled my temple (that is my body) with my own nature now that I have become a human being. . . . I have transformed all of my flesh into my own life. I have not been overcome by the decay of the flesh, but rather I have overcome it as God. . . . [So] whoever receives me into themselves through participation in my flesh will live, being wholly transformed into me, the one who can give life because I am from a life-giving root, that is, God the Father. (4.3 [1:240])

The fact that this is attributed to the Father in the text is now taken to confirm Trinitarian theology, and Cyril explains:

> that it is the custom of Christ the Savior for our benefit to attribute those things that exceed human power to the activity of the Father because Christ humbled himself when he became human. . . . The one who begat him accomplishes everything through him. . . . He grants then to the *oikonomia* with the flesh what is appropriate while he attributes to God the Father the acts that exceed human power. (4.3 [1:240])

Opposition to this is cut off by the question, "Who will endure the hair-splitting of the heretic any longer?" After all, "the holy and God-breathed Scripture" makes it explicit that "he is God by nature," not a participant in the life of another. Cyril will eventually go on to prove that

> this is the bread from heaven: the bread that comes through Christ, that is his body. It makes the one who has tasted it live forever . . . the divine nature does not deign to give only a little. It gives every gift superabundantly, even if the gift surpasses our understanding so that the more simple disbelieve it because of the magnitude of the grace. (4.3 [1:233–34])

Not for nothing has Cyril's interest in the efficacy of the Eucharist been identified as a key driver for his christological proposals.[54]

(3) *The Son is God by nature, completely removed from likeness with creation as far as his substance is concerned* (*Comm. Jo.* 5.4). The trigger here is John 8:23: "You are from below, I am from above; you are of this world, I am not of this world." Exegesis of the first clause of the verse precedes the thesis statement and leads up to it (5.3 [1:329–30]). The thesis itself is followed by consideration of the second clause (5.4 [1:331–34]), a case where treating the thesis as a chapter heading seems decidedly misleading. The first clause, Cyril suggests, does not follow very clearly on what has gone before, yet "these words" are "full of a hidden *oikonomia.*" Cyril will eventually state that "wise reasoning will convince us that 'from above' refers to the Son's begetting from God the Father," but first he writes of the Jews' ignorance and misunderstanding, all of which he knows because "he is God" and he "pierces the division of soul and spirit, joints and marrow, and he judges the thoughts and intentions of the heart" (Heb 4:12).

54. See Henry Chadwick, "Eucharist and Christology in the Nestorian Controversy," *JTS* 2 (1951): 145–64.

They imagined "he would leave Judaea," for they "did not acknowledge, after all, that he was God by nature; when they saw only his earthly body, they kept thinking that he was a human being, one of us." The second clause of John 8:23 "strips his statement of all obscurity," and presents "more clearly what he has said enigmatically." This is what "above" means: "God surpasses everything that comes into being, not by spatial exaltation . . . ; rather he outstrips originate beings by the ineffable superiority of his nature. The Word says that he is not a work but a fruit and offspring of this nature." There is a radical distinction between Creator and creature, and this is affirmed right there in the text of scripture—indeed, Christ himself endorses anti-Arian dogma, according to Cyril.

(4) *The Son is in no way less than God the Father but equal and similar to him in nature* (*Comm. Jo.* 10.1). This thesis interrupts reflection on John 14:28, which speaks of Christ's departure and return, then adds, "If you loved me, you would rejoice that I am going to the Father, because my Father is greater than I." Cyril has been enlarging upon the grief of the disciples at Jesus's departure, and the words he uses are to prevent their despondency, making it a word of comfort also for the readers of the gospel. But now he turns to the second half of the verse and notes how "he turns the occasion for grief into a reason for joy" (*Comm. Jo.* 10.1 [2:200–203]). He cross-references Paul's statement that it was better "to depart and be with Christ" (Phil 1:23) and uses it to "ascend to the mystery of Christ." He then paraphrases Philippians 2:6–7, which is referenced some forty times across the commentary and will become a classic reference point in the ensuing controversy. There follows yet another exposition of the purpose of the incarnation:

> to direct us all to the full knowledge of virtue, and through the incomparable power of his miracles to prepare us to behold the power and glory and exceeding authority that is in his divine nature; . . . to persuade those who had sunk to extreme ignorance to recover their understanding once again and to stop worshipping the creature rather than the creator and instead sign on with the one who is truly God by nature. (*Comm. Jo.* 10.1 [2:201])

To this catalog is added the fact that he overthrew the might of death, destroyed the power of sin, and so on. Understandably, then, "the holy disciples," not to mention we ourselves, desire "to be ever present with him."

But then Cyril needs to explain that "it was necessary, when the *oikonomia* for us was suitably accomplished, for him to return to his own glory and equality with God the Father." Alluding again to Philippians 2 and his humiliation, he states that

> while he was still on earth, though he was true God and Lord of all, he was thought to be no greater than one of us, at least by those who did not know his glory. (10.1 [2:201])

But "when the mystery was accomplished on our behalf . . . he showed the powers above that he was God." Psalm 24 celebrates his ascension and return; the Father set him at his right hand, and "no suspicion of inferiority" should jeopardize the "equal honor for the Son."

Cyril now recognizes that he has wandered off the Johannine passage and returns to showing "how sweet and desirable and precious it is for us always to be with Christ our Savior." However, he is soon back to those doctrinal issues, explaining why he said here "My Father is greater than I" and referring that statement to his presence as human, not to his sitting at God's right hand. Again the terminology of Philippians 2 dominates: he said it "as one who still has the appearance of a slave since the time had not yet come for him to be reinstated." His "natural place" was "equality with the Father" (*Comm. Jo.* 10.1 [2:203]). Cyril acknowledges he has written plenty about the equality of Son and Father, but he cannot eschew further words against "a certain ignorant heretic" before continuing with his exegesis. This includes the warning that "if he is not God by nature then we still worship the creature rather than the creator" (10.1 [2:206]). Indeed, it is a good few pages of invective and argument before he returns to John 14:29, the prediction which itself reinforces the conviction that "he is truly ascending to God the Father in heaven to rule with him and to take his seat with him as God and as the one begotten of him by nature as God" (10.1 [2:207]). The one speaking to the disciples in the farewell discourses of John's Gospel is, in Cyril's view, the divine Word/Son incarnate, a point confirmed by the second thesis in book 10.

(5) *The Son is of the same substance as God the Father, not a different or foreign nature as some twisted people say* (*Comm. Jo.* 10.2). This thesis introduces discussion of the true vine. The Father is the vinegrower, notes Cyril, and he "does not stand idly by while the Son nourishes us and keeps us in good condition in the Holy Spirit. Setting us right is the work of the entire, as it were, holy and consubstantial Trinity." For, "everything is from the Father, through the Son and in the Holy Spirit." Christ is the vine and we are the branches, and "even though he calls the Father the vinegrower you should not say he is of a different substance." That is not the point here: "he wants to show that the divine nature is both the root and the source of the spiritual fruit bearing and life that we have." The whole point of the illustration is not their "dissimilarity"; it has "nothing at all to do with the definition of their essence." Christ's "teach-

ing has a different goal." Again Cyril attacks "the insane heretic" for his false exegesis, and indeed section 10 of Athanasius's *On the Opinion of Dionysius* demonstrates that this text had been in contention in the Arian controversy. For Cyril the passage is about our "participation in the body of Christ and his precious blood" as "we are united so that he is in us and we are in him." Clearly for Cyril the prime target remains Arian exegesis, while one principal driver is his concern for the efficacy of the Eucharist.

This sample of Cyril's propositions is far from comprehensive, but surely enough has been considered to show how his commentary is dominated by concern about Arian exegesis, especially in the numbered theses that punctuate each book. However, it is precisely this anti-Arian reading of John's Gospel that generates themes that would become paramount in Cyril's defense of his position in the christological controversy: both the completeness of the human nature and the unity of Christ's person have emerged in the material already discussed.

2.2.1.3. Understanding the Oikonomia with the Flesh

Like Apollinaris, Cyril found it vital to differentiate between "God enfleshed" and "man inspired," between the incarnation of the truly divine Word of God and the inspiration of saints and prophets.[55] So already here, before the outbreak of controversy, Cyril is warning against the tendency of partitive exegesis to divide the Christ and produce "two Sons." We should consider a few examples:

(1) In the first chapter of the second book of his commentary, Cyril notes that in his debate with Nicodemus (John 3:12–15) Jesus states "that the Son of Man descended, refusing, after he became human, to be divided into two persons." He will not have it that "the temple taken from the virgin . . . is one son and the Word who appeared from the Father is another, except insofar as there is a distinction between what is appropriate to each one by nature. . . . Ultimately Christ is one from both, indivisible in sonship and God-befitting glory." Somehow the properties of each are conferred on the other:

> For now he says, "the Son of Man has descended from heaven," but at the time of his suffering he is afraid, terrified and distressed, and he himself is recorded as undergoing the sufferings that are appropriate to the humanity alone. (*Comm. Jo.* 2.1 [1:100])

55. See above, pp. 115–16 in section 1.1.

(2) In chapter 2 of book 4 of his commentary, while reflecting on John 6:53—the saying about eating the flesh of the Son of Man and drinking his blood—Cyril states that "his holy body too is no less life-giving, since it is in some way brought together and ineffably united with the Word who gives life to all." It is "counted as his" and "considered to be one with him." After his incarnation he is "indivisible" despite the fact that the Word from the Father and the temple from the Virgin are not the same in nature. They are one "by that coming together and ineffable concurrence." Moving to John 6:54 the unity is again underlined: instead of saying "my body" will raise up those who eat it, he says "I" will raise them up "on the grounds that he is not different from his own flesh. . . . [H]e refuses to be at all divided into a pair of sons after the union" (4.2 [1:238]). Cyril is still exercised by this as he comments on John 6:69:

> he would be understood as Christ [= anointed] by likeness to us and not in the same way as he is the Son. However, he is still one and unique—both by nature and by excellence, both before the flesh and with the flesh. He is not two as some think, who do not seem to understand the depth of the mystery. (*Comm. Jo.* 4.4 [1:258])

(3) Commenting on the phrase "I am the light of the world" (John 8:12), Cyril notes that he does not say, "In me is the light," but "I am the light," and suggests "that is so no one divides the Christ into a pair of Sons after the *oikonomia* of the incarnation." There is "one Lord, Jesus Christ," as Paul says (*Comm. Jo.* 5.2 [1:318]).

(4) Faith is "in the Son of God" (John 9:35), suggests Cyril, "not in a human being like one of us but in the incarnate God." When he reaches John 9:37 he spells it out:

> There are now some who think they are Christians who do not understand accurately the point of the *oikonomia* with the flesh. They dare to separate from the Word of God that temple that was assumed for us from the woman, and they divide the one true Son into two sons just because he became a human being. (*Comm. Jo.* 6.1 [2:51])

Philippians 2 is once again cross-referenced to show what the incarnation means. But:

> They say that the only begotten Son of God the Father, that is the Word who was begotten of his substance, is one, and the son of the woman is another.

> Since the divinely inspired Scripture proclaims the Son and Christ to be one, how could they not be full of ungodliness when they divide the one true Son into two? In that he is God the Word, he is thought of as different from the flesh. In that he is flesh, he is thought of as something different from the Word. However, in that the Word of God the Father became a human being, the distinction between the one and the other will have no force at all because of the ineffable union and conjunction. There is one and only one Son, both before and after he came together with the flesh. (6.1 [2:52])

On a number of other occasions Cyril insists there is no dyad or pair of Sons or Christs and protests against dividing or separating the temple from the Virgin and God the Word, insisting that, as Paul says, there is one Lord Jesus Christ (1 Cor 8:6).[56] Clearly he is already aware of the disturbing outcome in some quarters of the anti-Arian partitive exegesis and anticipates the protestations he will keep making once the controversy breaks.

However, in commenting on what he reads in John's Gospel, Cyril himself regularly appeals to "the *oikonomia* with the flesh" to account for all those things which, as they cannot pertain to the divine nature, must be referred to the human condition, such as tears, fear, weakness, ignorance, suffering, advancing or being promoted, receiving from or being sent by the Father—all those marks of inferiority cited by the Arians. Furthermore, Cyril constantly affirms that "flesh" means the whole creature, body, soul and mind. Thus, he purports to affirm the full humanity of the Christ, and indeed upholds the validity of partitive exegesis, despite his focus on the reality of Christ's divine nature. How does he do this? In his mind, it seems, the correct differentiation is between the Logos in his divine nature and the Logos incarnate. This, however, has two consequences. First, he runs the risk of his Christology seeming docetic, just as Athanasius had before him. At points in the *Commentary on John's Gospel* the Word almost seems to be playacting. Thus, when faced with Jesus's inquiry concerning Lazarus, "Where have you laid him?" (John 11:34), Cyril writes this: "he pretends to be ignorant, even though he is God by nature and knows all things"; for he has to insist that "his question conveys no ignorance on the part of him who for our sakes became like us" (*Comm. Jo.* 7 [2.90]). Second, despite his constant refrain about the flesh having a soul and a mind, he has always faced the charge of

56. See *Comm. Jo.* 8 [2:103] (frag. on John 12:23); *Comm. Jo.* 9 [2:134] (on John 13:31–32); [2:146–47] (on John 14:1); *Comm. Jo.* 10 [2:197] (frag. on John 14:24); *Comm. Jo.* 10.2 [2:215]; *Comm. Jo.* 12.1 [2:378–79].

Apollinarianism, for the Word so dominates the flesh which was "his own" that this supposedly whole man has no role to play. Indeed if he had some active role in the story of salvation he would in Cyril's mind be an inspired man rather than the enfleshed Logos.

But perhaps the attribution of Apollinarianism and crypto-docetism has been too hasty, and it is the commentary before us, rather than the slogans of the controversy, which in the end can take us deeper into Cyril's fundamental conception and indeed its scriptural basis. What I want to suggest here is that the *Commentary on John's Gospel* enables a more satisfactory account of what so often seems a paradoxical position. It is here that Cyril has to address the issues concerning Christ's knowing yet not knowing, grieving yet not grieving, fearing yet not fearing, willing yet not willing, and suffering yet not suffering.

It is time to explore more passages:

(5) In book 4 of his commentary Cyril discusses in the first chapter how it is that two wills seem to operate in the one Christ, something with which Apollinaris had great difficulty but something which Jesus's statement in John 6:38–39 seems to demand: "I have come down from heaven not to do my own will, but to do the will of the one who sent me."[57] Cyril reckons that "on the surface this statement may seem difficult"; indeed, "one might expect us to fall into insuperable difficulties from our opponents because of this statement" (*Comm. Jo.* 4.1 [1:216]). In other words, at first sight this seems to support the "two Sons" approach. Cyril takes the context seriously: the will of the Father is that none should be lost, that he should come down from heaven to nullify the power of death, and for that purpose he did not refuse to undertake things he would prefer not to—indeed, he willingly endured everything for us, though he would not have willed to suffer if his purpose for us could have been accomplished without suffering. "The suffering on the cross is both unwilled in a sense by Christ our Savior and willed because of us and the good pleasure of God the Father." Cyril cross-references Gethsemane and adds:

> Since the Word was God, immortal and incorruptible, and he was life itself by nature, he could not cringe before death. . . . Since he has come to be in the flesh, however, he yields to enduring what is proper to the flesh, and he allows himself to cringe before death when it is at the door so that he may show himself truly human. (4.1 [1:217])

57. See above, p. 116.

As we read on it becomes apparent that, despite first impressions, this is no charade.

> If it is possible, Father, he says, without undergoing death to obtain life for those who have fallen into death, if death may die without me dying . . . let this cup pass. . . . But if this may happen in no other way, not as I will, but as you will. You see how weak human nature is found to be, even in Christ himself, as far as that nature is concerned. But the Word, who is united to it, raises up in it courage worthy of God and re-educates it to a vigorous determination so that it does not entrust itself to what seems right to its own will but follows the divine purpose.

The apparent tension between the two wills Cyril turns not just into Christ's willing acceptance of his saving role but even into an exemplary case of human receptivity to the will and purpose of the divine Word, so as to overcome human terror in face of death. He also implicitly upturns the Apollinarian assumption that if Christ had a human soul or mind it would inevitably be in an adversarial relationship with the indwelling Word. For Cyril the new Adam's obedience recapitulates and reverses human resistance to accepting the will of the Father—at least if we correlate this discussion with his frequent cross-references to Paul as well as his articulation elsewhere of the overarching biblical narrative of fall and redemption. "The Spirit is willing but the flesh is weak," Cyril notes. He is clear that Christ was not unaware that it is "far beneath God-befitting dignity to seem inferior to death and to feel fear because of it." But he concludes that "death was not willed by Christ both because of the flesh and because of the ignominy of the suffering, but at the same time it was willed" for the eventual "salvation and life for all."

(6) We commented earlier on Cyril's treatment of Jesus's apparent ignorance in John 11:34 (*Comm. Jo.* 7 [2:90]).[58] Another frequent motif is found when Martha meets Jesus: "she errs concerning the truth . . . in that she addresses him not as God but as one of the saints" (7 [2:86]). In other words, Martha recognized him as only a man. This is evident from the fact that she "even gently hints that he is at fault for delaying and not coming immediately when he would have been able to help" (John 11:21–24). However, her subsequent response (John 11:25–27) is "a confession of faith," as she shifts from "a Christ or a son of God" to "the Christ, the Son of God," so showing that

58. See above, p. 151. As noted above, our manuscript evidence for book 7 of the *Commentary on John's Gospel* comprises only fragments.

her faith "is in the Son, not in a creature" (*Comm. Jo.* 7 [2:87]). Thus Martha becomes an example to the faithful under instruction.

Mary's meeting with Jesus, however, generates another kind of response:

> he condescends to her and reveals his human nature by weeping and being troubled when he sees her weeping, and the Jews who had come with her weeping. . . . Since Christ is not only God by nature but also human, he undergoes human experience with the rest of us. (*Comm. Jo.* 7 [2:89])

At first this seems a typical anti-Arian point. However, Cyril continues: "When grief begins to stir in him and his holy flesh inclines to tears he does not allow it to indulge those tears without restraint, as we often do," and then he exploits the extraordinary Johannine language suggesting violent emotion and agitation. He reads John 11:33, usually now rendered as "deeply moved in spirit," to mean "he was troubled *by* the Spirit" and explains that "by the power of the Holy Spirit he rebukes his own flesh," while the flesh, "since it cannot bear the movement of the divine nature within it, trembles and gives the appearance of being troubled" (*Comm. Jo.* 7 [2:89]). That, Cyril thinks, is what his agitation refers to; "otherwise," he asks, "how could he have experienced trouble?" The question presumes, as ever, that the divine nature must be trouble free, but now Cyril underlines this fresh notion that the flesh

> is being rebuked by the Spirit and taught to have feeling beyond its own nature. That is, after all, why the almighty Word of God came to be in the flesh, or rather became flesh, so that by the energies of his Spirit he might strengthen the weaknesses of the flesh, free its nature from feelings that are too earthly, and transform it, as it were, to only such feelings as are pleasing to God. Now it is an infirmity of human nature to be tyrannized by grief. But this infirmity, along with the others, is neutralized first in Christ so that this benefit may extend to us as well. (*Comm. Jo.* 7 [2:89])

Once more, then, we are being urged to understand how the natural responses of the creaturely flesh are overridden by the divine power of the indwelling Logos, but intriguingly the whole point is that this is exemplary and pedagogic, demonstrating the same possibility for other creaturely human beings. A little further on Cyril will again write:

> he fiercely rebuked his grief and the tears that would flow from his grief. As God, he rebukes his human nature like a teacher, commanding it to be brave in sorrowful situations. (*Comm. Jo.* 7 [2:91])

The narrative context, of course, makes this particularly applicable to grief in the face of death, and Cyril had already put Christ's weeping in the whole context of salvation:

> The Lord weeps when he sees the man who was made in his image succumb to corruption . . . so that he may put an end to our tears. That is also why he died, to free us from death. (*Comm. Jo.* 7 [2:90])

Rather than for Lazarus in particular, it seems, "he actually wept out of pity for human nature as a whole."

These comments are woven into a paragraph that is focused on the weeping as an exemplary act:

> he does no more than weep, and then immediately checks his tears. This is so he does not appear cruel and inhuman as he teaches us not to give in excessively to grief over the dead." (*Comm. Jo.* 7 [2:90])

This reinforces an earlier point: Cyril turns Jesus's joining in Mary's weeping into pastoral advice not "to correct those in throes of mourning" (*Comm. Jo.* 7 [2:89]). But here he adds, "It is one thing to be sympathetic, another to be effeminate and unmanly"—he has "allowed his flesh to cry a little, even though he is by nature tearless and immune to all grief," yet he also "immediately checks his tears."

Cyril's attitude here must surely be informed by contemporary ethical attitudes toward the mastery of excess passion. On approach to the tomb, Jesus is again "troubled": Cyril takes that to refer to "the will struggling with a sort of movement" (*Comm. Jo.* 7 [2:91]). This enigmatic statement, I suggest, provides a clue to the meaning of his notorious paradox: *apathōs epathen* indeed enables this chapter's illuminating insight and demands something of a digression.[59]

Excursus on *Apatheia*

In ancient philosophy *apatheia* was not only a presumed characteristic of the divine; it had long been a significant, if contested, ethical ideal, particularly but not only among the Stoics, and latterly among

59. My previous inchoate treatment of this can be found in my article "A Reconsideration of Alexandrian Christology," *JEH* 22 (1971): 103–14.

Christian ascetics such as Evagrius.[60] The Aristotelian alternative was *metriopatheia*—moderation of the passions. Some philosophers actually thought that, like the divine, the soul was impassible by nature; indeed, the Neoplatonist Plotinus could call psychological sufferings *apathē pathē*, just as Cyril could suggest that the impassible Logos suffered without suffering—*apathōs epathen*.[61]

Apatheia did not imply, as Jerome mockingly suggested, "insensibility like that of a stone" (*Ep.* 133)—indeed Stoics found it compatible with *eupatheiai*, which included joy, kindness, goodwill, and even love, while Evagrius states that "love is the offspring of impassibility" (*Praktikos* 81). After all, true love of another requires detachment from the selfish desire to possess and control. Those positive virtues were not classed as *pathē*, then, for *pathos* implied passivity, *being subjected to* something external or even internal, not being in control—hence its inappropriateness to the divine. Disturbance and agitation were the *pathē* from which to be freed, and that meant exercising rational judgement as to whether fear, anxiety, anger, jealousy, lust, and so on were appropriate responses to the situation, rather than giving in and succumbing to such destructive emotions.

Propatheiai, otherwise known as "first movements," were involuntary: shuddering, pallor, tears, sinking feelings. But these were not yet treated as *pathē*—indeed, *apatheia* meant the will to take control and not give way to such involuntary reactions. The following statement attributed to Posidonius captures this widely accepted ethical principle, though its exact terminology (associating *pathē* more closely with "movements") reflects complex debates about the most appropriate psychological analysis:

> For it is necessary both that this [the rational element] should acquire understanding of the truth and that the emotional movements (*hai kata pathos kinēseis*) should be blunted through habituation to good practices, if one is going to display a person with better character.[62]

60. For a comprehensive study of the complexities of debate across philosophical and Christian literature, see Richard Sorabji, *Emotion and Peace of Mind: From Stoic Agitation to Christian Temptation* (Oxford: Oxford University Press, 2000).

61. Plotinus, *Enneads* 3.6.1, as quoted by Chadwick, "Eucharist and Christology."

62. As quoted by Sorabji, *Emotion*, 96, from Galen, *On the Placita of Hippocrates and Plato* 5.5.29.

Propatheia may be said to have normally constituted "the frontier between being involuntarily subject to external forces and being an agent who initiated self-directed actions."[63] From Origen to Evagrius, *logismoi* (bad thoughts or temptations) functioned in a similar way: not yet sins, but potentially so if not resisted.

Of particular interest is the way Didymus the Blind exploits the notion of *propatheia*. A respected Alexandrian teacher who had lived to the age of eighty-five and died as the fourth century ended, he was one of the first to espouse positive arguments for acknowledging the human soul of Christ, thus resisting Apollinarian Christology within the so-called "Alexandrian" tradition. Neither soulless flesh nor divinity needs food or sleep, he suggested; therefore, the ineffable incarnation was not without soul. Indeed, the weaknesses and passions of Jesus Christ described in scripture should be attributed to his fallible human soul; he assumed not merely bodily pains and weaknesses but also psychological tensions and mental suffering (*Trin.* 3.21).[64] The soul of Jesus was no different in nature from that of other human beings, but he remained sinless in spite of temptation and the possibility of succumbing to it. Transcripts of Didymus's teaching on the Psalms and Ecclesiastes were discovered among the Tura Papyri, and these show the complex ways in which Didymus used *propatheia* in his exegesis.[65] For example, he describes how Judas moved from Satan's initial prompting (*propatheia*) to the act of betrayal as well as accounts for Christ's temptations and his agony in Gethsemane: because disturbance within "remains as a deliberation within Christ's own mind, it is properly called a *propatheia*, and does not constitute the passion of 'fear.'"[66] Indeed, Didymus affirms that Christ's human soul is never separated from the divine Word by thought or idea or disturbance, but it does experience that agitation called *propatheia*, which is not itself sin but tempts the rational soul to give in: "it would have no glory or dignity or praise or crown if it were not agitated."

---

63. Richard A. Layton, "*PROPATHEIA*: Origen and Didymus on the Origin of the Passions," *VC* 54 (2000): 262.

64. Cf. M. F. Wiles, "The Nature of the Early Debate about Christ's Human Soul," *JEH* 16 (1965): 139–51.

65. For the following discussion and quotations, see Layton, "Origin of the Passions" and also his book *Didymus the Blind and His Circle in Late-Antique Alexandria* (Urbana: University of Illinois Press, 2004).

66. Layton, "Origin of the Passions," 280–81.

This, then, is the philosophical and ascetical context for Cyril's comments on Jesus checking his tears as he meets Mary; Cyril actually wrote, "he experiences grief beginning to 'move' within, but does not permit his flesh to 'suffer' this [*touto pathein*]."[67] The Evangelist, he now writes, is amazed at his tears, as indeed were his enemies, for "those who achieve the pinnacle of philosophy and have a brilliant reputation in it shed tears with the greatest reluctance because they use their manliness to overcome every misfortune" (*Comm. Jo.* 7 [2:90]). As noted just before our excursus, Cyril understood "troubled" as "the will struggling with a sort of *movement*," in other words, with a *propatheia*. It struggles "according to its power, because it fiercely rebuked his grief and the tears that would flow from his grief" (*Comm. Jo.* 7 [2:91]). So although Christ suffered (*epathen*) he did so with *apatheia*; that is, he was not subjected by the weakness of the flesh or the flinching of the soul but overcame these "first movements" or *propatheiai*. Maybe *apathōs epathen* did not seem quite so impossibly paradoxical to Cyril, and his hearers or readers, as it does to us. For it was, as Cyril insists, pedagogic and exemplary, and it is hardly to be understood as simply the dominating and inexorable suppression of the flesh assumed by the impassible Logos within. True he does set alongside these comments the movement of the divine within rebuking and teaching the human nature, yet he also presumes the willing cooperation of the rational human soul to deal with the involuntary *propatheia* of grief and reach *apatheia* in itself.

(7) In a fragment from book 8 of his commentary, Cyril comments on John 12:27–28: "Now my soul is troubled. And what should I say—'Father, save me from this hour?' No, it is for this reason I have come to this hour. Father, glorify your Son" (*Comm. Jo.* 8 [2:105–7]). Modern commentators often suggest that these verses are the Johannine equivalent to the Synoptic Gethsemane narrative. Cyril does not make that connection here, but his discussion confirms our reading of the previous passages explored. He makes the following points:

- The human nature is easily troubled; the divine power is "inflexible." The thought of death "attempts to trouble" Jesus, but the power of the divine nature "immediately subdues the passion."
- It was necessary that "he show himself . . . a man born of a woman, not in appearance and fantasy . . . experiencing the full human condition except for sin."

67. Compare the English translation quoted above, p. 154: "When grief begins to stir in him . . . he does not allow [the flesh] to indulge those tears without restraint."

- Human emotions were "profitably stirred up in Christ, not that the emotions should prevail . . . but that once stirred up, they should be cut short by the Word. Our nature is thus transformed, first in Christ, into a better and more divine condition. . . . In Christ, as the first fruits, human nature was returned to newness of life. . . . That is why he is called 'second Adam' by the divine Scriptures."
- Just as he hungered and thirsted, so he accepted "the mental anguish that comes from suffering, since that is a human characteristic." This makes it clear that he had a rational soul: as he experienced passion belonging to the flesh, so also "passion of the rational soul." In particular, he experienced anguish in anticipation of what is going to happen—namely, the crucifixion.
- The passion of fear "belongs neither to the impassible divinity nor to the flesh"—it "belongs to the thought processes of the soul." "The Word of God, then, united to himself the entire nature of a human being in order to save the whole person. For what is not assumed is not healed." Cyril notably adopts here the classic anti-Apollinarian slogan used by Gregory of Nazianzus.[68]
- He "transforms the passion of fear into courage, practically saying: Death is nothing."

Cyril now turns to the prayer offered in John 12:28, making the usual point that Christ makes his request to the Father as a human being while also recognizing that the cross is the hour of glory. "He subjected himself to suffering willingly for us." That this was voluntary on his part, and not because he was overtaken by the hostile acts of the Jews, is a refrain repeatedly rehearsed by Cyril. It is a point that coheres not just with elements of the Johannine narrative (e.g., it is often noted how Jesus is in control of his own arrest in John 18:4–6) but also with the notion that it was with *apatheia* that he suffered—he was neither passive nor subject to anything beyond his control but willed to undergo the passion for our salvation. Once again Cyril's discussion culminates in the suggestion that this was an exemplary act:

> He says this also as an example to us that we should pray not to fall into temptation, but once we have fallen into trials, we should bear them nobly and not avoid them but pray to be saved by God. (*Comm. Jo.* 8 [2:106])

Cyril is clear that just as "death was destroyed" by "the Savior dying," so too "the passions of the flesh." So, "if he had not been afraid, our nature

68. See above, p. 116 in section 1.1.

would not have been freed from fear"; if he had not grieved, been troubled and alarmed,

> there would be no escape from these conditions. For every human experience, you will find the same corresponding experience in Christ. (*Comm. Jo.* 8 [2:107])

Passions are stirred up "not to overcome him as they do us," but so as to destroy them, "transforming our nature to a better condition."

***

In the light of the passages now reviewed we can see that even though much of what Cyril writes can appear on the surface to imply that the power of the divine nature simply overrides the frailties of the flesh assumed—indeed, there are reasons why Cyril has been accused of crypto-docetism and unconscious Apollinarianism—yet, that is not the whole story. The presence of the Logos within enables the complete human nature assumed by the Word to succeed where Adam failed, to find, even in the midst of suffering, the *apatheia* which is the soul's mastery of its agitation, the peace of mind which accepts the will of the Father and receives the power of the Spirit. In Christ the human *ego* was the instrument of salvation by being entirely receptive of the re-creating presence of the Logos, so achieving its own *apatheia*. As human he was our teacher and example, reversing Adam's disobedience and demonstrating humankind's true being as receptive of divine grace and responsive to the divine will.

2.2.1.4. Cyril's View of the Johannine Christ

When it comes to the passion narrative, Cyril for the most part follows through the story quite straightforwardly. He does, however, draw out a number of consistent motifs, most of which have already been anticipated—the voluntary nature of his suffering and death; the exemplary character of his acceptance of the mockery and ignominy to which he is subjected; the release from sin, suffering, and death effected for all humankind; the recapitulation and reversal of Adam's fall; and so on. Two final passages are worth exploring, however, as they provide overviews of the Christology Cyril deduces from the Johannine Gospel.

(1) In chapters 8–9 of the eleventh book of his *Commentary on John's Gospel*, Cyril comments on John 17:9–11, part of what is known as Jesus's high priestly prayer. Cyril opens with this statement:

> He once more mediates as a human being, the reconciler and mediator between God and human beings. And as our truly great and all-holy high priest, he appeases the wrath of the Father by his prayers, sacrificing himself for us. He himself is the sacrifice and the priest; he himself is the mediator; he himself is the spotless victim, the true lamb "who takes away the sin of the world" (*Comm. Jo.* 11.8 [2:282])

Cyril goes on to describe Moses as a type and shadow of Christ's mediation, asking for mercy and establishing the sacrificial system. "But Christ appeared in the last days as a high priest and mediator, superior to the types and outlines in the law." The one who "asks as a human being, also grants as God," he writes, and then develops Christ's role as "atoning sacrifice" (1 John 2:2) and mediator. When it comes to John 17:11, which reads, "Holy Father, protect them by your name that you have given me, so that they may be one, as we are one," he comments:

> He always maintains the combination of two facts into one. I am referring to the human nature, which possesses lowliness like ours, and the divine nature, which is pregnant with the highest glory of all. . . . After all, he is God who became human, holding a kind of middle position, as it were, by the ineffable and unspeaking concurrence of the two, so that he does not depart from the limits of the true divine nature, and neither does he completely leave behind those of the human nature. (*Comm. Jo.* 11.9 [2:284])

Cyril now elaborates on Christ's self-chosen humiliation—his humbling of himself willingly for us. Then again he emphasizes how his statement

> always and elegantly preserves for us the double character so that in the same statement, we see him who is God by nature speaking and also a true human being. He skilfully combines the lowliness of the human nature with the glory of the ineffable nature, and he blamelessly and irreproachably maintains an equal claim on both. (*Comm. Jo.* 11.9 [2:285])

This, Cyril asserts, is not dragging Christ down to the inferior precisely because it was a voluntary emptying. "He always remains what he was and is and will be, but he lowered himself for us to what he was not before."

(2) While dealing with the Evangelist's summing up of his purpose in John 20:30–31 in book 12, Cyril decides to "add the following" and launches into a tirade against those

> who out of ignorance split up the faith and then try to teach others to think that there are two christs. They cut him up into a human being, properly speaking, and God the Word, properly speaking, even after the completely ineffable and incomprehensible union and coming together with the body. (*Comm. Jo.* 12.1 [2:378–79])

Cyril invites us to probe further the meaning of the flesh's union with him and discover that "the Word is one entity with his flesh without being changed into flesh." The nature of the Word is "unalterable and unchangeable and admits of no turning whatsoever"; but in accordance with scripture "we maintain . . . that Jesus is one Christ and one Son." As an analogy he compares this union to the inseparable union of soul and body in one human being, an analogy fraught with potential misunderstanding. Be that as it may, this section of the *Commentary on John's Gospel* sets out in summary form the key principles that will inform Cyril's position as the christological controversy develops.

2.2.1.5. Cyril's Commentary on John's Gospel: Concluding Observations

This perhaps rather over-long exploration of Cyril's *Commentary on John's Gospel* evidently offers a prime example for exploring our principal question about how scriptural exegesis and doctrine related to one another. Engagement with this commentary has reinforced the picture sketched in this chapter's first section. The anti-Arian settlement had generated doctrinal propositions. These then shaped the reading of scripture, while exegesis of scripture generated ever more propositions coherent with the fundamental insight that God's Word was in every sense divine. All this, however, raised further questions about how the fully divine Logos could possibly be incarnated as a human being, a truth to which scripture clearly bore witness. Two approaches were emerging, each with roots in Athanasius's anti-Arian exegesis. One of these Cyril constantly expounds as he interprets the narrative and discourses of the gospel; the other he repeatedly repudiates, despite maintaining its essential insights in his own way. Thus is the ground prepared for those two approaches to come into conflict. It is time to explore other post-Nicene exegesis of John's Gospel.

2.2.2. *Other Post-Nicene Commentary on John's Gospel*

Maurice Wiles has done pioneering work on the relevant commentaries and homilies on the Gospel of John. The eighth chapter of his book *The Spiritual Gospel* sets out to compare Cyril's commentary with that of Theodore of Mopsuestia, the latter being extant in Syriac.[69] Wiles's work also weaves in occasional references to the work of John Chrysostom. We will rehearse Wiles's findings and then concentrate on Chrysostom's eighty-eight *Homilies on John's Gospel*.[70]

Wiles expresses surprise at how much all these commentators have in common. The surprise is prompted by Cyril's eventual attacks on Diodore and Theodore as well as his fourth anathema against anyone who "distributes between two persons or hypostases the terms used in the evangelical and apostolic writings, whether spoken of Christ by the saints or by himself about himself."[71] Those sharp confrontations during the controversy predispose the reader to expect greater divergences in these commentaries, even though they belong to the period prior to its outbreak. Wiles attributes the commonalities to shared presuppositions, presuppositions which, in his view, constitute "a straitjacket . . . to which the message of the Gospel will not succumb."[72]

The first common presupposition is that there are "certain things which cannot on any account be ascribed to divinity," notably "any kind of change." Two other presuppositions include the inapplicability of preexistence to the flesh or human nature, and the inapplicability "to the Word of God" of "anything that would imply an inferiority to the Father." So "widely differing conclusions are ruled out from the start by these accepted principles."[73] Wiles identifies the foot-washing episode as one exception generating real difference in exegesis: Theodore ascribes the action to "our Lord's man," whereas for Cyril "it is of the essence of the meaning of the sign that it is the act of one who is Lord of all"—a sign of humility and self-emptying. However, this is just taking different options within the same kind of "two-nature" analysis, and the fundamental similarity of approach required by an unquestioning adoption of those common presuppositions means that differences are only detectable by observing how each maneuvers around the exegetical problems posed.

69. See Wiles, *Spiritual Gospel*, 129–47. Syriac text with Latin translation of Theodore of Mopsuestia by J. M. Vosté, *Theodori Mopsuesteni Commentarius in Evangelium Johannis Apostoli*, 2 vols., CSCO 115–16 (Leuven: Peeters, 1940).

70. Text of John Chrysostom's *Homilies on John's Gospel* from PG 59; English translation, unless otherwise noted, from Thomas Aquinas Goggin, trans., *Commentary on Saint John the Apostle and Evangelist*, 2 vols., FC (Washington, DC: Catholic University of America Press, 2000). See also the translation in *NPNF*[1] 14.

71. Wiles, *Spiritual Gospel*, 130–31.

72. Wiles, *Spiritual Gospel*, 136.

73. Quotations in this and the following paragraph taken from Wiles, *Spiritual Gospel*, 131–35.

So Wiles shows how the two-nature exegesis is "regularly employed by Theodore in a neat and systematic way," this "alternation of reference" even taking place "within the context of a single verse or saying," despite everything in the gospel being "attributed to the one person." He illustrates this by reference to John 16:28: "I came out from the Father and am come into the world; again I leave the world and go unto the Father":

> None of this can be applied literally to Christ's divine nature, because movement is inapplicable to divinity. But the first half cannot be applied at all to Christ's human nature which has no original or natural communion with the Father. It must therefore refer to his divine nature in a non-literal sense. The second half, however, cannot refer to the divine nature, even in a metaphorical sense, because it implies progress towards God. It must refer to the taking up into the Godhead of Christ's human nature. The two halves of the one saying, therefore, must refer to the two different natures.

Nevertheless, Theodore does appeal to "the unity existing between the two natures" as justifying this combination and uses the same appeal to deal with awkward texts, such as John 3:16 or 6:33, which prove not easily susceptible to his two-nature exegesis.[74] Apart from such exceptions, however, Theodore "applies the principles of two-nature exegesis simply and directly."

By comparison Cyril seldom applies the two-nature exegesis "with the neatness and precision of Theodore"—the "intermingling and apparent confusion is of the essence of the system." Two natures may be distinguishable "in thought," but "the unity of the person of Christ is the more fundamental reality." Wiles notes Cyril's attacks on "those who would divide Christ into two sons," and reckons that Cyril is able "to do more justice to divine condescension." Yet he also notes the risk Cyril runs of his language being taken to denote "pretence" on the part of the divine Word acting as human.[75] In the next several pages Wiles explores how these exegetes deal with Jesus's ignorance, his prayers, and his emotion. We have already seen how Cyril wriggled through these issues, and it is perhaps surprising to find that Theodore does not, apparently, deal with them more easily by simply referring them to the

74. E.g., John 3:16 seems "to associate suffering with the divine nature, by asserting it of the only begotten Son," and John 6:33 seems "to assert the heavenly preexistence of Christ's body" when it speaks of "the bread of God which comes down from heaven." See Wiles, *Spiritual Gospel*, 134–35.

75. Wiles, *Spiritual Gospel*, 135–38.

human nature. The questions implying ignorance he explains away very much as Cyril does. John 17 he turns into prophecy rather than prayer, prophecy spoken for the sake of the disciples; emotion is referred to Jesus's human soul or anger at the Jews' faithlessness and Judas's treachery, while grief is hardly to the point when he is just about to raise Lazarus to life again, so it must be exemplary. Yet again the commonalities are exemplified.

And perhaps most striking of all is the fact that these commentators regard "the application of the two-nature exegesis" as "a means of making clear the actual intentions of Jesus as he spoke." They assume that "Jesus is both God and man with a perfect right to speak as either," and "alternation from one mode of speaking to the other" depended on "the situation of the Gospel setting" or the pedagogic need to provide believers with "a clear conception alike of the Lord's divinity and of his incarnation." So

> All three commentators[76] are agreed in applying this principle to the controversy between Jesus and the Jews which followed the sabbath healing of the man by the pool of Bethesda. Jesus justifies himself by an assertion of his oneness with the Father (John v. 17). When this arouses the fury of the Jews, Jesus rewords his assertion in language which at least appears to give him a humbler relation to the Father and which refers to his human nature (John v. 19, 20). He then goes on to lay claim to the two divine functions of raising the dead and judging the world, but finally redresses the balance once more and clips the wings of their anger by asserting that the ability to do these things is given to him as Son of Man by the Father (John v. 26, 27).[77]

This kind of thing we have already observed in Cyril's work; it is, however, particularly characteristic of Chrysostom's homilies to revel in such alternation between the divine and fleshly, whether on the part of the Evangelist or of Jesus himself. To Chrysostom we now turn.

Before examining the Christology that emerges from Chrysostom's *Homilies on John's Gospel* it is worth acknowledging the striking difference in atmosphere compared with Cyril's "more dogmatic" commentary, pedagogic though these homilies evidently are. The preacher's principal objects are, to borrow a phrase, "parsing the broken heart of humankind, and praising the loving

76. John Chrysostom has by now been drawn into the comparison of Theodore and Cyril.

77. Quotation here and earlier in the paragraph from Wiles, *Spiritual Gospel*, 139.

heart of Christ."[78] As he moves through the gospel narrative, Chrysostom is constantly sketching the motives and fears, the hopes and intentions, the misconceptions and needs of the characters in the story, not least so as to draw out morals for his audience, while each of his homilies, as ever, ends with a hortatory section more or, all too often, less coherent with the previous exegesis. All his favorite themes are to be found—the positive virtue of almsgiving and the damaging nature of pride and vainglory, avarice and gluttony, anger and envy, fear and depression—and often they emerge within exegesis of the gospel narrative itself, as may be shown by a few examples:

- Homily 16 opens with reflection on "the destructive power of envy," and this enables John the Baptist's witness to Christ (John 1:19–27) to shine with the light of self-effacement. The homily climaxes with a warning against pride (*Hom. Jo.* 16.1).
- Homily 29 picks up similar themes with respect to the apparent rivalry between the disciples of John and those following Jesus (John 3:22–30): "He did not seize upon glory for himself, but sent his listeners off to Christ," and we are taught by this "that vainglory is the cause of all evils, for it led them to envy" (29.1, 3).
- Homily 37 opens with "the profit to be derived from the sacred scriptures," which are "sufficient for every need," "a treasury containing every sort of remedy" against "senseless pride," the "fire of concupiscence," and the "love of riches." The sacred scriptures also enable one "to despise pain, or to cultivate cheerfulness and acquire patience," by following the example of the paralytic, "waiting for 38 years, and each year seeing others cured," while himself "still burdened with his malady" (37.1). This had already inspired reflection in the previous homily on how easily most of us give up when prayer is not answered (36.2).
- Homily 69 opens with Chrysostom urging his hearers "to flee the passions that corrupt the soul," especially those that "give rise to many sins" such as avarice and vainglory. This is rooted in the text of John 12:43: "they loved human glory more than the glory that comes from God" (69.1).

I could go on, but let that be enough to make the point. Needless to say, Jesus himself becomes exemplary in facing insult, and even death, without fear.

78. This apt phrase describes a fictional mid-twentieth-century Presbyterian preacher in the American Midwest in Marilynne Robinson's novel *Home* (London: Virago, 2008), 52.

The pedagogy of Chrysostom's homilies, however, is not confined to moral concerns. For faith involves matters of truth, and the dangers of Arian and Sabellian thinking are as significant for him as they are for Cyril. It hardly needs saying that the Johannine Prologue is expounded as affirming the truth about the divine Logos against Arian misreading. That a mere fisherman could produce this teaching shows it is not "human but divine and heavenly" (*Hom. Jo.* 2.6). The Evangelist passes over the Father and focuses on the Word because God the Unbegotten was already recognized as First Cause, whereas the Only-begotten was not known. He does not discuss "substance" because it is impossible to say "what God is in substance—but everywhere he reveals Him to us through His works" (2.8). Chrysostom emphasizes the absolute priority of God as Creator; and in his third homily picks up the distinction between the Son of God and adopted sons of God, a point underlined further in a much later homily by insisting on the significance of the definite article used with reference to "the Word," "the Son," "the Lamb," "the Christ," "the prophet," "the true Light," and "the Good Shepherd" by contrast with "many lambs and prophets and Christs and sons" (18.2). "Safeguarded by this article," says Chrysostom, "He has nothing at all in common with the creature." Back in the third homily he argues that "'was' indicates eternity," and "the Son of God is before not only time, but all previous ages, since He is their Creator and Maker" (3.2). John gave first place to his eternity, but in case anyone should say he was Unbegotten, he added, "He was with God"—not "in God"—"so making clear to us his eternity as to person." It is noticeable how grammatical details are exploited to substantiate doctrinal conclusions.

Chrysostom next leads us into an imaginary dialogue with someone claiming the Son was created, quoting classic Arian prooftexts (*Hom. Jo.* 3.3). He insists that he "infinitely transcends the created universe," and his response to an appeal to Acts 2:36, which reads "God made Him Lord and Christ," is to ask why the words "this Jesus whom you crucified" were added to Acts 2:36: "Are you ignorant that some words are said of his pure nature [as God], others of his incarnate nature?" The problem is if you refer them all absolutely to Christ's Godhead, then "you will also conclude that God can suffer." A picture of blood flowing forth "from the Deity itself and its ineffable nature," of the divine being "pierced and cut by nails, instead of Christ's flesh, in the crucifixion," is dismissed as blasphemy, while the designations "Lord" and "Christ" are attributed not to his "essence" but to his "rank," not to his "power" but to his "anointing." The statement in Acts under discussion "refers entirely to the humanity [of Christ]." The anti-Arian partitive exegesis is being vividly deployed to protect the divine nature from involvement in suffering, anticipating the way in which this would become a prime anxiety of the so-called Antiochenes. Further appeal to texts such as Acts 17:31, where he is referred to as "a man appointed," are countered by the statement that

> Christ did not reveal His Godhead to us all at once. At first He was thought to be the Prophet and the Christ, but merely man; later it appeared from His deeds and words what He was . . . Inasmuch as they were not then able to understand clearly about His Godhead, He therefore treated of matters pertaining to His humanity, in order that their hearing, having been exercised by these ideas, might become prepared for the rest of His teaching. (*Hom. Jo.* 3.4)

Later homilies will demonstrate how this progressive disclosure is played out in the narrative of the gospel. Chrysostom now insists that "neither John nor anyone else—whether Apostle or Prophet—said he was a creature." As he himself said so many lowly things of himself "for the sake of teaching humility," he would "certainly not have failed to say so" if he had been a creature. But "as a matter of fact, he did exactly the opposite," says Chrysostom (*Hom. Jo.* 3.4), quoting various words found later in the gospel to demonstrate his "complete equality with Him," including:

- I am in the Father and the Father in me (John 14:11)
- He who sees me sees also the Father (John 14:9)
- As the Father raises the dead and gives them life, even so the Son also gives life to whom he will (John 5:21)
- My Father works even until now, and I work (John 5:17)
- Even as the Father knows me and I know the Father (John 10:15)
- I and the Father are one (John 10:30)

The fourth homily turns to the incarnation and raises a question that we have already found Cyril addressing:

> John merely hints briefly at the incarnation by saying further on, "And the Word became flesh." Why does he omit all the other details—His conception, His birth, His upbringing, growth—and discourse to us about His eternal generation? (*Hom. Jo.* 4.1)

For Chrysostom it is all too easy to focus on the human story as did Paul of Samosata. The Evangelist's sights are set higher, yet the incarnation is not neglected.[79] He warns his hearers to think of the Word as neither "a work of the Creator" nor "simply a word." This Word is "a Being, a distinct Person, proceeding from the Father Himself without alteration," a fact indicated by the text itself: "with God" reveals "His co-eternity." It is "a very human way of speaking" to jump to the conclusion that as Son he is younger than or subject to the Father. "Our discussion at present is about God, not about human nature." Hebrews 1:3 captures the point with its image of sunlight bursting forth from the sun's substance. With further argument Chrysostom leads his audience to grasp the utter difference between Creator and creature. Arianism is clearly still the prime target, and it takes Chrysostom another half-dozen homilies to work his way through one argument after another arising from the fourth-century struggles over the Father-Son relationship.

Finally in homily 11 he reaches "the Word became flesh." Again like Cyril, he insists that he

> in no wise lowered His own nature by this descent, but elevated us, who had always been in a state of ignominy and darkness, to ineffable glory. . . . His substance was not transformed into flesh, but remaining what He is, He thus took the form of a slave. (*Hom. Jo.* 11.1)

Both sides constantly cross-reference, or allude to, Philippians 2:7 in their language about the incarnation.

Now, however, we discern another Antiochene concern: this was not "an appearance, an act, an allegory"—it was "His assuming real flesh," and his being "made flesh" is not to be taken as parallel to his being "made a curse" (Gal 3:13). Yet it was not that "His substance changed into flesh, but that, after assuming flesh, His substance remained intact"—if it had changed he would no longer be God. Yet this was no mere appearance:

> By their union and conjoining, God, the Word, and the flesh are one, not as a result of commingling or disappearances of substances, but by some ineffable and inexplicable union. (*Hom. Jo.* 11.2)

We should observe here the willingness to affirm a union that "He Himself knows," even if we do not and cannot understand it. As much as Cyril, Chrysostom wanted to affirm the union but worried about the possible implication whereby the mediator becomes a hybrid of the two—mixture

79. Quotations in the rest of the paragraph from *Hom. Jo.* 4.1–3.

and confusion would be dangers the Antiochenes would discern in Cyril's "hypostatic union."

For Chrysostom, the relationship between the "substances" is best captured in the image implied by the second half of John 1:14: "dwelt among us" signifies that the flesh constituted the dwelling place of the unchangeable divine substance. That dwelling place and the one dwelling within it are to be differentiated. He quotes Amos 9:11: "I will raise up the tabernacle of David that has fallen"—it was "our human nature" that had had "an irreparable fall" and "it was not possible to raise it up" unless its original Creator were to reform it "by the regeneration of water and the Spirit." So "He dwells always in this tabernacle, for He put on our flesh"—a mystery both "awesome and ineffable" (*Hom. Jo.* 10.2).

So much for the Prologue. Once Chrysostom is into the narrative of the gospel he consistently relays the Evangelist's portrayal of a single central character—the one person of Christ—responding to various scenarios in action and word. Yet there is constant oscillation between the "lowly" and the "lofty" as that response is geared towards the misconceptions, needs and fears of the people, both then and now. Chrysostom hardly needs to emphasize the union simply because there is one *prosōpon* condescending to teach appropriately Jews or disciples, unbelievers or half-believers, sometimes demonstrating his real human presence, sometimes pointing to his actual divine origin, adapting what he says and does to the divine pedagogical purpose.[80] This observation of how the unity of the one *prosōpon* comes across in Antiochene exegesis of the gospel surely illuminates its use as a kind of technical term in the subsequent controversy. Cyril never understood it—for him *prosōpon* was too weak, implying just "outward appearance" or even "role."[81] Here it is clear that it points to the single person of Jesus Christ speaking and acting as one. Yet distinguishing the natures was of fundamental importance: the anti-Arian partitive exegesis remained crucial, yet there is hardly a single passage justifying the slur of teaching "two Sons."

It is time to consider a few passages:

(1) *Homily 21*: In the previous couple of homilies on John 1:41–49, Chrysostom had shown how Jesus "began to reveal his Godhead." Now reaching John 1:49–50 Chrysostom shows how Jesus leads Nathaniel to deeper understanding: Nathaniel's confession of him as Son of God associates the title

80. These homilies constantly substantiate the approach of Rylaarsdam in his study of *John Chrysostom*.

81. See below chapter 5, 1.2.

with king of Israel, so the title "Son of God" does not have the same meaning as when Peter confessed him "Son of God" at Caesarea Philippi; for "Peter confessed the Son of God as true God, while Nathaniel confessed Him as mere man." The Son of God is not king of Israel only, but of the whole world, Chrysostom explains, then suggests:

> As if the greater and better part were lacking this confession, He added the remaining words . . . "Amen, Amen, I say to you you shall see heaven opened, and the angels of God ascending and descending upon the Son of Man." Do you perceive how He gradually led him up from the earth and made him think of Him no longer merely as man? (*Hom. Jo.* 21.1)

(2) *Homilies 24–28*: these deal with Jesus's discourse with Nicodemus, who came by night and was "still held back by Jewish weakness." Yet Jesus "revealed to him the most sublime teachings, obscurely, to be sure, but nevertheless revealed" (*Hom Jo.* 24.1). Nicodemus, though acknowledging he had come "a teacher from God," was "still clinging to earth, still had a human opinion of him," treating him as "a prophet." Chrysostom affirms that

> the object which Christ strove to attain was not so much to make known His own dignity as to convince men that He was doing nothing in opposition to His Father. Therefore, He often appeared to be measuring His words to their limited understanding. (24.2)

Chrysostom contrasts this reserve with his miracles, suggesting that his opponents could dismiss claims made "on the basis of his words alone," but facts spoke for themselves. Nicodemus thought "he was uttering something complimentary," yet he had come nowhere near "true knowledge of Him." Often Christ spoke obscurely to induce questions and greater attentiveness, as he did here with Nicodemus, who asks: "How can a man be born when he is old?" Nicodemus in his perplexity "dragged what was said down to the lowliness of the flesh" (24.2–3).

The following homilies explore the notion of spiritual birth implied by Jesus's response and lead Nicodemus into "the ineffable meaning of this mystery" (26.1). However,

> when Jesus is at the point of arriving at teachings which are sublime, He frequently restrains Himself in consideration of the weakness of His hearers and does not dwell for long on subjects befitting His greatness, but rather

> on those which condescend to their lowliness. If the sublime and great is even said once, it is sufficient to establish that dignity as far as is possible for us to hear it, but unless things that are more lowly and approaching the understanding of the hearers were spoken repeatedly, lofty ideas would not easily be grasped by the ordinary listener. It is on this account, accordingly, that more of His words were lowly than sublime. (27.1)

Where he spoke in limited and earthly terms it is to be attributed to the limitations of his hearers; yet the point of his scaling "His remarks to the weakness of the listener" arose from "a desire to lead him gradually upward" (27.1).

Chrysostom now turns to John 3:13: "No one has ascended into heaven except the one who descended from heaven, the Son of Man." How is this connected to what is gone before? Well, Nicodemus had acknowledged Jesus as a teacher from God but had not yet realized he is more than a prophet. The term Son of Man does not simply mean his humanity; he "here called his entire Person, so to speak, by the name of its lesser part . . . for it was his custom frequently to name the whole from his Godhead and as often to name it from his humanity." Chrysostom has not been distracted into the kind of two-natures contortions that Wiles found in Theodore's exegesis of John 16:28—a text with equivalent exegetical problems.[82] Indeed he offers little or no focus on Christology as he moves on through the rest of John 3, dwelling on the passion, the saving love of God, judgment, and forgiveness. The whole discussion with Nicodemus presumes the one person of the Word, the Son incarnate, speaking enigmatically and with reserve about his real identity as he adapts his teaching to the level of the hearer.

(3) *Homilies 38 and 39*: here Chrysostom sums up Jesus's defense against the Jews over breaking the Sabbath by commenting:

> He made His defence neither as Man alone, nor as God alone, but now as one, again as the other. He united the two truths to be believed: both the condescension of the incarnation and the dignity of His Godhead. It is for this reason that in the present instance He made His defence as God. If He were to speak to them always from a human point of view only, they would have persisted in the same lowly opinion of Him. Therefore, in order to prevent this from happening, He brought His Father into the discussion. (*Hom. Jo.* 38.3)

82. See above, p. 164, note 74.

Next Chrysostom takes up the Jews' suspicion that by breaking the Sabbath and calling God his own Father he made himself equal to God; he is concerned to answer those who exploited that suspicion to denigrate the claim as untrue, appealing also to the words, "The Son can do nothing of himself" (John 5:19). Clearly Arians are again in mind. Chrysostom insists that it means he cannot do anything in opposition to the Father, and this was put more starkly to indicate that "his equality is undeviating and complete," and "results from identity of purpose and power and strength" (*Hom. Jo.* 38.4). This becomes a refrain as he tackles the ongoing debates in John 7–8, not to mention passages such as John 10:25–30. He is far more concerned about Arian misreading than any other christological question, as would be borne out by detailed study of Chrysostom's exegesis of the farewell discourses (homilies 73–80).

Homily 39 turns to the claim that judgment has passed to the Son (John 5:22–23), and Chrysostom tackles the deduction that the Son should therefore be called Father. He firmly makes the distinction between Father and Son, while insisting that, even if "He has the Father as cause," one should not imagine any difference of substance or inferiority of divinity: his coming as Judge proves his equality to the Father. Surveying the sequence he has traced, Chrysostom points out how

> He varied his discourse weaving together both lofty and lowly phrases and sentences, so that what he said might be readily accepted by those who were then present, and those who come afterwards might not be misled, since in truth they would receive from the lofty expressions the correct idea regarding the rest. . . . And so we have a correct explanation, and one worthy of God, for His speaking with humble words: namely, His condescension and His teaching us to act with moderation. (*Hom. Jo.* 39.1)

Chrysostom continuously challenges those who suggest that the Son's power or honor or glory is not equal to that of his Father, or that the one sent and the one sending cannot be of the same substance. The problem is "confining the discussion within human limits," and not appreciating that "all these things were said for no other reason than that we might know of that First Cause, and that we might not fall into the error of Sabellius." To dispel the "erroneous idea" of the Jews that he had not come from God "he placed before them not so much the lofty ideas of himself as the humble ones," saying he was "sent," taking "refuge in the Father, putting aside, for the time being, his own autonomy." They simply would not have "accepted his words" if "he had made all his statements in accordance with his proper dignity" (*Hom. Jo.* 39.2). Chrysostom both imagines himself into the situation implied by the Johannine narrative and arms his congregation against false doctrinal deductions, but it is the old heresies of Arius and Sabellius that preoccupy him.

As he works his way through chapter 5 the same points emerge time and again: from statements "of humble tenor" to "those couched in accordance with His proper dignity" Christ endeavors to make his words acceptable, implying identity and equality with the Father, on the one hand, and on the other condescension in the incarnation. Consider the following extracts:

> Do you perceive that the words which seem to be especially humble are the very ones that have sublime meaning concealed in them? What He implied is some such truth as this: not that the Father wills one thing and He another, but, "Just as an individual soul has one will, so My will and the Father's are one." Now, do not wonder if He has spoken of so close a union.
>
> If He discoursed on these matters in a somewhat human fashion, do not be surprised. They still considered Him as merely man. Therefore, it is very necessary in such instances not only to search out the meaning of what is said, but also to take into consideration the suspicious attitude of His hearers and to hear His words as addressed to that suspicion.
>
> He is speaking in human language and addressing Himself to the suspicious attitude of His listeners. Inasmuch as, beginning from the former discussion, He had uttered His words, now in divine fashion, again in human fashion, He once again repeated this same procedure and said, human-wise: "My judgment is just."
>
> And what is it that I have said? That the excessive humility of His words is of itself convincing in a particular manner to the intelligent, persuading them, when they have received His words, not to interpret them readily in a lowly sense but to prepare to ascend to the sublimity of the thought. And it even easily raises up by degrees those disposed to cling to the earth. (*Hom. Jo.* 39.4)

(4) *Homilies 48 and 49*: we find one of the few passages that specifically uses two-natures terminology. Finding it puzzling that Jesus at first avoided Judea and then later ran the gauntlet of Jewish hostility (John 7), Chrysostom states:

> It was not in order that he might obtain the reputation of speaking in riddles that John spoke in this way. Perish the thought! On the contrary, he did this to make it clear that at one time Christ's divinity was being attested; at another, His humanity. When he said 'He could not' he was speaking of Him as a Man who did many things even in a human way; but when he asserted that He stood in their midst and they did not seize Him, he was, of course, proving the power of His Godhead. And this is so for in fleeing Christ was acting as a Man, and in making His appearance He was acting as God; in both cases, genuinely. The fact that He was not seized even though surrounded by those who were plotting against Him was proof of His invincibility and inviolability; while His withdrawal confirmed and strengthened the doctrine of the incarnation. (*Hom. Jo.* 38.1)

Chrysostom comments on the way in which this "shut the mouths" of various heretics.

Opening the following homily, however, Chrysostom adds that

> The actions performed by Christ in a human way were so performed not merely for the purpose of confirming the Incarnation, but also that He might instruct us to virtuous living. For, if He did everything as God, whence would we be able to learn what we ought to do when faced with trials outside the realm of our experience? (49.1)

The exemplary character of Christ's actions, especially his response to persecution and suffering, is made ever more apparent as the *Homilies on John's Gospel* move through the passion narrative (homilies 83 and 84). The humility displayed by the foot-washing is also a case in point (homilies 70–71). It is all part of the divine pedagogical purpose and provides an explanation for awkward facts such as Christ's praying to God though himself being God. The prayer in John 17, for example, is for the instruction of the disciples—after all teaching is better done by example than through mere words (80.1; 83.1). Chrysostom the preacher never passes up an opportunity to point out the exemplary character of Christ's words and actions.

(5) *Homilies 63–64*: As he met Mary weeping at Lazarus's death, Christ "asked a non-committal question and so condescended to their weakness. Further, in order to confirm the fact of His human nature, He wept a little" (*Hom. Jo.* 63.1). Chrysostom suggests in homily 63 that this had the effect of attracting crowds for the subsequent miracle: "he knew that grief arouses sym-

pathy." He asked them where they had laid him so as to avoid forcing himself on them, "to act at their request, so as to free the miracle from all suspicion of fraud." The Evangelist "was at great pains to mention repeatedly that he wept and that he groaned." This was so that

> you might learn He truly did assume our nature. For, as he clearly asserted greater things of Him than the other Evangelists did, he also spoke here of Christ's human nature in a much more humble strain than they. (63.2)

In fact mentioning his grief here made up for the fact that in the passion narrative he omitted the agony in the garden and asserted that "he cast his enemies prostrate on the ground," referring to John 18:6.

> In speaking of his death, indeed, Christ asserted: "I have the power to lay down my life" (John 10.18), and there he said nothing in lowly human fashion. That is the reason why, even in His Passion, the Evangelists attributed to Him much that is human, to prove by this means the genuineness of the Incarnation. Now, Matthew did so by means of His agony, and His becoming troubled, and his [bloody] sweat, while John accomplished this by Christ's grief. If He were not truly possessed of our human nature, He would not have been overcome by grief once and then again a second time. (63.2)

In the following homily, Chrysostom comments on the prayer of Jesus in John 11:41:

> I have often said—and I now repeat—that Christ did not have His own dignity in view as much as our salvation, nor was He thinking of how He might say something great, but how He could attract us. Therefore, sublime and great utterances from His lips are few, and these, obscure; while humble and ordinary ones are many, and are interspersed in His words in abundance. (64.1)

Chrysostom notes how often his "sublime teaching" turned off his contemporaries leading to charges of blasphemy and persecution, whereas humble words attracted people to believe, so surely "the entire reason for the lowly utterance was that He spoke for the sake of His hearers" (64.1). Chrysostom is again circumventing the Arian deduction that this was not condescension but a reflection of his inferior nature. His condescension is for the sake of adaptation to the weakness of those being instructed. Chrysostom is back arguing for equality with the Father and calling in the Johannine prooftexts (5:21, 23; 10:30, 37; 12:45; 14:9). Even the Father, who did not assume flesh, condescended to allow "statements of humble tenor to be made of himself," as when he called to Adam "where are you?" (64.2). Chrysostom adds other problematic Old Testament texts and enlarges upon the matter at some length before returning to the immediate issue: how was it that Christ needed the help of prayer? Would that not be a sign of weakness? It was, of course, for the sake of the people around him—to demonstrate that he had been sent by the Father. So why, asks Chrysostom, did he not say, "in the name of the Father, come forth," rather than "Lazarus, come forth"? His answer is: "Because it was a mark of His wisdom to show condescension by His words, but authority by His deeds." Chrysostom is adamant that he performed his works "by his own power." Ultimately his prayer is an indication of complete agreement with the Father, not an indication that he was ignorant or weak, stemming "not from His true dignity but from His condescension." "Enemies of the truth," however, assert that it was

> to show the Father's superiority to Him. Yet, actually, His saying this was not proof of the Father's greater excellence, but an abject humiliation of Himself and an assertion that as Man He was not above human nature. For, to pray is not in accord with the dignity of God the Father nor of Him who shares His throne." (64.3)

So it was the hearers' unbelief that prompted Christ to pray. Their immediate response was not marvel but plots to kill him; they still call him a "man," despite receiving "such a great proof of His Godhead." The old struggle with Arianism determines the way Chrysostom handles the classic problems of weeping and praying, and it is the motif of condescension that provides an explanation: the "subject" who speaks or acts remains the Logos. Chrysostom's reading of the Johannine narrative is closely parallel to the kenotic Christology of Cyril. There is no distinct human subject in the Christ to whom these human reactions are attributed; rather lowly human words are adopted for the sake of the people listening as part of the divine pedagogical purpose, and the charges of "pretence" and "crypto-docetism" are potentially applicable to Chrysostom's approach as much as to Cyril's.

***

Enough passages have been explored to show that Wiles's insistence on how much all these commentators have in common is borne out. So too is the more recent tendency to suggest that Chrysostom's fundamental approach to Christology is virtually "Alexandrian": "the divine Son predominates over his assumed humanity," and Chrysostom's understanding of the person of Christ is "quite different from that of Theodore," sounding "more Alexandrian than Antiochene."[83] Comparing different examples of Johannine exegesis in the post-Arian world, one might wonder whether the christological controversy need ever have happened, let alone how applicable the labels are to distinct "schools" or "traditions."

And yet, it is evident that the Nicene settlement did pose new exegetical questions when it came to articulating or conceptualizing the incarnation, and there were incipient differences of approach which, once insisted upon or exaggerated, could inflame the sensitivities of those committed to certain prior assumptions. The christological positions discernible in exegesis, then, reflect the two divergent traditions that we found emerging in the period, and yet they are remarkably similar. What is intriguing is the way in which the problems and differences could appear to reflect tensions within the New Testament itself—the Epistle to the Hebrews demanding acknowledgement of the two natures, and the Johannine narrative requiring response to the *kenōsis* or condescension of one identified as truly divine. Frequent recourse to Philippians 2:5–11 is characteristic of both Chrysostom and Cyril, and in controversy each side will emphasize different aspects of that apparently determinative text. To sample the literature of the controversy we must soon turn.

3. Doctrine and Scriptural Exegesis: Toward Some Conclusions

This exploration of the way in which the Gospel of John and the Epistle to the Hebrews were being expounded before the christological controversy but after

83. Rylaarsdam, *John Chrysostom*, 139–40, who quotes from Chrysostom's *Four Discourses on Lazarus*: "I have never left the assumed humanity unharmonised with the divine operation, (acting) now as man, now as God, but the divine operation indicating the nature and with the human operation making the Incarnation credible, teaching that the humbler things are to be referred to the humanity and the nobler to the divinity, and by this unequal mixture of actions, interpreting the unequal union of the natures" (PG 50:642–643). Rylaarsdam cites in note 228 the work of Camillus Hay, "Antiochene Exegesis and Christology," *Austrian Biblical Review* 12 (1964): 10–23; Hay, "St. John Chrysostom and the Integrity of the Human Nature of Christ," *Franciscan Studies* 19 (1959): 298–317; Grillmeier, *Christ in Christian Tradition*; Donald Fairbairn, *Grace and Christology in the Early Church* (Oxford: Oxford University Press, 2003).

the struggle with Arianism offers working examples of how scripture and doctrine would interact with one another in the hermeneutical process. Common to all are implicit assumptions about doctrine being enshrined in and proved from scripture, although agreed formulae, already established to exclude false interpretations, have now set the parameters within which interpretation takes place. If Cyril makes that transparent, it is equally true for Chrysostom, a point worth further discussion.

By now it has become a truism that questions and curiosity generate heresy, and Chrysostom shares that perspective. However, in his *Homilies on John's Gospel* Chrysostom makes a number of remarks about scripture which, gathered up, may at first sight appear to contradict that. The most frequent concerns the need not to skim or read superficially but to plumb the depths of the sacred scriptures, to search for hidden treasure and to dig deep.[84] He twice compares this to miners working a goldmine, not ignoring the smallest vein, purifying the gold, separating it from earth; so with scripture not a jot or tittle is to be passed over casually. Indeed, "heretics go astray because they seek to know neither the point of view of the speaker nor the attitude of his hearers"—without probing the text "many ridiculous conclusions will follow" (*Hom. Jo.* 36.1; 40.1).

As we have seen, this probing happens through posing questions about what is going on in a dialogue or narrative. On the other hand, constantly asking the question "how?" like Nicodemus is a typical recipe for "untimely curiosity":

> This word 'how' is the expression of doubt and does not belong to those whose faith is firm, but to those who are still of the earth. . . . In this way, also, heretics persevere in heresy, hunting down this expression everywhere. Some say: 'How was he made flesh?' while others: 'How was he born?'—subjecting that infinite Being to the weakness of their reasoning. Therefore, they who are aware of this must flee such untimely curiosity. . . .
>
> Do you see how, when a man wrests spiritual things to his own reasoning, he both utters absurdities and seems to be raving and intoxicated, since he is unduly examining words, beyond what is pleasing to God, and does not accept the deposit of faith? . . . in the end, he trumped up foolish trifles and ridiculous questions. . . .
>
> Therefore, since we know these things, let us not examine into the things of God by reasoning and let us not submit divine things to the order prevailing among us, nor subject them to the necessity of nature, but let us

84. *Hom. Jo.* 21.1; cf. 25.1; 41.2; 50.1; 57.1; 58.1; 84.3.

> think of them all reverently, believing as the Scriptures have said. He who is curious and meddlesome gains no profit; in addition to not finding what he seeks he will pay the extreme penalty. You have heard that He begot Him; believe what you have heard, but do not seek out 'how'; and do not on this account deny the begetting. This would be the part of utter senselessness. (*Hom. Jo.* 24.2–3)

More than once Chrysostom references the call in John 5:39 to "Search the Scriptures."[85] Yet, the fact that Jesus says this to the scribes and Pharisees shows that they had no benefit from studying the scriptures, and they indeed "even suffered harm thereby" (*Hom. Jo.* 52.1). It is hardly a surprise that the implied parallel is the error of heretics. Yet on the basis of John 5:39 and 2 Timothy 3:16–17 scripture is treated as arms to take up against heretics (*Hom. Jo.* 40.4) necessary to oppose the teaching of Marcion and Valentinus, who relied on pagan philosophy in denying both creation and resurrection. We should "glorify God, not by our faith alone, but also by our life. . . . For *purity of life is no benefit if one's doctrines are corrupt*, just as, therefore, contrarywise, sound doctrines are no advantage if one's life is immoral" (66.3). For Chrysostom correct doctrine is important.

So, like any good teacher, Chrysostom encourages the asking of questions and the probing of the text. Yet he warns, like so many before and since, that human reasoning leads to heresy. This apparent inconsistency, however, may well be the clue to how he sees the relationship between scripture and doctrine. To lift texts out of context and then take their superficial meaning as scriptural doctrine feeds into heretical deductions based on human reasoning, whereas to probe the narrative import of the context, to see what is at stake in argument, to explore the pedagogical intent of Jesus as he speaks and acts, and to do all this informed by scripture's own manner of speaking and overarching meaning is to discern the intent of the Holy Spirit and the true apostolic teaching, teaching which turns one away from both wickedness and blasphemy, and ensures coherence between one's way of life and one's way of belief.[86] For Chrysostom *dogma* retains the broad sense of "teaching": it is teaching how to think, indeed, but also how to live. Yet, his historical and cultural context makes him constantly aware of the need to wean his audience away from heresies old and new, so that "doctrine" is becoming, slowly but

85. *Hom. Jo.* 40–41 treat John 5:39 in context; other references include 15.1; 57.1; 58.1.
86. See, e.g., *Hom. Jo.* 36.1 and 66.3.

surely, the "truth" received from the apostles and enshrined in scripture, "the deposit of faith" to be accepted.[87]

How much more is this true of Cyril's *Commentary on John's Gospel*! As we have seen, the content of belief seems to have become paramount, so that its definition in dogmatic propositions has virtually become the prime purpose of exploring the scriptural text. Thus the implied understanding of the relationship between doctrine and scripture is narrowing. True, I have given reasons for not assuming that his claim to "a more dogmatic exegesis" excludes broader pedagogical aims, and for acknowledging how time and again in the commentary he moves from the narrative to spiritual and mystical meanings; for typology and the fulfillment of Old Testament precursors and patterns are of particular importance to his understanding not just of the gospel but indeed of the liturgy. And yes, for Cyril too the formation of Christian believers certainly did involve the ethical dimensions of Christian life. However, "the interpretation of the divine mysteries is extremely difficult," Cyril states in his preface to the *Commentary on John's Gospel*; his discourse is to muster forces for battle against erroneous opinions. That is the context of his claim to offer *dogmatikōtera exēgēsis*, words that Maxwell translates as "I will direct the discussion at every point to a *doctrinal explanation*" (*Comm. Jo.* 1 [1:3, my italics]). The meaning of *dogma* is surely narrowing, and, as the christological controversy will show, scripture increasingly becomes the source of "proofs" establishing propositional deductions to be accepted as dogmatic truth.

87. Cf. quotations above from *Hom. Jn.* XXIV.2–3, ET *FC* vol. 1, pp. 238–40.

5

Two Nature, One Christ?

PART 2, THE DEPLOYMENT OF SCRIPTURE IN DISPUTE

So we come to the christological controversy, which culminated in the Chalcedonian Definition of 451. It is not my intention to add to the many accounts already in existence of the sequence of events, the characteristics of the supposed two sides of the debate, or the extant literature that enables reconstruction of the process and the issues.[1] As in the case of the Arian controversies (chapter 2), I will map out some basic points to set the context for the following discussion, which will then focus predominantly on the use of scripture in the debates:

- The catalyst of the controversy was, of course, the difference between Cyril of Alexandria and Nestorius, bishop of Constantinople, over whether *Theotokos* was an appropriate title for the Virgin Mary. Athanasius possibly provided precedent, but the debate revealed two distinct approaches to understanding the nature of Christ.[2] It is doubtful whether more long-standing "Word-Flesh" and "Word-Man" traditions lay behind those approaches rather than the new questions posed by the Nicene settlement. The issues arose, surely,

1. E.g. R. V. Sellers, *Two Ancient Christologies: A Study in the Christological Thought of the Schools of Alexandria and Antioch in the Early History of Christian Doctrine* (London: SPCK, 1940); Sellers, *The Council of Chalcedon: A Historical and Doctrinal Survey* (London: SPCK, 1953); Grillmeier, *Christ in Christian Tradition*; F. Young, *From Nicaea to Chalcedon*, ch. 5; Susan Wessel, *Cyril of Alexandria and the Nestorian Controversies: The Making of a Saint and a Heretic*, OECS (Oxford: Oxford University Press, 2004).

2. See the quotation in chapter 2, p. 37. Note the reference is to *C. Ar.* 3, a work whose authenticity is questionable, though it may already have been transmitted as Athanasian.

because once the traditional hierarchical approach to mediation had been broken apart by insistence on the ontological gap between Creator and creatures, mediation came to be located in the person of the incarnate Word, and it was not easy to conceive of how the divine could cohere with a creaturely nature so as to provide the required bridge across the gap.

- In broad terms we may say that the "Antiochenes" focused on that utter differentiation between Creator and creatures, to the extent that giving an account of the one Christ became virtually impossible—at least in the eyes of their opponents, who accused them of preaching "two Sons," the Son of God and the Son of David.
- Again in broad terms we may say that the "Alexandrians" so focused on the Word as the one who became incarnate and was the subject of all the incarnate experiences that in the eyes of their opponents they (1) compromised the true divinity of the Word by attributing to it movement, change, and suffering; (2) undermined the true humanity of the incarnate one by focusing on the flesh as the instrument of the Word; and (3) implied by their insistence on the union a kind of mixture, thus maintaining still the errors of Apollinaris.
- Accounts of the controversy tend to focus first on the issue of the human soul of Jesus, and second on what might be called the "technical terms" of the debate—the meanings given to *ousia*, *physis*, *hypostasis*, and *prosōpon* in these arguments about conceptualizing the person of Christ. It is not my intention to go over that ground again, except insofar as this is demanded by the material under discussion, but rather to explore the appeal to apostolic tradition and the crucial use of scriptural proof.
- It is undoubtedly true that each side had soteriological interests that significantly affected their approach to the distinct roles of divine and human in the saving drama of incarnation. These interests had surely shaped potentially divergent readings of scripture since the Nicene settlement. As ever, how to make sense of scripture lay at the heart of the matter, and certain key texts, many already in dispute between Athanasius and the Arians but also others, are particularly prominent in the controversial literature.

At the time, of course, each side passionately rejected the views of the other side as heretical—this debate was no academic seminar! However, for once we are in a position to hear the voices of both parties directly—it is not the case that one triumphant side was able to suppress the "heretical" views of the other, as we have found so often before. From each side certain names would be carried into posterity to designate false options (such as Nestorian, Eutychian), but in the long run they came to represent extremes as agreements were negotiated and other names (Theodoret, for example)were rehabilitated—though, in stating that, we should not overlook the exception that proves the rule, namely, the long-term rejection of Chalcedon in Syrian and Coptic Orthodox traditions. From all the material available, what is to be examined in this chapter has been selected to illustrate the process of interpretation and counterinterpretation. Some readers may be daunted by the detail and may wish to be directed to summary sections,[3] but the to-and-fro of argument is what reveals the exegetical process, together with the underlying conceptualities, which shaped each side's doctrinal position. At times we may be tempted to conclude that we are listening to a dialogue of the deaf—they have so much in common, yet they persist in projecting onto each other their own presuppositions about what the other teaches rather than discerning the truth for which the other is contending. Observing the to-and-fro of argument, we can see how it was largely about making sense of scripture not only in terms of the rationality of the time but also in respect of the truths already established by earlier authorities.

The first section of this chapter will review key polemical material produced in the initial heated stages of the controversy, that is, up to and through the divided Council of Ephesus in 431 and the Formulary of Reunion in 433. Nestorius's provocative sermon, Cyril's objections, and the ensuing correspondence will introduce a blow-by-blow account of how Cyril's highly controversial twelve anathemas were challenged and defended. The second section will turn to material produced after the supposed peace of 433, with examples of each side publishing literary dialogues purporting to engage in more measured debate of the issues, though ultimately, of course, offering propaganda as they sought to persuade and convince the reader of the truth of their own viewpoint. The chapter's climax will necessarily be consideration of the scriptural basis of the doctrinal position reached at the Council of Chalcedon in 451.

1. Polemics and the Rhetorical Appeal to Scripture and/or Precedent

It has been suggested that a crucial factor in Cyril's success in getting rid of Nestorius was his framing of the controversy in terms of a replay of Athanasius

3. See, for example, sections 1.4.8; 2.1.5; 2.1.6; 2.2.4; 2.3; and in section 2 as a whole, note the supplementary headings.

against Arius, and that "while Cyril adhered to the Symbol of Nicaea, placing his Christology within its synodal decrees, Nestorius preferred the context of Scripture."[4] The selected letters, tracts, and sermons will confirm this at a superficial level, though it will become clear that what was really at stake was appropriate interpretation, whether of scripture or of accepted creedal definition, given both sides' acceptance of creed and scripture as articulating true doctrine and as mutually supportive.

1.1. Nestorius's First Homily against Theotokos

The circulation of this homily triggered upset among the monasteries of Egypt and Cyril's initial letter in response.[5] We begin by noting the pervasive scriptural allusions or quotations. Initially they reinforce generalizations about those "who profess that they know God, but, as it is written, they deny him by what they do" (Titus 1:16) or "do not understand either the words they employ or the things they are talking about" (1 Tim 1:7). Doctrinally more to the point, one can discern scriptural perspectives behind the opening emphasis on the Creator and divine providence, on God's fashioning of "me in my mother's womb" and subsequent care and preservation through manifold gifts, of which the incarnation proves to be the climax:[6]

> Without male seed, he fashioned from the Virgin a nature like Adam's (who was himself formed without male seed) and through a human being brought about the revival of the human race. "Since," Paul says, "death came through a human being, through a human being also came the resurrection of the dead." (1 Cor 15:21)[7]

A grasp of Irenaean "recapitulation" would seem foundational for Nestorius, who now turns to what would become the issue at stake, tackling inquirers who, "blinded with regard to the dispensation of the Lord's incarnation," ask "Is Mary Theotokos . . . or is she on the contrary *anthrōpotokos*?" A rhetorical battery of challenges to such people deploys biblical texts:

4. Wessel, *Cyril of Alexandria*, 153.

5. Latin text and Greek fragments in Friedrich Loofs, *Nestoriana: Die Fragmente des Nestorius* (Halle: Niemayer, 1905), 249–64; English translation in Richard A. Norris Jr., *The Christological Controversy* (Philadelphia: Fortress, 1980), 123–31.

6. Loofs, *Nestoriana*, 250; Norris, *Christological Controversy*, 123.

7. Loofs, *Nestoriana*, 251; Norris, *Christological Controversy*, 124.

> Does God have a mother? . . . Is Paul, then, a liar when he says of the deity of Christ, "without father, without mother, without genealogy" [Heb 7:3]? Mary, my friend, did not give birth to the Godhead (for "what is born of the flesh is flesh" [John 3:6]). A creature did not produce him who is uncreatable.[8]

Nestorius goes on to argue that the Father has not just recently generated God the Logos from the Virgin, quoting John 1:1; nor did the Holy Spirit create God the Logos, quoting Matt 1:20. Rather, he formed out of the Virgin a temple for God the Logos, a temple in which he dwelt. Then, from the problem of attributing birth to God, Nestorius turns to the impossibility of the eternal God dying and insists that "he raised up what had collapsed, but he did not fall," quoting Psalm 14:2, explaining how "God saw the ruined nature . . . , took hold of it . . . , held on to it while remaining what he had been, and lifted it up high."[9] It is worth noting Nestorius's commonsense analogy: if you were wanting to lift up someone who had had a fall, you would join yourself to the hurt person and lift, but you would remain what you were while thus joined to another. This "conjunction" is how Nestorius envisages the relationship of the incarnate God with the temple in which he dwelt.

Now, to counteract interpretation of Philippians 2:6—"he was in the form of God"—to imply that "his nature was transitory and has been altered," Nestorius quotes Hebrews 1:3. He admits "was" occurs in John 1:1, but that is because "the question concerned the original subsistence of the being which carried the humanity." Paul, Nestorius claims, recounts "that the [divine] being has become incarnate and that the immutability of the incarnate deity is always maintained after the union." He then emphasizes that Paul did not here name him "God the Logos" but rather "Christ," explaining that this is

> an expression which signifies the two natures, and without risk he applies to him both the style "form of a slave," which he took, and that of God. The descriptions are different from each other by reason of the mysterious fact that the natures are two in number.[10]

Nestorius adds that Christian proclamation must include both that "Christ as God is unaffected by change," and that he is "benevolent" and "takes 'the form of a slave' while existing as he was." He was "not altered after the union,"

8. Loofs, *Nestoriana*, 252; Norris, *Christological Controversy*, 124.
9. Loofs, *Nestoriana*, 253; Norris, *Christological Controversy*, 125.
10. Loofs, *Nestoriana*, 254; Norris, *Christological Controversy*, 126.

but was "revealed as both benevolent and just." This is then expounded in terms of Christ's death for sinners, quoting from Romans 5:7 and 3:23–25, showing how when tempted (Matt 4:1–10) Christ reverses Adam's fall (Gen 3:5) and capping this with Philippians 2:8, Colossians 2:14, and Ephesians 1:7. Enlarging on humanity's case against the devil's oppression, and the second Adam's reversal of Adam's sin, Nestorius asks why he was sinless yet "reckoned with the transgressors" (1 Pet 2:22; Isa 53:12) and then focuses on the second Adam's obedience crossing out Adam's disobedience, quoting John 12:31 to establish victory over the devil. Romans 8:34 clinches it.[11]

> Our nature, having been put on by Christ like a garment, intervenes on our behalf, being entirely free from all sin and contending by appeal to its blameless origin, just as the Adam who was formed earlier brought punishment upon his race by reason of his sin.[12]

This point Nestorius rubs home, insisting it was "the assumed man, as a human being" who had the opportunity "to dissolve, by means of the flesh, that corruption which arose by means of the flesh." The burial "belonged to this man, not to the deity." It was "his feet" that "were fastened down by nails," and he was the one formed by the Holy Spirit in the womb. Furthermore, it was "this flesh" of which "the Lord said to the Jews, 'Destroy this temple and in three days I will raise it up'" (John 2:19). "Am I the only one who calls Christ two-fold?" Nestorius asks—surely Christ calls himself "both a destroyable temple and God who raises it up." And how about that gospel saying, "Why do you seek to kill me, a man, who have spoken truth to you?" (John 8:40). Yet Christ is not "a mere man"—he is "at once both God and man." Apollinaris is challenged: if he were God alone, he would have had to have asked, "Why do you seek to destroy me who am God?"

> What, in fact, he says is, "Why do you seek to kill me, a man?" This is he who says, "My God, my God, why have you forsaken me?" [Matt 27:46]. This is he who suffered a death of three days' duration. But I worship this one together with the Godhead because he is a sharer in the divine authority; "for let it be apparent, men and brothers," says the Scripture, "that the remission of sins is preached to us through Christ" [Acts 13:38]. I adore him as the instrument of the Lord's goodness.[13]

11. Loofs, *Nestoriana*, 254–58; Norris, *Christological Controversy*, 126–28.
12. Loofs, *Nestoriana*, 258; Norris, *Christological Controversy*, 128.
13. Loofs, *Nestoriana*, 260; Norris, *Christological Controversy*, 129.

Nestorius now draws together further scriptural quotations to reinforce his saving message and the reasons for his adoration.[14] He sums this up thus:

> I revere the one who is borne because of the one who carries him, and I worship the one I see because of the one who is hidden. God is undivided from the one who appears, and therefore I do not divide the honor of that which is not divided. I divide the natures, but I unite the worship.[15]

This emphasis on unity will conclude the homily:

> We confess both and adore them as one, for the duality of the natures is one on account of the unity. Hear Paul proclaiming both the eternity of the Only Begotten's deity and the recent birth of the humanity, and the fact that the dignity of the association or conjunction has been made one. "Jesus Christ," he says, "is the same yesterday, today and forever [Heb 13:8]. Amen."[16]

Prior to that conclusion, however, Nestorius firmly states: "that which was formed in the womb is not in itself God," "that which was created by the Spirit was not in itself God," and "that which was buried in the tomb was not in itself God." "If that were the case," he says, we would be "worshippers of a human being and worshippers of the dead." Yet "the one who was assumed is styled God because of the one who assumed him," and "the demons shudder at the mention of the crucified flesh: they know that God has been joined to the crucified flesh, even though he has not shared its suffering." It is those denials that would prove to be "red rags to a bull" when read by Cyril and the Alexandrians, despite all the stress on unity, as well as the confession that the Son of Man would appear as judge on the clouds with power and great glory (Matt 24:30) because "he is joined to omnipotent deity."[17]

So it is true that this homily does not appeal to the Nicene Creed, but rather builds its position on the basis of scripture. Yet, clearly, it is informed by the post-Arian, post-Apollinarian context: the Antiochene anxiety to safeguard what may be called the "Godness of God" is fundamental. It rests, however, on more than that concern. There is a recognition that the reversal of human disobedience required human obedience: "He did not dissolve the debt by

14. In order, Eph 4:32; Col 2:1–3; John 8:26; Eph 2:14; Rom 3:25; Col 1:18; 2 Cor 5:19; Phil 2:6–7; John 12:32–33; 10:9; Phil 2:9–11.

15. Loofs, *Nestoriana*, 260; Norris, *Christological Controversy*, 130.

16. Loofs, *Nestoriana*, 263–64; Norris, *Christological Controversy*, 131.

17. Loofs, *Nestoriana*, 262; Norris, *Christological Controversy*, 130–31.

an order, lest mercy violate justice"[18]—it could not happen simply by divine fiat. Utilizing scriptural quotations Nestorius not only reclaims the notion of recapitulation, traditional since Irenaeus, but almost anticipates Anselm: it was by the mediation of the "debt-ridden nature" (human nature, in other words) that Christ "paid the debt back as a son of Adam":

> Because of his disobedience in the case of a tree, Adam was under sentence of punishment; Christ made up for this debt . . . "having become obedient" [Phil 2:6] on a tree. That is why Paul said, "He took away the handwritten bond of our sins, which stood against us, nailing it to the cross" [Col 2:14].[19]

As noted above, it was "the assumed man" that "had the opportunity to dissolve . . . that corruption which arose by means of the flesh." In other words, Nestorius assigns to the human nature an indispensable role in the achievement of reconciliation. God set forth Christ as "the pledge of peace" (Eph 2:14) and "as an expiation" of divine wrath (Rom 3:25). What Nestorius appeals to here is not, as is often thought, a Pelagian moral victory on the part of Christ's human nature with some kind of exemplary efficacy for humankind in general; rather the obedience of the second Adam crosses out the disobedience of the first—indeed, the willing obedience of the assumed man is an act of atonement, the payment of a debt only payable by the offending party if reconciliation is to be effected. Observing this has been this chapter's illuminating moment. As mediator Christ brings together parties divided by an offense committed by one against the other, and that necessitates the active involvement of both parties. It could not happen simply by divine fiat but required some kind of partnership.

Scripture, then, both at the level of prooftexts and at the level of the overarching story from creation to final judgment, is indeed the bar against which Nestorius measures his teaching. Yet his understanding is informed by a reading of scripture shaped by long-standing tradition—the old narrative of recapitulation long since developed by Irenaeus coupled with post-Nicene sensitivities about the utter differentiation between Creator and creatures.

1.2. Cyril's Second Letter to Nestorius

In his *Second Letter to Nestorius* (*Ep.* 4) Cyril articulates the issues with sufficient clarity that it would eventually be inscribed into the Acts of the Council

18. Loofs, *Nestoriana*, 255; Norris, *Christological Controversy*, 126.
19. Loofs, *Nestoriana*, 256; Norris, *Christological Controversy*, 127.

of Chalcedon, thus being enshrined as a classic statement of Christian doctrine.[20] That Council would also reaffirm both the Creed of Nicaea and the version of the Nicene Creed established at the Council of Constantinople, refusing to devise a new creed but adding a definition of how it was to be read. As we shall see, Cyril's letter anticipates that move by mounting his argument from the Nicene Creed.

First, however, Cyril addresses slanders against himself, which he claims certain parties were advancing in Constantinople, rhetorically exploiting scripture's language with allusions to Romans 3:14 and warning that they will face ultimate judgment.[21] He then reminds Nestorius of his episcopal responsibilities toward the laity, suggesting he keep in mind the consequences of causing even one of the "little ones" who believe in Christ "to stumble" (Matt 18:6). Scripture thus lies on the surface of his text from the beginning (*Ep.* 4.1–2).

Next, however, Cyril states that to get the right balance in one's teaching means forming "our own minds" in accordance with the orthodox views of the "holy fathers," "testing ourselves to see if we are in the faith, as it is written" (the allusion is to 2 Cor 13:5). That introduces an appeal to "the holy and great synod," which

> stated that "the only-begotten Son," "begotten" by nature "of the Father," "true God of true God," "light from light," the one "through whom" the Father made all things, "came down, was incarnate, made human, suffered, rose again the third day, and ascended into heaven." (*Ep.* 4.3)

That does not mean saying that the Logos was changed by becoming flesh—and as we have seen, Nestorius would certainly agree with that—nor

> that he was transformed into a complete man consisting of soul and body, but instead we affirm this: that the Word hypostatically united to himself flesh enlivened with a rational soul, in a manner mysterious and inconceivable, and became man, and was called "Son of Man." (*Ep.* 4.3)

20. Greek text and English translation of the *Second Letter to Nestorius*, Cyril's fourth overall epistle, in Lionel R. Wickham, ed. and trans., *Cyril of Alexandria: Select Letters* (Oxford: Clarendon, 1983), 2–11. Note also the Greek text and English translation in T. H. Bindley and F. W. Green, *The Oecumenical Documents of the Faith* (London: Methuen, 1950), 95–97 and 209–11, and the English translation in Norris, *Christological Controversy*, 131–35. My own translation in quotations is influenced by the available English versions.

21. Romans 3:14 likewise alludes to Ps 9:28 LXX (10:7 in the Masoretic Text).

Cyril reinforces the point that this was neither "by way of will or divine favour" (in other words, similar to the grace given to the saints) nor the assumption of just *prosōpon*. He seems to imply by this mere "outward appearance" or even "role" by contrast with a substantial or hypostatic union, even though, as Wickham notes, in Trinitarian theology *hypostasis* and *prosōpon* had become equivalent.[22] The Antiochenes might object to Cyril's caricature of their position, but he is surely driving home how inadequate any insistence on outward union is when there is inner division. What he really wants to indicate is that in the Nicene Creed there is one subject of all the statements in the second clause, and that one subject is the eternal Logos of God who also became incarnate. He admits that the difference between the natures was not abolished by the union, but insists on them being joined together to make "one Christ and Son from both" (*Ep.* 4.3).

Now Cyril applies this christological understanding to the birth from a woman. His divine nature did not originate there and certainly did not require a second birth; rather "for us and our salvation" he united humanity to himself substantially and issued from a woman. It was not the case that "initially an ordinary man was born of the holy Virgin and then the Word simply settled on him"; rather, by "making his very own the birth of his own flesh," united indeed "from the very womb," "he is said to have undergone fleshly birth" (4.4). One is almost tempted to suggest that Cyril has granted Nestorius's point that birth cannot be attributed to the divine, though of course Cyril has found a formula to make it seem possible. Similar statements are next made about his suffering: it is not that "God the Word suffered blows, nail-piercings or other wounds in his own nature"—the impassibility of the divine is a consequence of his incorporeality. Again that is a point with which Nestorius would wholeheartedly agree. But, like Athanasius, Cyril insists that it was "his own body" which suffered, and so "he is said to have suffered for our sake," for "within the suffering body was the Impassible." The same kind of thing has to be said about his dying: the Word of God, life itself, indeed the life-giver, is of course immortal and incorruptible, but "is said to have suffered death for our sake" since "his own body 'tasted death for everyone by the grace of God,' as Paul says" (Heb 2:9). Cyril recognizes the absurdity of thinking he experienced death with respect to his nature. So too with the resurrection: it was not as if he succumbed to corruption—rather it was his own body that was raised (*Ep.* 4.5).

So, Cyril concludes, this is how we confess one Christ and Lord, not "worshipping" a man "along with" the Word—the very notion of "along with" runs the risk

22. Wickham, *Select Letters*, 6 n. 7. On *prosōpon*, cf. chapter 4 above, 2.2.2 (p. 170).

of division. One and the same Christ is the object of worship, for "the Word's body is not dissociated from him." He presides with the Father, "one in union with his own flesh—not two presiding sons." The notion of two Sons is further challenged: without substantial union you end up with "a distinction between the particular man honored with the title 'Son' on the one hand, and the Word of God, natural possessor of both the name and the reality of sonship, on the other" (4.6).

The final paragraph of the letter challenges the alternative notion of a union of *prosōpa*—this is totally inadequate for an orthodox account of the faith. Appeal is made to John 1:14: scripture states "he became flesh," not that "the Word united to himself *anthropou prosōpon*." Cyril may have built his argument up from the Nicene Creed, but it is scripture that clinches it. He alludes also to Hebrews 2:14 in interpreting what John 1:14 means:

> he shared flesh and blood like us, made our body his own and issued as a man from a woman without abandoning his being God and his being begotten of the Father but remaining what he was even when he assumed flesh. (*Ep.* 4.7)

This is what the holy fathers meant, and this is why they dared to call the holy Virgin *Theotokos*, asserts Cyril.

Finally, Cyril underlines the fact that he has written this to ensure "the peace of the churches and for the priests of God an abiding bond of unbroken love and harmony." It is this ecclesial stance, surely, which undergirds his appeal to tradition—to the holy fathers and the Nicene Creed. But does this mean less interest in scripture? Surely for Cyril any contrast between scripture and the traditions to which he explicitly appeals would be inconceivable. Superficially there is a contrast between Nestorius's constant reference to scripture and Cyril's recourse to patristic authority. But given Cyril's vast exegetical output we can hardly gainsay his interest in scripture, and in the light of what we have previously seen of his propensity to distil the meaning of scripture into doctrinal propositions, we must surely affirm that for him the propositions of the creed constitute the agreed understanding of the sense of scripture as the ultimate, though not always entirely transparent, source of true teaching and right belief—that is, of fundamental Christian doctrine.

1.3. *Nestorius's Second Letter to Cyril*

This letter is Nestorius's reply to what he calls "the rebukes which your astonishing letter brings against us," professing to forgive them, as "what it deserves is a healing generosity of spirit," even though "it does not permit silence."[23] He quotes back at Cyril his summary of what "the great and holy synod" stated and urges more careful attention, quoting from 1 Timothy 4:13–16. By "reading superficially" rather than "giving heed" as Paul urged, Cyril had failed to perceive that on his interpretation the Synod teaches "the passibility of the Logos who is co-eternal with God."[24] With closer examination,

> you will discover that the divine chorus of the Fathers did not say that the co-essential Godhead is passible or that the Godhead which is co-eternal with the Father has only just been born.[25]

Nestorius now gives his exegesis of the Nicene Creed, pointing out that

> they first of all establish, as foundations, the titles which are common to the deity and the humanity—"Lord" and "Jesus" and "Christ" and "Only Begotten" and "Son"—and then build on them the teaching about his becoming human and his passion and resurrection, in order that, since the titles which signify and are common to both natures are set in the foreground, the things which pertain to the sonship and lordship are not divided and the things peculiar to the natures within the unitary sonship do not get endangered by the suggestion of a confusion.[26]

He then suggests that they were following Paul's instructions and cites Philippians 2:5–8 to show how, referring to the divine act of becoming human and intending to mention the passion, "he first points to the title 'Christ'"—in other words, he focuses on the title "which is common to the two natures." Indeed, Paul anticipates the potential suggestion that "God the Logos is passible" and

> he inserts the word "Christ," because it is the term which signifies the impassible and the passible essence in one unitary person, with the result that Christ is without risk called both impassible and passible—impassible in the Godhead but passible in the nature of the body.[27]

23. Latin text and Greek fragments in Loofs, *Nestoriana*, 173–80; English translation in Norris, *Christological Controversy*, 135–40. Quotation here from Loofs, *Nestoriana*, 174; Norris, *Christological Controversy*, 135.

24. Loofs, *Nestoriana*, 174; Norris, *Christological Controversy*, 135–36.

25. Loofs, *Nestoriana*, 174–75; Norris, *Christological Controversy*, 136.

26. Loofs, *Nestoriana*, 175; Norris, *Christological Controversy*, 136.

27. Loofs, *Nestoriana*, 176; Norris, *Christological Controversy*, 137.

Thus Nestorius appeals to scriptural usage to interpret the Nicene Creed.

Next he develops his argument against attributing birth to the Logos. First, he states that "the holy fathers" did not speak of "birth" when considering the economy of "coming to be in a human being." To cut a long story short, he recommends the "distinction of natures" according to the "special characteristics of humanity and divinity," the "conjunction of these natures in one person" along with the denial that the Logos needed a second birth from a woman and the confession that the Godhead is impassible, both of which points Cyril had, of course, admitted. Nestorius wants to focus on the "primary issues" and what he could not understand was Cyril's reintroduction "as passible and newly created one who had first been proclaimed as impassible and incapable of second birth." It is as if the qualities naturally attaching to the Logos as God "are corrupted by conjunction with his temple," and that temple is denigrated despite its crucial role "on behalf of sinners," an argument supported by allusion to parts of the homily we surveyed earlier, especially its use of John 2:19. As far as Nestorius is concerned:

> Everywhere in Holy Scripture, whenever mention is made of the saving dispensation of the Lord, what is conveyed to us is the birth and suffering not of the deity but of the humanity of Christ, so that by a more exact manner of speech the Holy Virgin is called Mother of Christ, not Mother of God.[28]

Citing a variety of biblical texts,[29] he also claims that there are

> thousands of other statements warning the human race not to think that the deity of the Son is a new thing, or susceptible to bodily passion, but rather the flesh which is united to the nature of the Godhead.[30]

Hence Christ calls himself both Lord and Son of David—and Nestorius here enlarges on Matthew 22:42–44. The body, he concludes, is the temple of the Son's deity, "united to it by a complete and divine conjunction."

So, Nestorius argues, to attribute the characteristics of the flesh to the Son's deity "in the name of this association" is to entertain pagan errors or be infected with "the insane heresy of Arius and Apollinaris and the others." What

28. Loofs, *Nestoriana*, 177; Norris, *Christological Controversy*, 137.

29. In order, Matt 1:1, 16, 18; John 2:1; Acts 1:14; Matt 1:20; 2:13; Rom 1:3, 8:3; 1 Cor 15:3; 1 Pet 4:1; 1 Cor 11:24.

30. Loofs, *Nestoriana*, 178; Norris, *Christological Controversy*, 138.

offends Nestorius is the idea that the divine Logos was "fed with milk," participated in growth, or needed "angelic assistance because of his fearfulness at the time of the passion." He forebears mentioning "circumcision, sacrifice, tears and hunger," all of which "belong properly to the flesh as things which happened for our sake." Nestorius could have cited Athanasius, and he does refer again to "the holy fathers," but he insists "this is the message of the divine Scriptures." Making such proper distinctions is the way to speak "theologically both of the things which belong to God's love for the human race and of the things which belong to his majesty," citing again 1 Timothy 4:15. The letter is then signed off with expressions of confidence and hope in the expansion of the church, its right teaching, and its peace with quotations of Isaiah 11:9 and 2 Samuel 3:1 woven in and brotherly counsel reinforced by Paul's assertion that contentiousness is not customary in the churches of God (1 Cor 11:16).

Yes, Nestorius does have recourse to scripture more persistently than Cyril, but it is in order to explicate the doctrinal propositions of the "holy fathers" in a way that accords better with what Nestorius takes to be the sense of the biblical proclamation of salvation through the birth, death, and resurrection of Christ—the one who shared fully in our human nature while the divine nature dwelt within.

1.4. Cyril of Alexandria's Twelve Anathemas

To his *Third Letter to Nestorius* (*Ep.* 17) Cyril appended a list of twelve anathemas.[31] The letter speaks of recent synods in Rome and Alexandria, which had urged Nestorius by a certain date to "dissociate" himself from his "distorted doctrines" or else face deposition—he must "embrace the orthodox faith transmitted to the churches by the holy apostles and evangelists." It would not be enough for Nestorius just to affirm the Nicene Creed, since he had interpreted it in a "twisted sense"; rather he must "make a written acknowledgement on oath" whereby he anathematizes his "foul and unhallowed dogmas" (*Ep.* 17.2). The attached anathemas, effectively brief and pointed statements of the doctrinal issues at stake, spell out the negative and positive propositions that would attract the curse. In this section we will sample the protracted discussion of these notorious statements. The letter to which they are appended both an-

31. Greek text and English translation of Cyril's *Third Letter to Nestorius* (*Ep.* 17) in Wickham, *Select Letters*, 28–33. Greek text and English translation also in Bindley and Green, *Oecumenical Documents*, 108–15 and 212–19. My own translation in quotations is influenced by the available English versions.

ticipates and exegetes their meaning, and Nestorius offered a reply.[32] Besides this, they generated a pamphlet war—a couple of point-by-point rejoinders from the Antiochene party, one from the "Orientals" and the other from Theodoret, along with Cyril's reply to each and his further *Explanation of the Anathemas* produced at the Council of Ephesus.[33] An outline survey of this material and the argumentation from each side can be found in *From Nicaea to Chalcedon*[34]—here our principal concern will be how these propositions relate to scripture, and how scripture was exploited to prove or contest them. The anathemas themselves contain few quotations as such, though there are some obvious allusions. As we shall see, however, on each side arguments used in debating them were constantly justified by appeal to scripture.

1.4.1. Anathema 1

The first anathema baldly condemns anyone "who does not acknowledge Emmanuel to be in truth God and hence the holy Virgin 'Mother of God'—for 'fleshly-wise' [*sarkikōs*] she gave birth to the Word of God." The name Emmanuel, already a weapon in the debate, was clearly drawn from Matthew's quotation of Isaiah 7:14 (Matt 1:23); it would continue to figure as justification for calling the Virgin *Theotokos* and asserting that she gave birth *sarkikōs*—whatever that might mean. Cyril had expounded this in the final paragraph of the preceding letter, insisting that the Word, though God in every sense (quoting John 1:1), "substantially united human nature to himself and underwent birth *sarkikōs* from her womb" (*Ep.* 17.11).

To that adverb, *sarkikōs*, the opposition raised objections: it implies ordinary natural birth, and surely "God-befitting" would be preferable. But their biggest problem was with the attribution of change to the divine, and they cited

32. Nestorius's reply to the anathemas can be found in *ACO* 1.1.6:1–13.

33. Cyril's *Apology against the Orientals* (text in *ACO* 1.1.7:33–63) and *Apology against Theodoret* (text in *ACO* 1.1.6:107–46) preserved extensive quotations from the pamphlets to which he was replying. See further J. A. McGuckin, *St. Cyril of Alexandria: The Christological Controversy. Its History, Theology, and Texts*, VCSup 23 (Leiden: Brill, 1994). An English translation of Theodoret's counterstatements can be found in *NPNF*[2] 3 and István Pásztori-Kupán, *Theodoret of Cyrus* (London: Routledge, 2009), 172–87. A summary of the points made concerning each anathema can be found in Bindley and Green, *Oecumenical Documents*, 124–37. For the *Explanation of the Anathemas*, the Greek text is in *ACO* 1.1.5:15–25; English translation, unless otherwise noted, in Norman Russell, *Cyril of Alexandria* (London: Routledge, 2000), 175–89.

34. F. Young, *From Nicaea to Chalcedon*, 280–87. Cf. Bindley and Green, *Oecumenical Documents*, 124–37; and Clayton, *Christology of Theodoret of Cyrus*, 141–52.

biblical texts to underline God's changelessness (Ps 102:27; Heb 1:12; Mal 3:6). They deduced that his "becoming flesh" could not be taken any more literally than his becoming sin or a curse, alluding here, of course, to 2 Corinthians 5:21 and Galatians 3:13. Theodoret switched attention to Philippians 2:7: he "took" flesh. He was prepared to accept *Theotokos* with careful explanations to the effect that what she bore was the temple of the divine in which all the fullness of the divine dwelt bodily, making allusion here to John 2:21 and Colossians 2:9. Theodoret concludes: "The God-Word was not turned into flesh, but the form of God took the form of the servant."[35] Doubtless Theodoret was aware that in the letter preceding the anathemas, Cyril had used, with a rather different emphasis, the same words from Colossians.

Cyril's response appeals to the Nicene Creed to interpret John 1:14, admitting that the incarnation must have happened without change or mixture. To call the birth "God-befitting" surely implies no objection to *Theotokos*—an ordinary man does not, surely, have a "God-befitting" birth? It is ridiculous to suggest that he became flesh in the same way as he became sin or a curse; since he was sinless, the corollary would be that he was not really incarnate. And "indwelling a temple" must be inadequate to characterize the incarnation: 1 Corinthians 3:16–17 uses such language of God's presence in the saints. Cyril's *Explanation of the Anathemas* again insists that the Nicene Creed says that the same one who was God by nature partook of flesh and blood like us, an allusion to Hebrews 2:14, but admits that when he became man he did not undergo change or alteration into what he was previously not, quoting James 1:17. Change and mixture are both denied: even in the assumption of flesh he remained God; allusion is made to Hebrews 1:3. The first anathema he justifies on the grounds that some denied his birth according to the flesh: the correct confession states that Emmanuel is truly God and therefore the holy Virgin *Theotokos*.[36]

1.4.2. Anathemas 2 and 3

The second and third anathemas are concerned with what were becoming the "technical terms" of the debate—hypostatic or natural union versus conjunction. Again in discussion both sides draw on scripture. In his preceding letter Cyril had repudiated the idea that the Word had taken up residence in an or-

35. For Theodoret's first counterstatement, see *ACO* 1.1.6:110; English translation of Theodoret's counterstatements, unless otherwise noted, from Pásztori-Kupán, *Theodoret*.

36. Cyril, *Explanation* 5–6 (*ACO* 1.1.5:17).

dinary human being born of the holy Virgin; he was not a "God-bearing man." The one Christ "was anointed humanly alongside us" despite being giver of the Spirit "without measure" (John 3:34). Although the Word "dwelt among us" (John 1:14) and "all the fullness of the Godhead" is said to have dwelt "bodily" in Christ (Col 2:9) that does not mean that his dwelling in him is comparable to his dwelling in the saints (*Ep.* 17.4). In the later *Explanation of the Anathemas* Cyril would insist that 1 Timothy 3:16 indicates that "one and the same subject is called Son, before the Incarnation as the Word still incorporeal and after the Incarnation as the same Word now embodied." Picking up classic contentious texts from the Arian controversy Cyril refuses to regard as problematic Hebrews 3:1 or Romans 1:4—they simply apply to the incarnation. These points justify his insistence on the hypostatic union.[37]

Theodoret, however, can make no sense of this term, which is "alien and foreign to the divine Scriptures and to the fathers who have interpreted these." He is adamant that, if it means "mixture of flesh and Godhead," it must be repudiated.[38] To outlaw the term he appeals to John 2:19, Christ's own differentiation between himself and the temple of his body—a text we have already seen Nestorius deploying in a similar way.[39] As far as Theodoret is concerned, other terms simply are unclear and abstruse: the third anathema makes a distinction between joining by conjunction (*synapheia*) and a natural union by concurrence (*synodos*) but is there any real difference between the concurrence of separated parts and the conjunction of disconnected parts? As for "natural" union, "natural" suggests it is involuntary, like our experience of hunger, thirst, or sleep, a matter of necessity rather than freewill, so "the God-Word was conjoined to the form of the servant under the constraint of some necessity" rather than his *philanthrōpia*. That is not what Paul taught. Again Philippians 2:7 is brought into play, with insistence that Christ emptying himself was voluntary. Perception of the union implies previous perception of the division. Of course there is one Son and Christ, but no one can help speaking of the united natures as two: a human being is one though made up of two natures, the body and the immortal soul, and this analogy is then substantiated by Paul's references to the inner and outer man (2 Cor 4:16; Rom 7:22; Eph 3:17).[40]

Cyril in reply wants to make a distinction between a real union, which is indivisible, and a union of two independent natures conjoined *schētikōs*, by mere

37. Cyril, *Explanation* 8–9 (*ACO* 1.1.5:17–18).
38. Theodoret's second counterstatement (*ACO* 1.1.6:114).
39. See above, p. 187.
40. Theodoret's third counterstatement (*ACO* 1.1.6:117).

habit, which would imply two Sons. To take "natural union" as confusion or necessity is to misunderstand—the Logos could not be compelled to become human and suffer—the divine is not susceptible to suffering or necessity. In his later *Explanation of the Anathemas* he justifies "by nature" as equivalent to "in reality" on the basis of Ephesians 2:3: "we were *by nature* children of wrath." He insists that "the divinely inspired Scriptures" speak of one Son and Lord, and once again explains "Emmanuel" as the Word of God the Father, who has become incarnate and been made man, and who, as man, is no less God accommodated to human limitations by divine dispensation. For Cyril the incarnation means that the intangible has become tangible, the invisible visible, for the body capable of being seen and touched was united to God the Word, not something alien to him.[41]

1.4.3. Anathema 4

To the fourth anathema we have already made reference earlier.[42] In this anathema Cyril repudiates "partitive exegesis"—the allocation of terms to two *prosōpa* or *hypostaseis*, attributing some to a man conceived of as separate from the Word of God and some only to the Word of God the Father. In the preceding letter Cyril had already stated that the one, unique Christ has no duality, despite being conceived as compounded "out of two different elements." He instances the fact that one human being has no duality despite consisting of body and soul, a point we have already seen Theodoret make. Human and divine expressions are from one speaker. Cyril quotes John 14:9 and 10:30 as examples of Christ speaking of himself "in terms appropriate to God," alludes to Hebrews 1:3, and then says of John 8:40, "the limitations of his humanity do not make us any less conscious of him as God the Word" who, he reminds us, shares equality and parity with the Father. "According to the scriptures there is one Lord Jesus Christ," he states yet again (*Ep.* 17.8). Later in his *Explanation of the Anathemas* he turns immediately to Philippians 2:6, pointing to his voluntary self-emptying and deducing that "everything relating to his divinity and everything relating to his humanity alike belong to him." He enlarges yet again on the need to assign everything to a single *prosōpon*: a single human being cannot properly be divided into two *prosōpa*, even if consisting of soul and body, and the same is true of Emmanuel. We may recall Chrysostom's *Homilies on John's Gospel*, and the way he presents the one *prosōpon* as speaking now as

41. Cyril, *Explanation* 11 (*ACO* 1.1.5).
42. See above, p. 163.

God now as man.[43] This anathema applies to people who "divide him and set apart a distinct human being . . . saying there are two sons."[44]

Theodoret, however, with good justification given the history of the "partitive exegesis" approach, clearly thinks that despite his antiheretical reputation Cyril might as well be Arius or Eunomius, as he applies to God the Word "what was uttered humbly and suitably by the form of the servant," so implying that the Son of God is inferior, a creature. The old problematic texts are called up: how can one refer texts (such as Matt 27:46; 26:39; John 12:27; Matt 26:36 // Mark 13:22) not to mention all the other passages referring to weariness, sleep, ignorance, fear, and so on to the Son who is *homoousios* with God the Father (and the epithets are piled up: Creator of the universe, Almighty, and the like)? Theodoret spells out the resultant absurdities: the Father and the Son would appear to be not of the same mind; the Son's ignorance is incompatible with foretelling his saving passion; and other such crazy corollaries.

> Surely then these words are not of the God-Word but of the form of the servant, which fears death because death was not yet destroyed.[45]

Theodoret suggests these words were permitted to prevent docetism and insists on applying what is "God-worthily uttered and performed" to God the Word and connecting "what is uttered and performed humbly" to the form of a servant so as to avoid "the blasphemy of Arius and Eunomius."[46] In due course Cyril would be forced to climb down on this one, admitting the necessity of distinctions, repudiating mixture, yet still insisting that even though some things are said of Jesus Christ "humanly" and others "divinely," all apply to the one person of the incarnate Logos.

1.4.4. Anathemas 5–9

Anathemas 5–9 condemn various aspects of the adoptionist position that Cyril understood the Antiochenes to hold: the understanding of Christ as a divinely inspired man, for whom the Word was his God or master; the idea that Jesus was a man energized by God the Word, the glory of the Only-begotten being attached to an essentially different entity; the assertion that this assumed man

43. Cf. chapter 4, 2.2.2, above.
44. Cyril, *Explanation* 13–14 (*ACO* 1.1.5:19–20).
45. Theodoret's fourth counterstatement (*ACO* 1.1.6:121–22).
46. Theodoret's fourth counterstatement (*ACO* 1.1.6:122).

should be worshipped and called God along with God the Word; and the suggestion that Christ was glorified and empowered by the Spirit to do miracles. Cyril's preceding letter had already spelled out the necessity of rejecting the idea of a God-bearing man (*Ep.* 17.4), and he had mocked the possibility that the one Christ was slave and master of himself: as man, with due regard to the self-emptying, he had, of course, said he was like us subject to God and under the law (an allusion to Gal 4:4), even though as God he was the lawgiver (*Ep.* 17.5). Cyril's letter had also addressed the issue of co-worship, a matter to which we shall return. Again, the letter had also recognized that according to John 16:14 Christ had said he would be glorified by the Spirit, but stated this should not be interpreted to mean that "the one Christ and Son was deficient in glory and acquired it from the Holy Spirit"—rather "he used his own Spirit in his mighty acts to show his own Godhead" (*Ep.* 17.10). Cyril then noted that, of course, the Spirit was a distinct *hypostasis*, but he was not alien to him: as the Spirit of Truth he was poured out by Christ, who is the Truth, just as much as poured forth from the Father.[47]

The Orientals firmly repudiated the idea that their formulae implied that Christ was energized simply like a man, a prophet, an apostle, or a righteous individual; they asserted the scriptural basis for language like "energizing" (e.g. Eph 1:19–20) and for doing signs by the power of the Spirit and insisted that he was energized "as a Son."[48] In the end, however, they failed to answer Cyril's main point: how is the "man assumed" different from a saint or a prophet? How can this be described as the incarnation of God the Word?

On anathema 5 Theodoret stated that God the Word shared like ourselves in flesh and blood and also in immortal soul (Heb 2:14 is in play again, though with that significant addition), but he certainly was not changed into flesh.[49] In his *Explanation of the Anathemas* Cyril would make almost identical statements, explaining John 1:14 in terms of Hebrews 2:14 and using Luke 3:6 to establish that "inspired Scriptures habitually refer to the human being as flesh."[50] Theodoret, however, had gone on to insist on the distinction of natures, while worshipping "the one who took and that which was taken as one Son." Cyril's *Explanation of the Anathemas* would deplore Nestorius and his followers for using the words but not saying that the Word of God became incarnate *in*

47. Some may find it interesting that Cyril would give support to the *filioque*, the subsequently controversial Western version of the Nicene Creed, which states that he proceeds from the Father *and the Son*.

48. *ACO* 1.1.7:47.

49. Theodoret's fifth counterstatement (*ACO* 1.1.6:126).

50. Cyril, *Explanation* 16 (*ACO* 1.1.5:20–21).

reality: for him that meant becoming "a man like us while remaining what he was." Cyril was still obsessed by their apparent view that "the Word of God dwelt in someone born of the holy Virgin like one of the saints," and by the way they regarded this "man set apart on his own" as "the recipient of joint worship and joint glorification." Cyril would spell out the scriptural testimony to God dwelling in us through the Holy Spirit (2 Cor 6:16, alluding to Lev 26:11 and Ezek 37:27; 1 Cor 3:16; John 10:35–36), insisting that

> God does not dwell in Christ in the same way as he does in us. For Christ was God by nature, who became like us. He was the one and only Son even when he became flesh.[51]

Theodoret, however, had defended the term "God-bearing man" on the grounds that many of the holy fathers used it, naming the great Basil and explaining that they called him this "not because he received some share of the divine grace, but as possessing all the Godhead of the Son united."[52] To establish this he quotes Colossians 2:8–9, a text we have already noticed both sides exploiting. A series of biblical texts (Gal 4:7; John 15:15; Isa 7:14; 9:6; 49:3, 6) he then deploys against the next anathema, distinguishing the form of a servant (Phil 2:7 yet again) from the Son, but then suggesting that after the assumption he was no longer servant and therefore to be confessed as "God on account of the form of God united with it," and named "Emmanuel." But what was formed from the womb was not God the Word but the form of the servant. "The God-Word was not made flesh by being changed, rather assumed flesh which had a rational soul."[53] The brief response to the seventh anathema insists that the form of a servant was glorified by the form of God.[54] The eighth anathema confirms that "the doxology we offer to the Lord Christ is one": he is "at once God and man" but "we shall not shrink from speaking of the properties of each natures."[55]

Anathema 8 shows how deeply Cyril had been offended by Nestorius's explanation of how they worshipped the assumed man along with the Word—Emmanuel should be venerated with a single worship, a single act of praise offered because the Word was made flesh. In the *Third Letter against Nestorius*

51. Cyril, *Explanation* 17 (*ACO* 1.1.5:20–21).
52. Theodoret's fifth counterstatement (*ACO* 1.1.6:126).
53. Theodoret's sixth counterstatement (*ACO* 1.1. 6:128).
54. Theodoret's seventh counterstatement (*ACO* 1.1. 6:130).
55. Theodoret's seventh counterstatement (*ACO* 1.1.6:132).

he had quoted Nestorius's statements about venerating and calling God the assumed alongside the assumer: "to say this," he asserted, "is once more to divide him into two Christs and to posit man separately on his own and to do the same with God." Cyril had then enlarged on the story of passion and resurrection, insisting that, despite being impassible in his own nature, it was "the very Son begotten of God the Father" who "suffered in flesh for our sake," who "trampled on death" so becoming "in his own flesh" the "first-born of the dead" and "first-fruits of those asleep." In the process of bringing out how this was accomplished through the power of one who was Life and Resurrection in himself, he quotes or alludes to several texts (Heb 2:9; John 11:25; Col 1:18; 1 Cor 15:20) and admits that "the resurrection of the dead" is said to have come about "through man" (1 Cor 15:21), but the power of death is broken through the Word of God (*Ep.* 17.6). Clearly he had in mind Nestorius's homily, which not only had spoken of worshipping the man assumed, but had also, as we observed earlier, attributed to that human being rather than the Logos the actual death and resurrection that achieved salvation on behalf of the rest of humanity.

In his later explanation of anathema 8 Cyril focuses on baptism, quoting Paul: "all of us who have been baptized into Christ were baptized into his death," buried and raised that "we might walk in newness of life" (Rom 6:3–4). For Cyril this is dependent on there being one Lord Jesus Christ who is the Word of the Father, and "we have been taught to worship him as someone who is one being and truly God," quoting Hebrews 1:6. It was "the Only-begotten" who "became the first-born when he appeared as a man like us," he states, alluding to Romans 8:29. To worship a man "along with but separately" from the Word of God, instead of recognizing "a true union into a single Christ and Son and Lord and honouring him with a single worship," is to incur the consequences of anathema 8.[56]

Anathema 9 criticized the idea that Christ was glorified by the Spirit, and his miracles were done by the Spirit's power. Theodoret's attack is hard-hitting in its accumulation of scriptural references and the charge that Cyril has anathematized not just current orthodox believers but even the "heralds of truth," the writers of the gospels, the apostles, and even Gabriel.[57] The words of annunciation to Mary (Luke 1:34–35), along with the announcement to Joseph (Matt 1:20) are quoted along with Matthew 1:18, followed by the Lord's own words in the synagogue (Luke 4:17, 21), those of Peter's sermon in Acts (Acts 10:38), those

56. Cyril, *Explanation* 23 (*ACO* 1.1.5:22–23).

57. Theodoret's ninth counterstatement (*ACO* 1.1.6:133).

of Isaiah (11:1–2; 42:1), and finally the words of the Lord himself (Matt 12:28) and of John the Baptist (John 1:33). Cyril "has not only anathematised prophets and apostles or even the archangel Gabriel, but extended the blasphemy even to the Saviour of all himself." Theodoret reaffirms the anointing of Christ with the Spirit and his casting out demons by the Spirit, explaining it was not God the Word who was formed by the Holy Spirit and anointed but the assumed human nature. He is willing to accept that the Spirit of the Son was his own to the extent that it is of the same nature and proceeding from the Father, but if what Cyril means is that the Spirit is "out of the Son or having his origin through the Son," then this is "blasphemous and impious." He quotes John 15:26 and 1 Corinthians 2:12 as upholding the procession of the Spirit from the Father—the proper outcome of the debates about Trinitarian theology that he surely thought Cyril had blurred. The Orientals also challenged Cyril's statement on Trinitarian grounds. Cyril's later *Explanation of the Anathemas* reiterates his view that "he worked miracles because he possessed the Holy Spirit which is from him and essentially innate within him as his own property." What he really objects to is the idea of him being a man like one of the saints, with the consequence that "the power by which he operated through the Spirit was not his own but rather was one external and appropriate to God"—indeed, that "he received his ascension to heaven from the Spirit as a grace."[58]

Our survey of the debates over anathemas 5–9 must surely have given the impression that the two sides were talking past each other. Cyril does at one level hear what the Antiochenes are saying, but he hardly grasps the significance—all he hears is an emphasis on the human nature of Christ, which suggests adoptionism. Theodoret and the Antiochenes also hear at one level what Cyril is saying, but they cannot help jumping to the conclusion that both Godhead and humanity are compromised and Arian and Apollinarian doctrines resurgent. Each is convinced that key scriptural texts justify their own views and run counter to the opposition's interpretation. We turn now to the final three anathemas, which perhaps reveal the issues that were really at stake, issues concerning fundamentally different readings of the salvation proclaimed in scripture and the mode of its achievement.

1.4.5. Anathema 10

The tenth anathema shows how profoundly Cyril failed to understand Nestorius's insight that atonement could not be achieved simply by divine fiat, that

58.Cyril, *Explanation* 25 (*ACO* 1.1.5:23).

the "debt-ridden nature" had its own indispensable part to play in reparation and reconciliation (the illuminating observation made earlier when rereading Nestorius's sermon). It is worth quoting the anathema in full:

> Divine Scripture says Christ has been made "High Priest and Apostle of our confession" (Heb 3:1) and "gave himself up for us as a fragrant offering to God the Father" (Eph 5:2). So whoever says that it was not the Word of God personally who was made our High Priest and Apostle when he became flesh and man as we are, but another woman-born man separate from him, or whoever asserts he made the offering for himself too instead of for us alone (for he who knew no sin did not need an offering), let him be anathema. (*Ep.* 17.12)

One might be forgiven for reading the opening of this anathema as simply a particular example of those different readings that emerged from response to the Arian controversy. It is an old familiar text: Hebrews 3:1. The Antiochenes insist on partitive exegesis; he is "apostle" *as human* not as Logos or Son of God. Cyril instead insists that it is the Word himself who is made "apostle" when made flesh. Here, however, to this is added high priesthood and the offering of sacrifice—Hebrews is clearly in mind still though some of the language is drawn from Ephesians. In his *Third Letter to Nestorius* Cyril had already explained that the priesthood and sacrifice should not be attributed to a different "man": the only-begotten Son of God is made mediator (1 Tim 2:5) by offering himself as a fragrant sacrifice to God the Father (Eph 5:2) and indeed to the Holy Spirit, so being the agent of peaceful reconciliation. Hebrews 10:5 and the following verses were used to substantiate this: here the Epistle quotes a modified version of Psalm 40:6–8 to indicate that obedience is preferable to sacrifice: "a body you have prepared for me" and "I have come to do your will, O God." Cyril explains:

> He proffered his own body as a fragrant sacrifice for us and not for himself. What need had he, God as he is, utterly transcending sin, of offering or sacrifice on his own behalf? (*Ep.* 17.9)

He insists that "all have sinned and fallen short of the glory of God," quoting Romans 3:23, but as "this was not his condition," clearly it was "on our account and our behalf" that "the true lamb was sacrificed." For Cyril the whole act was an act of God on our behalf—a divine fiat indeed.

It is perhaps not surprising that the Orientals reacted to this with the old arguments: God cannot be the subject of many texts in the Epistle to the Hebrews—how can God offer prayers and supplications with many tears? How can God learn obedience through suffering? Theodoret makes several of the same points. The Epistle to the Hebrews shows "the weakness of the assumed nature," he states; the unchangeable nature did not change into flesh and learn obedience by experience—the Logos is not a creature. The one who is of David's seed was made high priest and victim and offered himself to God as a sacrifice, though he did this "having in himself the God-Word from God, united and inseparably conjoined to him."[59] In the course of his argument Theodoret quotes in full Hebrews 5:1–3, which, in speaking of high priests in general, states that a priest offers "as for the people *so also for himself*." Continuing with Hebrews 5:4, 7, and 10, he asks who this is and concludes it was not "God the Word, the impassible, the immortal, the incorporeal," for he wipes away tears (Isa 25:8) and gives joy and gladness (cf. Psalms), adding further texts to confirm his divine character, such as John 16:15 and Colossians 1:15. The one assumed was mortal, passible, afraid of death and fulfilled all righteousness (Matt 3:15). This one took the name of the priesthood of Melchizedek, for "it was beset by the infirmity of nature, and was not the almighty God-Word." Theodoret adds Hebrews 4:5 and states: "It was the nature taken from us for our sakes which in the trial experienced our sufferings without sin, and not the one who for our salvation had taken it." It was "the one of David's seed, who being free from all sin became our high priest and victim." He offered himself on our behalf to God, "having in himself the God-Word from God, united and inseparably conjoined to him."

Theodoret's response would seem to have reinforced Cyril's determination to oppose this way of thinking. In his explanation he first underlines the fact that "though Lord of all by nature he brought himself down to our level and took the form of a servant," being called "our high priest and apostle" because of "the limitations of the human condition." He repeats the point that "he gave himself up for us as a fragrant offering to God the Father" (cf. Eph 5:2 again), quoting Hebrews 10:14 to underline the fact that "by a single offering he has perfected for all time those who are sanctified." He then protests against those who "maintain that it is not the incarnate Word of God himself who is called both apostle and high priest of our confession (Heb 3:1 again), but another human being apart from him," including those who suggest that he "gave himself up as a sacrifice to God the Father *not only for us but also for himself*" (my italics). Cyril uses 1 Peter 2:22 to confirm his sinlessness and the fact that "he had no need of sacrifice on his own behalf."[60]

59. Theodoret's tenth counterstatement (*ACO* 1.1.6:136–37).
60. Cyril, *Explanation* 27 (*ACO* 1.1.5:24).

The point of difference between Cyril and Theodoret would seem to hinge on whether the sacrifice was offered "on his own behalf"—Theodoret presuming his solidarity with humankind, highlighting his "fulfilling all righteousness," while acknowledging his sinlessness. What we have in Theodoret's response is certainly less clear than what we found in Nestorius's earlier homily, and Cyril may be excused perhaps for not seeing the point. Yet this anathema may well imply a real doctrinal difference. In our previous chapter we briefly noted how important for Cyril was the overarching biblical narrative of fall and redemption and the fact that old Adam was recapitulated in the second Adam.[61] But whereas recapitulation for Cyril, as for Athanasius, involved the restoration of the Logos to humankind, renewal of the image of God in which Adam was created, an act of divine rescue and re-creative power, for the Antiochenes reconciliation would seem to involve the recapitulation and reversal of the act of disobedience that caused estrangement—indeed, a sacrificial offering for atonement, not just on behalf of, but *on the part of* humankind. Was this more widely held than just by Nestorius himself? It is worth digressing a little to explore how much this was a common Antiochene approach, not only by retracing our steps to see whether Chrysostom's *Homilies on Hebrews* show traces of this perception, but also by probing what we have from Theodore of Mopsuestia.

True, Chrysostom does not spell it out in quite the same terms as Nestorius had, though, of course, Chrysostom did insist that Christ was high priest as man, interceded as man, as man was able to share and symphathize with our experiences of suffering and temptation, and indeed as man offered his own body "that he might offer a sacrifice able to purify us, for this cause he has become man" (*Hom. Heb.* 5.2). He was himself victim, priest, and sacrifice (17.3–4). Chrysostom's principal interest in these homilies was the superiority of Christ's priesthood and sacrifice compared with the provisions of the old covenant—it was, once for all, an effective medicine for sin (17.5). Following Hebrews itself, he uses the "types" of the old covenant to show how Christ's sacrifice was more effective: thus, blood is purifying, but the blood of bulls and goats is surpassed by the blood of "the Body prepared by the Spirit" (15.5), not least because it is able to purify not just the flesh but also the soul (16.5). As we noted before, Christ as Mediator entered the holy of holies (i.e., heaven) with a sacrifice that had the power to propitiate the wrath of the Father, making peace for us, enabling forgiveness and reconciliation (16.2; 17.2); sin was overcome, suffered violence, and was destroyed by the very fact it was not punished (17.5)—"we

61. See above, pp. 140 and 141; also my article "Theotokos."

had offended, we ought to have died, he died for us" (16.2). Nor should we overlook the importance of Chrysostom's emphasis on the conquest of temptation. It is certainly exemplary, for Chrysostom suggests that our high priest demonstrates that "it is possible even for one in afflictions to go through them without sin" (7.5) and elsewhere insists on our freewill—"it depends on us . . . we must first choose the good; and then he leads us" (12.5). Yet it is more than exemplary, indeed essential, to establish victory over the devil, and so overcome the power of death (4.6; 5.1–2). Even though Chrysostom is clear that, being without sin, he did not "die as owing the debt of death, nor yet because of sin," it would seem implicit that salvation required an act *on the part of* humankind, not just on its behalf, to reverse the old propensity to succumb to temptation, to purify what had been contaminated, to offer some kind of recompense for disobedience, and to put sin, death, and the devil at a disadvantage.

So, at least in the homilies we have considered, the idea of the humanity of Christ bearing our death penalty seems to be there subliminally, though less clearly spelled out than by Nestorius. It is much more evident, however, in what we have of the writings of Theodore of Mopsuestia, who stated explicitly that it was "in order to make satisfaction for all others" that

> he underwent death as *the payment that our nature owes*, in order that, by dying in accordance with what is required of human nature, and then by rising from the dead by means of divine power, there would be a new beginning for all other humans who have died in accordance with their nature. (my italics)[62]

Referring to Philippians 3:21 and 1 Corinthians 15:48–49, he indicates that as we all "conformed to Adam according to our present state, so we will be made conformed to Christ our Lord in the future." Elsewhere he insists that "we are all one human being by reason of our nature," paralleling Adam as the beginning of our present life with Christ in whose resurrection we will all share, and whose body we become when united to him in baptism.[63] Recapitulation is clearly of such fundamental importance to Theodore that a key element

62. The works of Theodore are not easy to access but may be sampled in the selections translated by Frederick G. McLeod, *Theodore of Mopsuestia* (London: Routledge, 2009). This passage is found on pp. 88–89, which is a translation of a Greek text of PG 66:1009.

63. McLeod, *Theodore*, 119, a translation of the Latin text found in H. B. Swete, *Theodori Episcopi Mopsuesteni in Epistolas B. Pauli Commentarii*, 2 vols. (Cambridge: Cambridge University Press, 1880, 1882), 1:57; cf. McLeod, *Theodore*, 101 and 106 for further statements about the solidarity of humankind in Adam and in Christ.

in his protests against the allegorists lies in their refusal to take the story of Adam literally.[64] How can they account for the existence of "the disobedient one" or the introduction of "the sentence of death"?[65] The "assumed man" had to grow in virtue and battle against spiritual passions as much as those of the body so as to reverse that condemnation.[66] "The sentence of death for everyone has been abolished," he states, quoting Romans 8:1–2.[67] Elsewhere, quoting Hebrews 2:10 Theodore writes:

> See how clearly he says that God the Word has made the assumed man perfect through sufferings and has called him the leader of salvation[68]

In fact, he had unique assistance from the indwelling Word, but

> we will not assert that the man had no voluntary part [to play], for he did prefer the good; in fact he purposely desired to accomplish the greatest good and to hate evil.[69]

This perfect fulfillment of righteousness for our sake is predominant, and Theodore is explicit that, if it was the Godhead that conquered, then "nothing he did would benefit us."[70] Yet it came out of cooperation: when John the Baptist said, "Behold the Lamb of God," this signified his humanity—the one to undergo death because "he is a 'body' that has been offered for the whole world." But what follows—"who takes away the sin of the world"—is "in no way applicable to the flesh. For it was not in his power to take away the sin of the world. This is certainly the work of the divinity."[71] On Philippians 2:5–11, though positing the union of Assumer and the one assumed, Theodore indicates that the one who was actually crucified and died in accordance with his nature was human:

64. For the wider cosmic implications of recapitulation in Theodore's thought, see McLeod's introduction to *Theodore.*

65. McLeod, *Theodore*, 120–21. Greek text in Swete, *Pauli Commentarii*, 1:73.

66. Theodore, *Inc.* 7 (PG 66:980); translation quoted from McLeod, *Theodore*, 134; cf. *Inc.* 15 (text in Swete, *Paul Commentarii*, 2:311).

67. From the Syriac of his *Catechetical Homilies* 5.14; translation quoted from McLeod, *Theodore*, 159.

68. McLeod, *Theodore*, 138 (PG 66:985).

69. Theodore, *Inc.* 14 (PG 66:989), translation quoted from McLeod, *Theodore*, 141.

70. Theodore, *Inc.* 15. Latin text in Swete, *Paul Commentarii*, 2:311; translation quoted from McLeod, *Theodore*, 142.

71. Theodore, *Inc.* 10 (PG 66:983–84); translation quoted from McLeod, *Theodore*, 137.

> For was it not a human being who humbled himself and obeyed unto death, all the way to the cross, by bringing death upon himself, a death that God imposed upon our nature as a punishment from the beginning? The one assumed by God the Word was able to overcome death because of his union, and was willing to endure his passion for our salvation.[72]

Thus, human nature had a vital role to play, but it is not simply the achievement of a moral victory; it has greater salvific significance by being placed in the overall context of recapitulation and conceived as reparation for what had gone wrong. Behind Nestorius's homily there surely lies the thought of Theodore.

Furthermore, that such ideas were shared among the Antiochenes is surely confirmed by the fact that Theodoret himself spelled out similar points more clearly elsewhere than in his response to the anathemas. We may sample a few of his statements from his *On the Incarnation of the Lord*:[73]

> [On Rom 8:3–4: "he condemned sin in the flesh"] He did this not to justify the man he assumed, but—as he says—so that the righteousness of the law might be fulfilled in us. . . . The benefaction of our Saviour extends to the whole nature of humankind: as with our forefather Adam, we both share the curse and have all arrived under the [power] of death like him; in the same way we also appropriate the victory of the Saviour Christ . . . the righteousness of our Saviour means the deliverance from the former [state of condemnation].

> [Against Apollinaris] If the assumed nature did not possess a human mind, then it is God who fought against the devil, and God is crowned in victory. Yet if God is the winner I gained nothing from the victory, as not having contributed to it with anything. . . . I have been deprived of victory, [because] God fulfilled all righteousness.

> By enduring these things, he achieved our salvation. Because the servants of sin were liable to the punishment of sin, therefore he, who was immune from sin and pursued rightousness in all respects, accepted the punishment

72. Theodore, *Comm. Phil.* 2:5–11. Quoted in McLeod, *Theodore*, 114. Syriac text from E. Sachau, ed., *Theodori Mopsuesteni Fragmenta Syriaca* (Leipzig: Engelmann, 1869).

73. These translated selections are from Pásztori-Kupán, *Theodoret*. They are all drawn from the reattributed *De incarnatione Domini* (PG 75:1419–78).

> of sinners. By the cross he repealed the sentence of the ancient curse, for [Paul] says: "Christ had redeemed us from the curse of the law, being made a curse for us: for it is written, 'Cursed is every one that hangs on a tree'" (Gal 3:13 and Deut 21:23).

So did Cyril ever get to grips with this point? It is worth a quick look at one of the homilies preached by Cyril during that disastrously split Council of Ephesus. It suggests that he had some inkling by then of what the Antiochenes were saying about reparation and indeed, given his allusions to 1 Peter 1:18 and 1 Corinthians 6:20, of the strength of their appeal to the scriptures on this point. Yet he saw it rather differently, anticipating Anselm in his own way:

> we were redeemed for a price, not with perishable things, such as silver and gold, but with the precious blood of Christ, like that of a lamb without blemish or spot. But how can the blood of a common man, of one who is similar to us, be [sufficient] ransom for the world? And how, also, did one man die on behalf of all, that he may enrich all?[74]

For Cyril the restoration of humankind had to be an act of God.

1.4.6. Anathema 11

Anathema 11 is concerned with Cyril's most fundamental commitment, namely, the power of the Eucharist to impart life and immortality. Let us again quote in full:

> Whoever does not acknowledge the Lord's flesh to be vitalizing and to belong to the Word of God the Father but says it belongs to somebody different joined to him by way of rank or merely possessing divine indwelling instead of being vitalizing, as we have said, because it has come to belong to the Word who has power to vivify everything, shall be anathema. (*Ep.* 17.13)

According to Cyril's *Third Letter to Nestorius*, when "we perform in church the unbloody sacrifice" what we receive is not "mere flesh, or the flesh of a man hallowed by some kind of connection with the Word." Rather "the actual life-giving flesh of the Word himself" is received "when we approach the sacramental gifts and are hallowed participants in the holy flesh and precious

74. *Homily* 5 (*ACO* 1.1.2:92–94). English translation from Wessel, *Cyril of Alexandria*, 304.

blood of Christ, Saviour of us all." The Word is by nature life, and by becoming one with his own flesh he rendered it life-giving. Cyril quotes John 6:53: "unless you eat the flesh of the Son of Man and drink his blood," pointing out that as ordinary human flesh it could not be life-giving—it is only because it is the very own flesh of the one "who for us has become and is named 'Son of Man'" (*Ep.* 17.7).

Apropos this anathema, the Orientals accuse Cyril of Apollinarianism: confusion of the natures is the result of speaking of "his own flesh" rather than recognizing the flesh was ours. Theodoret too thinks Cyril talks of the flesh in the same way as Apollinaris, neither mentioning it was intelligent nor accepting that the assumed man was complete. He agrees that the flesh is life-giving because it is united with the "life-giving Godhead," but there is no escaping the two natures implied by that.[75] Constantly we have found Cyril defending himself against these very charges: of course "flesh" means "man in completeness," or "flesh with a soul and a mind," and of course the union is without confusion. But the later explanation of this anathema simply reiterates the point about the Eucharist being

> the very own body and blood of the Word who endows all things with life. For ordinary flesh cannot endow with life. The Saviour himself testifies to this when he says: "The flesh is of no avail; it is the spirit that gives life" (John 6:63). Because it became the Word's own flesh it is therefore regarded as life-giving and actually is so. "As the Father sent me, and I live because of the Father, so he who eats me will live because of me" (John 6:57). Since Nestorius and those who think like him ignorantly weaken the power of the mystery, that is why this anathema has rightly been drawn up.[76]

1.4.7. Anathema 12

So to the final Anathema 12, which puts starkly the troublesome issue of divine suffering. Again we quote in full:

> If anyone does not acknowledge that the Word of God suffered in the flesh, and was crucified in the flesh, and experienced death in the flesh, and became the first-born from the dead, seeing that as God he is both life and life-giving, let him be anathema. (*Ep.* 17.12)

75. Theodoret's eleventh counterstatement (*ACO* 1.1.6:142–43).
76. Cyril, *Explanation* 27 (*ACO* 1.1.5:24).

Earlier in his *Third Letter to Nestorius* Cyril had made the following statement:

> We confess that the very Son of God the Father, the Only-begotten God, impassible though he is in his own nature, has (as the Bible says) suffered in flesh for our sake and that he was in the crucified body claiming the sufferings of his flesh as his own impassibly. By nature Life and personally the Resurrection though he exists and is, "by God's grace he tasted death for every man" (Heb 2:9) in surrendering his body to it . . . "by God's grace" . . . he tasted death for every man, harrowed Hell and came back to life the third day. (*Ep.* 17.6)

He adds that though the resurrection of the dead is said to have come about "through man" (1 Cor 15:21); this is to be interpreted as through the incarnate Word of God who broke the power of death.

The Orientals have a habit of quoting Cyril's own words against the statements in his anathemas, and here they point out that Cyril himself admitted the impassibility of the Godhead, yet to say "God suffered in flesh" implies divine passibility—a degradation of the Deity. Theodoret goes for the logic: "Passions are proper to the passible, for the impassible is above passions"; therefore it was "the form the servant" that suffered,

> the form of God of course being together with it, and permitting it to suffer on account of the salvation brought forth out of the sufferings, and making the sufferings its own through the union.[77]

The distinction is underlined: it was not God who suffered, but the man taken of us by God," and he quotes Isaiah 53:3. Life itself is not killed, but "the one who has the mortal nature." John 2:19 is quoted to show that "the one who was of David" was destroyed while "the Only-begotten God-Word, born impassibly of the Father before the ages, raised up the destroyed one."

In his explanation Cyril begins by admitting that "the Word of God the Father is impassible and immortal. For the divine and ineffable nature transcends suffering." He adds that this is what is "superior to corruption and anything that normally causes us grief." Impassibility is as important to him as to the Antiochenes, but for him it is the precondition for victory over sin and death. The Word is impassible "in his essential being" and

77. Theodoret's twelfth counterstatement (*ACO* 1.1.6:144).

> he made his own the flesh that is receptive of death, that by means of that which is accustomed to suffering he might take these sufferings to himself on our behalf and for our sake and deliver all of us from both corruption and death.[78]

Cyril is still haunted by what he sees as the useless idea that the one "who endured the precious cross for our sakes and experienced it" was just "an ordinary man to be regarded as separate and distinct from the Word of God the Father." According to the scriptures, 1 Peter 4:1 in particular, the Lord of glory himself suffered in the flesh.

The discussion of anathema 12 is relatively brief, then, each side repeating well-known assertions. Yet the significance of this anathema is surely profound, casting its shadow over all the others. Cyril is determined that the Logos is the subject of the incarnate experiences and will not let go of the paradox that the impassible suffers and the immortal dies. For the Antiochenes this is unquestionably blasphemy—if the Son is *homoousios tōi Patri* yet *pathētos*, then God the Father must be passible. So to what extent would it be fair to say that the latter argue from a predetermined concept of divinity while Cyril allows philosophical presuppositions to be challenged by the Christian revelation? That is surely a false contrast. Cyril repeatedly accepts that the divine nature is impassible: in one of his homilies at Ephesus he states that "the nature of the Word is unchangeable and immutable, and it cannot suffer even a 'shadow of change'" (Jas 1:17), basing this "philosophical" idea in scripture, just as we have seen the Antiochenes do.[79] Both sides for good reason found in scripture and tradition the basic confession of God as the ultimate transcendent Creator God, source of all life, utterly other, just and impartial—beyond change or corruption—and therefore, in their view, unquestionably *apathēs*. True, Cyril was persistently heard to compromise this with his emphasis on the Word's *kenōsis*—his self-emptying—and his notorious phrase *apathōs epathen*. Yet, to suggest any modification of the fundamental concept of divine *apatheia* would surely have been inconceivable to Cyril, particularly given what we discovered in the previous chapter when exploring his *Commentary on John's Gospel*.[80] And yet, maybe Cyril's emphasis there on the Word's free choice to assume the form of a slave, suffer, and die does imply a concept of such creative freedom as to override the supposed constraints of his own di-

78. Cyril, *Explanation* 31 (*ACO* 1.1.5:25).

79. See above, e.g., p. 186 for Nestorius and p. 191 for Cyril. Quotation from Cyril's *Homily* 2 (*ACO* 1.1.2:94–96). English translation in Wessel, *Cyril of Alexandria*, 319.

80. See above, pp. 154–60.

vine nature—potentially the second illuminating insight of this chapter. More than the Antiochenes, Cyril was prepared to let philosophical presuppositions be challenged by the gospel.

1.4.8. The Nub of the Issue—Different Understandings of What Was Required for Salvation

In fact, however, both sides were determined to do justice to scripture and to avoid replaying false, easy solutions to the paradoxes, solutions already dismissed with the condemnation of those who had become bywords for heresy: Arius, Apollinaris, Paul of Samosata, not to mention the docetists and adoptionists of old. They had so much in common that it is perhaps not altogether surprising that once Nestorius was out of the way John of Antioch and Cyril of Alexandria could agree on a *Formulary of Reunion*. And yet, have we not found that at root there were different readings of scripture that underlay different emphases in appeal to the Nicene Creed, the key doctrinal statement that neither side would think of challenging? Rather than disagreements and misunderstandings over terminology, which there certainly were, the nature of the saving act of recapitulation was surely the really divisive issue, because it inevitably generated instinctive negative reactions to key elements of the other side's position, persistent mishearings of the fundamentally scriptural case each side was pressing. It would ultimately become imperative to embrace the truths to which each side pointed, namely, the full involvement of both Godhead and humanity in the incarnate medium of reconciliation. For, on the one hand (the Antiochene arm), the sin that had disrupted the relationship of humankind with its Creator required some kind of reparation *on the part of humankind*, though it was itself also an act initiated and assisted by the very Word and Son of God out of *philanthrōpia*. On the other hand (the Alexandrian wing), no ordinary human being could adequately perform this act of mediation—only the Word of God could heal the wounded creature and restore the image of God, though this certainly required willing and humble receptivity on humanity's part. It was these dynamics, at once both divergent and convergent, their drivers essentially scriptural, that now necessitated some kind of dogmatic definition in agreed formulae.

1.5. The Formulary of Reunion

Despite the débacle of the Council of Ephesus in 431, John of Antioch and Cyril of Alexandria found their way to an agreed statement in 433. It was admittedly the result of pressure from the imperial government, and yet it has been noted that Cyril's efforts and expense to get the support of imperial officials was pricey: "the bankrupting size is the sincerest testimony to Cyril's wish for a united Church and should, in fairness, bring him credit."[81] Envoys engaged in negotiation and carried letters; Cyril's one stipulation was that the condemnation of Nestorius should stand, though willing to differentiate Nestorius's teaching from that of others in the Antiochene camp.[82] In one of his letters to John of Antioch, Cyril welcomed the proposed formulary, setting it out in full:

> We confess, then, our Lord Jesus Christ, the only-begotten Son of God, Perfect God and Perfect Man of a rational soul and body; before the ages begotten from the Father as to His Godhead, and in the last days the Selfsame for us and for our salvation, (born) of Mary the Virgin as to his Manhood; the same co-essential with the Father as to Godhead and co-essential with us as to Manhood, for there was a union of Two Natures, whereby we confess One Christ, One Son, One Lord. And according to this idea of the unconfused Union we confess the holy Virgin to be Theotokos, because that God the Word was incarnate, and lived as Man, and from the very conception, united to Himself the temple which He took of her. And with regard to the evangelic and apostolic sayings concerning the Lord, we know that theologians make some common, as relating to One Person, and distinguish others, as relating to Two Natures, interpreting the God-befitting ones of the Godhead of Christ, and the lowly ones of His Humanity.[83]

Each side had made concessions: the Antiochenes embraced *Theotokos*, whereas Cyril embraced the explicit affirmation of two natures, passing over his controversial "one-nature" formula. Each side had secured key points: Cyril the single subject of the narrative, the Antiochenes the principle of partitive exegesis. The preamble noted that the statement was "not by way of supplement . . . making no addition at all to the Creed of the holy fathers put forth at Nicaea." It was the faith "as we have held from the first, having received it both from the divine scriptures and from the tradition of the holy fathers" and "it suffices both for all knowledge of orthodoxy and for the exclusion of all heretical blasphemy."

81. Wickham, *Select Letters*, xxv; cf. 66–67 n. 8.

82. E.g., Cyril's letter *To Acacius of Melitene* (*Ep.* 40.9–10, 15–19); see the translation in Wickham, *Select Letters*, 44–57.

83. Text and English translation of the Formulary in the relevant epistle (unnumbered, but elsewhere enumerated as *Ep.* 39) in Bindley and Green, *Oecumenical Documents*, 142 and 221.

Though not a new creed, the statement is, of course, couched in the language of creedal confession, and though taken to encapsulate the gist of the scriptures with respect to the issues at stake, it barely alludes to biblical texts as such. A few basic terms like "only-begotten Son of God" and the "temple which he took" ultimately derive from scripture, but they are used alongside nonscriptural language, such as the Nicene *homoousion*, "unconfused union," and so on in order to specify exactly what is meant. Here are the doctrinal propositions about the incarnation which we found missing from Cyril's *Commentary on John's Gospel*, now prepared and ready to stand alongside those Trinitarian theses.[84] A process of heated debate about the implications of scripture had generated the formulation of such agreed doctrinal propositions.

2. Revealing Dialogues

Yet this was by no means the end. Another twenty years would pass before the classic definition was reached at Chalcedon in 451. Already in his letter accepting the *Formulary of Reunion* we find Cyril attempting to deflect continuing suspicion on the part of the Antiochenes that his doctrine is Apollinarian and Patripassian.[85] Further letters of explanation and self-defense indicate his ongoing need to justify his accommodation to the other side—his own side clearly remained suspicious of the language of two natures, whilst the charge of Apollinarianism continued to rankle.[86] The issues had not been put to bed, despite repeated appeal to their common commitment to the doctrine of Athanasius's *Epistle to Epictetus*, though perhaps it is telling that Cyril makes persistent reference to the existence of corrupt versions of the text.[87] This is the ongoing situation in which were composed the dialogues to which our attention now turns.

Around 438 Cyril wrote *On the Unity of Christ*, which has been described as "one of his most mature theological works."[88] Some ten years later Theodoret composed the *Eranistes*. If the context for Cyril remains the need to justify

84. See above, chapter 4.

85. Cyril, *Letter to John of Antioch* (*Ep.* 39).

86. Cyril, *To Acacius of Melitene* (*Ep.* 40.12–14, 20); *To Eulogius* (*Ep.* 44); *First Letter to Succensus* (*Ep.* 45.5–6). Translation of all *Letters* in Wickham, *Select Letters*.

87. Cyril, *Letter to John of Antioch* (*Ep.* 39); text and English translation in Bindley and Green, *Oecumenical Documents*, 144 and 223; cf. also *To Acacius of Melitene* (*Ep.* 40.21), *To Eulogius* (*Ep.* 44); *First Letter to Succensus* (*Ep.* 45.11).

88. See the introduction to *On the Unity of Christ*, trans. John Anthony McGuckin (Crestwood, NY: St. Vladimir's Seminary Press, 1995), 30.

his own position, for Theodoret it was renewed controversy over the views of Eutyches, which would prove to be the immediate lead-up to the Council of Chalcedon. Each was doubtless producing propaganda, seeking to induce or confirm the reader's grasp of the truth. Yet the dialogue form necessarily sets up debate, enabling us to gauge something of how each side heard and responded to the other's arguments, especially their appeal to and interpretation of scripture. It is perhaps not surprising that when I first attended to the relationship between doctrine and scripture I turned to these dialogues.[89] A major question now is whether each had listened sufficiently closely to the other to be able faithfully to represent the opposing position, or indeed grasp the significance of the critique offered to their own, particularly with respect to the manner in which scripture is deployed to develop and substantiate doctrinal propositions.

2.1. *Cyril of Alexandria:* On the Unity of Christ

On the Unity of Christ follows a pattern Cyril had already used in his seven *Dialogues on the Trinity*, the *dramatis personae* being identified in the text as *A* and *B* respectively.[90] Persona *A* sketches out recognizably Arian and Nestorian teaching without specific attribution; persona *B*, confessing himself "so put out by all this" and "afraid" about "where this teaching will all end" (*Un. Chr.* 716 [51]), then begins to ask questions, sometimes suggesting what the others might say, often agreeing with *A*'s exposition. More often than not, *B* is just a stooge representing the reader who is to be led to the truth by the arguments of *A*, who clearly represents Cyril's own position.

The most striking thing about this work, now that we have considered Cyril's position earlier in the decade, is the lack of reference to the Nicene Creed, previous authorities, or named heretics, the predominance of debate being around scripture and its intent. Frequent affirmations are made to the

89. See my article "Exegetical Method and Scriptural Proof: The Bible in Doctrinal Debate," StPatr 19 (1989): 291–304, which explores the first dialogue of Theodoret's *Eranistes*; it is also the case that of all the material in these two christological chapters, the section on Cyril's dialogue was the first to be drafted.

90. Citations of *On the Unity of Christ* follow the Greek text in G. M. de Durand, ed., *Deux dialogues christologiques*, SC 97 (Paris: Cerf, 1964), 302–514; Greek text may also be found in the edition in volume 7 of Pusey, *Cyrilli Archiepiscopi Alexandriae*. English translation, unless otherwise noted, in McGuckin, *On the Unity of Christ*. Citations of the page numbers of McGuckin's translation appear in brackets.

effect that a point is in accord with, or in disagreement with, "God-inspired scripture."[91] For example:

> Surely our exposition follows the mind of the scriptures? (*Un. Chr.* 729 [69])

> The mind of the holy scriptures does not admit anything like this. (744 [88])

Throughout the dialogue there is a wealth of scriptural references adorning the conversation; barely a single page is without biblical quotation or allusion—indeed there are over three per page on average. So, from the beginning scriptural quotations enhance conventional points: "Man shall not live by bread alone, but by every word that comes from the mouth of God" (Matt 4:4; Deut 8:3) shows how "the Word of God is food for the mind and spiritual 'bread that strengthens the heart of man'" (cf. Ps 104:15), while pagan love of elegant expression and small regard for the truth are dismissed by quoting Paul (Rom 1:21). The *B* character agrees and adds Isaiah 44:20 (*Un. Chr.* 714–715 [49–50]). Further texts are gathered to blacken heretics, as a couple of sentences sum up the position of Arians and Nestorians without naming them:[92]

> In effect the first group, insofar as lies within their power, drag down the Word born of God the Father from the heights of divinity even before his incarnation, while the second group have decided to wage war against the Word even in his incarnation. (*Un. Chr.* 715 [51])

The latter find unreasonable the idea that

> he inflicted flesh upon himself and took up the limitations of this self-emptying, that is, became man and "appeared on earth and engaged with men"; God-inspired scripture will cry out against both forms of madness. (715 [51])

It is worth noting that the text quoted here is Baruch 3:38—a text long since exploited by the Monarchians to claim that it was the one and only God who came down to earth in Christ. Now that the Word of God was conceived as fully divine rather than as some kind of mediating being (the initial response

91. E.g., Cyril, *Un. Chr.* 716–717, 727–728, 744, 757, 760 (51, 53, 65, 67, 88, 106, 109).

92. Texts used to decry heretics include Acts 20:30; Prov 26:11; 2 Pet 2:21–22; Heb 2:6; 1 John 2:19; Prov 9:18 LXX.

to Monarchianism), to make sense of this appearance on earth and "becoming man" required fresh articulation against what were perceived to be inadequate conceptions. Without a doubt this is all about making sense of scripture.

In this dialogue Cyril spirals around the familiar issues, returning over and over again to the same basic points in a way that can become very repetitive. So, rather than pursuing the debate blow by blow, we will abstract key topics, introducing them in the order in which they first appear, then following through later returns to the same topic.

2.1.1. Son by Nature, Son by Grace

It is no surprise that the opening issue (*Un. Chr.* 716–717 [52–53]) concerns the Nestorian denial that the holy Virgin is the Mother of God, which means "they must also deny that Emmanuel is God." It was pointless, then, for the Evangelist to translate Emmanuel as "God with us" (Matt 1:23; cf. Isa 7:14). Yet that is "exactly how we ought to name the one that is born of the holy virgin according to the flesh," as we are taught "through the voice of the prophet." Persona *B* suggests that the opposition does accept that the Word of God was present helping us and "saving everything under heaven through the one that was born of a woman." For *A*, however, that interpretation is not strong enough: surely God was with Moses and Joshua, a point made in phrases drawn from biblical texts (Ps 136:12; Josh 3:7). So "why are neither of them called Emmanuel? Why does this name apply only to the one who was so wondrously born of a woman, according to the flesh, in these last times of the world?"

For Cyril, Matthew 1:23 identifies the nub of the problem: "Emmanuel" must mean that the presence of the divine Word in the incarnation is different from the presence of God in other cases. This theme will recur in the dialogue. At one point *B* tries to explain that the opposition does not intend to teach two Sons or two Christs—to that extent Cyril does seem to have realized that it was an unfair charge:

> they say that the Word of God the Father, who is Son by nature, is one; but that the man who is assumed is by nature son of David. . . . He has come to such dignity and has the sonship by grace, because God the Word dwells within him. (*Un. Chr.* 737 [80])

But for *A* this is senseless: How can they say there is not a duality of sons when they split off man and God from each other? Cyril maintains what he sees as the logic of their position. However, the point he then takes up is the difference between being son by grace and Son by nature. After all the Word also dwells in us, as Paul indicates with the words, "that Christ may dwell in your hearts" (Eph 3:14–17); and "he is within us by the Spirit 'in whom we cry out, Abba Father'" (Rom 8:15). So "we too are sons and gods by grace." To say the same of Jesus is "wicked and foolish," and the ensuing conversation pinpoints why (*Un. Chr.* 737–740 [80–83]). First, if not by nature, the Sonship is an addendum that could be lost, but, more importantly, if he is not truly Son but stands alongside us who have sonship by grace, it undermines the Son's ability to grant adopted sonship to others. The gospel parable of the tenants in the vineyard demonstrates the difference. To protest that the one who is son of David is not Son of God by nature just leads to their duality of sons, and the mystery of Christ, the incarnation itself, becomes false and superfluous. *A* cites Matthew's account of Jesus challenging the Jewish teachers: "What do you think of Christ? Whose son is he? . . . How then did David call him Lord?" (Matt 22:42–45); then he adds verses from Hebrews 1 and Ephesians 1:21, which speak of his Sonship and sitting on the throne above all thrones and every name that can be named. Scripture in Cyril's eyes consistently differentiates the true Son from sons by grace.

The same fundamental argument appears again later on when *B* suggests that they say "he dwelt within a man" (*Un. Chr.* 749–750 [96]). *A* mocks the idea that he is a mere "inhabitant"—that, as one who dwells in Nazareth is called Nazarene, so he should be called "mannish" rather than "man." But then he mounts a more telling argument: scripture shows that "the fullness of the Trinity dwells within us through the Spirit," for that is why Paul says, "Do you not know that you are the temple of God and that the Spirit of God dwells within you?" (1 Cor 3:16), and Christ himself states, "If anyone loves me he will keep my word and my Father will love him, and we shall come to him and make our abode with him" (John 14:23). However,

> neither the Father nor the Holy Spirit have ever been called a man because of the fact that they dwell within us. These people are making a mockery of the mystery of the incarnation. Dogmas of the church . . . are twisted round by them to the point of deformity. (*Un. Chr.* 750 [96–97])

Their mistake is to reduce the Son to the status of "the apostles and prophets." *B* protests that Acts 3:22 and Hebrews 3:1 show that he was indeed called prophet and apostle, but *A* responds that the reason "why he is named prophet, apostle, and priest," is that he was "made like his brethren in all things" when he assumed the form of a slave. That, of course, alludes to what have proved to be absolutely key passages during the controversy, namely Hebrews 2:17 and Philippians 2:5–11. There is a recognition here that scripture text can be ranged against scripture text, and what matters is the overarching narrative context, or conceptual scheme, within which the texts are read coherently.

2.1.2. Kenōsis: *John 1:14 and Philippians 2:5–11*

Returning to the sequence of the dialogue, we find *B* with a question about the "Emmanuel" argument (*Un. Chr.* 717 [53]): "Then how should we understand that God was born of a woman? Does it mean that the Word took up his being in her and from her?" Persona *A* protests at the idea that "the Only Begotten could ever be the fruit of flesh": as God he was "ineffably begotten by nature from the Father and coeternal." What clinches it for *A* is John 1:14: "the Word became flesh."

The problem now is the verb "became." The unhinged opposition seems to suggest that it "inevitably and necessarily signifies change or alteration." *B* substantiates this and offers biblical justification of that view: Lot's wife becoming a pillar of salt (Gen 19:26) and Moses's staff becoming a serpent (Exod 4:3). *A*'s riposte consists of texts that cannot be taken to signify such transformation, such as "the Lord became my refuge" (Pss 94:22; 90:1), so it is "impious and absurd" to "presume" change rather than "applying some wisdom and turning instead to what is much more fitting and applicable to the unchangeable God." We should notice here the nature of the exegetical argument. This is not about possible literal, metaphorical, or symbolic senses, but rather about appropriate meaning given the subject and context. When it comes to the applicability to God of ordinary, everyday language, the plain meaning may need to be critically modified or extended though perhaps not evacuated. Determining this is a rational and deductive process on the basis of biblical parallels or theological presuppositions. This is not the first time we have noted this process of making sense of scripture, nor will it be the last.

Now we find *B* pressing for further explanation (*Un. Chr.* 718–719 [54]). *A* switches to Philippians 2:5–8 (reinforced by Heb 1:3 and 12:2). As we have seen, there was constant cross-referencing and interplay between the Philippians 2 passage and John 1:14 in the course of the controversy; we shall find it again in Theodoret's dialogue. Here it is worth taking something of an overview of the main import of Cyril's constant appeal to the Philippians passage across the dialogue.

For Cyril the point is that the Word "submitted himself to being emptied" and made the flesh "his very own." It was the only-begotten Word who became man.

> He did not disdain the poverty of human nature. . . . The same one was at once God and man, and he was "in the likeness of men" (Phil 2:7) since even though he was God he was "in the fashion of a man" (Phil 2:8). He

> was God in an appearance like ours, and the Lord in the form of a slave. (*Un. Chr.* 718–719 [55])

In other words there is one subject of the whole passage, namely the Logos, who willingly "emptied himself." Cyril keeps returning to "his acceptance of servile limitations" (721 [58]), to the way he voluntarily abased himself "to our condition out of tender love" (722 [59]), to his self emptying and humbling of himself to assume the form of a slave. His Christology is fundamentally kenotic, despite his constant affirmation that he remained what he was, and despite his appropriation of the quasi-docetic language of Philippians. It was, of course, this quasi-docetism, in the form of an apparent Apollinarianism, which disturbed the other side, and in places in this dialogue *A* attempts to preempt this by asserting that

> the body which he united to himself was endowed with a rational soul, for the Word, who is God, would hardly neglect our finer part, the soul, and have regard only for the earthly body. (*Un. Chr.* 726 [64])

Somewhat later on *B* tries to say that when the other side talks about "assumption," they too base their view on the Philippians passage, drawing attention to the words "taking the form of a slave," an intervention that certainly indicates Cyril's awareness of the Antiochene use of this very passage. However, *A* urges that the "proper conclusion" is

> that the one assumed in this inseparable union has become the personal property of the one assuming, and while Jesus is God, the one and only true Son of God, the Word of God the Father born of God before all ages and times, nonetheless the same one, in these last times of the present age, has been born of a woman according to the flesh, for the form of a slave belongs to no other, but was his very own. (*Un. Chr.* 734 [75])

Later still in the dialogue, *A* again insists that when he "assumed the form of a slave" it was "not as if he joined a man to himself, as they would say, but rather that he himself came in that form, while even so remaining in likeness to God the Father" (758 [108]).

Meanwhile, however, *B* has drawn attention to the reason for the opposition's insistence on the "conjunction" of the Word with "one who is of David's line":

> "He became obedient to the Father even to death, death on a cross. So God has highly exalted him and granted him the name above every name"

> (Phil 2:5–9), and this name is God. . . . [But] how could the Only Begotten, who is from God by nature, ever be given what he already possesses? (*Un. Chr.* 741 [85])

It is important to remember that this Philippians passage was the first of those controversial texts which Athanasius had had to tackle in the first book of his *Orations against the Arians* (1.40–41).[93] Arians had been using it, along with other texts, to argue that the Son was adopted, promoted, or rewarded. Athanasius had insisted that the passage showed how he descended so as to be exalted, that "humbled" and "exalted" are spoken of his human nature, and "because of the flesh he bore."

> For as Christ died and was exalted as man, so, as man, is he said to take what, as God, He ever had, that even such a grant of grace might reach to us. (*C. Ar.* 1.42)

Now in Cyril's dialogue, *B* recognizes that this old issue needs to be addressed. *A*'s response, of course, is to object to considering the "one who is of David's line" separately and on his own, and to inquire how he could be the one who preexisted and assumed the form of a slave (*Un. Chr.* 741–742 [85])—in other words, *A* insists again that there has to be one subject of the text's narrative of descent and ascent, and sense cannot be made of it by dividing aspects of it between two separable entities.

The Philippians 2 passage is again quoted in full further on in the dialogue (*Un. Chr.* 769–771 [121–23]). The issue now is the honor of sitting at the right hand: *B* asks how the Word could receive something he already had. Surely "the name above every name" must have been given to "the man who was assumed." *A* is worried about introducing a

> new or recent god among angels and men, one that holds the glory of the Godhead not essentially within his own being, but as something added on from outside, and as if only by the will of God the Father.

He suggests that the name was given by the Father to the Word "made man for our sake." That is why he said, "The Father is greater than I" (John 14:28) despite having "exact equality" with him—"he enjoyed the highest eminence in humility" and "held what belongs to him by nature (that is, to be worshipped

93. See above, chapter 2, pp. 33–34.

by all) as a gift because of his humanity." John 17:5 explains Philippians 2:10–11, and John 1:1 explains Philippians 2:6. *A* is back, drawing attention to the overall narrative of descent and ascent.

Consistently for Cyril, then, the point is that the Word submitted himself to "the limitations of the manhood" (*Un. Chr.* 742 [86]) and made the flesh his very own so as to redeem it from sin and death; as he originally put it, he did not "change himself into flesh" or "endure any mixture or blending," but "he is said to have undergone a birth like ours, while all the while remaining what he was" (*Un. Chr.* 718–719 [54–55]). This is the meaning of "became flesh" and the reason why "we affirm that the holy virgin is the Mother of God."

Cyril first introduced the Philippians text to explain the meaning of John 1:14. So now we return to that initial discussion of how "became" is to be understood. There *B* had taken up the issue on behalf of the other side, arguing that, since scripture speaks of him becoming "sin for our sake" and "a curse for us" (2 Cor 5:21; Gal 3:13), even though clearly "this does not mean he really became a curse and sin," surely "he became flesh" should be understood in the same way (*Un. Chr.* 719–720 [55–56]). *A* agrees that his becoming a curse belongs to the "economy" and the incarnation, relating it to all the things that happened through his willing *kenōsis*: being tired, hungry, and so on. However, this is not strictly parallel to his becoming flesh—he became accursed to get rid of the curse and became sin to bring an end to sin, but he did not come to suppress the flesh but rather to exhibit in his own body "the incorruptibility and imperishability of flesh." Again this is spelled out with allusion to Pauline texts (especially 1 Cor 15:17 and 45). If it is not the flesh that is redeemed and raised, "the whole sense of the mystery is lost to us," including the efficacy of the Eucharist. "Where," he asks, "is that revitalisation of human bodies which is achieved by participation in his holy flesh and blood?" (*Un. Chr.* 720 [57–58]). Again we note that this sacramental point was perhaps one of the most important drivers shaping Cyril's thinking.[94]

Returning to the fundamental issue, *A* proceeds to appeal to Hebrews to show "that he 'became like us in all things except sin'" (Heb 4:15), quoting at length Hebrews 2:14–17 and explaining that "this likeness in all things" had "a kind of beginning" with his "birth from a woman," even though "the Word was God" (John 1:1). Then *B* explains that the opposition regards it as "unfitting" to attribute "a second birth from a woman" to "the Word who was ineffably and incomprehensibly born from God the Father" (*Un. Chr.* 721 [58–59]).

94. See above, e.g., p. 146 and the references to Henry Chadwick's seminal article, "Eucharist and Christology," in note 54.

A accuses them of suggesting that "his decision to undergo a voluntary self emptying for our sake was misguided" and launches into a summary of the fundamental narrative of God the Father engendering the Son and saving the whole human race through the incarnation, supporting it with quotations of Romans 6:5 and 2 Corinthians 8:9. He continues:

> When they say the Word of God did not become flesh, or rather did not undergo birth from a woman according to the flesh, they bankrupt the economy of salvation, for if he who was rich did not impoverish himself, abasing himself to our condition out of tender love, then we have not gained his riches but are still in our poverty, still enslaved by sin and death, because the Word becoming flesh is the undoing and the abolition of all that fell upon human nature as our curse and punishment. (*Un. Chr.* 722 [59–60])

This basic narrative is reinforced with questions about how without it certain texts of scripture could possibly be true:

> how could it be that the "blood of Jesus cleanses us from all sin" (1 John 1:7) . . . ? And how has "God the Father sent his son born of a woman, born subject to the law" (Gal 4:4)? Or how has "he condemned sin in the flesh" (Rom 8:3)? (*Un. Chr.* 722–723 [60])

These soteriological themes will be taken up further at a later stage.

Meanwhile, the important thing is our transformation: "Just as we bore the image of the earthly, so shall we bear the image of the heavenly (1 Cor 15:49), that is to say, of Christ" (723 [61]). He is heavenly man, not because he brought down his flesh from heaven (Cyril is again defending himself against the charge of Apollinarianism), but because the Word who is God "came down from out of heaven and entered our likeness, that is, submitted to birth from a woman according to the flesh" and "came in the form of a slave" while remaining what he was—indeed it is repeatedly reaffirmed that he remained Lord of all things even when he came down, here confirmed by John 3:31. The Philippians passage again hovers in the background, and now texts are marshalled against scoffers (Hab 1:5; Acts 13:41), for "indeed, the mystery of Christ runs the risk of being disbelieved precisely because it is so incredibly wonderful." The paradoxes, such as the invisible made visible and the immaterial made touchable, are spelled out. But we can already see Cyril's fundamental line of argument: the whole story of our renewal and restoration depends upon the life-giving Logos really sharing in our fleshly condition, and how could this be unless by

> appropriating a human body to himself in such an indissoluble union that it has to be considered as his very own and no one else's? This is how he transmits the grace of sonship even to us so that we too can become children of the Spirit, in so far as human nature had first achieved this possibility in him. (*Un. Chr.* 725 [63])

The discussion of how the Word became flesh has brought us back around to the first theme: we become sons by grace because he is Son by nature.

2.1.3. *Appropriate Naming, Appropriate Worship*

Now if that is all so, then the blasphemy of the opponents is clear, for "they are denying that Christ is really God and Son" (*Un. Chr.* 726 [64]). This initiates a discussion of the attribution of appropriate titles. *B* sets out the problem from the standpoint of the opposition:

> they say that the title of Christ is the only proper designation for the one who is born of a woman of David's race, since he was anointed by the Holy Spirit. But the Word of God needs no such anointing in his own nature, for by nature he is holy. Is it not true that the title Christ presupposes some kind of anointing has taken place? (*Un. Chr.* 726 [65])

That Christ means "anointed" is agreed, but *A*'s attempt to disallow the point as merely referring to a role (with more scriptural quotations, namely Ps 105:15 and Hab 3:13) is dismissed: "Really they do not want the title Christ applied to the Word born of God the Father, since in his own nature, as God, he was never anointed," states B. Again we recall how this issue played out earlier in the Arian controversies, and how Athanasius attributed the anointing to the "flesh." Here *B* adds: "They would also maintain that this too is one of those names which we cannot use about the Holy Spirit or the Father himself." *A* appears as foxed by this as we feel, so *B* explains their Trinitarian scruples:

> There are many varied titles which the inspired scriptures apply to the Son. He is called: God, Lord, Light, and Life, as well as King, Lord of Hosts, Holy One, and Lord of All. If someone wished to apply all these titles to the Father himself, or to the Holy Spirit, he could do so without error. This is because in a single nature there can only be one excellence of dignities. They argue from this that if the title Christ is truly appropriate to the Only Begotten, then it should be, like the other titles, equally applicable

> without distinction to the Father himself and to the Holy Spirit. Given that it is entirely inappropriate to apply this title to the Father or to the Holy Spirit, then neither can it be right to apply it to the Only Begotten. (*Un. Chr.* 727 [65–66])

Their conclusion is, of course, that it belongs to the one who is of the line of David. *A*, perforce, agrees to the point in general, an indication, perhaps, that Cyril has taken some opposition arguments seriously—indeed, we shall find exactly this kind of Trinitarian argument as an opening gambit in Theodoret's dialogues. However, Cyril's way out of it is to insist that "Christ" does apply to the Only-begotten "after the manner of his self-emptying" and the "economy of the flesh." Here Cyril is putting down a marker: you cannot thus differentiate scriptural titles or statements applied to the one enfleshed Logos—divine and human characteristics are interchangeable in this unique case. As already noted, he likewise objects to dividing the subject in the Philippians passage.

Persona *B* now attempts to justify the opposition's standpoint, and to affirm their rejection of the idea that they teach "two Sons":

> they maintain that God the Word assumed a perfect man who was of the line of Abraham and David, as the scriptures say, . . . a man complete in his nature, composed of a rational soul and human flesh. . . . They say that God the Word conjoined this man to himself in an entirely new way, bringing him to death as is the law among men, but raising him from the dead . . . (adding Eph 1:21). (*Un. Chr.* 728–729 [67–68])

This "inseparable conjunction" means they do not "speak of two Sons or two Lords; for "this man is connected with him (= God the Word), and participates in him and thereby shares in the very title and honour of the Son." That *B* can set this out so clearly shows that Cyril had understood what his opponents were saying, but *A* is horrified. This completely overthrows

> the divine and sacred kerygma which has proclaimed One Lord Jesus Christ, the Son of God, truly the Word of God the Father who was made man and incarnated so that the same one is equally God and man, and that to him alone apply all the divine and human characteristics. (*Un. Chr.* 729 [68–69])

It goes against "the holy Fathers and all the God-inspired scriptures." He reverts to John 1:14 and repeats his objection to a view that turns "the mystery of the economy in the flesh completely on its head." In their argument one cannot see how God the Word abased himself to a self-emptying (*Un. Chr.* 730 [69–70]). We are back to using Philippians 2:5–8 to interpret "the Word became flesh."

However, in thus developing and restating what it is all about, a new issue arises: the opponents' account suggests that "the one who is of the line of David and Abraham" is the one enthroned and "the Only Begotten is the Patron and Promoter of that man by whom we were saved." The specter of anti-Arian exegesis raises its head again, as the consequences of attributing promotion, not to the Word but to the flesh, comes home to roost. For

> they steal the worship from him who is really the Son, and persuade us to worship someone conjoined to him in some kind of relationship instead. (*Un. Chr.* 731 [71])

Quoting Romans 10:6–9, *A* accuses them of giving divine honors to a man and worshipping a person apart from "the Word who shone forth from God the Father's very being." Multiple scriptural quotations challenge the validity of their claim that the association of a man with God justifies co-worship as if he were a god.[95] Besides, this conception surely implies that "something of an unequal nature must be added to the holy and consubstantial Trinity, so as to receive worship and share in the same glory" (*Un. Chr.* 732 [72–73]). To avoid this they need more than the idea of mere conjunction—indeed, that of union. Conjunction, assumption, and attachment are terminologically inadequate because, implying difference, they could apply to anyone called upon to assist, like Amos (73 [74–75]). *Mutatis mutandis* we are again back to that first theme, and the difference between a son by grace and the Son by nature.

So now it is becoming increasingly necessary to explain what is meant by "union" (a topic to which we shall return later). This eventually leads to *A* making the following statement: "both the recent characteristics of humanity, and the eternal characteristics apply to him" (*Un. Chr.* 748 [93–94]). The question of appropriate naming is back, together with the rejection of partitive exegesis assigning different elements in the gospel narratives either to the divine nature or to the humanity of Christ. Examples here include: (1) John the Baptist's

95. For a human being associated with God, Cyril here appeals to Num 16:11 and Exod 16:8 (murmuring against Moses and Aaron is implicitly murmuring against God); 1 Sam 8:5 (rejection of Samuel equals rejection of God); Matt 25:40 ("whatever you do to the least, you do to me"); Ps 63:8 ("my soul is bound to you"); 1 Cor 6:17 ("whoever is bound to the Lord is one spirit with him").

statement, "Behold the Lamb of God who takes away the sin of the world" (John 1:29): thus he indicates that he is a man and calls him a lamb, yet says "he is no different to the one who takes away the sin of the world, and indeed attributes to him this great and vast dignity which befits God"; and (2) Peter's confession (Matt 16:16): he "gazed upon the Logos, not nakedly or without flesh, but as he was revealed in flesh and blood"—if he was "only a man" he would not have needed that special revelation from the Father to which Jesus's response attests. Other texts (e.g., John 10:37–38) show how his "ineffable glory" he had "as his own," not as someone else's or as a gift of grace. Further on in the dialogue we find an acknowledgement of the resultant paradoxes:

> we see in Christ the strange and rare paradox of Lordship in servant's form and divine glory in human abasement. That which was under the yoke in terms of the limitations of man was crowned with royal dignities. (*Un. Chr.* 753 [101])

As ever, scripture texts are deployed to reinforce the point that in his *kenōsis*, Christ assumed everything that went along with it, so as to ennoble human nature by "making it participate in his own sacred and divine honours." For Cyril this participation is only appropriate if the human nature is integral to, rather than appended to, the Word incarnate.[96]

2.1.4. Human Limitations, Suffering, Redemption

In response to that statement of the paradoxes, *B* quotes Hebrews 5:7–9 and Matthew 27:46: praying for release, learning obedience, and crying out, "My God, my God, why hast thou forsaken me?"—surely "such things are not at all applicable to God the Word." *A*, of course, attributes all this to the economy. The exemplary pattern of Christ's suffering is developed: he showed that in temptation we should resort to prayer, asking for courage, and he demonstrated

> how far the limits of obedience should extend, by what wonderful ways it comes, how great is its reward, and what form it has. This was the reason Christ became our model in all these things. . . . [1 Pet 2:20–21 is quoted.]

96. Cf. Cyril, *Un. Chr.* 767 (119). In discussion of 2 Cor 13:4: "Though indeed he was crucified out of weakness he lives now from the power of God," *A* states: "it is the one 'who is weak' in the flesh, insofar as he is revealed as man who 'lived from the power of God,' a power indeed not alien to him but integral, since he actually was God in the flesh."

> And so the Word of God became an example for us in the days of his flesh, but not nakedly or outside the limits of the self emptying. . . . This was why he extended his prayer, and shed a tear, at times even seemed to need a savior himself, and learned obedience, while all the while he was the Son. (*Un. Chr.* 754–755 [102–3])

It was initial work on this dialogue that first opened for me the question whether Cyril's notorious phrase *apathōs epathen* was to be understood as exemplary (i.e., the illuminating insight of chapter 4). Here it is clear that Cyril could not stomach the idea that "he was a broken man." *B* refers to Matthew 26:38 and 39 (Gethsemane), and *A*'s response is that to think "Christ had fallen so low into such faint heartedness as to be so 'sorrowful and cast down' that he could no longer bear his suffering but was overcome by fear and mastered by weakness" is to deny he was God. "He presumably gained no benefit at all from his divine dignities" (*Un. Chr.* 755–756 [104–5]). We recall the *Commentary on John's Gospel* and Jesus's exemplary mastering of human fear and weakness.[97] Cyril will eventually insist that the salvation of humanity from suffering, corruption, and death could only have been achieved by divine power.[98]

Meanwhile *A* quickly moves beyond the merely exemplary—"he would undo our abandonment by his obedience and complete submission" (*Un. Chr.* 756–757 [105]). Called second Adam, in him "you see human nature made clean," a point backed up with scriptural references (Rom 5:14: 1 Cor 15:22). Recapitulation and the reversal of Adam's disobedience are important. But for the moment *B* persists with his problem texts and the discussion briefly reverts to the issues of partitive exegesis. He inquires whether *A* means that it is "in complete disagreement with the sacred scriptures to think or to say that the assumed man used these human expressions as one who was abandoned by the Word who had been conjoined to him." *A*, of course, regards that as "blasphemy" and "madness," though no doubt it would suit the opposition:

> they split up and completely divide his words and attributing something as proper solely to the only begotten, and others to a son who is different to him and born of a woman. In this way they have missed the straight and unerring way of knowing the mystery of Christ clearly. (*Un. Chr.* 757–758 [106])

97. See chapter 4, pp. 158–59.
98. See below, p. 235. Cyril, *Un. Chr.* 775–776 (130).

To *B*'s query whether "one must not divide the words or acts in this way," *A* gives a firm negative, but perhaps glosses it a bit by adding:

> at least not as referring to two persons or two hypostases divided from one another and completely diverging into distinct and separate spheres. For there is only one Son, the Word who was made man for our sake. I would say that everything refers to him, words and deeds, both those that befit the deity, as well as those which are human. (*Un. Chr.* 758 [107])

B pursues the matter, however, by asking whether it would be proper to attribute weariness (John 4:6), hunger (Matt 4:2), and sleep (Matt 8:24) to God the Word, and *A* admits that "such things would not be at all fitting to the Word, if we consider him nakedly, as it were, not yet made flesh or before he had descended into the self-emptying." But "just as we say that the flesh became his very own, in the same way the weakness of that flesh became his very own in an economic appropriation according to the terms of the unification." *B* tests this out by asking about other texts (John 14:9; 10:3; 8:40)—"Are we to apply both sets of sayings to one and the same subject?" And the answer confirms it: "Christ is in no way divided, but is believed by all those who worship him to be the one and only true Son" (*Un. Chr.* 758 [107–8]).

Once again we are replaying the exegetical debates with Arianism. For *B* persists with those old questions: What about Jesus advancing in stature and wisdom and grace (Luke 2:52)? What about his suffering and death (*Un. Chr.* 759–761 [110–13])? With respect to each, a battery of texts is deployed to give essentially the same answer. His flesh and his blood were his own: the Word is made one with it (*Un. Chr.* 761 [111]). When *B* cites the opposition's use of Hebrews 2:10 to suggest that it was the Word who "perfected the leader of our salvation through sufferings, that is, the one who is of the line of David," *A* counters first by saying that "in that case we have no longer been redeemed by God but by the blood of someone else," then by quoting the whole context of descent and ascent, of being made like his brethren (Heb 2:9–17) (*Un. Chr.* 762–764 [112–15]). We recognize Cyril's old critique of the Antiochene focus on the fact that it was the human nature that died the redemptive death, but here Cyril makes little more of the point. He surely has not fully understood their insight into the role of "the assumed man" in atonement and reconciliation.

Now *A* affirms that "the Word who shines forth from God's essence is his proper Son," reasserting the point, however, that "he is not given to us nakedly, as it were"—"he did not suffer in the nature of the godhead, but in his own flesh" (*Un. Chr.* 764 [114–15]). Spelling this out with reference to other texts (Col 1:15–18; Heb 12:2; 1 Cor 2:8), *A* baldly states "he suffered in the flesh for us, and on our behalf," though later adding that "even if he is said to suffer in the flesh, even so he retains his impassibility insofar as he is understood as God" (*Un. Chr.* 766 [117]). To the opposition, says *B*, this paradox—the same one suffering and not suffering—seems "like a fairytale and indeed verges on the incredible. For either as God, he has not suffered at all, or alternatively, if he is said to have suffered, then how can he be God?" (*Un. Chr.* 766 [117]).

Cyril has, it seems, appreciated the opposition's protests, and will affirm yet again that "in his own nature he certainly suffers nothing" (769 [121]), but through *A* he now suggests that their insistence on this just demonstrates feebleness of mind—an inability to allow for the Only-begotten to take the initiative and find a way voluntarily to take on suffering through his own body and then to raise it to life. Elsewhere in the dialogue we find:

> It was not impossible to God, in his lovingkindness, to make himself capable of bearing the limitations of the manhood. (*Un. Chr.* 737 [79])

This would seem to confirm the illuminating insight that Cyril's stress on the voluntary nature of the Word's *kenōsis* does indeed bespeak a refusal to limit the possibilities open to the divine: the God Word has freedom from the constraints even of his own inherent nature—a daring thought beyond his opponents' imagining. Here he explains: "The manner of the economy allows him blamelessly to *choose* both to suffer in the flesh, and not to suffer in the Godhead" (*Un. Chr.* 766 [118]; my italics). A body was prepared for him by the Father, and then he came in that body to do the Father's will (Heb 10:5–7; cf. Ps 40:6–8 LXX) (*Un. Chr.*769 [121]). So the "recapitulation of all things was perfectly accomplished through him and in him." Yet again the Philippians 2 passage is rehearsed to confirm this, and its implications teased out once more. It was to destroy death that he came in our likeness (769 [121–22]).

After spiraling back over points made before, the discussion next focuses on this "destruction of death and the banishing of corruption from the bodies of men [*sic*]" as "something the Son *wanted to do*" (my italics), a point confirmed by Wisdom 1:13–14 and 2:24 (*Un. Chr.* 772 [125]). It could only happen through the incarnation, which implanted life into "a body subject to corruption" that he had "made his own." *A* briefly outlines points we have observed in Cyril's *Commentary on John's Gospel*: his approach to the passion "in a way befitting a man, in the fashion of prayer," and his reluctance yet willingness to "do what would cause him grief" for the sake of the resurrection, quoting Matthew 26:39 (Gethsemane), Colossians 1:18 (firstborn of the dead), 1 Corinthians 15:20 (firstfruits of those that sleep). Further discussion establishes that he is the "Last Adam": "a second beginning for those on earth, to transform the nature of man in himself [*sic*] into a newness of life in holiness and incorruptibility through the resurrection from the dead" (*Un. Chr.* 773 [126]).

Appeal is now made to baptism (quoting Matt 28:19; Rom 6:3; Eph 4:5) with the following summary statement:

> [Paul] certainly would not say that we were baptized into someone who was a distinctly different son of the line of David. Since he is God by nature, he is conceived of as beyond suffering, and then he chose to suffer so that he might save those under corruption, and so became like those on earth in all respects, and underwent birth from a woman according to the flesh. As I have said, he made his very own a body capable of tasting death and capable of coming back to life again, so that he himself might remain impassible and yet be said to suffer in his own flesh. (*Un. Chr.* 773 [127])

This is supported by another battery of quotations from scripture: Matthew 18:11 (saving what was lost); John 10:11, 18 (the good shepherd, laying down his life); 1 Corinthians 5:7 (Christ our Passover is sacrificed); 1 Corinthians 6:19–20 (we were bought at a price; not our own; one died for all); 2 Corinthians 5:15 (those for whom Christ died no longer live for themselves but for the one who died on their behalf and rose again); Galatians 2:19–20 (died to law to live to God; crucified with Christ); Hebrews 13:12 (sanctified by his own blood); Colossians 1:21–22 (reconciled in his own fleshly body through his death). For Cyril the passion is the voluntary act of the incarnate Word suffering in his own flesh in order to redeem humankind from death by the power of his life.

For *B*, however, it remains "a terrible dishonor" to say that the Word of God suffered, and "it brings our noble mystery into disrepute." *A* retorts with Hebrews 12:2 and 1 Peter 4:1: "'despising the shame' he chose to 'suffer in the flesh' for our sake, according to the scripture." *A* insists that

> suffering in the flesh, and rising from the dead, he revealed our nature as greater than death or corruption. What he achieved was beyond the ability of our condition, and what seems to have been worked out in human weakness and by suffering was really stronger than men and a demonstration of the power that pertains to God. (*Un. Chr.* 775 [130])

For Cyril it is fundamental that we cannot save ourselves; our redemption depends upon the impassibility and incorruptibility of God the Word enabling his own flesh to rise through suffering and death. He acknowledges that this is "altogether ineffable" and "there is no mind that can attain to such subtle and transcendent ideas."

> The force of any comparison falters here and falls short of the truth, although I can bring to mind a feeble image of this reality which might lead us from something tangible, as it were, to the very heights and to what is beyond all speech. It is like iron, or other such material, when it is put in contact with a raging fire. It receives the fire into itself, and when it is in the very heart of the fire, if someone should beat it, then the material itself takes the battering but the nature of the fire is in no way injured by the one who strikes. This is how you should understand the way in which the Son is said both to suffer in the flesh and not to suffer in the Godhead. (*Un. Chr.* 776 [130–31])

For Cyril the paradoxes of scripture whereby the impassible suffers and the immortal dies are essential to his understanding of salvation. Some account has to be given of this inseparable union, not least because it is the flesh that becomes life-giving as the living bread of the Eucharist (776–777 [131–32]).

2.1.5. *Union Rather Than Conjunction*

Already we have found arguments in this dialogue urging the inadequacy of "conjunction" as a model for the coming together of Godhead and human nature in the Savior and the necessity of "union"—this indeed pervades the whole. We need to scroll back to pick up the discussion from the point where we put this theme to one side.[99]

Earlier *A* had spoken of the Word "appropriating a human body to himself in such *an indissoluble union* that it has to be considered his very own body and no-one else's" (*Un. Chr.* 725 [63]; my italics). This becomes a refrain throughout the dialogue. It is the union that enables him to transmit "the grace of sonship even to us," with 1 Corinthians 15:47–49 here substantiating this.[100] Taking up the theme, *A* next insists that the union is "customary," indeed it has "come down to us from the holy Fathers"—so why do they abandon it and

99. See above, p. 229. Cyril, *Un. Chr.* 733 (73).
100. Cyril, *Un. Chr.* 725 (63–64); cf. 756–757, 772 (105, 125).

prefer "conjunction" (733 [73])? Union in no way causes confusion, rather "the concurrence is one reality of those things which are understood to be united." The word "unity" is not simply used of "things which are simple and homogenous" but can also apply to "things compounded out of two." But they divide the one incarnate Son into two; "they reject the union and call it conjunction, something any other man could have with God." The discussion loops around various scripture texts, contrasting Amos as an "assistant" with the *kenōsis* of Philippians 2 as well as other points already noticed (733–734 [74–76]). Eventually it returns to the issues of confusion and change, and another key statement is made by *A*:

> Godhead is one thing and manhood is another thing, considered in the perspective of their respective and intrinsic beings, but in the case of Christ they came together in a mysterious and incomprehensible union without confusion or change. *The manner of this union is entirely beyond conception.* (*Un. Chr.* 735 [77]; my italics)

B, however, is not satisfied with this agnosticism and keeps pressing the point: how can we envisage a single Christ? And how can mixture or confusion be avoided?

So *A* is provoked into providing analogies, conceptual models that go some way toward enabling a kind of understanding:

(1) The first is the single nature of the human being, which is nevertheless "not homogeneous but really composed of two things," namely "soul and body." Interestingly the point is given roots in scripture: Paul's reference to our "inner" and "outer" being (2 Cor 4:16) is cited, and to this is added the point that just as in our case scripture often refers to the whole by a part (e.g., "all flesh" in Joel 2:28 and "seventy souls" in Deut 10:22), so Emmanuel may simply be called "Only begotten or God from God" without this implying that he is "separated from the flesh or indeed the manhood." It is perhaps not surprising that in the post-Apollinarian situation *B* regards this as inevitably involving confusion and mixture, even though it is clearly meant as an analogy. In fact we have found Theodoret using the same analogy in his response to the third anathema, and it will be given extended treatment in his dialogues, as we shall see.[101]

(2) The second analogy is directly drawn from scripture—an enigmatic type or prophecy:

101. See p. 198 above and pp. 248–49 below.

> For he came down in the form of fire onto the bush in the desert, and the fire played upon the shrub but did not consume it . . . this event was a type of a mystery, of how the divine nature of the Word supported the limitations of manhood; because he chose to. Absolutely nothing is impossible to him (Mark 10:27). (*Un. Chr.* 737 [79])[102]

This "fire" image we have already seen adapted to explain *apathōs epathen*: iron hammered in the fire but the fire remaining unaffected (776 [130–31]).[103]

Conceptualizing the union may be beyond the limits of human rationality, but union rather than conjunction is the only way the transformation of human being can be effected. The climax of the dialogue sums this up by reference to the life-giving power of the Eucharist. *A* asks:

> If the flesh that is united to him, ineffably and in a way that transcends thought or speech, did not become the very flesh of the Word, directly, then how could it be understood as life-giving? He himself says: "I am the living bread which has come down from heaven and gives life to the world . . ." (John 6:51, 33) (*Un. Chr.* 776 [131])

How could this be, he continues, "if it is the flesh of a different son than him, someone appropriated by him in a conjunction of relationship?" And "how could the flesh of anyone else ever give life to the world if it has not become the very flesh of Life, that is of him who is the Word of God the Father?"

B replies with John 6:53: "unless you eat the flesh of the *Son of Man*" (my italics)—"they say" this should be understood as the body and blood, not "of God the Word" but "of the man assumed by him." For *A* this completely undermines "the mystery of piety" (1 Tim 3:16) and destroys both the *kenōsis* (Phil 2:7–8) and the recapitulation (Eph 1:10). If it was this separate "Son of Man," rather than the Only-begotten, who said "the bread I shall give is my flesh for the life of the world" (John 6:51), then it was not "the Lord himself who saved us" (Isa 63:9 LXX) "but one of our own number" (*Un. Chr.* 777 [132]). For Cyril that is what really offends. He has heard what "they" are saying but never grasped the point. For him

102. Cf. chapter 3, 2.3.1, for the association between the burning bush and the incarnation.
103. See above, p. 235.

> There was no other way for the flesh to become life-giving, even though by its own nature it was subject to the necessity of corruption, except that it became the very flesh of the Word who gives life to all things.

And back comes the fire analogy:

> There is nothing astonishing here, for if it is true that fire has converse with materials which in their own natures are not hot, and yet renders them hot since it so abundantly introduces to them the inherent energy of its own power, then surely in an even greater degree the Word who is God can introduce the life-giving power and energy of his own self into his very own flesh;

with the triumphant conclusion:

> We can see this is his very own flesh since he is united to it unconfusedly and unchangeably and in a manner he alone knows. (*Un. Chr.* 777 [132–33])

So to "define the doctrine of faith correctly and without error," to be "lovers of the doctrines of the truth who follow the track of the faith of our holy fathers" and "not to be carried away from the right path," we must "believe that there is only one Son of God the Father" and "understand our Lord Jesus Christ in one person," attributing "both the divine and human characteristics" to the same one, "the birth and the suffering on the cross." *A* signs off with Philippians 2:10–11 (*Un. Chr.* 778 [133]).

2.1.6. *Review of Cyril's Handling of Scripture as Source of Doctrine*

Throughout Cyril has been in teaching mode, determined to convey how his *dogma* (i.e., teaching) derives from scripture and to articulate the correct reading of scripture according to the tradition of the holy fathers. What seems remarkable—indeed a confirmation perhaps of the maturity of his thinking here—is the absence of appeal to his controversial slogans, or indeed to the supposed "technical terms" of the controversy, and the profound concentration on scripture as the ultimate source of correct doctrine. The complexity of scripture is handled (1) by subtlety in the treatment of language—the way divine reference stretches human terminology, even conceptuality, beyond ordinary meanings; (2) by frequent testing of text against text; (3) by constant interplay between particular texts and the overarching biblical narrative from creation to redemption through the descent and ascent of the God Word, the Only-begotten, life itself; and (4) by acknowledgment that what scripture reveals and offers is received through baptism and in the liturgy. It would be hard to claim that this does not convey a valid reading of scripture within the terms already established by the tradition of the holy fathers to which Cyril appealed.

And yet, could it be said that, despite accommodation with those with whom he had been in conflict, Cyril was still failing to appreciate certain insights that they offered into further layers of meaning to be found in scripture?

2.2. *Theodoret:* Eranistes

In the introduction to his edition of the Greek text of Theodoret's *Eranistes*, Gerard H. Ettlinger writes: "The *Eranistes* represents the high point in Theodoret's opposition to Cyril, and is perhaps the most original work to stem from Syria in the fifth century."[104] Yet Cyril had died some three or four years earlier than the time of Theodoret's dialogues. In a notorious, but possibly inauthentic, letter (*Ep.* 180), Theodoret supposedly surmised that the dead might be so annoyed at Cyril's company as to send him back, and he hoped that the undertakers would lay a very big heavy stone on his grave to prevent that! Maybe the reason for these dialogues was that he feared Cyril had indeed returned! In 448 Eutyches was condemned, but Theodoret himself was confined to his diocese of Cyrus by imperial decree, then to be deposed in the following year by the synod in Ephesus, which reinstated Eutyches. The tensions building up to the Council of Chalcedon would have seemed to him like a replay of those twenty-year-old disputes. Indeed, a study devoted to Theodoret's Christology argues that in the *Eranistes* he was still confronting the old issues faced in the 430s, his basic position remaining essentially the same, with Eranistes in the dialogues representing the Alexandrian Christology of Cyril, Dioscorus, and Eutyches as Theodoret perceived it.[105]

In his prologue (*Eran.* 61–62 [160–61]) Theodoret first explains that he calls his work *Eranistes* or *Polymorphus* as the heretics he has in view pick up their ideas from many sources, producing a patchwork from such as Marcion,

104. Gerard H. Ettlinger, ed., *Theodoret of Cyrus: Eranistes* (Oxford: Oxford University Press, 1975), quote from 3. Translation of *Eranistes* from *NPNF*² 3; citations include the page numbers from Ettlinger's text in brackets.

105. Clayton, *Christology of Theodoret.*

Valentinus, Apollinaris, Arius and Eunomius, among others.[106] Then, he indicates that he intends to write in dialogue form, with questions and answers, propositions, solutions and antitheses, with the to and fro made clearer for the less well educated by writing the names of the questioners and respondents in the margin rather than incorporating them in the body of the text as did "the wise Greeks of old," notably Plato, of course. He names the dialogue partners as Eranistes and Orthodoxus—you can hardly miss which character is meant to be his own mouthpiece. He begs his readers to put truth to the test as he sketches the content of his three dialogues: (1) *atreptos*—the Son is immutable; (2) *asynchytos*—the union of Godhead and humanity is unconfounded; and (3) *apathēs*—the divinity of the Son is impassible.

The very titles indicate a prime Antiochene concern—that the "Godness" of the God-Word incarnate in Christ should not be compromised. In other words Theodoret remains haunted by what has been described as the "Arian syllogism" whereby the Word itself must be the subject of the human experiences and therefore must be other than fully divine.[107] Yet, despite the apparently abstract titles signifying such a doctrinal or conceptual approach, there is hardly a page of Ettlinger's Greek text that does not have a list of biblical allusions or quotations at its foot—a concrete sign of the central role scripture played in these christological debates. My earlier study of the first dialogue set out to show that the exegetical methods deployed in doctrinal controversy were not essentially different from those to be found in commentary and homily.[108] The focus here shifts to the question how prior doctrinal commitments shaped the reading of scripture and vice versa. Rather than picking out recurrent themes, as we did in Cyril's case, we will follow Theodoret's far less repetitive arguments in linear fashion.

106. The word *eranistes* seems to imply a "picker up of scraps," while *polymorphus* implies "multiform."

107. Clayton, *Christology of Theodoret*, throughout argues that the "Arian syllogism" remains at issue for Theodoret, referring the term "Arian syllogism" to F. A. Sullivan, *The Christology of Theodore of Mopsuestia* (Rome: Analecta Gegoriana, 1956). The major premise was that the Logos is the subject of the human experiences, the minor premise that whatever is predicated of the Word must be predicated *kata physin*, with the conclusion that the Word is limited in nature and passibly affected by the sufferings of Christ, so divine *ousia* cannot be predicated of the Word.

108. F. Young, "Exegetical Method and Scriptural Proof."

2.2.1. Atreptos—*Immutable*

The participants agree to search for truth and not depend on human reasoning—rather they will trace the footprints of the apostles, the prophets, and the saints who followed them. This means that they both acknowledge one substance of God—Father, Son, and Holy Spirit—as taught by holy scripture, both old and new, and by the fathers in council at Nicaea. Then they carefully distinguish between *ousia* and *hypostasis*, illustrating the distinction from Genesis 6:7 and Psalm 49:20 (48:21 LXX), applying it to what the Trinity has in common and what designates their individuality, and quickly agreeing that *atreptos* applies to the Son as to the Father and the Holy Spirit (*Eran.* 63–66 [161–62]). We recall how Cyril in his dialogue apparently attributes exactly this kind of argument to the opposition.[109] We also note how important to Theodoret is this appeal to doctrine already agreed and established.

Here, however, Orthodoxus immediately puts Eranistes on the spot over John 1:14: how is it, he inquires, that emphasizing this gospel text you attribute mutation to the immutable? Eranistes refuses to accept that he became flesh by mutation—rather it happened "as he himself knows" (*Eran.* 66 [162]). Pressed further Eranistes resorts to stating that all things are possible to God (Matt 19:26), Theodoret thus attributes to Eranistes a point we have observed in Cyril's dialogue.[110] Orthodoxus responds by quoting Psalm 102:27 (101:28 LXX) and Malachi 3:6 to prove divine unchangeability, having pointed out that, of course, creatures can be changed by their Creator (*Eran.* 67 [163]).

They now differ over whether it is appropriate to inquire into such matters. Eranistes is presented as insisting that "the manner of his enfleshment escapes me, but I have heard that the Word became flesh." In other words, Theodoret did recognize his opponents' wish to take the language of scripture seriously, but insists on pursuing the problem of its meaning and implications. Exploring potential analogies Orthodoxus takes change to imply that the thing in question ceases to be what it was. Yet Theodoret clearly knew that the Alexandrians confessed that the Word did not change, for he put into the mouth of Eranistes these words: "continuing still to be what he was, he was made what he was not" (*Eran.* 67 [163]). It seems, however, that Theodoret could make no sense of this. Either there was change, or else "the Word became flesh" must be understood as the Word "taking" the seed of Abraham—Orthodoxus thus proposes to interpret John 1:14 in terms of other scriptures, here adducing

109. See above, 2.1.3.

110. See above, 2.1.4, and further discussion in 2.2.3, below.

Hebrews 2:16. It seems that Cyril had correctly diagnosed the Antiochene inability to understand "became" as meaning anything other than change: we recall his recourse to scripture texts to counter this.[111]

Here scripture will soon appear to drive the discussion as the implications of that are explored. Meanwhile, however, Orthodoxus extracts agreement that the seed of Abraham must be endowed with a rational soul as well as a body. Eranistes is then worried about two Sons, a point Orthodoxus rather sharply dismisses—if the Word is changed into flesh there is not even one Son, just flesh (*Eran.* 69 [164])! Eranistes worries that the statements in John 1:14 and Hebrews 2:16 are inconsistent; so Orthodoxus takes him through a string of prophetic and apostolic texts to establish he was God but sprang from the Jews as man.[112] Eranistes eventually retorts with a text we already saw Cyril exploiting, that old favorite from Baruch 3:35, 37: "This is our God. . . . Afterward he showed himself upon earth and conversed with us."[113] God was actually seen on earth—the prophet does not speak of flesh or humanity, Eranistes insists, but only of God (*Eran.* 70–72 [164–65]). Again Theodoret seems fully aware of typical Alexandrian arguments.

That quotation provokes exploration of the invisibility of the divine nature (*Eran.* 73 [165]), which is then proved from various biblical texts (1 Tim 1:17; 6:16b; Bar 3:38; John 1:14a), and the consequent necessity of a body for it to be seen. Eranistes insists on the plain meaning of the Baruch text, but they agree to investigate, Orthodoxus stating he wants no recourse to human reason—he will yield only to scripture. He introduces 1 Timothy 3:16: "God was manifest in flesh," claiming that through the visible the invisible is seen (*Eran.* 74–76 [166–67]). But then they get distracted by the sequel in that verse—they question whether the angels could see God. That leads to further discussion about divine theophanies in scripture (to Abraham at Mamre, to Isaiah in the temple, to Micah, Daniel, and Ezekiel, not to mention Moses), both agreeing that God accommodates the divine glory to the capacity of those who see God in visions or likenesses—God's *ousia* remains invisible, John 1:18 and Exodus 33:20 having been adduced along the way. First Timothy 3:16 is pressed home: the flesh is what makes visible the invisible, even to angels: they too see not the divine *ousia*, but such glory as may be accommodated to their capacity.

But the flesh is a veil. Eranistes is troubled by that, but he accepts it on the

111. See above, 2.1.2.

112. The texts include, in order, Gen 12:3; Gal 3:16; Gen 49:10; Mic 5:2; together with Heb 7:14; Matt 2:5–6; Rom 9:5.

113. See above, 2.1.

basis of Hebrews 10:19–22 (*Eran.* 76 [167]), while Orthodoxus refers back to Genesis 49:10, which had figured among the prophecies adduced earlier and also speaks of the veil. They agree that it points to the incarnation when it speaks of the scepter not departing from Judah, and it goes on: "his *parousia* the nations expect; he washes his own garment in wine, and his own veil in the blood of the grape." Reference to the coming of Christ to the gentiles is so obvious to them that it does not need discussion, but they do search for the proper reference of the rest of the verse. It is associated with "I am the vine," and with the flowing of water and blood from the Savior's pierced side, and so with the Eucharist: "for as we call the mystical fruit of the vine after the holy blood of the Lord, so he named the blood of the true vine the blood of the grape" (*Eran.* 77 [167–68]). A similar line of argument associates his body with bread. Orthodoxus presses the point that the bread and wine are symbols of his body and not of his Godhead (78 [168]), then he turns to Hebrews: God did not require sacrifice or offering but prepared a body for the Savior who as high priest offered the body he had taken. Eranistes now worries that this suggests the Virgin gave birth only to a body—taking a body is not the same as being made flesh. Orthodoxus reverts to the original charge: not even Valentinus, Marcion, and Manes dared attribute mutation to the immutable (80–81 [168–69]).

Next Psalm 89 is examined (*Eran.* 84 [170]): the promise made must refer to our Savior and not to Solomon or Zerubbabel, Eranistes eventually agreeing that "the promise goes beyond the bounds of human nature"—David's seed shall endure forever. So Orthodoxus presses home the point that Jesus Christ is plainly called seed of David in his humanity, adding Isaiah 11:1 (the stem of Jesse) and showing that the succeeding verses cannot refer to a "mere man," for the one who sprang from the root of Jesse possessed all the powers of the spirit. Eranistes accepts the prophecies and suggests that here is reference to God. Orthodoxus replies, not only God but man. Apostolic preaching confirms the prophecies (Peter in Acts 2:30–31; Paul in Acts 13:23; 2 Tim 2:8; and Rom 1:1–3), and the conclusion is that the Lord Christ sprang from the seed of David according to the flesh and had not flesh only but also a soul (*Eran.* 86–87 [172]).

Eranistes still wants to assert the plain sense of John 1:14, but Orthodoxus wants to understand it *eusebōs*, that is, in an appropriately pious sense: that by taking flesh and a rational soul he is said to have become flesh. For Orthodoxus all the covenants, promises, and so on are void, and we are not raised nor can we sit in heaven if the God-Word took nothing of our nature. He moves to what follows in John 1:14, namely, he dwelt "in us": the flesh he took was a kind of temple (*Eran.* 88–89 [172–73]). Then comes the classic Antiochene move: Philippians 2:5–8 provides the exegesis of John 1:14. He took the form of a slave, and the *morphē doulou* means human nature just as *morphē theou* means divine nature. After further quibbles about John 10:33 and 9:16, and clarification that in the Philippians passage "the form of a servant" really does mean human nature, not human likeness, just as "the form of God" means the divine nature, Eranistes seems to cave in and requests examples of how John 1:14 has been read by "the old teachers of the Church" (*Eran.* 88–89 [173]). There follows the first florilegium: Orthodoxus quotes many patristic authorities, not least those names he thinks the opposition would take particularly seriously (91–111 [174–82]).

The florilegia in the *Eranistes* have generated considerable interest, but our immediate concern is rather to review the interaction of doctrine and scripture in this debate. Looking back, at first it might seem that established doctrine, together with reasonable deductions from it, has priority, as they agree that the Son shares the divine *ousia* with the Father and the Spirit, and so must be *atreptos* as they are. It even looks as if Theodoret is ready to allow this to challenge scripture's apparent plain sense: the Word cannot have straightforwardly become flesh because that presupposes mutation. But in fact, of course, he is looking for ways to interpret the text appropriately in the light of other scriptures. Eranistes might seem to be presented as literalistic, but actually his evident concern is to do justice to what scripture actually says—he is nervous of overinvestigation. In fact, both sides are struggling with the problem of the limitations of human language and conceptuality when it comes to the divine: religious language is always problematic because it speaks of a reality beyond human comprehension. Theodoret clearly grasped the fact that the Alexandrians were prepared to attribute impossibilities to God, yet he feared the consequences for the utter "otherness" of the divine Being, which could hardly be alienated from itself. Clayton has suggested that Theodoret was limited in his conceptuality—he could only imagine three possibilities, two of which were outlawed: either he took flesh, or mutated into flesh, or seemed to appear in flesh (docetism).[114] Thus it looks as if the conceptual argument has priority. Yet it is evident that scripture played a determinative role in debating the issues, the exegetical process being a rationalistic inquiry into meaning and reference through offering substitutes, paraphrases, equivalents, synonyms, alternative expressions, or other biblical texts.

Our exploration of Cyril's dialogue likewise showed that what was at stake

114. Clayton, *Christology of Theodoret*, 223.

had nothing to do with possible literal, metaphorical, or symbolic senses, all of which could equally be deployed in the course of argument, but was rather about appropriate meaning given the subject and context. The plain meaning of limited human language might need to be critically modified or extended, though perhaps not evacuated. Here Orthodoxus insists on investigation—on making sense of scripture by engaging in a rational and deductive process on the basis of biblical parallels or theological presuppositions. Eranistes pleads for serious engagement with the given language of scripture and an appropriate intellectual humility—for with God nothing is impossible. These differences in approach underlie divergent articulations of the doctrine to be found in the biblical material.

2.2.2. Asynchytos—*Uncompounded*

The title might suggest that the focus of this dialogue will be on the need to resist Apollinarian "mixture" or any notion of the God-Man as a hybrid—like an unproductive mule, neither horse nor donkey. Surprisingly little of the discussion, however, follows that path explicitly. Rather, as the first dialogue concentrated on the integrity of the Godhead, so this one largely deals with the integrity of Christ's humanity, and the underlying reasons for this concern prove not on the whole to be the issues about history, human moral virtue, or soteriology, the themes that have attracted modern scholars to Antiochene Christology. Rather, the integrity of the humanity was as important as the integrity of the Godhead because otherwise the essential difference between Creator and creature would be jeopardized. The doctrine of creation remained as fundamental as ever; the underlying purpose of Theodoret's insistence on the two unimpaired natures was to uphold that long-standing gulf between Creator and creature that had been distinctive of Christianity since the second century, consistently taught as biblical, and crucially contested in the Arian controversy. The latest illuminating moment came with this insight, along with the perception that those typically Alexandrian emphases, *kenōsis* and *theopoiēsis*, may well be unspoken targets in these dialogues—both being misread by Theodoret as compromising that fundamental distinction. As we work through this second dialogue, though primarily focusing on the way scripture is deployed in argument, we will read between the lines to trace hints suggestive of this perspective.

At the end of the first dialogue, after the florilegium, Eranistes had conceded on the basis of all the authorities quoted that the Word of God was immutable and took flesh. Now Orthodoxus first establishes that they are indeed still agreed that "he took flesh" and also that "flesh" must include body and soul; but then he asks what kind of soul. The Apollinarian distinction between the "vegetative" (vital or life-giving) soul and the "rational" soul (the mind) is at issue, and Genesis 2:7 is used to show how only one soul was involved in the formation of the first human being, one soul being confirmed as scriptural by Matthew 10:28 (par. Luke 12:4–5), Genesis 46:20 (LXX), and Acts 20:10. Eranistes is obliged to agree that "the form of a servant" was complete. Orthodoxus presses the point that, with the intention of renewing the blurred divine image, "the Creator assumed the nature in its entirety, and stamped the imprint far better than the first" (*Eran* 112–113 [183]). The integrity of the humanity is indeed the prime issue.

Eranistes's reaction is to inquire what, in that case, one should call Jesus Christ: man or God? Orthodoxus quotes scripture to demonstrate that he is both God and man.[115] But Eranistes concludes from these texts that "the Lord Jesus is God only," stating that "since he became man without being changed but remained just what he was before, we must call him just what he was" (*Eran.* 114 [184]). Orthodoxus, of course, retorts that we should "confess both natures, both that which took and that which was taken." Eranistes proposes that the Savior should rather be named by the nobler nature. In response Orthodoxus first deploys scripture to show that the composite human being is not consistently called "soul" rather than "flesh."[116] He then asks what is wrong with calling Christ "man" once he has been confessed as God given all the compelling reasons for doing so. Eranistes demands to know those compelling reasons. At some length Orthodoxus points to the prevalence of heretical opinions and the need to defend the humanity of Christ (*Eran.* 116–120 [184–86]). John 8:40, Acts 2:22, and Acts 17:30–31 provide scriptural endorsement, reinforced with 1 Timothy 2:1–5: "mediator" indicates Godhead and manhood (*Eran.* 121–122 [187]). To Eranistes's objection that Moses was a mediator but only man, Orthodoxus replies with a long digression on the notion of "type," appealing to the Epistle to the Hebrews, particularly Melchizedek (Heb 6:20; 7:1–3) (*Eran.* 123–127 [187–89]). But the underlying issue would seem to be a difference in the understanding of mediation: one sense of mediation may be found in Moses acting as intercessor or mediator between estranged parties, but for Theodoret mediation consists in conjoining essentially different natures in the mediating person of Jesus Christ.

115. Matt 1:21; Luke 2:11; John 1:1, 3–4.

116. Texts adduced include Gen 6:3 LXX; Gal 1:15–17; Ps 65:2; Isa 40:5; Ezek 18:4, 20; Lev 5:1.

Eventually they revert to the topic in question, the appropriate naming of the Savior (*Eran.* 127 [189]). Eranistes insists on calling him God as he is God's Son, but Orthodoxus adds that he called himself "Son of Man." Eranistes agrees that "man" belongs to him according to the *oikonomia* and, challenged as to whether that was real or imaginary, has to admit that he was named "man" prior to the passion. Orthodoxus demonstrates the attribution of "man" to Christ after the passion and resurrection with a string of texts.[117] Heretics need to be persuaded, the ignorant need to learn. Classic passages (John 10:32–33; Matt 22:42–46) are reinforced with several other texts (Matt 15:22; 20:31; 21:9; Luke 19:40; 24:30; 2 Tim 2:8) to lead to the conclusion that instruction was given about the Godhead to those who were ignorant and about the resurrection of the flesh to those who denied it. So two natures should be confessed. Eranistes immediately affirms two before the union but asserts one after their combination (*Eran.* 128–132 [190–91]).

The timing of the union is now the overt question, though the ensuing discussion also touches on its manner—the stated topic of this dialogue. Eranistes proposes the exact moment of conception. Orthodoxus, however, quickly establishes that Eranistes accepts the Word's preexistence but denies the preexistence of the flesh, so proving that before the union there was only one nature. Pursuing the logic further he insists that it is after the incarnation that "we speak properly of two, that which took and that which was taken." Eranistes still wants to uphold one nature after the union, proposing the Alexandrian formula "out of two natures," rejecting natural analogies like gilded silver or solder composed of lead and tin, and affirming a union that is "ineffable and passes all understanding." Orthodoxus persists in asserting that, incomprehensible though the manner of the union may be, after the union each nature remains unimpaired—this is what divine scripture teaches. Eranistes demands to know where. "Everywhere," Orthodoxus claims. Induced to specify, he quotes John 1:1–3. Eranistes will not separate God the Word from the flesh; Orthodoxus will not either, but also refuses confusion. Eranistes once more affirms one nature after the union (*Eran.* 132–134 [192]). At first sight appeal to scripture might seem incapable of settling the issue, but Orthodoxus tries John 1:1–3 again, putting the genealogies of Matthew and Luke alongside it. Immediately he is accused of dividing the only-begotten Son into two persons. Orthodoxus affirms that he knows and adores one Son of God, the Lord Jesus Christ, but he has been taught the difference between Godhead and humanity. The debate goes on, endeavoring to determine how

117. 1 Tim 2:5; 1 Cor 15:21–22; Acts 2:22; 7:56.

being Creator of Adam could possibly be compatible with being son of Adam's descendants (*Eran.* 134–136 [193]). Notice here how the contrast is set up in terms of Creator and creature.

Orthodoxus reverts to the problem of change. Eranistes confirms that he accepts God's immutability, and again agrees that the Word took flesh and was not changed into flesh. Orthodoxus insists that this means the natures were not confounded, appealing again to the Evangelists. Here Luke 2:51 and John 2:4 are contrasted and Matthew 22:42 is set against the acceptance of the name "Son of David" elsewhere, while John 8:58 is opposed to Mark 6:1 and the claim is made that scripture is full of similar passages, all pointing not to one nature but to two. Eranistes's old charge that two natures equals two Sons is met with the proposal that "he who says Paul is made up of soul and body makes two Pauls out of one" (*Eran.* 136–137 [194]). This shifts the debate to the soul-body analogy.

Orthodoxus is primarily concerned about confusion—if conceptually soul and body are distinguishable, why not the two natures of Christ, even though in both cases the qualities of each are applicable to the one person? He is clear that when arguing about the nature of Christ we should

> give to each its own, and recognise some as belonging to the Godhead, some as to the manhood. But when we are discussing the Person we must then make what is proper to the natures common and apply both sets of qualities to the Saviour, and call the same being both God and Man, both Son of God and Son of Man, both David's son and David's Lord, both seed of Abraham and Creator of Abraham, and so on. (*Eran.* 139 [195])

This passage reminds us of Chrysostom's presentation of the one person who may speak as God or as man in his exegesis of John's Gospel.[118] Clayton rightly argues against the supposition that Theodoret is now admitting the *communicatio idiomatum*—rather it is a statement of his long-standing doctrine of "prosopic union."[119] Perhaps it is telling that, while Theodoret has Eranistes accept this statement, he also puts into his mouth the suspicion that the "real position" of Orthodoxus appears "to dissolve the union," that real position

118. Cf. chapter 4, 2.2.2.

119. The burden of Clayton's argument throughout his *Christology of Theodoret* is that there was no significant change in Theodoret's position between 431 and 451. Apropos the *Eranistes* see especially 230, 235–36.

being "that in discussing the natures we must give each its own properties" (*Eran.* 139 [195]). In other words, Theodoret is aware of how his views differ from those of the Alexandrians. The "names" of each nature may be referred to the person of our Lord Jesus Christ, but no properties or predication exchanged between those two distinct natures.

Orthodoxus now accuses Eranistes of granting "an unconfounded union to soul and body," yet venturing to say "that the Godhead and manhood of Christ have undergone mixture and confusion." Eranistes, of course, is equally anxious to avoid confusion, yet confesses to shrinking from "asserting two natures lest I fall into a dualism of sons" (*Eran.* 140 [195–96]). Orthodoxus acknowledges the dilemma, but he is still haunted by the memory of Arius and Eunomius attributing inferiority to the Son on the basis of Matthew 26:39 and John 12:27. How would Eranistes respond to them? His answer is a distinction between the *theologia* and the *oikonomia*—in the "economy" the Son of God made man shows weakness of the flesh and of the soul, and scriptures are cited to confirm the latter (John 10:17–18; 12:27; Matt 26:38; Acts 2:31). Keeping up the argument with various heretics, Orthodoxus approves Eranistes's answers and his scriptural citations, only to mock him in the end for admitting three natures (i.e., body, soul, and Godhead), and so three Sons! Eranistes feels trapped and reverts to refusing two natures after the union (*Eran.* 140–143 [195–96]).

In response to Orthodoxus's demand for explanation, Eranistes maintains "that the Godhead remains and that the manhood was swallowed up by it." Orthodoxus scorns such pagan follies—Theodoret perhaps has myths of *apotheōsis* in mind. The subsequent discussion, though focused on Christology, may imply that he regarded *theopoiēsis* as implying absorption, so blurring the distinction between Creator and creature. He begins by asking how a nature absolute and uncompounded, comprehending the universe, inapproachable and infinite, could have absorbed the nature which it assumed. Eranistes proposes an analogy: like the sea receiving a drop of honey that disappears as it mingles with the ocean's water. Orthodoxus soon shows how inappropriate that is—those two are natures alike in key respects, such as both being liquid. He offers alternatives—light pervading the atmosphere, fire diffused through metal. These, he claims, are unconfounded mixtures: iron is not damaged by contact with fire but retains its nature. That Cyril played with the iron-fire analogy in his own dialogue is interesting, but note to what different effect: for Cyril the fire utterly pervades the iron (as it did the burning bush), but for Theodoret iron and fire remain distinguishable, indeed, unadulterated by their union.[120] Here Eranistes agrees that the assumed nature was not destroyed—rather it was taken up into the substance of the Godhead (*Eran.* 143–145 [197]).

The ostensible topic of this dialogue is now center stage; yet the debate has proceeded without reference to scripture, treading over territory debated among philosophers, both Stoic and Neoplatonic, particularly as they tried to conceptualize the relationship between soul and body.[121] Scripture reappears as the timing of the Logos's absorption of the flesh again comes into question. Eranistes once more suggests the conception. Orthodoxus, however, has no difficulty in showing how Eranistes's concept of the union as absorption is incompatible with the gospel narratives—being a babe in the womb or a toddler, being circumcised, hungry and thirsty, walking about, falling asleep, and so on. After the union "the manhood did not lose its own nature" (*Eran.* 146 [198]). Eranistes backtracks: the moment of change into Godhead came after the resurrection. Now he is confronted with the postresurrection appearances, and they argue about whether the risen Christ needed food, or only seemed to eat, and what the resurrection life might be like with various scripture quotations along the way. Orthodoxus eventually concludes: after the resurrection "the nature of his body was preserved and was not changed into another substance," though he does find he has to account for change into incorruption and immortality by defining mortality and corruption as accidents. Eranistes feels obliged to backtrack again, attributing the transformation into Godhead to the ascension, only to find Orthodoxus able to produce further scriptures indicating that his body persists in heaven and the bodies of the saints will be transformed into the likeness of his glorious body (*Eran.* 147–150 [199–200]). Again we find hints that, for Theodoret, Christology cannot be pagan *apotheōsis*, nor can *theopoiēsis* be transformation into the divine, for Creator and creature are alien natures.

So the union cannot imply the absorption of humanity into divinity, and Orthodoxus has still another trick up his sleeve. The eucharistic elements are symbols of his body and blood, and the image must have an archetype: so even now the body of the Lord is a body, not changed into Godhead but filled with divine glory. Eranistes's appeal, as an analogy to the change effected in the bread and wine at the consecration, is not acceptable, for Orthodoxus is clear that they retain their own nature despite being treated as what they have become and being venerated as such: so too after the resurrection the body

120. See above, 2.1.5.

121. Cf. Clayton, *Christology of Theodoret*, 238–41.

remains but, now immortal and incorruptible, it is adored as the Lord's body. Eranistes still thinks the risen Lord should be called "God"; Orthodoxus resorts to scripture, appealing to John 6:51 and Hebrews 13:8 (*Eran.* 151–152 [200–201]). Eranistes finally demands that Orthodoxus demonstrate that "the saints who have shone of old in the Church," whom he aims to follow, divided the natures after the union. So we run into the second florilegium (*Eran.* 153–188 [201–16]), the climax of which consists of quotations from Apollinaris indicating, to Eranistes's amazement, that despite introducing the idea of "mixture" even he recognized the distinction of the natures after the union.

The second dialogue, then, has been another object lesson in how scripture functioned in the context of doctrinal debate. As so often before, we have seen doctrinal positions established through argument about the conceptual implications of scriptural statements, and conceptual claims then being tested against the words or narratives of scripture. Indeed, the questions at issue prove to have been predominantly conceptual. True, scripture was deployed to establish that the humanity was intact and, as the argument proceeded, scripture remained the reference point, but each participant had a different perception of its implications, not least because prior conceptions of the divine nature, not to mention conceptions of human nature, determined both argument and scriptural exegesis. For Theodoret their conjunction in Christ must not be allowed to dilute either one of the two natures: this is inexorably a conceptual argument, a doctrinal matter on which scripture offers no canonical ruling as such. Yet it is assumed on both sides that the validity of any conclusion requires scriptural endorsement.

But the crucial question remained: which account was truer to those foundational documents? What Theodoret seems not to have grasped, haunted as he was by Arian exegetical reasoning, is that the Alexandrians dared to allow scripture the authority to challenge some of those prior conceptions. It is noticeable that the Alexandrian notion of *kenōsis* is never discussed, and so the possibility of divine love overriding other divine attributes remains beyond Theodoret's comprehension. For him the divine nature could not be impaired or alienated from itself, and that, of course, becomes all the more apparent as the third dialogue turns to divine impassibility.

2.2.3. Apathēs—*Impassible*

The third dialogue raises the crucial issue of the passion: Who or what suffered on the cross? Orthodoxus initiates the discussion by recapitulating their agreement that the Word became incarnate not by being changed into flesh but by taking perfect human nature. The scriptures, along with the church's teachers, clearly taught that after the union he remained as he was—unmixed, impassible, unchanged, uncircumscribed—and that he preserved unimpaired the nature he had taken. Then Theodoret has Eranistes ask, "Who, according to your view, suffered the passion?" Orthodoxus replies, "Our Lord Jesus Christ." Eranistes suggests that that means "a man gave us our salvation." Orthodoxus denies this: "Have we ever confessed that our Lord Jesus Christ was only a man?" Eranistes asks for a definition as to what Orthodoxus does believe Christ to be; the answer is "incarnate Son of the living God." They confirm that that means he is God. So, says Eranistes, God underwent the passion (*Eran.* 189 [216–17]).

Orthodoxus immediately suggests that it is not as simple as that: if he was nailed to the cross without a body, one might assign the passion to the Godhead, but if he was made human by taking flesh, why exempt the passible from the passion and subject the impassible to it? Eranistes wants to affirm that the reason he took flesh was precisely so that the impassible might undergo the passion by means of the passible, which for Orthodoxus is a contradiction in terms (*Eran.* 189–190 [217]).

Eranistes then shifts the issue: the divine nature is immortal, flesh is mortal, and the immortal was united with the mortal precisely so as to taste death through it. Again Orthodoxus demurs: that which is by nature immortal does not undergo death even when conjoined to the mortal. Eranistes demands proof, and Orthodoxus replies with the soul-body analogy: it is the body that dies, not the immortal soul. The ensuing discussion, with biblical allusion or quotation of Genesis 2:17 and Matthew 10:28, determines that death is a penalty for sin, that both body and soul sin but only the body dies, the soul being chastised in the afterlife; so it is impossible for the immortal to die. How on earth, then, can God the Word, Creator of mortal and immortal natures, partake of death? Eranistes still insists that he shares death and Orthodoxus still regards this as impossible; after all, his immortal nature means that even the devil—the very teacher and inventor of iniquity—did not incur death, so "do you not shudder at the idea of saying that the fount of immortality and righteousness shared death?" (*Eran.* 190–194 [217–18]).

It now becomes clear that Theodoret did understand how important it was to the Alexandrians that the Word underwent the passion voluntarily, for here he attributes this response to Eranistes: he suffered because he willed to suffer and shared death because he wished it. Instead of accusing us, he suggests, you ought to be praising the immensity of his love for humankind (194 [219]). That Theodoret could thus chide his own spokesperson shows that he did appreciate the force of the opposition's arguments. But Orthodoxus cannot conceive of the Lord God wishing anything inconsistent with the divine nature: God is able to do all God wishes, and what God wishes is appropriate and agreeable to God's own nature. Eranistes falls back on the protestation made in the first dialogue that all things are possible to God, quoting Job 10:13 (LXX). Here the matter is taken up and discussed more fully than previously. To begin with Orthodoxus puts the text in context: the kind of thing to which it refers is God's creation of Job. As Eranistes presses the point, Orthodoxus then accuses him of suggesting that it was possible for God to sin. Eranistes is gradually led to affirm that what is possible for God is what God wishes, and God cannot wish sin since it is foreign to the divine nature. Orthodoxus has won the point and pursues other impossibilities for God, through logic and scriptural citation, particularly Hebrews 6:18 and 2 Timothy 2:11 and 13. They are impossible because they are foreign to God's nature (*Eran.* 194–197 [219–20]). Theodoret has clearly recognized that he needs a fuller answer to statements such as the one we found in Cyril's dialogue:

> It was not impossible to God, in his lovingkindness, to make himself capable of bearing the limitations of the manhood. (*Un. Chr.* 737 [79])[122]

So it is that the third dialogue develops points made previously, reinforcing fundamental arguments from the earlier dialogues, now focused in particular on the passion and what it accomplished. For Eranistes John 3:16 and Romans 5:10 affirm God's love taking the initiative to reconcile us through the death of the Son; for Orthodoxus the distinction of natures is the only way to articulate this, as God he remained incapable of suffering, but the body which suffered was his own body (*Eran.* 197 [220]). That this claim makes sense is argued from scripture: Isaac's blindness must be attributed not to his soul but his body, and so too the paralytic's sickness—we make such a distinction, though it is not explicit and the natural union of soul and body is not undercut. So, too, in the case of the Savior: we make the distinction between the temporal and the eternal, the Creator and the created, what belongs to the Godhead and what to the humanity. Eranistes states that scripture says the Son of God underwent the passion; Orthodoxus agrees it was not any other, but, distinguishing impassibility and passion, we attribute passion to the passible body and confess no passion undergone by the impassible nature (*Eran.* 198–200 [221]). The ensuing discussion goes over much of the same ground again: Eranistes worries about separating the body from the

122. See above, 2.1.4.

Godhead, Orthodoxus about attributing things like weariness to the Godhead, which contradicts Isaiah 40:28–29. The union of unlike natures being conceded, however, the person of Christ receives both, though to each nature one should assign its own properties. Eranistes consents but not to dividing one Son into two, and scripture, he asserts, does not teach the distinction of natures but says the Son of God died (Rom 5:10). Again the body-soul distinction is applied to scriptural examples: they buried Abraham, Sarah, Isaac, Rebekah, and Leah (Gen 49:31), but it was actually the body not the soul that was buried. The analogy is drawn out: the natures of Christ, though connected, should be distinguished in thought, for the impassible, immutable and immortal divine nature should not be represented as mortal and passible (*Eran.* 200–203 [223]).

Orthodoxus turns to Hebrews 2:11–15: it was the Creator who, by means of a mortal body, undid death's dominion. It was his immortality and impassibility, he implies, that overcame death, by allowing death to claim unjustly a body kept blameless and free from sin and then raising it. Eranistes does not immediately follow the argument, so there is further explanation: death is punishment for sinners, but unrighteously and against divine law death seized the sinless body of the Lord, so he raised it, promising release to those imprisoned (*Eran.* 204–206 [223–24]). There follows some discussion of how it was that all humanity, saints as well as sinners, were mortal, and how those justifiably punished could be rescued through Jesus Christ. Appeal is made to Romans 5:15–19 and 1 Corinthians 15:20–22: the apostle names Christ from the nature he assumed because it is in this nature that he is comparable to Adam. The justification, struggle, victory, death, and resurrection are all of the human nature that we share with him. Speaking of this nature is not dividing it from the Godhead but referring what is proper to the humanity (*Eran.* 206–207 [224]). Thus Theodoret's understanding of salvation certainly involves the reversal of Adam's failure being successfully achieved by the human nature assumed. Yet we should probably infer that talk of *natures* is not really talk about *individual subjects*—Adam and the humanity of Christ are somehow corporate or universal "heads" of a race first gone wrong then put right. If so, both sides in the debate tended to subsume the particular man, Jesus, into a generalized human nature. The idea of two natures was not meant to mean "two Sons." Yet the attribution of actions and experiences—the struggle, the victory, the passion—to the human nature was not unreasonably understood as turning the human nature into a subject (i.e., an individual). Furthermore, as Clayton has argued, "Theodoret can understand predication of an attribute to the Word strictly and only in the sense of attributing it to him as a *hypostasis* arising out of the one divine *ousia-physis*," thus conflating the divine nature and the particular person of the Trinity—God the Word—in such a way as to deny the possibility of attributing certain actions and experiences to him as subject.[123] Given both of these moves, the accusation "two Sons" is perhaps comprehensible—indeed, not altogether inappropriate—whatever the protestations.

Indeed, Theodoret recognized that an Eranistes would still be worried. He is now presented as citing Romans 8:32: God "spared not his own Son," and asks, "What Son is this?" "The one and only Son of God," replies Orthodoxus, "but he was not delivered up without a body." He turns to Abraham's sacrifice of Isaac: God said that Abraham had not withheld his only son, but was he actually slain? Eranistes takes the commonsense position that this refers to Abraham's willingness to sacrifice his son—in other words his understanding seeks the essential meaning rather than the literal sense. Orthodoxus invites him to take a similar view of the text in question (Rom 8:32) and so see that it was the flesh that was nailed to the cross. He goes on to develop that classic Abrahamic "type" of the passion in a way that suits his conceptuality. In both the Akedah and the passion there is a father, a well-beloved son, and a sacrifice; one son bore wood on his shoulders, the other son a cross. Other correspondences are sketched, and then the point clinched: a lamb was sacrificed, not the son himself! So the passion should be assigned to the flesh and impassibility to the Godhead. This extraordinary deduction is justified by Orthodoxus on the grounds that a type never exactly corresponds to its archetype—a point already developed with respect to Melchizedek in the second dialogue. The issue here is that Isaac and the lamb fit as different natures, but not insofar as there is separation of their divided persons. Orthodoxus hastens to affirm so close a union of Godhead and humanity as to understand one undivided person, acknowledged to be both God and man, visible and invisible, circumscribed and uncircumscribed, and so on (*Eran.* 208–210 [225]).

They then turn to further "types"—the sacrifices explored in the Epistle to the Hebrews and the two goats of the Day of Atonement ritual. There the goat that was let go prefigures the impassible Godhead, the one slain, the passible human nature. Eranistes jibs at likening the Lord to goats, whereat Orthodoxus cites John 3:14–15, the crucified Savior prefigured in the brazen serpent! Such moves are justified with reference to John 1:29, 36; Isaiah 53:7; 2 Corinthians 5:21; and Galatians 3:13. The weakness of such typology Eranistes now indicates by pointing out that two goats suggests two persons. Orthodoxus, however, regards it as impossible to prefigure with just one goat both passible and impassible natures, Godhead and humanity, referring to the sacrifice of two doves

123. Clayton, *Christology of Theodoret*, 223.

as similar. Eranistes objects to these enigmas, and we may feel some sympathy with his objection to such contentious exploitation of long-standing figural insights. Orthodoxus appeals to the apostle, citing Paul's use of Sarah and Hagar in Galatians (*Eran.* 210–211 [226]). Once again we are confronted with the fact that traditional typological exegesis could provide cogent material from which doctrinal deductions might be argued. It is assumed that truths obliquely indicated in prophecies, types, and enigmas confirm what has been arrived at by essentially conceptual argument.

Eranistes protests that in no way will he agree to divide the passion. He cites Matthew 28:6: "Come, see the place where the Lord lay." Orthodoxus elaborates his earlier point about the way we and the scriptures refer to the person when really it is the body that is buried. Then he rehearses material from the gospels to confirm the same case with respect to the body of Jesus. We need not go into detail, except to note that he refers to 1 Corinthians 15:3–4, and that introduces discussion of the context, namely the Corinthians' disbelief in resurrection. The point eventually arrived at is that a resurrection of God would never induce anyone to believe in general resurrection, since the difference between God and humans is incalculable—humans are mortal, God is Almighty. So the suffering, death, and resurrection belong to the body. The argument of 1 Corinthians 15 is followed at some length to show that as in Adam all die, so in Christ shall all be made alive. Eranistes still protests that this means Christ is only a man, which gives Orthodoxus the chance to assert yet again that he has repeatedly confessed that he is not only man but eternal God. Eranistes agrees that the apostle proves general resurrection by means of the Lord's resurrection, acknowledging that the argument depends on some kinship between the substance of the one and the other, but he would never consent to apply the passion to the human nature alone: he still wants to affirm that God the Word died in the flesh (*Eran.* 212–216 [226–28]).

So we are back going over old ground again, as this implies change, but the Trinity is immutable. First Peter 4:1 states that Christ suffered for us in the flesh. No problem with that, retorts Orthodoxus: we too "have learnt the canon of dogmas from the divine scriptures" (*Eran.* 216 [228]). Yet they take that scriptural statement in different ways: Eranistes identifies the Lord Christ as God the Word, while Orthodoxus differentiates God the Word—the eternal and incorporeal nature—from Emmanuel, God with us, the incarnate Word, both God and man. If God the Word made man is called Christ, surely there is nothing unreasonable in saying that God the Word suffered in flesh, thinks Eranistes (*Eran.* 216 [228–29]). The conceptual frameworks within which they read the text have different starting points, and so they can use scripture to deduce different things. Orthodoxus does not find in scripture any statement to the effect that God the Word suffered in flesh. Eranistes cannot believe it: you cannot mean you do not regard the Lord Christ as God the Word? But now Orthodoxus leads Eranistes into acknowledging that accepted doctrines are not all spelled out in scripture, taking the nature of the Holy Spirit as an example. Eranistes remains bothered about using nonscriptural language; Orthodoxus is clear that scripture never in so many words connects God with the passion. Eranistes agrees God never suffered apart from a body, but that for Orthodoxus is a kind of passion, not impassibility. Eranistes finally comes out with the Alexandrian paradox: *apathōs epathen*—he suffered impassibly. That is a ridiculous riddle to Orthodoxus: Whoever heard of impassible passion or immortal mortality? (*Eran.* 217–218 [229]). So again back to going over old ground—the divine shared in suffering. But what on earth can that mean? Did the divine nature feel the pain of nails going into the body? Antiochene favorite texts about the body being a temple are brought out again as well as Orthodoxus's fear of heresy (*Eran.* 220 [230]).

Pressed for further evidence Orthodoxus turns once more to the Eucharist. At the Passover the Lord pointed to the death of the lamb as a type and taught what body corresponded to that foreshadowing—they agree there is no reference here to the Godhead but to the body and blood (221 [231]). The resurrection appearances are again adduced: he showed them the body. Acts 2:29 raises issues about the soul and the resurrection, Orthodoxus eventually reasoning that the body severed from the soul underwent death and not the Godhead. Eranistes protests and quotes 1 Corinthians 2:8: "Had they known they would not have crucified the Lord of glory" (*Eran.* 221–224 [233]). The same old arguments reappear: it was the body of the Lord of glory that was nailed to the wood. In the course of the discussion they both agree that it is rash to add words to scripture, though to explain what is written and reveal the hidden meaning is pure and holy. The issue remains: what is the truth to be deduced from scripture about the particular conceptual issues at stake?

We reach a kind of summing up which introduces the third florilegium. Orthodoxus accepts Eranistes's statement that the peculiar properties of the natures are shared by the person, for on account of the union the same being is both the Son of Man and the Son of God, Son of David and Lord of David, adding that no confusion results from both having the same name: the reverent distinction of terms can lead to apparent contradictions finding agreement (*Eran.* 226 [233]). Orthodoxus expounds 1 Corinthians 2:8: they crucified the nature they knew, the human nature being ignorant of the divine, cross-referencing John 10:33. Eranistes finally appeals to the Nicene Creed, which states that the only-begotten, very God, of one substance with the Father, suffered and was crucified (*Eran.* 227 [233]). Clearly Theodoret was well aware of the Alexandrian appeal to this confession of faith and has to respond. So Orthodoxus recaps: after the union scripture applies to one person terms both of exaltation and humiliation. This is why the creed, after speaking of belief in the Father, does not simply continue, "and in the Son," but speaks rather of belief in our Lord Jesus Christ, the Son of God. After the incarnation God the Word is called Christ because the name Christ includes what is proper to the Godhead and the manhood. Yet some properties belong to one nature and some to the other, and Eranistes is led to agree that it is the Godhead which is *homoousios*, not the flesh. So, when it comes to the passion, we need to recognize the nature that submitted to it, avoid attributing it to the impassible, and attribute it to the nature assumed for the purpose of suffering. The creed anathematizes those who claim he was mutable and variable—the clauses condemning Arian tenets are quoted (*Eran.* 227–229 [234]). Orthodoxus develops again the point that if suffering and tasting death are attributed to the Son of God, then he underwent mutation and alteration, and he asserts that such expressions have been expelled from the church by the illustrious fathers, thus introducing the third florilegium (*Eran.* 229–253 [234–44]).

2.2.4. *Review of Theodoret's Handling of Scripture as the Source of Doctrine*

Just like Cyril, Theodoret has throughout been in teaching mode. In each case the character who is the author's spokesperson leads the dialogue partner toward the truth, inducing agreement through leading questions. Again, like Cyril, Theodoret tests scripture against scripture, assuming that the basis of doctrinal statements is to be found there, though literal or surface meanings might be misleading. It is notable that these questions about how scripture is to be interpreted recur in the dialogues, and so much of the discussion addresses the question how specific texts are to be read.

For Theodoret the exploitation of scripture by heretics, especially Arians but also docetists and Apollinarians, is a recurring concern. In the position of his opponents he not only uncovers a barely disguised docetism but also seems to detect the potential danger of projecting onto scripture the somewhat pagan notion of *apotheōsis*. These tendencies he meets by appeal to established doctrine—accepted Trinitarian tenets and especially the classic doctrine of creation out of nothing which, if not explicit, is ever implicit in the assumption of the utter difference between the Creator and all things created. This determined his prior conceptuality and from it flowed the logic of his position.

His conceptual cast of mind becomes all the more evident in his appendix to the dialogues, his summary demonstration in logical syllogisms of each of the three topics addressed in the dialogues (*Eran.* 254–265 [245–49]).

Yet this fundamental conceptuality was undoubtedly believed to be biblical teaching and demanded a hermeneutic that never blurred the distinction between creature and Creator. For Theodoret, this necessitated not merely partitive exegesis but the grounding of that exegesis in the reality of the Savior's two distinct natures, divine and human. Gavrilyuk's suggestion that when considering patristic thought impassibility should simply be treated as one among many apophatic qualifiers is both telling and misleading: telling in that divine *apatheia* contributes to the articulation of that fundamental differentiation; misleading in that it minimizes what for Theodoret was absolutely vital—the actual, indeed practical, fact that the divine was beyond being adversely affected or changed by anything external to the divine self.[124] How dire might be the consequences of rigid adherence to that conceptuality for grasping the truth of the incarnation can seem all too evident in the arguments of the *Eranistes*; neither Chrysostom's *synkatabasis* nor Cyril's *kenōsis* was conceivable.[125] Theodoret, it seems, missed their grasp of the overarching narrative of scripture in his concern to do justice both to the nature of God and the creatureliness of humankind—these were the key truths, as revealed in scripture and determined in established doctrine, at least according to his understanding.

And yet, Theodoret, it must be said, does more justice to the human dimensions of the gospel narratives, reads more truly the New Testament affirmations of atoning sacrifice made in and through the bodily offering of human obedience, and has his own grasp of the overarching biblical story, albeit a different one than Cyril's. His use of the old tradition of Christ's recapitulation of Adam, a tradition founded on key Pauline texts, suggests that his reading of scripture was in terms of the creation and re-creation of humankind as a creature meant to image the divine in a creaturely medium rather than as a being meant to be transformed into the divine through *theopoiēsis*.[126]

124. Paul Gavrilyuk, *The Suffering of the Impassible God: The Dialectics of Patristic Thought*, OECS (Oxford: Oxford University Press, 2004).

125. See chapter 4, 2.1.1.

126. See further my article "God's Image: The 'Elephant in the Room' in the Fourth Century?" StPatr 50 (2011): 57–71.

3. Scripture in Doctrinal Dispute: Some Conclusions

Repeatedly in these dialogues we have seen the two sides agreeing that it is to scripture they defer, not arguments of human reason. With some difference in approach both sides also defer to established doctrinal traditions. Yet it was precisely their sense of the right way to understand scripture and tradition in the face of fresh questions that drove their essentially didactic endeavors. These dialogues cannot give us direct access to the course of debates at the time; they are all slanted to the conclusions that suited their authors. Yet examining them side by side has enabled us to lift the curtain a little, to see not just the extent to which they did or did not hear what the other side was saying, but also to appreciate the profoundly important role scripture played in the controversy. Both sides claimed, usually justifiably, to be defending scriptural teaching, but each was focused on different aspects of the scriptural narrative and different key prooftexts because they differed in their overall conception of the implications of both Bible and creed for the incarnation. In this concluding section we will largely refrain from summarizing and repeating points noted in the process of our review and just draw out a few similarities and contrasts.

Let us begin with the themes we abstracted from Cyril's dialogues as a way of organizing his rather repetitive material. Theodoret never addresses most of those issues, though for Cyril they were clearly vital. We have observed already that Theodoret seems never to discuss *kenōsis*; nor does he consider Cyril's challenge to differentiate the Son of God incarnate from adopted sons or sons by grace. Bothered himself, we suspect, by any kind of *apotheōsis*, Theodoret does not engage with Cyril's charge that the two Sons doctrine meant they blasphemously offered worship to a divinized human being alongside the truly divine Son of God. He protests at the accusation of teaching two Sons, denying it time and again and using the language of union. But whereas the soul-body analogy implies for Cyril a union in which the Logos as subject assimilates the assumed, using it as an instrument to engage in human experience in the same way as the immortal soul shares in the experiences of the body, for Theodoret it implies two distinguishable natures, soul and body, reference to each of which may signify the one person in which the natures are conjoined. The same can be said regarding their common use of the iron-fire analogy: for Cyril the fire permeates and heats the metal; for Theodoret they are unconfusedly conjoined, each retaining its own nature. If we now consider Theodoret's major themes captured in the titles discussed above—*atreptos*, *asyngchutos*, *apathēs*—they obviously bypass Cyril's principal interests. Nor can it be said that Cyril's dialogue anticipated and addressed the particular focus of Theodoret's concern—to safeguard the difference between Creator and creature, to avoid any conception by which the divine might be alienated from its inherent nature. To that extent we find them talking past each other, even as the dialogues purport to engage with the slogans and proposals of the other party. These dialogues most surely do not give us access to actual discussions—only to each author's perception of the debate.

Yet when it comes to their constant appeal to scripture, we find the same key passages time and again, the same endeavor to deduce from wording or narrative the appropriate articulation of a doctrine concerning the truth of the Word's incarnation in Christ. Much they have in common, not least the same desire to prove their conceptions from scripture and the same recognition that you have to probe text and context to find true meaning. Yet in crucial ways their reading of biblical texts produces different outcomes. This is partly because of different ways of grasping the overarching narrative of scripture, partly because of differing instincts about the nature of salvation, this perhaps being shaped by differing anthropologies, and partly because of fundamental conceptual models, these deriving not simply from underlying philosophical differences but from differing reception of doctrines already established as scriptural in the tradition. To conclude we offer brief retrospection of two examples, one biblical text and one crucial topic:

(1) It is particularly striking that for both Cyril and Theodoret Philippians 2:5–11 was a key reference point for their doctrine, but they brought out different aspects of that text without really hearing what the other was saying. For Theodoret it was a classic statement of the two natures: the one who was *morphē theou* (in the form of God) took the *morphē doulou* (the form of a slave). For Cyril the key was to be found in the verb *ekenōsen*, he emptied himself: the subject of the entire narrative of humiliation and exaltation is the one in the form of God. Theodoret never seems to have grasped that nettle, the idea of *kenōsis*; indeed, he almost seems deliberately to avoid discussion of Cyril's favorite term. For Theodoret the one obedient unto death, even death on a cross, was the one in human likeness—this was the one whom God raised and graced with the name above every name. The Lord Jesus Christ confessed by every tongue is the incarnate one, both in *morphē theou* and in *morphē doulou*. The latter is brought through struggle and temptation, suffering and death, and raised to new life by the presence of the former. The body of the *morphē doulou* is offered as a sacrifice that frees humankind from sin and death. Cyril never quite grasped that: for him the taking of the *morphē doulou* by the *morphē theou* in itself re-constituted humanity in God's image, enabling *theopoiēsis*. His entire understanding of salvation is different.

(2) Both Cyril and Theodoret turn to the Eucharist to substantiate their views, appealing to the scriptures. We stated earlier that the climax of Cyril's

dialogue is his treatment of the life-giving power of the Eucharist: unless it was "the very flesh of the Word," it could not be understood to give life as attested in John 6:33 and 51.[127] The flesh and blood of a different son would be ineffective. God the Word has introduced the life-giving power and energy of his own self into his very own flesh: the analogy of metal and fire is offered. Theodoret also makes eucharistic points; indeed at some point in each of his three dialogues he turns to this subject. In the first, his exegesis of Genesis 49:10 associates the blood of the grape with the true vine (John 15) and the water and blood flowing from the Savior's side (John 19:34), which then suggests the association of his body with bread.[128] For Theodoret the important point is that the bread and wine are symbols not of his Godhead but of his body. In the second dialogue, reference to the Eucharist is used to dismiss absorption of the human in the divine. Again, the symbols are of his body and blood, and the image must have an archetype; therefore the body of the Lord is not changed into Godhead.[129] He resists the idea that the consecration of the elements indicates their transformation—they retain their own nature, though now venerated as the Lord's body and blood. In the third dialogue we find reference to the death of the Passover lamb—the Lord pointed to this as a type, referring not to the Godhead but the body and blood.[130] Each time references to the narratives and words of scripture substantiate the point. We recall the importance in Theodoret's soteriology of the offering of the body in sacrifice on the cross. However, one can easily hear Cyril's potential reaction: you might as well be speaking of the body of any one of us! What this would mean is that it was not "the Lord himself who saved us but one of our own number."[131] This was not simply a difference of emphasis in sacramental theology—it was about articulating the teaching of scripture so that the salvation offered by the gospel could be received and lived out in the liturgical and ethical life of believers.

These two examples surely mean that the debate cannot be dismissed as driven wholly by philosophical or anthropological preconceptions. It was certainly conceptual in its aim to articulate doctrine—to conceptualize the truth enshrined in the biblical text and narrative. But different readings of scripture and its message of salvation were also at stake. Doctrinal definition, as ever, emerged from the endeavor to make sense of scripture and as ever struggled with

127. Cf. 2.1.5 above, pp. 237–38.
128. Cf. 2.2.1 above, p. 243.
129. Cf. 2.2.2 above, pp. 250–51.
130. Cf. 2.2.3 above, p. 257.
131. Cf. 2.1.5 above, p. 237.

the reality that scripture points beyond itself to truths barely conceivable within the bounds of human reason, barely expressible within the limits of human discourse, barely susceptible to analogies drawn from within the created order.

Excursus on the Chalcedonian Definition

This is not the place for yet another discussion of the outcome of those twenty years of dispute. Was the Chalcedonian Definition arrived at in 451 just a compromise? If so, it barely established peace for any length of time—there remained suspicion of it in Egypt and in the East, and the resultant splits would last for centuries, with those in the Miaphysite tradition rejecting the formula "in two natures" and insisting on "out of two natures." Elsewhere, debates about the implications of the Definition have been perennial, continuing into our own day. It provides parameters but hardly a clear conceptual model for Christology. Suffice it to underline a few key points, in the Definition

- the creeds of Nicaea and Constantinople are explicitly reaffirmed as sufficient for orthodoxy;
- the issues in dispute are sketched, and key documents are received, including the synodical epistles of Cyril and Pope Leo's letter to Flavian, Archbishop of Constantinople;
- the ideas rejected by the Council are listed: a Duality of Sons; the passibility of the Godhead of the Only-begotten; a mixture or confusion of the two natures of Christ; the idea of two natures before the union and one nature after the union.

Then come the carefully balanced phrases of the Definition:

> our Lord Jesus Christ is One and the same Son, the Self-same Perfect in Godhead, the Self-same Perfect in Manhood; truly God and truly Man; the Self-same of a rational soul and body; consubstantial with the Father according to the Godhead, the Self-same consubstantial with us according to the Manhood; like us in all things, sin apart; before the ages begotten of the Father as to the Godhead, but in the last days the Self-same, for us and our salvation (born) of Mary the Virgin Theotokos as to the Manhood; One and the same Christ, Son, Lord, Only-begotten; acknowledged in Two Natures unconfusedly,

> unchangeably, indivisibly, inseparably; the difference of the Natures being no way removed because of the Union, but rather the property of each Nature being preserved, and (both) concurring into One Prosopon and One Hypostasis; not as though He were parted or divided into Two Prosopa, but One and the Self-same Son and Only-begotten God, Word, Lord, Jesus Christ; even as from the beginning the prophets taught concerning Him, and as the Lord Jesus Christ Himself hath taught us, and as the Symbol of the Fathers hath handed down to us.[132]

It is hardly surprising, given the terms in which the Definition sets out the doctrine of Christ, that most studies of the christological controversy have focused on explaining the "technical terms" that appear in that statement—*ousia*, *hypostasis*, *physeis*, *prosōpon*—tracing how they were used and what the participants meant by them. Scripture seems way over the horizon as far as this doctrinal text is concerned—never quoted and barely alluded to in any way. However, I hope this chapter has shown how grossly misleading it would be to conclude that the articulation of doctrine was remote from scripture. Indeed, we should take note of the fact that the documents received by the Council as spelling out orthodox views certainly indicated the scriptural basis for their christological statements, Leo's Tome, as well as the letters of Cyril, which we explored in the first section of this chapter. The whole controversy was for sure about making sense of scripture, both within that particular intellectual context and particularly with respect to inherited doctrinal traditions, but also in relation to the experience of salvation, ethical engagement, and liturgical participation.

---

132. English translation quoted from Bindley and Green, *Oecumenical Documents*, 234–35.

6

Doctrine and Scripture

SHAPING AND RECLAIMING THE MYSTERY

As we attempt to reach some conclusions about the relationship between doctrine and scripture, not only in early Christianity but also for the ongoing Christian tradition, we will begin by revisiting conclusions reached at the end of volume 1 and then once again enter into dialogue with Augustine to sharpen up the issues and inform further reflection.

1. Scripture and Doctrinal Development: Interim Conclusions

In scholarly circles there has been a long-standing suspicion that Christian doctrine is not to be found in scripture—that later developments under the influence of nonbiblical factors produced articles of belief in the form of creeds as well as definitions of the classic dogmas concerning the Trinity and the incarnation. We began this project by noting this widely perceived gap between doctrine and scripture and its exacerbation through the dominance of historico-critical reading: New Testament scholarship has long treated doctrinal reading as anachronistic. We considered two widely influential ways of addressing the gap:[1]

1. the approach of John Henry Newman, whereby continuities can be traced, development treated as legitimate, indeed providential, and the eventual outcome as rooted embryonically in scripture; and
2. that of Adolf von Harnack, whose "Hellenization" thesis demanded radical

1. See volume 1, chapter 1.

rejection of alien developments, implying a return to the simple gospel of Jesus unearthed by nineteenth-century historical reconstruction, namely, the Fatherhood of God and the brotherhood of man (to use its long-standing, but now politically incorrect, characterization).

With assumptions derived from either approach (or even from both once the "Hellenization" of the New Testament texts themselves was taken into account), modern scholarship rendered more and more problematical the coinherence of scripture and doctrine assumed by the early church. So we set out to construct a fresh account of how doctrine was distilled from scripture through often competing attempts to make sense of the teaching offered by the authoritative yet disparate collection of books in use in early Christian ecclesial communities. These we found more "school-like" than anything else in the sociocultural context of the time, for they offered teaching (*dogma*, *doctrina*) whose truth was grounded in those authoritative books.

At the end of volume 1 we offered some interim conclusions concerning the story of doctrinal development:[2]

1. The rule (canon) of faith and the canon of scripture were received together as the apostolic tradition before the end of the second century; thus from very early on scripture and basic Christian teaching were treated as coinherent. This clearly remained the case throughout the period covered in this second volume: finding the correct doctrinal articulation of what had been received through scripture and the baptismal creed was the aim of protagonists on all sides of the debates with which we have been concerned here.
2. The rule of faith, and subsequently the baptismal creeds, were understood to be summaries of scripture—indeed, to guide the reader in identifying the overall "hypothesis" of scripture, so discerning the unitive narrative, from beginning to end, as an account of creation, fall, and redemption under the providential oversight of the one true Creator God, to whom all human creatures would ultimately be accountable. The disputes reviewed in this volume were surely shaped by the need to consolidate the implications of this overall perspective in the face of proposals with the potential to undermine it by separating the ultimate God from the mediating actor in creation and redemption.
3. Construing scripture, whether with reference to particular prooftexts or the overall import of ostensibly contradictory material, raised such questions

2. See volume 1, chapter 7.

that the restatement in propositional terms of its prophecy and poetry, narrative and drama became inevitable, such propositions then providing hermeneutical guidelines for exegetical challenges. The material discussed in this second volume has surely made that process even clearer—indeed, the need for nonscriptural terms to clarify the fundamental "mind" of scripture became explicit.

4. The legacy of the second century was the promulgation of the countercultural doctrine of God as the transcendent Creator of everything out of nothing—hardly the outcome of "Hellenization." It was rather a distinctive deduction from scripture with enduring consequences for the doctrinal arguments we have subsequently traced in this volume.
5. Thus there was development and, given that the sense-making was within the context of Greco-Roman intellectual culture, there was more than a little "Hellenization"—both approaches certainly carry a measure of truth. The shift in perspective offered here arises from the perception that the process was nothing like some kind of automatic evolution, nor was doctrine an alien growth distorting scripture's profile. Rather sense-making was what it was all about. Through deduction, and through dispute about the appropriateness of the deductions, scripture was the genesis of a distinctive Christian discourse within that particular cultural ambit. Nothing we have found in this second volume would gainsay that.

Thus we carry forward and confirm those interim conclusions.

2. Methodological Questions concerning Doctrinal Reading of Scripture

However, in that concluding chapter of volume 1 we also expressed the hope that the "postmodern turn" might open up ways of closing that perceived gap for us, as in our own intellectual culture the focus on original, authorial, and historical meanings gives way to consideration of the text itself, readers' response, and the interaction between author, text, and reader as communication is triangulated, as well as to the validity of future meanings as the formative impact of the text becomes generative of new senses. The future potential of the text could perhaps justify the doctrinal readings that were the outcome of the process we have been tracing, while also facilitating our own fresh appropriation of such meanings. So we utilized Augustine's *Teaching Christianity* (*De doctrina christiana*) to draw out some parallels between his approach to hermeneutics and that of postmodern developments such as canon criticism and theological reading. It is surely evident that accepted exegetical method and received hermeneutical approach can determine the extent to which the gap between doctrine and scripture is experienced, and the "postmodern turn" seemed to ease the tensions.

Yet with respect to the Trinity and Christology there remains the suspicion that these traditional doctrines, hammered out from scripture in those early centuries, are not convincingly biblical, given the exegetical methods and hermeneutical assumptions through which they were deduced. I confessed earlier to having teased systematic theologians with carrying on regardless when modern approaches to reading scripture were so fundamentally different to those that produced the doctrines which they were trying to expound.[3] As Lewis Ayres has put it, "modern Trinitarian theology invokes some of the formulae produced within the fourth century but simultaneously argues that the theological methods that produced those formulae are untenable in modernity."[4] He acknowledges that Andrew Louth had earlier raised the question how we can accept the results of patristic interpretation when we do not accept their methods.[5] (Though, as we shall see, for Louth that was preparing the way for reappropriating the approaches of the past.) Naturally enough the historico-critical method made the presence of these doctrines in scripture anachronistic. Notorious are the strictures of R. P. C. Hanson:

> We may . . . allow that Athanasius had a firm grip of the ultimate drive or burden of the New Testament at least . . . [but] we cannot but observe the great gulf which divides him, and virtually all his contemporaries of whatever ecclesiastical complexion, from the moderns in his method of handling and presuppositions in approaching the text of the Bible.[6]

> It was . . . the presuppositions with which they approached the Biblical text that clouded their perceptions, the tendency to treat the Bible in an 'atomic' way as if each verse or set of verses was capable of giving direct information about Christian doctrine apart from its context, the 'oracular' concept of the

3. See volume 1, p. 247, citing my article "The 'Mind' of Scripture: Theological Readings of the Bible in the Fathers," *International Journal of Systematic Theology* 7 (2005): 126–41.

4. Ayres, *Nicaea and Its Legacy*, 386.

5. Ayres, *Nicaea and Its Legacy*, 386 n. 5, referencing Andrew Louth, *Discerning the Mystery: An Essay on the Nature of Theology* (Oxford: Clarendon, 1983), 100.

6. Hanson, *Search*, 843.

> nature of the Bible. . . . The very reverence with which they honoured the Bible as a sacred book stood in the way of their understanding it.[7]

In the face of such dismissals Louth attempted to revive the kind of view once espoused by John Henry Newman, namely that allegory—that is, the mystical interpretation—was necessary for discerning in scripture the dogmas of the faith: allegory "is a way of glimpsing the living depths of tradition from the perspective of the letter of the scriptures."[8] It is about "the deeper spiritual meaning" that even ancient critics of allegory were seeking. Newman had asserted that

> It may be almost laid down as an historical fact that the mystical interpretation and orthodoxy will stand or fall together.[9]
>
> The use of Scripture, then, especially in its spiritual or second sense, as a medium of thought and deduction, is a characteristic principle of the developments of doctrine in the Church.[10]

Apparently by contrast, Lewis Ayres stated that "patristic exegesis takes as its point of departure the 'plain' sense of the text," but he explains that this means "'the way the words run' for a community in the light of that community's techniques for following the argument of texts."[11] This does not, then, signify the literal sense as now generally understood—even though "grammatical techniques are the fundamental reading tools."[12] The "plain sense," he suggests, has "flexibiity" and may offer alternative possible readings that "result from its speaking about realities that are beyond comprehension."[13] It would seem that the "plain sense" is here so conceived as to include the notions that the fulfillment of a prophecy constitutes its plain sense, that texts are collec-

7. Hanson, *Search*, 848–49. Particularly robust had been both his estimate of Origen's failure to understand history and his criticism of Origen's commitment to allegory in his earlier work, *Allegory and Event* (London: SCM, 1959).

8. Louth, *Discerning the Mystery*, 96.

9. John Henry Newman, *An Essay on the Development of Christian Doctrine: The Edition of 1845* (Harmondsworth: Penguin, 1974), 340.

10. Newman, *Development*, 342.

11. Ayres, *Nicaea and Its Legacy*, 32.

12. Ayres, *Nicaea and Its Legacy*, 34–37.

13. Ayres, *Nicaea and Its Legacy*, 33.

tions of discrete oracles with meanings divorced from their context, and that figural, if not allegorical, reading may yield the plain sense.

So the apparently diverse terminologies in play would seem to be pointing in the same direction. What is clear is that we need a less broad-brush characterization—indeed, a more precise review of the strengths and weaknesses of the way scripture was deployed in the debates, and a reassessment of how far they betrayed or deepened the grasp of scripture's import. Are we persuaded that, whether we call it the "plain sense" or the "mystical interpretation," the way in which doctrines were derived from scripture can be accepted as employing lastingly valid interpretative techniques? Was the doctrinal outcome read into scripture rather than out of it—indeed, was it ultimately biblical or not? Despite the postmodern move beyond the historico-critical method, surely (1) allegory still provokes negative vibes—eisegesis not exegesis is the cry; (2) prooftexting, though still widely practiced in constructing the "biblical" view on one topic or another, is surely rightly regarded as delivering suspect exegesis given the abstraction of texts from their context; and (3) the christological interpretation of the Old Testament remains problematical, especially as the legacy of supersessionism and anti-Semitism is acknowledged. Such exegetical practices have been observed time and time again as we have explored the arguments deployed in the major doctrinal disputes of the fourth and fifth centuries. As we set out to review these questions and respond to them, let Augustine provide us again with a kind of summation and a dialogue partner, as he did at the end of volume 1.

3. Augustine's *On the Trinity*: Contemplating God through Scripture and Creation

Like *Teaching Christianity*, from which we drew previously, *On the Trinity* was composed off and on over a period of time.[14] Begun around 400, it was completed soon after 420 following a hiatus occasioned by the unauthorized publication of the incomplete manuscript. The work thus lies prior to the outbreak of the christological controversies in the East but largely beyond the heat of the struggles with Arianism—largely, I say, because there were Arians around

14. Latin text of *On the Trinity* in W. J. Mountain, ed., *On the Trinity*, 2 vols., CCSL 50–50A (Turnhout: Brepols, 1968); English translation, unless otherwise noted, in Edmund Hill, trans., *The Trinity: De Trinitate*, Works of St. Augustine 1.5 (Hyde Park, NY: New City, 1991).

still. Augustine had come across them in Milan, it seems, and the imminent fall of the Western Empire to tribes already converted to Arian Christianity would mean such issues were far from laid to rest.[15] Still, the point here is that Augustine's work is mostly not in controversial mode, though we certainly find him replaying pro-Nicene arguments and prooftexts in the first part of this work (books 1–7). The questions for us are whether Augustine's doctrine of the Trinity depends upon those methods that we find suspect, and whether the theology that emerges is a true reflection of the biblical material.

On the Trinity is largely a work of contemplation, an endeavor to understand the God who has been the object of Augustine's lifelong search and in whom he has placed his faith. "Unless you believe, you will not understand" (Isa 7:9 LXX) he quotes more than once (*Trin.* 7.6.12). In Genesis 1:26 it is "to our image and likeness" that God made humankind, so "it was the image of the trinity that was being made in man" (*Trin.* 12.5.5–6.7). In his *Confessions* Augustine had already suggested that to understand the Trinity disputants should reflect upon "the triad within their own selves," which he there identifies as being, knowing, and willing, while urging contemplation on how inseparable they are—"one life, one mind, and one essence, yet ultimately there is distinction, for they are inseparable, yet distinct" (*Conf.* 13.11.12).[16] We may recall that Gregory of Nyssa also looked for an analogy to the Trinity within an individual, suggesting mind, word, and love.[17] Such introspection is what will occupy Augustine in books 8–15, as he seeks some grasp of the God in whose image he was created while repudiating the idea that the image might be found in three human beings rather than one—that is too much like three gods (*Trin.* 12.5.5)! Thus his contemplation was informed and guided by scripture's affirmation of the image of God in humankind. First, however, he sets out what is to be believed, propounding this as the teaching of scripture.

3.1. From Doctrine to Scripture

It is clear that for Augustine, as we have repeatedly discovered for early Christian thinkers in general, correct doctrine determined the right reading of scripture. At the end of volume 1 we observed how Augustine briefly set out in *Teaching Christianity* (1.10–12) an account of the one God as Trinity, the love

15. Michel R. Barnes, "Anti-Arian Works," in *Augustine through the Ages*, ed. Allan D. Fitzgerald, OSA (Grand Rapids: Eerdmans, 1999), 31–34.

16. Translation from Henry Chadwick, *Confessions* (Oxford: Oxford University Press, 1992).

17. See chapter 3, 2.3.2.

of whom, along with love of neighbor, constitutes the subject matter (*res*) of scripture.[18] We found five key points:

1. The Trinity is "one supreme thing" or perhaps "the cause of all things; if indeed it is a cause." Already Augustine confesses that "to find any name that will really fit such transcendent Majesty" is not easy.
2. In fact, it is better to say that "this Trinity is the one God *from whom are all things, through whom all things, in whom all things*" (Rom 11:36).
3. "Thus Father and Son and Holy Spirit are both each one of them singly God and all together one God; and each one of them simply is the complete divine substance, and altogether are one substance."
4. So "the Father is neither the Son nor the Holy Spirit; the Son is neither the Father nor the Holy Spirit; the Holy Spirit is neither the Father nor the Son"; each is simply itself, in other words, though "the three possess the same eternity, the same unchangeableness, the same greatness, the same power."
5. Finally Augustine lodges their unity in the Father, their equality in the Son, and their harmony of unity and equality in the Holy Spirit.

In similar vein *On the Trinity* affirms from the start that "according to the scriptures Father, Son, and Holy Spirit in the inseparable equality of one substance present a divine unity, and therefore there are not three gods but one God" (*Trin.* 1.4.7). It rapidly acknowledges, however, that the narrative of scripture makes this a real puzzle, and that is the starting point for Augustine's explorations. How can this inseparable equality be understood when, according to scripture, "an utterance of the Father was heard which is not the Son's utterance" and "only the Son was born in the flesh and suffered and rose again and ascended" (*Trin.* 1.5.8)? It seems "the Father does some things, the Son others and the Holy Spirit yet others," so the Trinity is no longer inseparable.

Augustine's first recourse is to cite texts that establish that scripture does imply equality and inseparability. His second is to distinguish the "form of God" from the "form of a servant" to explain texts that purport to show the Son's subordination to the Father (to consideration of these prooftexting discussions, mostly already familiar to us from Athanasius and elsewhere, we will return). For us the initially significant point is that in the end the doctrine of inseparable equality radically modified the traditional christological reading of Old Testament theophanies. The old claim that in those appearances the Logos was somehow sent as the visible form of the invisible God would no longer do because it implied subordinationism.

18. See volume 1, chapter 6.

3.1.1. Beyond Christological Reading of Old Testament Theophanies

In book 2 Augustine embarks on an extended inquiry into

- "whether it was the Father or the Son or the Holy Spirit who appeared under these created forms to the fathers; or whether it was sometimes the Father, sometimes the Son, sometimes the Holy Spirit; or whether it was simply the one and only God, that is, the trinity without distinction of persons";
- "whether the creatures by which God would manifest God's self . . . to human sight were formed for this function alone; or whether angels . . . made themselves material media out of created material . . . or changed their own bodies . . . [for the purpose]";
- "whether the Son and the Holy Spirit were also being sent of old, and if they were, how such sending differed from the one we read of in the gospel." (*Trin.* 2.7.13)

Working through the classic appearances one by one, from Genesis through Exodus, Augustine addresses issues concerning physical manifestations of the incorporeal divinity, the ambiguity of the term "Lord," the fact that sometimes but not always one or another of the three must be identified as the voice heard, and so on. But the overall perspective is that the created order is entirely at God's disposal and "whenever God was said to appear to our ancestors before the Savior's incarnation, the voices heard and the physical manifestations seen were the work of angels . . . representing God's person" (*Trin.* 3.27).

We may observe one example of Augustine's exegetical argumentation (*Trin.* 2.10.19–11.21), namely the incident at Mamre when Abraham "entertained angels unawares" (Heb 13:2). The widespread and deep-seated tradition by which this narrative has been understood in Trinitarian terms is confirmed by the way in which it underlies the famous fifteenth-century Rublev icon of the Trinity. Augustine states that "Abraham saw three men, whom he invited in and entertained to a meal." But immediately he notes that scripture introduces the story with the words, "The Lord appeared to him" (Gen 18:1), and the conversation about the promise of a son to Sarah is all conducted in the singular. If only one man had appeared, Augustine muses, those who practice christological interpretation of such Old Testament theophanies (my phraseology) "would surely have been very quick to claim this was he [namely, Christ]." He raises a number of awkward questions about this and continues:

> But in fact three men appeared to him, and none of them is said to have been superior to the others in stature or age or authority. So why may we

> not take the episode as a visible intimation by means of visible creations of the equality of the Triad, and of the simple identity of substance in the three persons?

It is impossible, Augustine notes, to identify one of the three as superior and "to be taken to be the Lord the Son of God while the other two are his angels." Holy scripture itself provides evidence against such a view, he says, contrasting the following episode where the two angels appearing to Lot are consistently treated as two whereas "Abraham was talking to three and called him Lord in the singular."

Such exegetical treatment of the details we might be tempted to dismiss as rationalistic overplay, but undoubtedly Augustine's argumentation could facilitate respect for the then often threatened distinction between the sending of the Son in the New Testament and Old Testament theophanies of the one God mediated through creaturely media. Furthermore, as Hanson put it, "The traditional centuries-old, much-used, one can almost say Catholic, concept of the pre-existent Christ as the link between an impassible Father and a transitory world . . . was abandoned. This was rather a return to Scripture than a development of dogma."[19] So, by taking the Trinitarian concept of God with the utmost seriousness, what was enabled was a reclamation of the one Creator God of whom the Old Testament scriptures clearly speak; a sense that it really is God at work in the world, not some kind of lesser (almost semi-divine) mediating being but rather the one God, now understood through the mystery of threefold yet unitive activity in creation and redemption. The old economic Trinitarianism necessitated subordinationism, but Augustine's engagement with scripture, informed by Trinitarian doctrine, meant that God's very own engagement with the creation and its creatures must lie at the heart of any biblical doctrine of God. Pro-Nicene theological reflection involved the abandonment of the traditional christological reading of those Old Testament theophanies, an observation that perhaps might ease some of the scepticism of modernity about patristic exegesis.

3.1.2. The Rule of Faith as the Key to Scripture's Teaching

Throughout this study we have found scriptural exegesis shaped by the rule of faith, treated as the one thing enabling readers to read this disparate collection of books according to the right hypothesis enshrined in the apostolic tradition.

19. Hanson, *Search*, 872.

We suggested at the end of volume 1 that in book 1 of *Teaching Christianity*, despite its idiosyncratic framing, Augustine was indeed setting out the rule of faith in his own inimitable way as the *res* (realities) of which scripture speaks. This was his *inventio*—the rhetorical exegete's identification of what the text was all about. Scripture's teaching was "Love God and love your neighbor," so this he identified as the criterion for correct exegesis. But scripture's subject matter was our exile from God and return, the overarching story of creation, fall, redemption, and eschaton enshrined in the rule of faith. What of *On the Trinity*?

Again Augustine does not follow the traditional path of setting out the rule of faith or a creed as the summary or doctrinal framework essential to the right reading of scripture. Yet, to an eye trained by the material covered in this study of doctrine and scripture in early Christianity, such an overview would seem to be key to grasping Augustine's Trinitarian reading of the Bible. Some have interpreted the two parts of *On the Trinity* in terms of faith and reason; for Augustine it was certainly a case of setting out what is to be believed, then searching for how it is to be understood.[20] Yet, at key points in the work as a whole the doctrinal summation of scripture's unitive story surfaces and surely provides the fundamental context for Augustine's contemplation.

In his translation of *On the Trinity*, Hill characterizes book 4 as "one of the most difficult"—indeed, there is much here to puzzle the modern reader, especially Augustine's number symbolism.[21] Yet Hill on the same page also treats it as "one of the most important," suggesting that

> the Son of God's mission was to be the mediator between men and God; the accomplishment of this mission required him to be incarnate and to offer himself as an acceptable sacrifice on our behalf; he cannot meaningfully be said to have been sent until he began to accomplish this mission; he did not do this until the New Testament; and so we conclude he was not sent until the New Testament.

That analysis certainly highlights the progression from Augustine's treatment of the Old Testament theophanies to his engagement with the incarnation.

But perhaps there is more to be said about the role of book 4. It begins with allusion to the very parable we found Augustine using in *Teaching Christian-*

20. See the introduction to Hill, *Trinity*, 22–23. Hill contests this as a common view among Catholic interpreters; it is almost suggested by Henry Chadwick, *Augustine* (Oxford: Oxford University Press, 1986), 91.

21. See the introduction to book 4 in Hill, *Trinity*, 147.

ity: “I was struggling to return from this ‘far country’ (Luke 15:13) by the road he has made in the humanity of the divinity of his Son” (*Trin.* 4.1). We were once in exile, so God “sent us sights suited to our wandering state” through sheer grace. For “we needed to be persuaded how much God loves us.” Now Augustine introduces reflection on the opening chapter of John’s Gospel, on our enlightenment through the incarnation, and on our purification through “the blood of the just man and the humility of God,” so “becoming a partaker of our mortality he made us partakers of his divinity.” Thus the doctrinal framework of the apostolic tradition enshrined in the rule of faith so shapes the reading of scripture as ultimately to justify Trinitarian and christological conclusions. Augustine sits alongside Irenaeus, Athanasius, and many others in this movement from doctrinal tradition to doctrinal reading of scripture.

Again, books 12–14 incidentally map the doctrines of fall and redemption summed up in the rule of faith. Explicitly Augustine is engaged in sketching “a likeness or comparison of things known to us” from which “we are able to believe so that we may love the as yet unknown God” (8.4.8). As already outlined, he found this in the human psyche, made in “our” image: “it was the image of the trinity that was being made in man, and this is how man would be the image of the one true God, since the trinity itself is the one true God” (12.5.7). But rapidly Augustine moves to the ease with which “the soul, loving its own power” and “by the apostasy of pride” essentially does its own thing, disrupts the commonality intended by God, and turns away from the image that “can only be preserved when facing him from whom its impression is received.” We now find a compressed version of the story we have previously traced Augustine telling in the *City of God*,[22] as *On the Trinity* 13 sketches faith in renewal through the incarnation, our justification, the worsting of the tempting devil by “God the Son obeying God the Father even unto death on the cross” (Phil 2:8).

On the Trinity has been described as “an integral theological anthropology, a structure in which diverse doctrinal themes are woven together in an account of how human acting, designing and thinking come to participate in the action of God.”[23] This characterization reinforces how deeply Augustine’s mind was formed by his own take on the basic rule of faith and the long traditional reading of the overarching story of scripture as an account of fall and redemption, a viewpoint underlying all his major writing, including both the *City of God* and the *Confessions*. His very spirituality was formed by the narrative or “type” of fall and redemption that he saw shaping his life, and indeed the life of every

22. See volume 1, chapter 6, excursus on original sin.

23. Rowan Williams, “*De Trinitate*,” in Fitzgerald, *Augustine through the Ages*, 845–51.

human being, and so this treatise *On the Trinity*, which at first sight appears doctrinal, indeed profoundly intellectual, turns out to be as deeply attuned to the pilgrimage of the heart as the *Confessions*.

As observed before, to read scripture "Christianly" is surely to read it coinherently with this deeply traditional framework, long perceived to be apostolic. So is it read into scripture or out of it? Surely the burden of these two volumes has been that the doctrinal articulation of scripture's overall meaning was both vital and valid, and the continuing identity of Christianity depends upon our capacity to embrace this coinherence. It is from this reading that the one God comes to be identified as Father, Son, and Holy Spirit, the three names into which every believer is baptized. At the end of *On the Trinity*, Augustine prays:

> Directing my attention toward this rule of faith as best as I could, as far as you enabled me to, I have sought you and desired to see intellectually what I have believed. (*Trin.* 15.28.51)

3.1.3. Countertexts and How to Deal with Them

Problematic for the Trinity's equality was the very "sending" of Son and Spirit to which we have seen Augustine devoting such attention—it could imply their inferiority to the Father who sent them. Indeed, Augustine admits that "many things are said in the holy books to suggest, or even state openly that the Father is greater than the Son" (*Trin.* 1.7.14). In Augustine's eyes the basic problem with the heretics' exegesis lay in transferring "what is said of Christ Jesus as man to that substance of his which was everlasting before the incarnation and everlasting still."

So the classic texts come up: "My Father is greater than I" (John 14:28)—"how could it be otherwise with him who emptied himself taking the form of a servant?" asks Augustine, alluding to Philippians 2:7. As so many others before him, he refers back to Philippians 2:6, which as a whole shows that he is the Father's equal by nature though the Father's inferior in the form of a servant. Nor should we assume that 1 Corinthians 15:24–25 implies Christ ceases to reign when he hands the kingdom to the Father (*Trin.* 1.8.15–10.21).

And, of course, that notorious wisdom passage in Proverbs 8 could also be addressed according to "this rule for understanding the scriptures" whereby "two resonances" can be distinguished, "one tuned to the form of God in which he is, and is equal to the Father, the other tuned to the form of a servant which he took and is less than the Father" (*Trin.* 1.11.22). In the form of

God, Proverbs 8:25 says, "before the hills I begot you," but in the form of a servant Proverbs 8:22 says, "The Lord created me in the beginning of his ways" (*Trin.* 1.12.24). Thus Augustine rehearses those long-standing but awkward pro-Nicene responses to the surely more commonsense exegesis of the heretics. And we are left doubting if such exegetical moves could ever be regarded as valid. Doctrinal controversy had forced distinctions that often seem inappropriate; the text is grotesquely manipulated and we surely need to acknowledge that.

But does that invalidate the doctrines thus defended? Or does it point to the need to move beyond overprecision at the verbal level to a more imaginative appropriation of semi-poetic texts such as Proverbs 8:22–31? Much of volume 2 of this study has been spent charting the less than satisfactory consequence of applying the rule to which Augustine appeals here, namely a divisive Christology. Two doctrinal moves made by Augustine, taken together with an allusion to this Proverbs text made in *Teaching Christianity*, might perhaps ease our exegetical caveats, though it will take us on quite a journey to get there.

His first interesting move is to shift the distinctions between the persons of the Trinity from individual roles or characteristics to relationship; indeed, surely we might agree that God's relationship, whether with creation or personified Wisdom, is potentially the subject matter of Proverbs 8:22–31. But let us digress a little to consider the arguments whereby Augustine makes the doctrinal move to focusing on relationship rather than individuality. The inseparability of the divine activity necessitates that no one of the three acts independently of the others, and so none can have a role absolutely distinct from the others—we have already seen the effect of this in relation to the Old Testament theophanies. So the question arises what the three might be in their distinctiveness.

In book 5 Augustine admits "our thoughts are quite inadequate to their object" and "cannot be measured by the standard of things visible, changeable, mortal and deficient" (*Trin.* 5.1.1–2) and then sets the context of further discussion by getting involved in abstract reasoning about substance and predication. It is impossible to predicate anything of God as that would imply change or participation in something other than God (5.4.5–7.8); as Rowan Williams puts it, "God has no qualities that are incidental to God's being what God is."[24] So God's being is, in itself, good, great, just, and so on, and so is each of the three. Later, books 6–7 tackle what this could possibly mean with respect to wisdom; after all Paul had written, "Christ, the power of God and the wisdom of God" (1 Cor 1:24). Eventually Augustine picks up this point about predica-

24. R. Williams, "*De Trinitate*," 847.

tion and simplifies the issues by stating that "With God to be is the same as to be wise," so

> the Father is not wise with the wisdom he has begotten; otherwise he did not beget it, but it begot him. . . . So the Father is himself wisdom, and the Son is called the wisdom of the Father in the same way as he is called the light of the Father, that is, that as we talk of light from light, and both are one light, so we must understand wisdom from wisdom and both are one wisdom. (*Trin.* 7.1.2)

So, says Augustine, "the Father and the Son are together one being and one greatness and one truth and one wisdom. But the Father and the Son are not both together one Word, because they are not both together one Son." The Son is called Word "only in relationship to him whose Word he is, just as he is Son in relationship to the Father, but he is wisdom in the same way as he is being. . . . So Father and Son are together one wisdom because they are one being." One is unbegotten and the other begotten, but that does not mean "they are not one being," for these are terms of relationship, not definitions of being. Back in Book 5 Eunomian definitions of God as "unbegotten" are his target: "when the Father is called unbegotten, it is not being stated what he is, but what he is not." We recall the Cappadocians making this very point. For Augustine the meaning of the terms "unbegotten" and "begotten" lies not in substance but in relationship.

> So although begotten differs from unbegotten, it does not indicate a different substance, because just as son refers to father, and not son to not father, so begotten must refer to begetter, and not begotten to not begetter. (*Trin.* 5.7.8)

Augustine moves from discussion of predication to treating the Greek distinction between *ousia* and *hypostasis* as "rather obscure," and the Latin *substantia* and *personae* as not much better:

> In very truth, because the Father is not the Son and the Son is not the Father, and the Holy Spirit who is also called the 'gift of God' (Acts 8:20; John 4:10) is neither the Father nor the Son, they are certainly three. . . . Yet when you ask "Three what?" human speech labors under a great dearth of words. So we say three persons, not in order to say what precisely but in order not to be reduced to silence. (5.9.10)

The notion of relationship Augustine now develops further: everything distinctive said of each of the three is not said with reference to that particular self but "only with reference to each other or to creation" (5.11.12). The triad can be called great, good, eternal, omnipotent, and so on, but "the triad cannot in the same way be called Father," nor can "the trinity be called Son," but the terms imply relationship. Relationship can also be attached to the Holy Spirit as gift: it is implied in the very idea of the "gift of the giver" and the "giver of the gift" (5.11.13).

So much for Augustine's first doctrinal move; now to the second, namely, his determination not to allow the rule that he has enunciated for understanding scripture to create a divisive Christology. Again we need a bit of a digression to observe his one-person Christology. Christ's anointing with the Holy Spirit happened when the Word became flesh,

> that is when a human nature without antecedent merits of good works was coupled to the Word of God in the virgin's womb so as to become one person with him. (*Trin.* 15.25)

The grace of God is particularly evident, Augustine suggests, in that neither we nor even "the man Christ" deserved on merit "the privilege of being joined to the true God in such a unity that with him he would be one person" (13.17.22).

> When I read "The Word became flesh and dwelt amongst us" (John 1:14), in the Word I understand the true Son of God and in the flesh I acknowledge the true Son of Man, and each joined together into one person of God and man by an inexpressible abundance of grace. (13.19.22)

Thus, to quote Henry Chadwick, "Augustine saw Christ as able to bring redemption because in one person he is both God and man. The God-Man is the way and the ladder by which God enables us to rise from the temporal to the eternal."[25] In Daley's discussion of this one-person Christology, the following is cited from one of Augustine's sermons:

> Therefore he is the "mediator between God and human beings" because he is God with the Father and because he is human among humans. . . . Divinity without humanity is not a mediator, humanity without divinity is

25. Chadwick, *Augustine*, 53–54.

> not a mediator; rather, between divinity by itself and humanity by itself the mediator is the human divinity and divine humanity of Christ.[26]

In the one person of the God-Man, then, Augustine has implicitly shaped a theory of mediation to replace the old hierarchical ladder:

> So it is that the Son of God, who is at once the Word of God and the mediator between God and men, the Son of Man, equal to the Father by oneness of divinity and our fellow by taking humanity, so it is that he intercedes for us insofar as he is man, while not concealing that as God he is one with the Father. (*Trin.* 4.8.12)

The God-Man mediates through his very being. Such "conjoining of natures" we found before in the work of Theodoret.[27] Cyril, we may likewise recall, also located mediation in the very person of Christ.[28]

So far our discussion may seem tangential to the exegesis of Proverbs 8:22–31, but what it does is help to shift the nub of the issue. Modern scholarship has been happy to explore the "wisdom" Christology of certain New Testament texts, and postmodernism might allow that the tracing of those "future" resonances of Old Testament language, images, and themes could remain potentially valid.[29] The sense that Jesus Christ was the embodiment of God's wisdom is evident in Paul's writings, underlies the cosmic Christ of Colossians 1:15–20, and almost certainly informs the Johannine Prologue. It was, of course, by hindsight that such moves were made as the earliest Christians sought to understand the figure of Christ, yet they were fruitful in the discovery of precursors, prophecies, and hints. Such insight into continuities in the overarching biblical story of God's engagement with the world is hardly invalidated. So we can surely take it that Proverbs 8 points to God's wisdom flowing out, as it were, into creative and re-creative engagement with God's initial purpose and intentions. According to Augustine, behind such "outflow" is the inseparable activity of the Trinitarian relationship; there is nothing "strange . . . in his being sent . . . because he is 'a certain pure outflow of the glory of almighty God'" (Wis 7:25).

26. *Sermon* 47.12.21 [401–11] (PL 38:310); cited by Brian E. Daley, *God Visible: Patristic Christology Reconsidered* (Oxford: Oxford University Press, 2018), 160.

27. See chapter 5, 2.2.2.

28. See chapter 4, 2.2.1.1–2.

29. See volume 1, chapter 7.

Like everyone else, then, Augustine read this passage christologically. And elsewhere, in a context where Arianism was not on the horizon, Augustine shows us in an unforced way, indeed quite naturally, how it could make sense to read Proverbs 8:22–31 as the pro-Nicenes did. In *Teaching Christianity* we find Augustine stating:

> Christ, of course, is the one who wished to offer himself . . . to be the way there for those who have come to the beginning of the ways; that is, he wished to take flesh to himself. That is the meaning of the text, "The Lord created me in the beginning of his ways"; that is where those who wish to arrive must begin from. (*Doctr. chr.* 1.34, 38)[30]

Reminded now by Augustine that Christ himself said, "I am the way, the truth and the life" (John 14:6), we might take a bit more notice of the context in Proverbs. All through the preceding verses in Proverbs 8 Wisdom is calling us to follow her. Thus the passage taken as a whole might surely be read as pointing beyond itself to Wisdom as Creator yet become creature so as to be the way for us, so adumbrating the incarnation for our sake of the one begotten of God. Augustine could even have had Proberbs 8 in mind when he wrote, "I am struggling to return from this far country (Luke 15:13) by the road [= way] he has made in the humanity of his divinity of his only Son" (*Trin.* 4.1). Read doctrinally alongside New Testament insights, the text that seemed most problematic in the face of Arianism turns out to have unexpected future resonances. That, I confess, is one of my unexpected moments of illumination for this chapter!

Yes, the christological deployment of that text was reading doctrine into scripture. It was attributing a new sense to a particular passage through reading by hindsight. But by Augustine's time the reading community of the Christian church had long endorsed this future of the text, and Augustine's way of taking it surely eases our discomforting sense that the pro-Nicenes were manipulating it in entirely unconvincing ways. It now simply sits alongside many other texts that became prophetic within traditional Christian reading of scripture.

3.1.4. Prophecy, Typology, Allegory: Essential to Doctrinal Reading?

So we must remind ourselves that Augustine did think that the Old Testament is only fully understood in the light of the New, and despite his revised stance

30. English translation from Edmund Hill, trans., *Teaching Christianity: De Doctrina Christiana*, ed. John E. Rotelle, Works of St. Augustine 1.11 (Hyde Park, NY: New City, 1996).

towards the Old Testament theophanies, he certainly adopted the traditional reading of the books of the old covenant as prophecy, often veiled yet fulfilled in Christ. This we failed to address at the end of volume 1, and perhaps there was some excuse, for it has been stated that:

> Study of the *Enarrationes in Psalmos* colors in large gaps that are left blank by the common assumption that Augustine's views on scripture are all found in the *De Doctrina Christiana*. In the early edition of *De Doctrina Christiana* 1–3, the reflection of his own practice of prophetic, Christological and ecclesiological interpretation is conspicuous by its absence, while in the later addition to Book 3 the merely formal treatment of the *totus Christus* fails to convey the axial position it held in his own exegesis.[31]

Indeed Augustine's critical appropriation of Tyconius's *Book of Rules* hardly does justice to his own exegetical practice. It is tempting to be distracted into considering the massive collection of his treatment of the Psalms over his time as priest and bishop. However, we will simply note here that "Augustine channeled all the Psalms into a richly variegated figurative sense," for "the comprehensive mystery underlying all of Scripture is Christ and the Church" (*Enarrat. Ps.* 79.1),[32] and now go on to explore the material that can be found in *On the Trinity* which bears on this issue.

Already in Augustine's review of the Old Testament theophanies we may find examples of prophetic and typological reading, with allegorical spin-offs, the most telling example arising from the Exodus passage where Moses is told that he cannot see the Lord's face and live, but God will set him at a lookout in a rock, cover him as he passes, and let him see the Lord's back (Exod 33:20).[33] We recall how this passage was exploited by the Cappadocians, both to rub home how little we know of God and as a sign of the incarnation.[34] Augustine tells his readers that "this is usually understood, not inappropriately, to prefigure the person of our Lord Jesus Christ, taking his 'back' to mean his flesh, in which he was born of a virgin, died and rose again," thus echoing the way it was taken by Gregory of Nyssa. His face, however, is "that form of

31. Michael Cameron, "*Enarrationes in Psalmos*," in Fitzgerald, *Augustine through the Ages*, 295.

32. Cameron, "*Enarrationes*," 290. The quotation of *Enarrations on the Psalms* here also comes from Cameron.

33. Latin manuscripts differ regarding the word rendered here as "lookout" (*specula* or *spelunca*); see Hill's note in *Trinity*, 121.

34. See chapter 3, 1.3 and 2.3.

God in which he 'did not think it robbery to be equal with God' the Father (Phil 2:6), and which of course no man can see and live." Augustine offers two reasons why not: the first is that we shall see him "'face to face' only after this life" (1 Cor 13:12), then "when he appears we shall be like him, because we shall see him as he is" (1 John 3:2); the second is that even in this life "to the extent that we perceive in a spiritual way the Wisdom of God . . . , we die to fleshly, materialistic attachments." From this starting point Augustine ponders the sight that everyone yearns to behold who aims to love God with all his heart and soul and mind," spelling out Matthew 22:37–39, then returning to the Moses narrative: "But while 'we are away from the Lord and walking by faith not sight' (2 Cor 5:6), we have to behold Christ's back, that is his flesh, by this same faith." The catholic church is now represented by the rock, and standing there anyone "who believes his resurrection may safely look upon the pasch of the Lord, that is the passing of the Lord, and upon his back, that is his body, to his own good" (*Trin.* 2.16.28–17.31). Augustine implies that some such interpretation of the story about Moses is required, for "we must not allow ourselves to be so befogged by literal-minded materialism that we imagine the Lord's face to be invisible and his back visible. Both of course were visible in the form of a servant; in the form of God—away with the possibility of such thoughts!" (*Trin.* 2.17.31).[35]

In his final book, Augustine discusses "figures of speech which the Greeks call 'tropes'" (15.8.14–9.15). Translation of this into Latin distracts him momentarily, and he concludes, "Some of our translators, unwilling to use a Greek word for the apostle's phrase 'these things are put in an allegory' (Gal 4:24), have translated with a circumlocution and said, 'these things are signifying one thing from another.'" There are various kinds of allegory, states Augustine, and among them one called enigma. He quotes 1 Thessalonians 5:6 (on keeping awake and sober) as an example of an allegory that is not an enigma, as its metaphorical sense is obvious. An enigma, then, is an obscure allegory, such as Proverbs 30:15: "the bloodsuckers had three daughters." When Paul referred to allegory, it is not found "in words, but in fact," and before he explained it, its meaning was obscure. Paul argued that "the two testaments are to be understood for the two sons of Abraham," and this kind of allegory "could specifically be called an enigma."

In the context of Book 15 all this is to explain how we now see "through a mirror" and "in an enigma" (1 Cor 13:12), as we, being in God's image, find trinity in ourselves. The exegetical implications are not spelled out further. Yet

35. See also Hill's gloss of the Moses story in *Trinity*, 123 n. 57.

it is clear that scripture's enigmas are important to Augustine as signs pointing to realities beyond themselves. Examples can again be found earlier in book 3 of *On the Trinity* (3.9.19–20). There Augustine reflects on the work of angels in representing God through miracles and signs as well as the prophetic words and actions found in scripture. He mentions the bronze serpent lifted up in the wilderness (Num 21:9), describes how "a rod was used to mean something and changed by angelic skill into a serpent" (Exod 4:3), and points to Jacob setting up a stone after his dream to signify God (Gen 28:18). Signification is the main point—he even includes "the bread which is . . . consumed when the sacrament is received." To put this in the terms used in *Teaching Christianity*, these are *res* (things in their own right) but also *signa* (signs of something else). Moses's rod-*cum*-serpent and Jacob's stone are signs, and what they signify is Christ. With cross-references to Numbers 21:9, Philippians 2:8, John 3:14 and Romans 6:6 he explains:

> Serpent stands for death (which was caused by the serpent in paradise). . . . So the rod turned into a serpent means Christ turned into death, and the serpent turned back again into a rod means Christ transformed in the resurrection—the whole Christ with his body the church at the end of time; this is the meaning of the serpent's tail, which Moses caught hold of to turn it back into a rod again. (*Trin.* 3.9.20)

Besides this, the pillars of cloud and fire represent the Lord and the Holy Spirit (3.9.21). All these "enigmas" are "signs"—this Augustine takes for granted, along with all the other exegetes of the ancient church.

How within our culture prophetic and figural meanings of the Old Testament might be appropriated is a big question but, in one way or another, to read the Old Testament Christianly surely involves some kind of acceptance that within the overarching narrative of the scriptures God was preparing the way for the "sending" of the Son and the Spirit in a new way, and it was through the prompting of the Spirit of Truth, leading into all truth (John 16:12), that Christians were inspired to reread the scriptures so as to discern hints as to God's purposes and clues to the identity of Jesus Christ. Such reading produced types, figures, and enigmas that offered an imaginative biblical code subsequently exploited over the centuries in Christian art and literature. Perhaps the shift to postmodern recognition of the way significant texts have a "future" in which original or past meaning might be superseded could facilitate some reclamation of a rich inheritance sidelined by historico-critical reading. But the question this raises is whether the doctrines of Trinity and Christology depend upon such "mystical" or allegorical reading. Is it not rather that these doctrines facilitate such a symbolic and imaginative reading of the scriptures?[36] It was my argument in the second part of chapter 3 that the Trinitarian settlement was liberating—"the key to a heuristic process of symbolic association that draws participants into the biblical story and into richer depths of contemplation and worship."[37]

We have been considering the move from doctrine to scripture in Augustine's discussion; it is time to turn to the converse move from scripture to doctrine.

3.2. *From Scripture to Doctrine*

3.2.1. *Deductions by Prooftext*

Augustine assembles positive testimonies to argue for his basic concept of inseparable equality. The first chapter of John's Gospel proves that the Word was God and, since all things were made by him, he cannot have been made himself, so he is not a creature (*Trin.* 1.6.9). Thus Augustine rehearses the classic pro-Nicene argument whereby a radical distinction between Creator and creature is affirmed, and shows how it is to be deduced from scripture. First John 5:20 then proves he is "true God," and so 1 Timothy 6:16—"who alone has immortality"—does not "refer to the Father alone but to the one and only God which the trinity is," for "life everlasting can scarcely be mortal," and that is what the Son of God is since we are made immortal "by becoming partakers in his life everlasting" (*Trin.* 1.6.10). With reference after reference, through book 1 Augustine builds up a positive scriptural case for the Son's equality with the Father, "consubstantial and co-eternal in the oneness of the three" (1.6.13). Indeed, to back up the three, he next shows how we can deduce that the Holy Spirit is also not a creature from Romans 1:25, which abominates worship (*latreuein*) of the creature rather than the Creator. The Greek word *latreuein*, as distinct from *douleuein*, he explains, indicates the kind of service given to gods in worship and, using *latreuontes*, Philippians 3:3 speaks of serving the Spirit of God. The argument is then bolstered by reference to 1 Corinthians 6:19, "your bodies are the Temple of the Holy Spirit," and alluding to 1 Corin-

36. See my treatment of serpents in *God's Presence: A Contemporary Recapitulation of Early Christianity* (Cambridge: Cambridge University Press, 2013), 250–56.

37. Above, p. 78.

thians 6:15 Augustine then states, "If things that are the members of Christ are the Temple of the Holy Spirit, then the Holy Spirit is not a creature," clinching it with 1 Corinthians 6:20: "Glorify God therefore in your bodies."

As noted already, the rest of book 1 turns to problem texts and how to handle them, the culminating arguments being devoted to the seemingly ambiguous relationship between the activities of Father and Son in John's Gospel, especially with reference to judgment. The method of argument throughout involves testing text against text in a process of making plausible deductions from the plain sense of New Testament texts; doctrinal conclusions so far do not require mystical, prophetic, or allegorical reading.

So Augustine certainly did assemble collages of texts abstracted from context, and he will do so time and again. Throughout our second volume we have observed examples of prooftexting as well as the gathering of instances to show particular scriptural usages. But we have also noted a certain scepticism about whether that procedure could solve the problems—remember Gregory of Nazianzus's comments noted in chapter 3.[38] In any case the approach is surely paralleled by the methodology of Kittel's *Theological Dictionary*, and besides, any thematic study of the scriptures, of which there are multiple examples in modern scholarship, would surely do likewise. The biggest difference between Augustine's procedure and that of the modern scholar lies not so much in method as in indiscriminate deployment of scriptural material from across the canon with no attempt to distinguish distinctive features, Johannine and Pauline texts reinforcing one another, sometimes with texts from Isaiah, Psalms, or wisdom literature thrown in alongside. Indeed, Augustine's rhetoric throughout the entire work employs scriptural quotations and allusions from anywhere and everywhere to reinforce whatever point he is making. Unsurprisingly the employment of such quotations in the first half of *On the Trinity* (on what we believe) outweighs their use in the second half (on how to understand what we believe) by roughly a five-to-three ratio. Yet, no other text is so frequently referred to as 1 Corinthians 13:12, the verse which substantiates the search for Trinitarian analogies in the mirror and enigma of the mind purified and turned toward God. Consistently Augustine returns to the Johannine Prologue, to Philippians 2:8–11, to 1 Corinthians 1:24 and 1 Timothy 2:5 and 6:15–16. It is by reading across from such passages that he shows how more ambiguous statements in scripture may be read in terms of the Trinity or the Son's mediatorial incarnation.

38. Chapter 3, 1.1.

3.2.2. *The Doctrinal Implications of Scripture as a Whole*

Augustine certainly did not simply rely on prooftexts to justify reading the doctrines of Trinity and incarnation from scripture. Athanasius had appealed to the "mind" of scripture to justify using nonscriptural terms; Augustine does that implicitly if not explicitly, for it is on his understanding of scripture's overall import that the whole of *On the Trinity* is built. It is worth endeavoring to discern that implicit understanding, for it is the true grounding of the doctrines Augustine seeks first to specify and then understand in the course of his fifteen books. I identify five key elements, some of which have been anticipated in earlier discussions.

(1) *It is scripture itself that summons its readers to the search for God and to the contemplation of God.* This is Augustine's prime quest in *On the Trinity*. "Seek his face always" (Ps 105:3–4) has been described as the "theme-setting text."[39] This verse appears in the prologues to books 1, 10, and 15, reinforced in the last case by Isaiah 55:6. The consummation, when God will be all in all, will be face-to-face contemplation; the pure in heart will see God, and this will be the reward of faith (*Trin.* 1.8.17–10.21). Meanwhile scripture provides signs and pointers, adapting its language to babes needing milk (1 Cor 3:1–2). If at first Augustine's discussion just goes over the classic issues of anthropomorphism in scripture (*Trin.* 1.1.2–3), this is transcended by a lively awareness of the almost sacramental role of both creation and scripture as vehicles conveying us on the search, despite "the difficulties presented by the holy scriptures in their multifarious diversity of form" (2.1.1). We shall see face to face, but meanwhile we see in a mirror, in enigmas and symbols (1 Cor 13:12 hovers in the background throughout), and this is what drives the long exploration of how the Trinity is reflected in its creaturely image, the human mind. Scripture implies the God characterized in doctrinal propositions and creedal affirmations.

(2) *It is scripture that both demonstrates the need for Christ's mediation and shows how it has happened.* Purification is required before there is any hope of contemplation of God; indeed, the mind, which in one sense is God's image, needs transforming and perfecting before it can be a true reflection of God. Much of *On the Trinity* assumes Augustine's understanding of the fall, the deception of the devil, original sin, and the need for redemption—matters set out more fully elsewhere in his voluminous writings.[40] Book 4 of *On the Trinity* begins with our exile, our sickness, and the sheer love and grace of

39. Hill, *Trinity*, 68 n. 11.

40. See volume 1, chapter 6, excursus on original sin.

God, quoting Romans 5:8 and 8:31, followed by the Johannine Prologue: the light shines in the darkness of human foolishness, blindness and unbelief as the Word becomes flesh, and Christ died for us while we were yet sinners.

> Our enlightenment is to participate in the Word. . . . Yet we were absolutely incapable of such participation and quite unfit for it, so unclean were we through sin, so we had to be cleansed. Furthermore, the only thing to cleanse the wicked and proud is the blood of the just man and the humility of God. So God became a just man to intercede with God for sinful man. (*Trin.* 4.2.4)

Augustine thus deduces from scripture the key reason why God made "a road . . . in the humanity of the divinity of his only Son" (4.1.1). For

> he applied to us the similarity of his humanity to take away the dissimilarity of our iniquity, and becoming a partaker of our mortality he made us partakers of his divinity. (4.2.4)

The sacrificial act of death and resurrection on the part of the God-Man enables our old human nature to be stripped off as we are crucified with him and the new human nature to be put on (Eph 4:22):

> By his death he offered for us the one truest possible sacrifice, and thereby purged, abolished, and destroyed whatever there was of guilt, for which the principalities and powers had a right to hold us bound to payment of the penalty; and by his resurrection he called to new life us who were predestined, justified us who were called, glorified us who were justified (cf. Rom 8.30). (*Trin.* 4.13.17)

We have seen how this atoning act of paying our penalty was significant also to Nestorius and the Antiochenes but perhaps missed by Cyril.[41] Like Cyril, however, Augustine focused on the power, as well as the sheer grace, which demonstrated God's love for us: God dealt with us in such a way that we could progress "*rather in his strength*" than our own (my italics), arranging it so that "the power of charity would be brought to perfection in the weakness of humanity" (4.1.2). Thus the overarching scriptural narrative requires a mediator to unite true divinity with true humanity. Augustine is surely true to the

41. On Nestorius and Cyril, see chapter 5 above.

import of the scriptures here, and perhaps better able to articulate this than either the Antiochenes or the Alexandrians. He anticipated Chalcedon's paradoxes while articulating mediation through the one person of Christ. Doctrine as set out thus is perhaps the only way to capture the implications of the New Testament. If so, there is no gap: scripture and doctrine are coinherent.

(3) *It is scripture then that requires the true divinity of the mediator*. Somehow this must be understood without jeopardizing scripture's own insistence on the one God. In his final prayer Augustine sets out the parameters clearly:

> Truth would not have said, "Go and baptize the nations in the name of the Father and of the Son and of the Holy Spirit" (Matt 28:19), unless you were a triad. Nor would you have commanded us to be baptized, Lord God, in the name of any who is not Lord God. Nor would it have been said with divine authority, "Hear O Israel, the Lord your God is one God (Deut 6:4), unless while being a triad you were still one Lord God. (*Trin.* 15.28.51)

The demands of scripture, and of performative liturgy derived from scripture, had long fostered a Trinitarian account of the one God, no matter how hard to conceive within the limitations of creaturely minds. Grasping the reality that it really was and is God and none other who was and is present bringing healing and sanctification through Christ and the Spirit was fundamental to Augustine's search, and so to contemplation of the mystery of the relationship between the three, each and all equal and inseparable in the divine attributes and activities. Scripture's signs asked to be articulated thus.

(4) *It is scripture that insists on creation by the one God, distinguishing the Creator from creatures*. Like other pro-Nicenes Augustine is adamant that none of the three are creatures formed from nothing but they are the one Creator. We have already observed the way he used 1 Corinthians 8:6 and the Johannine Prologue as he built up scriptural testimonies in book 1: all things were made by the Son who is equal to the Father. Similarly we found New Testament testimonies from which to deduce the fact that the Holy Spirit is also "God and not a creature," namely, the argument from worship of God's Spirit (*Trin.* 1.12). All this is reinforced in Augustine's prologue to book 9:

> What we have to avoid is the sacrilegious mistake of saying anything about the Trinity which does not belong to the creator but rather the creature. (9.1.1)

The ontological gap between Creator and creature is affirmed. Elsewhere we find:

> So there is an uncreated nature which created all natures great and small, and is without doubt more excellent than those natures it has created. (14.16)

This nature is God, of whom it is written, "from him and through him and in him are all things" (Rom 11:36). It is not only "the authority of the divine books which assert that God is; the universal nature of things which surround us, to which we also belong, proclaims that it has a most excellent founder, who has given us a mind and natural reason," by which to distinguish which things are to be valued above others. And so "we rank the creator without a shadow of doubt above created things" (*Trin.* 15.4.6).

Yet Romans 1:20 and Genesis 1:26, each of which is quoted at least half a dozen times, encouraged Augustine to find signs and symbols in creation as he did in scripture, things that point beyond themselves to God, not least his suggested trinities in the human mind, which share equality and inseparability. Summarizing his work he writes that he has spent time "over the things that God has made in order through them to get to know him who made them," reinforcing this procedure by quoting from the book of Wisdom: "For from the greatness of the beauty and of the creature the creator of these things can knowably be seen" (Wis 13:1–5). Creation is almost "sacramental" as an outward and visible sign through which the Creator may be discerned.

But in the end all the attributes of God to which creation points must belong to all three as God, so a trinity (rather than unity) is not necessarily signified.[42] Furthermore, Augustine is at pains to uncover the profound difference between the creature and the Creator, which means that the trinities identified within the human mind are but inadequate sketches (*Trin.* 15.7.11–9.15).[43] So it is the faith enshrined in the scriptures and the teaching of the church that indicates that the one creator God is a trinity, and it is the "sacrament" of Christ's incarnation, death, and resurrection that provides the ultimate grounds for Trinitarian faith.

It is worth looking at Augustine's use of that word "sacrament." It occurs first in book 4 with reference to Christ's death and resurrection, "a sacrament for the inner man and a model for the outer one."

> As a sacrament of our inner man he uttered that cry, both in the psalm and on the cross, which was intended to represent the death of our soul: "My God, my God, why have you forsaken me?" (Ps 22:1; Mark 15:34) (*Trin.* 4.3.6)

42. See discussion in *Trin.* 15.4.6–6.10.
43. Cf. the discussion of "enigma," p. 284 above.

This Augustine explains in terms of Romans 6:6: our "old man" was crucified together with him. This crucifixion of the inner man is identified as the sorrows of repentance, the torment of self-discipline, "a kind of death to erase the death of ungodliness in which God does not leave us." Then Augustine suggests that "the Lord's bodily resurrection is a sacrament of our inner resurrection," as well as a "model for our outer man's resurrection." Our double death, of both soul and body, Augustine finds balanced by Christ's single death, for he was "not a sinner" and "had no need to be renewed in the inner man." Here by "sacrament" Augustine would appear to mean something like "sacred sign."

Later in book 4 we find "sacrament" used to mean the incarnation, the Word made flesh: "in this sacrament . . . lies the salvation of all who believe, hope and love" (4.20.27). First Timothy 3:16 follows in the form "the great sacrament of piety which was manifested in flesh, justified in spirit." Augustine's usage reflects the fact that the Latin translation, here and elsewhere (e.g., Ephesians and Colossians) represented the Greek *mysterion*. It is the "mystery" of Christ, the sacred sign of salvation through the "sacrament" of Christ's mediation that points to the reality of God as Trinity, and therein lie the overall implications of scripture.

Thus Augustine challenges our historico-critical suspicions of anachronism and asks us to reconsider what are the implications of scripture. We might perhaps find somewhat alien to our intellectual sensibilities the prooftexting argumentation of an Athanasius in controversial mode, though surely his *On the Incarnation* enables us to see what drove all that. Maybe Augustine helps us to see those exegetical controversies more sympathetically. Can we not affirm with them that the New Testament in its overall gospel message demands recognition of the real presence of the one true creator God in the person of Christ and the work of the Holy Spirit? An incarnational reading requires a Trinitarian reading.

(5) *It is scripture that commands us to love God and our neighbor*. At the end of volume 1 we found that in *Teaching Christianity* Augustine treated the double love command as the criterion for scriptural exegesis. It is hardly surprising, then, that both the theme and the relevant texts punctuate *On the Trinity*.[44] It is worth exploring a number of key discussions.

In book 8 Augustine speaks of loving what is good and lyrically describes the goodness of "the earth, with its lofty mountains and its folded hills," a good farm with fertile land, a good house "with its harmonious symmetry of architecture," the goodness of animals, fresh air, food, a human face with "a cheerful

44. E.g., Matt 22:37–40; John 14:15, 21, 23; 15:12, 17; 16:27.

expression and a fresh complexion," and the good heart of a friend with its "loving trust." Even riches can be put to good use. Then there is the sky with its heavenly bodies, then angels, then speech and song. Augustine continues:

> This is good and that is good. Take away this and that and see good itself if you can. In this way you will see God . . . the good of every good. . . . That is how we should love God. (*Trin.* 8.3.4)

He proceeds to talk in somewhat Platonic terms of good this and good that participating in the good, perceiving good itself by putting particulars aside and so perceiving God. "And if you cling to him in love, you will straightway enter into bliss." Loving other things for their goodness and "so clinging to them that you fail to love the good itself which makes them good" is an occasion for shame. "So the good the soul turns to in order to be good is the good from which it gets its being soul at all," and it is not far away, "for in it we live and move and are" (Acts 17:28) (*Trin.* 8.3.5). We need to "cling to this good in love, in order to enjoy the presence of him from whom we are, whose absence would mean that we could not even be" (8.4.6).

There are ways in which this passage fills out the previous point about creation and all that is in it offering a kind of sacrament or sacred sign whereby God is known. But as we shall see, it is also a significant move given Augustine's ensuing struggles to provide an answer to the question how we can love what we do not know, for we still walk "by faith not sight" (2 Cor 5:7). Is it even possible to love something unknown? If not, no one can love God before knowing him. True, "to behold and grasp God . . . is only permitted to the pure in heart" (Matt 5:8), yet from scripture Augustine deduces that faith enables loving what is unknown, for "where are faith, hope and charity to be found if not in the spirit that believes what it cannot see, and hopes and loves what it believes?"

Augustine now explores imagination—in brief, he argues that it does not matter exactly how we picture to ourselves characters in the biblical story: "the physical face of the Lord" is "pictured with infinite variety by countless imaginations," but the one face he actually had is not "relevant to salvation." What does matter is that we think of him "specifically as a man" and believe "that God became man for us as an example of humility and to demonstrate God's love for us." For his birth and death provides "a medicine to heal the tumor of our pride and a high sacrament to break the chains of sin." Thus "we firmly believe those things because we think of them in terms of general and specific notions we are quite certain of" (8.4.7).

This principle is then applied to the "desire to understand as far as it is given us the eternity and equality and unity of the trinity." We have to "believe before we can understand," and that means that we must not let our imagination run riot—false belief means hope is vain and love unchaste. But the question remains: "how then are we to love by believing this trinity which we do not know?" What we need is a "likeness or comparison of things known to us we are able to believe, so that we may love the as yet unknown God" (8.4.8). This then drives his attempt by introspection to find trinities within the human mind that can be treated as somewhat analogous to the one God who is Trinity, a project ultimately rooted not only in Genesis 1:26, but also 1 Corinthians 13:12—the deep relationship between knowing and loving.

This is further developed in book 9. There Augustine notes the trio: I myself, what I love, and love itself (*Trin.* 9.2.2). He then explores the mind knowing itself and loving itself, deducing a trinity of mind, love, and knowledge, drawing out the point that each is in itself, "yet they are in each other too," and so inseparable, for mind is "knowing or known or knowable" relative to its knowledge and "loving, loved or lovable" relative to the love with which it loves itself (9.5.8). Implicit, of course, is an analogy with the one God as Trinity. Now this may seem remote from anything in scripture, yet at its core is what Augustine discerns as lying at the heart of what scripture is all about.

For indeed, ultimately it is scripture that allows Augustine to resolve the problem of loving the unknown God. He links the two commandments and, with a range of other scriptural references, concludes: "if a man loves his neighbour, it follows that above all he loves love itself. But 'God is love and whoever abides in love abides in God' (1 John 4:16). So it follows that above all he loves God" (*Trin.* 8.7.10). The God who is love is present inwardly, and lowliness characterizes love, as shown by Christ, who said, "Learn of me" (8.7.11). All we have to do is love our brother and then love the love by which we love; that love, which is God, we know better than the brother we love—"better known because more present, better known because more inward to [us], better known because more sure." To be full of love is to be full of God (8.8.12).

The deep connection between loving God, loving oneself, and loving the neighbor is explored further in book 14. Loving oneself involves loving God—self-love of any other kind is against one's own interest—and when the mind loves God and so loves itself "with a straight, not a twisted love," it can "rightly be commanded to love its neighbour as itself" (14.11.15; 14.14.18). Augustine proceeds to reflect on the weakness and confusion that prevents this as well as the scriptural promises of renewal. For all his seemingly speculative—even perhaps contrived—constructions, the underlying perspectives have their roots in scripture's overarching narrative, within which each human being is invited to find self-understanding as fallen creature redeemed in Christ.

Thus scripture profoundly informs Augustine's doctrinal commitments and explorations.

4. Doctrine and Scripture: Complementary Ways of Attending to the Truth

4.1. Augustine's Two Ways of Knowing

As we have seen, Augustine expends much time and energy on the question how we can love what we do not know. Knowledge thus seems key; yet elsewhere in his spiraling discussions he makes a clear distinction between knowledge and wisdom, which seems to suggest a very different estimate of knowledge and its role. Different contexts perhaps point to two different ways of knowing. So let us consider his discussion in book 12.

"When we live according to God," Augustine states, "our mind should be intent on his invisible things and thus progressively be formed from his eternity, truth and charity." Yet, it is clear that "some of our rational attention, that is to say some of the same mind, has to be directed to the utilization of changeable and bodily things without which this life cannot be lived." That does not mean being "conformed to this world" (Rom 12:2), he explains, but it is a recognition of the need to act in the temporal sphere while having an eye on eternity, passing through the former, "setting our hearts on the latter" (*Trin.* 12.13.21).

Next Augustine notes that Paul treats knowledge and wisdom as different gifts of the Spirit (1 Cor 12:8) and finds "after searching the multiple stores of the holy scriptures" that Job 28:28 clarifies the difference: "piety is wisdom, while to abstain from evil things is knowledge." Wisdom, then, "belongs to contemplation, knowledge to action," for piety, "which in Greek is *theosebeia*," signifies "worship of God" (12.13.22). Much later on in book 14, deploying a version of another of his inner trinities—memory, understanding, and will—Augustine will state that it is when the mind remembers, understands, and loves not itself but the one by whom it was made that it becomes wise. Then "this trinity of the mind becomes the image of God," suggests Augustine (14.12.15). Elsewhere, however, he suggests that if "wisdom is concerned with the intellectual cognizance of eternal things and knowledge with the rational cognizance of temporal things, it is not hard to decide which should be preferred and which subordinated to the other" (12.15.25). This perhaps signifies a clear distinction that is blurred elsewhere by ambiguous usage of the word "knowledge." Here, it seems, it is reduced to the kind of rational understanding needed to function in this world; elsewhere, however, it can represent the kind of deep acquaintance with others, even God, which is required for loving. We may perceive some sort of connection between these two kinds of knowing, for in practice loving our neighbor involves the will to take action in the world. But these two kinds of knowing also seem to map onto the distinction Augustine makes between knowledge and wisdom. Indeed Augustine himself notes that wisdom may be called knowledge: he observes that in 1 Corinthians 12:8 Paul "clearly means the contemplation of God" (*Trin.* 12.13.22). But his purportive distinction between "intellectual cognizance of eternal things" and "rational cognizance of temporal things" might perhaps anticipate the kind of insight we need both to characterize and close the gap that we assume is inevitable between doctrine and scripture.

4.2. An Intellectual Journey of Discovery

To unpack that impenetrable statement let me, as briefly as possible, indulge in a little intellectual autobiography—an unexpected move in an academic work, perhaps, but in line with my references to moments of illumination throughout these volumes and their dedication to all who along the way have opened my eyes.

In the 1970s, with the arrogance and self-confidence of youth, I was involved with the group that produced *The Myth of God Incarnate.*[45] My contributions offered a historico-critical attempt to describe how Jesus came to be identified as Son of God and worshipped even in that biblically shaped "monotheistic" culture, eventually to be understood as God incarnate. The threat to the human, historical figure of Jesus from the semi-divine (unconsciously Arian) Savior of much popular Christian belief was my principal target, whereas the target of the volume's editor, John Hick, was the incoherence of the Chalcedonian Definition. It could be said that we were working in the province of Augustine's knowledge—rational comprehension of temporal things, a logocentric rationality bound by what we thought we could establish on the basis of the evidence and what we thought we knew. Most participants and readers alike jumped to the conclusion that "myth" meant mere figments of the imagination, though the one who suggested the title was fully aware

45. *The Myth of God Incarnate*, ed. John Hick (London: SCM, 1977).

of the ambiguity of the word, of the potential for myth to be true though not literal, rather pointing figuratively to the deepest questions about the human condition and its meaning. Indeed my own contribution shows how I sought some way of affirming the presence of God in the human Jesus, if only because I relied on it for theodicy—to be able to claim that on the cross the Creator God somehow entered and bore the consequences of the "gonewrongness" in creation, its suffering and sin. But the imperative then was "scientific" history, realism, and facts. How could this theodicy be defended intellectually alongside uncompromising focus on the "historical Jesus"?

At that stage I was influenced by the writings of Arthur Koestler. My scientist husband had introduced me to *The Sleepwalkers*—his history of science detailing the way in which breakthroughs came not through painstaking logical argument but by insight, unexpected correlations, and intuitions.[46] In another one of Koestler's works, *The Act of Creation*, I found him associating together a good joke, a poem, a scientific discovery, all involving what has come to be known as "lateral thinking"—seeing something in terms of something else by recognizing patterns, parallels, models, metaphors, and analogies.[47] Apparently inconsistent models could function in complementary ways alongside each other even in science, the classic example being the Uncertainty Principle whereby an electron's position may be calculated as if a particle or as if a wave but not both at the same time. I proposed a somewhat parallel strategy, confessing myself "driven to tell *two stories*, to think in terms of *two models*" which I set out thus:

1. The story of a man who lived as the "archetypal believer," who lived and died trusting in God, and accepted the bitter consequences of the stupidity of such a career and his inevitable failure.
2. The story of God being involved in the reality of human existence with its compromises, its temptations, its suffering, its pain, its injustice, its cruelty, its *death*; not running away from it, not pretending that all this does not exist, but transforming its darkness into light, demonstrating that he takes responsibility for all that seems wrong with the world that he created.

I described this as a Christology "which is not incredible in so far as Jesus is a real man in the human context, and a Christology which transcends the limits of human understanding and allows for the mystery and paradox of

46. Arthur Koestler, *The Sleepwalkers* (London: Hutchinson, 1959).
47. Arthur Koestler, *The Act of Creation* (London: Hutchinson, 1964).

belief in God." I now retrospectively discern some parallels between this and Augustine's two kinds of knowledge.

In the early 1990s I revisited Christology in an invited lecture entitled "From Analysis to Overlay: A Sacramental Approach to Christology."[48] I began with a parable: a group of friends walking along a coast path above cliffs, all with different competences so attending to the cliff in different ways—the geologist discussing strata, weathering, and the action of the ocean on the rocks, and the artist enabling a grasp of the whole, the beauty of its proportions, shapes, and colors, all enriching perception and contemplation through synthesis and analysis providing complementary perspectives.

I then explored the need for both in Christology. I spoke of the Chalcedonian Definition and the necessity of its analysis, for in the social setting of early Christianity there was generally confusion between gods and humans. By contrast, characteristic of Christianity since the second century had been a sharp distinction between Creator and creatures, as has been underlined repeatedly in the course of this study now. I explained how definition means determining what a thing is as distinct from other things, such differentiation being the beginning of analysis, and how this was the dominant issue in ancient philosophy—the question of a thing's "being" or substance—and how the equivalent for us is the question of identity. Chalcedon was about specifying the identity of Jesus Christ, but its analysis left a puzzle—indeed, an apparently impossible paradox. To claim that Jesus Christ was to be identified as fully God and fully human might seem as implausible as the idea of a centaur—a horse-man. And yet, the grounding analytical principle was that God could not be confused with any other existent thing, and "the Godness of God"—the otherness of the divine—was no small factor in the controversies, as we have seen. The analytical process was and remains essential: two distinct natures, divine and human, we dare not confuse, "yet we find, perhaps to our embarrassment, that we have to assert that Jesus Christ has to be identified as being wholly both."[49]

I then turned to the New Testament, particularly the writings of St. Paul, and there explored synthesis—the idea that "it is in the ambiguities produced by overlaying images and concepts that creative perceptions arise." I drew out

48. "From Analysis to Overlay: A Sacramental Approach to Christology" (paper presented as the Gore Memorial Lecture, St. Margaret's Westminster and Birmingham Cathedral, November 1993). Originally published in *Christ: The Sacramental Word; Incarnation, Sacrifice and Poetry*, ed. David Brown and Ann Loades (London: SPCK, 1996); republished in F. Young, *Ways of Reading Scripture*.

49. F. Young, *Ways of Reading Scripture*, 122.

the ambiguity implied in Paul's treatment of Christ as God's image. In the first place it is linked with divinity—Christ embodying God's wisdom (explicitly in 1 Cor 1:24, implicitly in 1 Cor 8:6 and Col 1:15); but then it parallels Christ with Adam, truly human, re-creating humankind as it was meant to be, forming that image anew in those baptized into Christ (Rom 5:12–14; 8:29; 1 Cor 15:21–22, 49; Col 3:9–10). Thus I showed how the notion that Jesus Christ is God's image "cannot be logically pinned down": it is about "perfect humanity . . . realised in Jesus" and about our transformation in him, but it is also about "the immanence of divine wisdom . . . God's self-revelation, the presence of God's own glory." Metaphors about mirrors and reflections, or about the imprint of a seal in wax, suggest that "Paul understood human nature to be stamped with the divine imprint, through and in Christ." Neither wax nor imprint was other than real. This is a synthetic way of seeing whole, as it were, the significance and identity of Jesus Christ.

My subsequent exegesis of 2 Corinthians 3, which in detail needs not detain us just now, drew out further this synthetic way of thinking by showing how Paul's thought overlaid different Old Testament texts so as to bring out a fresh understanding, such that Jesus Christ becomes a manifestation of the God of the scriptures, and the Spirit becomes the continuing transformative power of Jesus Christ in the lives of Christians. "The synthesis means that distinctions are not removed, but a union which is a sort of coinherence is perceived."

After exploring such synthesis in the traditions of Jewish and Christian mysticism, I returned to Chalcedon and suggested that it did work after all—for the very differentiation of the Creator from the creature meant that God did not suffer the same constraints as created things or beings that we know. Place, shape, time, structure—these belong to the material creation and are irrelevant to the nature of the totally "other" divine nature. So "there was no contradiction in the divine, as it were, occupying the same space as another entity. Divine being could be both differentiated from and mystically identified with another being . . . , human being could . . . receive God's impress." Through this overlaying of texts, this interpenetration, mediation could be understood "in terms of the whole character of God being 'imaged' in a wholly human medium." Surely this rings true to the Christology of Augustine, and to the intentions of those struggling with the inadequacies of human language and conceptuality in the controversies leading up to Chalcedon.

At the start of that lecture my parable had suggested that "wisdom is reached when synthesis and analysis work together," and that "there are profound analogies in the way in which all creative thought, artistic and scientific, is both 'inspired' and the outcome of conscious mental discipline." I had spoken of a split in modern apprehension whereby theology has come to be "treated as cold, critical, objective, rational, analytical, distanced, even irrelevant," rather than "the lifeblood of the Christian life." I suggested that "renewed confidence in the truth by which we live as Christians" could only come by "a reintegration of paths presently perceived as split." A few years previously such had been the burden of my inaugural lecture as Edward Cadbury Professor of Theology at the University of Birmingham, entitled "The Critic and the Visionary." The task was to address the university, one founded with an explicitly secular charter and dominated by science, engineering, and medicine, and explain my subject. To defend the unlikely presence of theology in that context, I called upon John Henry Cardinal Newman—after all he had founded his Oratory in the very same city. I appealed to his book, *The Idea of a University*, to challenge merely utilitarian values.[50] I then moved to dialogue with his *Essay on the Development of Christian Doctrine*.[51] For Newman, I suggested "faith was the reasoning of the religious mind." Indeed, "his contrast between faith and reason was really a contrast between two modes of rationality," and it was not "irrational to recognise the limits of rationality. Rationality could be enlarged by imagination." In these ways, Newman's theory of knowledge was "closely akin to that of the Fathers he loved so well." For both Gregory of Nazianzus and Newman, "religious language could never be precisely accurate, and knowledge of God was the fruit of grafting an attuned imagination onto strict moral and intellectual asceticism—the critical and the visionary."[52]

By now a certain consistency might be emerging from this personal story: a "two ways" approach to conceiving the truth about the way things are. So the work of Iain McGilchrist, *The Master and His Emissary: The Divided Brain and the Making of the Western World*, struck home as a remarkable consummation, at many levels confirming the position to which I had been stumbling for a long time.[53] With his expertise in neuroscience he showed

- how the divided brain enables two different ways of attending to things;
- how the left hemisphere in chickens focuses on individual grains to be pecked, in humans on specifics to be manipulated or controlled, on needs to be fulfilled, on mechanisms, data, and analysis (parts not wholes), de-

50. John Henry Newman, *The Idea of a University*, ed. M. J. Svaglie (San Francisco: Rinehart, 1960).

51. See volume 1, chapter 1, for my much more recent engagement with that work.

52. Esp. Gregory, *Orat.* 27—his first theological oration.

53. Iain McGilchrist, *The Master and His Emissary: The Divided Brain and the Making of the Western World* (New Haven: Yale University Press, 2009).

ploying logic and linguistic literalism, categorization, and propositional formulations;

- how the right hemisphere in chickens attends to a wider perspective, looking out for rivals or predators, and in humans grasps wholes, overall context, narrative, relationships, and facial recognition, while appreciating music, metaphor, humor, poetry—language being in a different register from that of the logocentric, analytic approach of the left hemisphere, thus generating insight and imagination: "It is the task of the right hemisphere to carry the left beyond, to something new, something 'other' than itself."[54]

McGilchrist's work ranks highly among my illuminating discoveries. Since my initial encounter with his work, his magnum opus, *The Matter with Things: Our Brains, Our Delusions, and the Unmaking of the World*, has provided not only more scientific data for distinguishing the brain hemispheres and their functions, but also more philosophical reflection on how humans know, what is worth knowing, and why the humanities matter alongside science—even why religion may give important access to reality.[55]

My initial discovery came as I was working on *God's Presence: A Contemporary Recapitulation of Early Christianity*. This was my attempt at pulling things together so as to produce a systematic theology in dialogue with the fathers of the church, the chapters being a series of essays on traditional doctrines and how they might be appropriated in our very different intellectual culture. There I suggested that the features just summarized "point to the integration we seek, challenging the logocentric narrowness of scientific materialism, and the atheism so aggressively associated with it, by taking up the critical reason into intuitive insight and wider wisdom." This, I argued, was anticipated by the fathers, again drawing attention to Gregory of Nazianzus's first theological oration (*Oration* 27):

> The best theologian, he suggests, is not the one who can give a complete logical account of his subject—for if God is beyond the grasp of human comprehension, then the normal processes of human logic are inapplicable. Rather the true theologian is one who "assembles more of Truth's image or shadow." Heretics he accuses of the clever tricks of logicians who perform acrobatics with words, twisting absurdity into apparently reasonable syl-

54. McGilchrist, *Master and Emissary*, 104.

55. Iain McGilchrist, *The Matter with Things: Our Brains, Our Delusions, and the Unmaking of the World*, 2 vols. (London: Perspectiva, 2021).

> logisms and quibbling sophistries—in McGilchrist's terms, the left-brain over-dominant. The true theologian must qualify by meditation, by purification of soul and body, and by genuine commitment to the subject—in other words, by a holistic recognition of the transcendence of the subject-matter, and the significance of embodiment—a right-brain outlook. Religious language is necessarily metaphorical and symbolic, but this does not mean it is irrational. . . . Knowledge of God comes partly through a balance between the analysis of apophaticism and the suggestiveness of analogy and synthesis, by which an overall viewpoint is taken of the way things are and how things point beyond themselves.[56]

This intellectual autobiography was introduced to unpack an earlier dense sentence, suggesting that Augustine's "distinction between 'intellectual cognizance of eternal things' and 'rational cognizance of temporal things' might perhaps anticipate the kind of insight we need both to characterize and close the gap that we assume is inevitable between doctrine and scripture."[57] Surely Augustine anticipated to a remarkable extent the "two ways" of attending to things that have been distinguished, recognizing in his own way that both are necessary. Maybe a rationality that deals in analysis, makes distinctions, manipulates data, and concentrates on discrete things has an essential clarificatory and practical role; but as McGilchrist shows, it can be limiting—indeed destructive—if it is not taken up into an imaginative and holistic grasp of reality, holding the parts in the flow of dynamic relationship rather than focusing on discrete identities: "if we are . . . to grasp at an *intellectual* level the primacy of metaphor and myth in understanding—we need the clarity, the ordering, the trying-to-make-sense-of-things that are the left hemisphere's forte."[58] But reliance on one hemisphere is insufficient:

> All that is to be known must initially "presence" to the right hemisphere (we have no other access); then be transferred to the left hemisphere so as to gain expression through re-presentation; and that re-presentation return to the right hemisphere. . . . As always we need the hemispheres to co-operate in fulfilling their proper roles.[59]

56. F. Young, *God's Presence*, 193–94.
57. Above, p. 296.
58. McGilchrist, *Matter with Things*, 2:1228.
59. McGilchrist, *Matter with Things*, 2:1228–29.

The articulation of doctrine in propositions was vital and valid, but only comes alive when embodied in the scriptural narratives and confessions that bring us into encounter with Christ.

4.3. The Gap Closed: Knowledge Becomes Wisdom

So how does this discussion both characterize and close that gap between scripture and doctrine?

First, it exposes the way in which scripture has been captured within the limitations of a logocentric rationality which, through the historico-critical approach, literalizing exegesis, and fundamentalist appeal to the veracity of facts, becomes "the rational cognizance of temporal things." Second, doctrine may likewise become rigid literalizing dogma, defining propositions, excessively precise inferences, and analytical deductions and distinctions. Time and again we have described it in terms of deducing propositions from scripture, attempting to define truth within the categories of human rationality; to pin things down, we might say, and to take control, not least in order to constrain wild (gnostic?) fantasies of the imagination or to counter damaging heretical syllogisms with more telling arguments. For, as the fathers repeatedly said, too much logic and sophisticated syllogisms end up in busybodying speculation beyond the limited capacity of the human mind. These left-brain tendencies, which try to tie things down into known categories, are surely at the root of the gap between scripture and doctrine in modern theology, each analyzed into separate parts, and separated from each other as belonging to different times (doctrine as anachronistic development) or different linguistic and cultural contexts (doctrine as Hellenization). This all fits with the argument of McGilchrist as philosopher that the dominance of the left-brain approach in Western education and culture in general has been a serious impoverishment, narrowing not just our conception of what constitutes rationality but our very grasp of reality.

Yet surely the characterization just offered is highly restrictive. After all, scripture is composed of narrative and poetry, symbolic motifs, and figural narratives that deepen literary links and typological connections across its various texts and so offer an invitation rather into a holistic encounter with reality—a right brain response? And as for doctrine, surely the perception actually found in these volumes is not so narrow: the rule of faith constantly provided the right-brain overview that allowed the multifarious material in scripture to be encountered as a whole. The need to view discrete doctrines as constituting a single beautiful building we found (in volume 1) emphasized by the catechist, Cyril of Jerusalem, may be in effect a left-brain move from parts to the whole. Yet, equally it can be seen as an exhortation to observe the whole as a single beautiful temple to doctrinal truth. Surely it was the "intellectual grasp of eternal things" that discerned the "hypothesis" of scripture and enabled the recognition of doctrine's coinherence with the scriptural canon. There was no gap, as the clarifications and specifications produced out of controversy and analysis were taken up into a wider vision, an imaginative grasp of the whole that was facilitated by what we might call doctrine's unifying ecology.

To close the gap, then, we need to reclaim the right brain's "intellectual cognizance of eternal things," to reintegrate analysis and synthesis, to let propositional statements clarify the mind without undermining intuitive insight into depths of truth that can only be approximately articulated, signified through metaphor and apparent paradox, signs, and shadows of mystical realities encompassing the multiplicity of things. The intuition of sacred mystery in encounter with the person of Jesus Christ led to sketching its shape in the doctrine of the Trinity and the Chalcedonian Definition so as to enable its apprehension, but then such doctrines are liable to be taken over by a (left-brain) theoretical rationality, which makes them its own and seeks to control, possess, and order them for its own ends. An intellect open to respect, receive, and respond (right brain) would reintegrate such doctrinal propositions into a more intuitive grasp of narrative flow, meaning, and relationships, and would be ready to admit humbly that it cannot know everything but receives in encounter with scripture's *skopos*, a sense of wonder and amazement. There are two ways of attending to things, two ways of knowing, but wisdom comes when they are in proper balance. Painting with a very broad brush, one could say that what the right brain encounters through the narratives, teaching, and poetry of scripture, the left brain clarifies through propositional doctrine, which not only constrains but enables the shaping of the Christian imagination when it is taken up into the perspective of eternal wisdom. We recall the poetry of Ephrem, the spirituality of the Macarian *Homilies*, and the theology of Gregory of Nyssa (see chapter 3). Doctrine and scripture are surely meant to be coinherent and together to break open our generally narrow conceptions of what might constitute rationality so as to appreciate the "intellectual cognizance of eternal things" in a way that might indeed enable us to find wisdom, to close that perceived gap, to "shape and reclaim the mystery" (to pick up the heading to this chapter). Oh yes, resorting to mystery is often regarded as a cop-out, and I plead guilty to making that point on occasion. But again let us hear the protest of McGilchrist:

> Mystery does not imply muddled thinking. On the other hand, thinking you could be clear about something which in its nature is essentially mysterious *is* muddled thinking. Nor does mystery betoken a lack of meaning—rather a superabundance of meaning in relation to our normal finite vision.[60]

It is in worship that the mystery of God's being and God's incarnation are present to us.

4.4. *Worship: Where Scripture and Doctrine Truly Coinhere*

We have already noted not only the passage (*Trin.* 14.1.1) where Augustine indicates that human wisdom is *theosebeia*, that is, "God's worship" for "behold, piety is wisdom" (Job 28:28) but also his reference (*Trin.* 15.28.51) to the baptismal formula "in the name of the Father, the Son and the Holy Spirit" (Matt 28:19), a text to which we have seen so many turn as the basis for affirming the Trinity. *On the Trinity* yields little on communal worship, yet the whole trea tise constitutes a search for appropriate means of contemplation prior to the face-to-face vision that the consummation will bring (*Trin.* 1.10.20–21), while Augustine's characteristic emphasis on loving God and loving one's neighbor for God's sake is by no means absent. For Augustine, as for the fathers more generally, there were none of our splits between doctrine and contemplation, scripture and prayer, action and reflection, theology and worship. There has been much in this volume to substantiate that observation, above all the engagement with Basil's treatise on the Holy Spirit.[61] But much else has shown how scriptural words and liturgical phraseology shaped doctrinal argument; conversely doctrine certainly shaped the prayers and praises of the worshipping community. This surely must be the context within which we might ourselves rediscover the coinherence of scripture and doctrine.

For indeed it is already there. Nor has the fact that worship is the appropriate starting point for theological reflection escaped some systematic theologians, such as Daniel Hardy and David Ford, or Geoffrey Wainwright.[62] As for the relationship between doctrine and scripture, we only need to consider how the communal reading of scripture, often according to lectionaries which

60. McGilchrist, *Matter with Things*, 2:1258.

61. See chapter 2.

62. David F. Ford, with Daniel W. Hardy, *Living in Praise: Worshipping and Knowing God*, 2nd ed. (London: Darton, Longman and Todd, 2005); Geoffrey Wainwright, *Doxology* (London: Epworth, 1979).

pattern the commemoration of Advent, Christmas, Lent, Passion, Easter and Pentecost, sits alongside recitation of the creeds in the structure of worship in many Christian communities, bringing together scripture and doctrine so that week by week, month by month, they interpret one another, implicitly if not explicitly. The context of worship brings out the doxological character of the creeds—too easily they can seem like articles of belief when in the context of liturgy they really are doxological, confessions of loyalty, the liturgical recitation of the sacred story into which believers are drawn so as to find their meaning, and into which scriptural lections fit and find their sense. One might add that the homily or sermon, with admittedly varying degrees of success, is the place where doctrine (in the broader sense of Christian teaching, including ethics) informs the exposition of the scriptures read. Certainly that was the case for the fathers, as is evident in chapter 4: Chrysostom's exegesis of both Hebrews and John was given as a series of homilies. It is in the context of the Eucharist (or communion service) that all this is reinforced for many Christian communities by the Great Prayer of Thanksgiving. As a result of the twentieth-century liturgical movement there are now similar liturgical patterns in use among both Catholics and Protestants whereby the lead-up to the consecration of the elements is the thankful rehearsal in prayer of the story of creation, fall, and redemption; that is, a form of the rule of faith—the very basis of Christian doctrine and of the Christian reading of scripture as a whole. Thus the context is made explicit for the commemoration of Christ's Passover sacrifice for us and for our reception of his body given for us and his blood shed for us.

Furthermore, it is in songs and hymns that congregations sing together doctrines and scriptures, celebrating the divine love whereby they are adopted into a world way beyond anything known on earth, which yet transfigures everything known on earth. At this point my Methodist self cannot resist the temptation to demonstrate how deeply both scripture and the doctrines of incarnation and Trinity are embedded in the hymns of Charles Wesley by offering a few examples, probably less well known than "Love Divine" or "Hark! the Herald Angels":

> Father, God, thy love we praise,
>   Which gave thy Son to die;
> Jesus, full of truth and grace,
>   Alike we glorify;
> Spirit, Comforter divine,
>   Praise by all to thee be given;

Till we in full chorus join,
  And earth is turned to heaven.

Thus praise necessitates calling on each of the three—they are co-glorified, as the fathers repeatedly affirmed.

One undivided Trinity
  With triumph we proclaim;
Thy universe is full of thee,
  And speaks thy glorious name.

Three Persons equally divine
  We magnify and love;
And both the choirs[63] ere long shall join
  To sing thy praise above:

Hail! Holy, holy, holy Lord,
  Our heavenly song shall be,
Supreme, essential One, adored
  In co-eternal Three.

Equal and inseparable: thus we learn to sing Augustine's doctrine alongside Isaiah's vision. Elsewhere Augustine's mediator, Philippians' *kenōsis*, and Athanasius's *theopoiēsis* are given voice:

Let earth and heaven combine,
  Angels and men agree,
To praise in songs divine
  The Incarnate Deity,
Our God contracted to a span,
  Incomprehensibly made man.

He deigns in flesh to appear,
  Widest extremes to join,
To bring our vileness near,
  And make us all divine:

63. An earlier verse refers to adoration from the heavenly host and the church below.

And we the life of God shall know,
For God is manifest below.

Then again, Charles Wesley indicates how the scriptures teach core Christian doctrines under the inspiration of the Holy Spirit:

Come then, divine Interpreter,
The Scriptures to our hearts apply;
And taught by thee, we God revere,
Him in three Persons magnify,
In each the triune God adore,
Who was, and is, for evermore.

Thus he expresses what Augustine, together with the church over the centuries, has accepted and celebrated in worship. To read scripture Christianly means reading it doctrinally. In the end there is no gap, for scripture was and remains the genesis of doctrine, and doctrine ensures that the complexities of scripture are brought into harmony as the revelation of how the one true God is for us Creator, Redeemer, and Sanctifier.

Seeing scripture whole requires doctrine, even the use of language and concepts not to be found therein, as Athanasius argued. Seeing doctrine whole requires the narratives of scripture in all their particularity, and the parables, metaphors, symbols, and signs of scripture in all their potential ambiguity and paradox. It is in worship that we find their coinherence as we read the scriptures according to the rule of faith and within the traditions of Christian worship. It is in worship that we find human language and conceptuality inadequate to the One whose name we seek to hallow. It is in worship that the stories and poetry, symbols, and signs of scripture make sense despite parable and paradox, and we discover that, like creation, scripture and doctrine together point beyond themselves in ways that are virtually sacramental.

And so to a meditative postlude.

5. Postlude: Three Meditations

Meditation 1 (after Augustine)

God of all being and my being, in the light of your glorious presence I discern a trinity, a trinity of truth, beauty and goodness. I open myself

- to receive from truth perspective on my *angst* and inadequacy—for I am but part of something so much bigger than myself and my self-concern;
- to receive from beauty perspective on my trivial preoccupations—for I belong to an order of creation that points to transcendence;
- to receive from goodness perspective on my experience of gonewrongness put right—for love plants germs of new possibilities in the midst of suffering and sin.

Goodness—surely I may correlate that with stories of exodus from slavery, of return from exile, of cross and resurrection—and so with the God of the Bible, who consistently and lovingly engages with the realities of creaturely existence, bringing order out of chaos, generating good in the midst of evil; and hesitatingly I may associate that goodness particularly with the Son of God, through whom are all things, including us (1 Cor 8:6), and who for our sake took flesh and became a human being, was tried and tested as we humans are yet without sin, who died and rose again that we might become created anew according to the image of God in him.

And beauty—surely I may correlate that with the wonders of the cosmos and the natural world created out of nothingness, with the awesome revelations of scientific research from genes to galaxies, with new life in spring, with the fractals of trees bursting into leaf and with birdsong, with human creativity, with ecstatic singing and dance, with the worship of psalms and hymns—and so with the one Creator God of the Bible, the source of existence, of blessing, of joyful and creative living, of harmony and community; and hesitatingly I may associate that beauty particularly with the Father from whom are all things, including us.

And truth—hesitatingly I may associate that particularly with the Spirit of Truth, the Paraclete who will teach, guide, and remind, the one who inspired the scriptures and inspires their reading; so that then surely I can find in scripture, already there and potentially there, the truth of the one God, Father, Son, and Holy Spirit, three in one and one in three, equal in being, inseparable in activity, distinct in relationship—truth in a mystery that stretches human language and conceptuality, teases the creaturely mind with puzzling ambiguities, yet integrates mind and heart in praise and worship informed by attention to scripture, to inner reflection, to deep contemplation, and song:

> Father, we adore you, lay our lives before you, how we love you.
> Jesus, we adore you, lay our lives before you, how we love you.
> Spirit, we adore you, lay our lives before you, how we love you.

Meditation 2 (after Augustine, with McGilchrist)

God, beyond yet within, in the depths of my consciousness I discern a trinity of head, heart and mind.

I open myself

- to recognize words of truth in my head—for I need guidance to act well in the world;
- to feel intimations of love in my heart—for I can love others well only if I know myself loved;
- to attend well with the whole of my mind to the whole of experience and find beyond tension integration, beyond paradox peace.

Head—surely I may correlate head knowledge with the Word of the Lord, commandments to be kept, promises to be fulfilled, the practical know-how, tools and values to be lived out in the kingdom of God; and this perhaps I may associate particularly with the incarnate Word, the Logos, who is the way, the truth and the life, who lived out on earth the commands he proclaimed and, bearing our judgement, gave his life for the life of the world.

Heart—surely I may correlate that with the overflowing love of God revealed in the scriptures and hesitatingly associate it particularly with the Spirit of the Lord, the giver of gifts for community formation, the inspiration of prophecy and poetry, narrative and music, creativity and contemplation, performance and liturgy.

Mind—hesitatingly I may associate that particularly with the Father, the source of Word and Spirit, in whom justice and mercy are integrated; but I may also correlate it with the integrative wholeness of the one God, darkly reflected in the mirror of myself, created in the Creator's image, head, heart, and mind, distinct yet inseparable, as are Father, Son and Spirit.

> Father, we adore you, lay our lives before you, how we love you.
> Jesus, we adore you, lay our lives before you, how we love you.
> Spirit, we adore you, lay our lives before you, how we love you.

Meditation 3 (after Augustine, with Gregory of Nyssa)

God of the beyond, in the luminous darkness of your singularity we discern a trinity, a trinity of love, knowledge and wisdom.

We open ourselves

- to receive from love the grace of purification—for we are all implicated in the mass of pollution and sin;
- to receive from knowledge hints of the beyond—for sacramental signs seen through a glass darkly are sufficient for faith and the love of God and neighbor;
- to receive from wisdom the humility of unknowing—for dizzy before infinite mystery we feel sensations of divine presence.

Wisdom—surely we may correlate that with the bronze serpent in the desert, the antidote to human wisdom (Num 21:9; John 3:14), and hesitatingly we may associate that wisdom particularly with the Son of God, through whom are all things (1 Cor 8:6; Rom 11:36), lifted up on the tree of life for our salvation, self-emptied in the foolishness of the cross (Phil 2:7–8; 1 Cor 1:25).

Knowledge—surely we may correlate that with the one creator God of the universe, who offered us the excitement of search and discovery, never to reach stale satisfaction but to press on pursuing the beyond, through parable and paradox, analogy and enigma, faith and hope; and hesitatingly we may associate that knowledge with the Father from whom are all things (1 Cor 8:6; Rom 11:36).

And love—hesitatingly we may associate love particularly with the Holy Spirit (1 John 4:7, 12–13, 16), in whom are all things (Rom 11:36), the love between lover and beloved—Father and Son, the love poured out upon us to sanctify, renew, and strip ready for contemplation of the God who is love when finally we see the Three-in-One face to face and know as we are known (1 Cor 13:12).

> Father, we adore you, lay our lives before you, how we love you.
> Jesus, we adore you, lay our lives before you, how we love you.
> Spirit, we adore you, lay our lives before you, how we love you.

Bibliography

Texts and Translations

Apollinaris. Text in *Apollinaris von Laodicea und seine Schüle*. Edited by H. Lietzmann. Tübingen: Mohr, 1904.

Athanasius. *Letters to Serapion concerning the Holy Spirit*. Greek text in *Athanasius Werke*. Vol. 1.4, *Epistulae I–IV ad Serapionem*. Edited by Dietmar Wyrwa. Berlin: de Gruyter, 2010. Translation in *Works on the Spirit: Athanasius the Great and Didymus the Blind*. Edited and translated by Mark DelCogliano, Andrew Radde-Gallwitz, and Lewis Ayres. Yonkers, NY: St. Vladimir's Seminary Press, 2011.

———. *On the Incarnation*. Text and translation in *Contra Gentes and De Incarnatione*. Edited and translated by Robert W. Thomson. OECT. Oxford: Clarendon, 1971.

———. *Orations against the Arians*. Text in *Athanasius Werke*. Vol. 1.2, *Orationes I et II contra Arianos*. Edited by K. Metzler, D. U. Hansen, and K. Savvidis. Berlin: de Gruyter, 1998; *Athanasius Werke*. Vol. 1.3, *Oratio III contra Arianos*. Edited by K. Savvidis and K. Metzler. Berlin: de Gruyter, 2000. Translation in *NPNF*[2] 4.

Athenagoras. *Embassy for the Christians*. Text and Translation in *Legatio and De Resurrectione*. Edited and translated by W. R. Schoedel. OECT. Oxford: Clarendon, 1972.

Augustine. *Confessions*. Translated by Henry Chadwick. Oxford: Oxford University Press, 1992.

———. *On the Trinity*. Text in *On the Trinity*. Edited by W. J. Mountain. 2 vols. CCSL 50–50A. Turnhout: Brepols, 1968. Translation in *The Trinity: De Trin-*

itate. Translated by Edmund Hill. Works of St. Augustine 1.5. Hyde Park, NY: New City, 1991.

———. *Teaching Christianity*. Text and translation in *De Doctrina Christiana*. Edited and translation by R. P. H. Green. OECT. Oxford: Clarendon, 1995; *Teaching Christianity: De Doctrina Christiana*. Translated by Edmund Hill. Edited by John E. Rotelle. Works of St. Augustine 1.11. Hyde Park, NY: New City, 1996.

Basil of Caesarea. *On the Holy Spirit*. Text in *Liber de Spiritu Sancto*. Edited by B. Pruche. SC 17. Paris: Cerf, 1947. Translation in *NPNF*[2] 8; *On the Holy Spirit*. Translated by David Anderson. Crestwood, NY: St. Vladimir's Seminary Press, 1980.

Cyril of Alexandria. *Commentary on John's Gospel*. Text in *S. Cyrilli Archiepiscopi Alexandriae in S. Joannii Evangelium*. Edited by P. E. Pusey. 3 vols. Oxford: Clarendon, 1872. Translation in *Cyril of Alexandria: Commentary on John*. Edited by Joel C. Elowsky. Translated by David R. Maxwell. 2 vols. Ancient Christian Texts. Downers Grove, IL: IVP Academic, 2013, 2015.

———. *Explanation of the Anathemas*. Text from *ACO* 1.1.5:15–25. Translation in *Cyril of Alexandria*. Translated by Norman Russell. London: Routledge, 2000.

———. *Letters*. In *Cyril of Alexandria: Select Letters*. Edited and translated by Lionel R. Wickham. Oxford: Clarendon, 1983.

———. *On the Unity of Christ*. Text in *Deux dialogues christologiques*. Edited by G. M. de Durand. SC 97. Paris: Cerf, 1964. Translation in *On the Unity of Christ*. Translated by John Anthony McGuckin. Crestwood, NY: St. Vladimir's Seminary Press, 1995.

Ephrem the Syrian. *Against Heresies*. Translation in Sebastian Brock. *The Luminous Eye: The Spiritual Vision of Saint Ephrem the Syrian*. Rev. ed. Kalamazoo, MI: Cistercian, 1992.

———. *Hymns*. Translations in *Ephrem the Syrian: Hymns*. Translated by Kathleen E. McVey. CWS. New York: Paulist, 1989; *Ephrem the Syrian: Select Poems*. Edited and translated by Sebastian P. Brock and George A. Kiraz. Provo: Brigham Young University Press, 2006; *Hymns on Paradise*. Translated by Sebastian Brock. Crestwood, NY: St. Vladimir's Seminary Press, 1990; Sebastian Brock. *The Luminous Eye: The Spiritual Vision of Saint Ephrem the Syrian*. Rev. ed. Kalamazoo, MI: Cistercian, 1992.

Eusebius. *Church History*. Text in *Eusebius Werke: Die Kirchengeschichte*. Edited by Eduard Schwartz. 2 vols. GCS 9. Leipzig: Hinrichs, 1908. Translation in *The History of the Church*. Translated by G. A. Williamson. Harmondsworth: Penguin, 1965.

Gregory of Nazianzus. *Orations*. Text in PG 37–38; Orations 1–12 and 20–43 in *SC*. Translations in *NPNF*[2] 7; Brian E. Daley. *Gregory of Nazianzus*. London: Routledge, 2006; F. W. Norris, with F. Williams and L. Wickham. *Faith Gives Fullness to Reasoning: The Five Theological Orations of St. Gregory Nazianzen*. VCSup 13. Leiden: Brill, 1991.

Gregory of Nyssa. *Against Eunomius*. Text in *GNO* 1 and 2. English translation in *NPNF*[2] 5.

———. Extracts from Gregory of Nyssa's mystical writings in *From Glory to Glory*. Translated by Herbert Musurillo, SJ. New York: Scribner's Sons, 1961.

———. *Homilies on the Beatitudes*. In *The Lord's Prayer, The Beatitudes*. Translated by Hilda Graef in *ACW*.

———. *Homilies on the Song of Songs*. Text in *GNO* 6.

———. *Life of Moses*. Text in *GNO* 7; *Grégoire de Nyssa: La vie de Moïse*. Edited by J. Daniélou. 3rd ed. SC 1. Paris: Cerf, 1968. Translation in *Gregory of Nyssa: The Life of Moses*. Translated by Abraham J. Malherbe and Everett Ferguson. CWS. New York: Paulist, 1978.

———. *On the Making of Humankind*. Text in PG 44. Translation in *NPNF*[2] 5.

———. *On Virginity*. Text in *GNO* 8. Translation in *NPNF*[2] 5.

Hippolytus. *Against Noetus*. Text in *Contro Noeto*. Edited by M. Simonetti. Biblioteca Patristica 35. Bologna: EDB, 2000. Translation in R. Butterworth. *Hippolytus of Rome: Contra Noetum*. Heythrop Monographs 2. London: Heythrop College, 1977.

———. *Refutation of All Heresies*. Text in *Hippolytus Werke: Refutatio omnium haeresium*. Edited by Paul Wendland. GCS 26. Leipzig: Hinrichs, 1916. Translations in *ANF* 5; and in Werner Foerster. *Gnosis. A Selection of Gnostic Texts*. Vol. 1, *Patristic Evidence*. Translated by R. McL. Wilson. Oxford: Oxford University Press, 1972.

Irenaeus. *Demonstration of the Apostolic Preaching*. In *On the Apostolic Preaching*. Translated by John Behr. Crestwood, NY: St. Vladimir's Seminary Press, 1997.

John Chrysostom. *Homilies on John's Gospel*. Text in PG 59. Translations in *NPNF* 14; *Commentary on Saint John the Apostle and Evangelist*. Translated by Thomas Aquinas Goggin. 2 vols. FC. Washington, DC: Catholic University of America Press, 2000.

———. *Homilies on Hebrews*. Text in PG 63. Translation in *NPNF*[1] 14.

Justin. *I Apology*. Text in *Iustini Martyris Apologiae pro Christianis*. Edited by Miroslav Markovich. PTS 38. Berlin: de Gruyter, 1994. Translations in *ANF* 1; *Justin, Philosopher and Martyr: Apologies*. Edited and translated by Denis Minns and Paul Parvis. OECT. Oxford: Clarendon, 2009.

———. *Dialogue with Trypho*. Text in *Iustini Martyris Dialogus cum Tryphone*. Edited by Miroslav Markovich. PTS 47. Berlin: de Gruyter, 1997. Translation in *ANF* 1.

(Ps.-)Macarius. *Homilies*. Text in PG 34. Translation in *The Fifty Spiritual Homilies and the Great Letter*. Translated by George A. Maloney, SJ. CWS. New York: Paulist, 1992.

Nestorius. *First Homily against Theotokos*. Latin text and Greek fragments on pages 249–64 in *Nestoriana: Die Fragmente des Nestorius*. Edited by Friedrich Loofs. Halle: Niemeyer, 1905. Translation on pages 123–31 in *The Christological Controversy*. Edited and translated by R. A. Norris. Philadelphia: Fortress, 1980.

———. *Second Letter to Cyril*. Latin text and Greek fragments on pages 173–80 in *Nestoriana: Die Fragmente des Nestorius*. Edited by Friedrich Loofs. Halle: Niemeyer, 1905. Translation on pages 135–40 in *The Christological Controversy*. Edited and translated by R. A. Norris. Philadelphia: Fortress, 1980.

Novatian. *The Trinity*: Text in *Novatiani Romanae urbis presbyteri De Trinitate liber*. Edited by W. Yorke Fausset. Cambridge Patristic Texts. Cambridge: Cambridge University Press, 1909; *Novatiani opera*. Edited by G. F. Diercks. CCSL 4. Turnholt: Brepols, 1972. Translation in *ANF* 5.

Origen. *Against Celsus*. Text in *Die Schrift vom Martyrium, Buch I–IV gegen Celsus* and *Buch V–VIII gegen Celsus, Die Scrift vom Gebet*. Edited by P. Koetschau. Origenes Werke 1–2. GCS 2–3. Leipzig: Hinrichs, 1899.

———. *Commentary on John*. Text in *Der Johanneskommentar*. Edited by E. Preuschen. Origenes Werke 4. GCS 10. Leipzig: Hinrichs, 1904. Translations in *ANF* 9; *Commentary on the Gospel according to Saint John*. Translated by R. Heine. 2 vols. FC 80, 89. Washington, DC: Catholic University of America Press, 1989, 1993.

Tertullian. *Against Hermogenes*. Text in *Contre Hermogène*. Edited by Frédéric Chapot. SC 439. Paris: Cerf, 1999. Translation in *Treatise against Hermogenes*. Edited by J. H. Waszink. ACW. New York: Paulist, 1956.

———. *Against Praxeas*. Text and translation in *Tertullian's Treatise against Praxeas*. Edited and translated by E. Evans. London: SPCK, 1948.

Theodore of Mopsuestia. *On the Incarnation of the Lord*. Text in PG 75. Translation in *Theodore of Mopsuestia*. Edited and translated by Frederick G. McLeod. London: Routledge, 2009.

———. *Theodori Episcopi Mopsuesteni in Epistolas B. Pauli Commentarii*. Edited by H. B. Swete. 2 vols. Cambridge: Cambridge University Press, 1880, 1882.

———. *Theodori Mopsuesteni Commentarius in Evangelium Johannis Apostoli*. Edited by J. M. Vosté. 2 vols. CSCO 115–116. Leuven: Peeters, 1940.

———. *Theodori Mopsuesteni Fragmenta Syriaca*. Edited and translated by E. Sachau. Leipzig: Engelmann, 1869. Translation in *Theodore of Mopsuestia*. Edited and translated by Frederick G. McLeod. London: Routledge, 2009.

Theodoret of Cyrus. *Eranistes*. Text in *Theodoret of Cyrus: Eranistes*. Edited by Gerard H. Ettlinger. Oxford: Oxford University Press, 1975. Translation in *NPNF*[2] 3.

———. *Theodoret of Cyrus*. Translated by István Pásztori-Kupán. London: Routledge, 2009.

Theophilus. *To Autolycus*. Text and translation in *Theophilus of Antioch: Ad Autolycum*. Edited and translated by R. M. Grant. OECT. Oxford: Clarendon, 1970.

Collections

Bindley, T. H., and F. W. Green, eds. and trans. *The Oecumenical Documents of the Faith*. London: Methuen, 1950.

Norris, Richard A., Jr. *The Christological Controversy*. Philadelphia: Fortress, 1980.

Staab, K. *Pauluskommentare aus griechischen Kirche, aus Katenenhandschriften gesammelt*. Münster: Aschendorff, 1933.

Secondary Literature

Anatolios, Khaled. *Athanasius: The Coherence of His Thought*. London: Routledge, 1998.

Ayres, Lewis. *Nicaea and Its Legacy: An Approach to Fourth-Century Trinitarian Theology*. Oxford: Oxford University Press, 2004.

Balthasar, Hans Urs von. *Presence and Thought: An Essay on the Religious Philosophy of Gregory of Nyssa*. Translated by Mark Sebanc. San Francisco: Ignatius, 1995.

Barnes, Michel R., and Daniel H. Williams. *Arianism after Arius: Essays on the Development of the Fourth Century Trinitarian Conflicts*. Edinburgh: T&T Clark, 1993.

Bates, Matthew W. *The Birth of the Trinity: Jesus, God, and Spirit in the New Testament and Early Christian Interpretations of the Old Testament*. Oxford: Oxford University Press, 2015.

Beeley, Christopher A. *Gregory of Nazianzus on the Trinity and Knowledge of God*. Oxford: Oxford University Press, 2007.

Biesen, Kees den. *Simple and Bold: Ephrem's Art of Symbolic Thought*. Piscataway, NJ: Gorgias, 2006.

Boersma, Hans. *Embodiment and Virtue in Gregory of Nyssa: An Anagogical Approach*. OECS. Oxford: Oxford University Press, 2013.

Brent, A. *Hippolytus and the Roman Church in the Third Century: Communities in Tension before the Emergence of a Monarch-Bishop*. VCSup 31. Leiden: Brill, 1995.

———. *The Imperial Cult and the Development of Church Order: Concepts and Image of Authority in Paganism and Early Christianity before the Age of Cyprian*. VCSup 45. Leiden: Brill, 1999.

Brock, Sebastian. *The Luminous Eye: The Spiritual Vision of Saint Ephrem the Syrian*. Rev. ed. Kalamazoo, MI: Cistercian, 1992.

Cameron, Michael. "Enarrationes in Psalmos." Pages 290–96 in *Augustine through the Ages*. Edited by Allan D. Fitzgerald, OSA. Grand Rapids: Eerdmans, 1999.

Chadwick, Henry. *Augustine*. Oxford: Oxford University Press, 1986.

———. "Eucharist and Christology in the Nestorian Controversy." *JTS* (1951): 145–64.

Clayton, Paul B., Jr. *The Christology of Theodoret of Cyrus: Antiochene Christology from the Council of Ephesus (431) to the Council of Chalcedon (451)*. OECS. Oxford: Oxford University Press, 2007.

Coakley, Sarah, ed. *Re-Thinking Gregory of Nyssa*. Oxford: Blackwell, 2003.

Daley, Brian E. *God Visible: Patristic Christology Reconsidered*. Oxford: Oxford University Press, 2018.

Daniélou, Jean. *Platonisme et théologie mystique: Essai sur la doctrine spirituelle de saint Grégoire de Nysse*. 2nd ed. Paris: Aubier, 1954.

Ernest, James. *The Bible in Athanasius of Alexandria*. Leiden: Brill, 2004.

Fitzgerald, Allan D., OSA., ed. *Augustine through the Ages*. Grand Rapids: Eerdmans, 1999.

Ford, David F., with Daniel W. Hardy. *Living in Praise: Worshipping and Knowing God*. 2nd ed. London: Darton, Longman and Todd, 2005.

Gavrilyuk, Paul. *The Suffering of the Impassible God: The Dialectics of Patristic Thought*. OECS. Oxford: Oxford University Press, 2004.

Golitzin, A. "Temple and Throne of Divine Glory: 'Pseudo-Macarius' and Purity of Heart, Together with Some Remarks on the Limitations and Usefulness of Scholarship." Pages 107–29 in *Purity of Heart in Early Ascetic and Monastic Literature*. Edited by Harriet A. Luchman and Linda Kulzer. Collegeville, MN: Liturgical, 1999.

———. "A Testimony to Christianity as Transfiguration: The Macarian Homilies and Orthodox Spirituality." Pages 129–56 in *Orthodox and Wesleyan Spiritu-*

ality. Edited by S. T. Kimbrough Jr. Crestwood, NY: St. Vladimir's Seminary Press, 2002.

Gregg, Robert, and Dennis Groh. *Early Arianism: A View of Salvation*. Philadelphia: Fortress, 1977.

Grillmeier, Aloys, SJ. *Christ in Christian Tradition: From the Apostolic Age to Chalcedon (AD 451)*. Translated by J. S. Bowden. London: Mowbray, 1965.

Gwynn, David M. *Athanasius of Alexandria: Bishop, Theologian, Ascetic, Father*. Oxford: Oxford University Press, 2012.

Hanson, R. P. C. *Allegory and Event*. London: SCM, 1959.

———. "Basil's Doctrine of Tradition in Relation to the Holy Spirit." *VC* 22 (1968): 241–55.

———. *The Search for the Christian Doctrine of God: The Arian Controversy, 318–381*. Edinburgh: T&T Clark, 1988.

———. *Tradition in the Early Church*. Philadelphia: Westminster, 1962.

Harrison, Verna. "Gender, Generation, and Virginity in Cappadocean Theology." *JTS* 47 (1996): 38–68.

Heine, R. E. "Hippolytus, Ps-Hippolytus and the Early Canons." Pages 142–51 in *Cambridge History of Early Christian Literature*. Edited by Frances Young, Lewis Ayres, and Andrew Louth. Cambridge: Cambridge University Press, 2004.

———. *Perfection in the Virtuous Life: A Study in the Relationship between Edification and Polemical Theology in Gregory of Nyssa*. Patristic Monograph Series 2. Cambridge, MA: The Philadelphia Patristic Foundation, 1975.

Hick, John, ed. *The Myth of God Incarnate*. London: SCM, 1977.

Holman, Susan. *The Hungry Are Dying*. Oxford: Oxford University Press, 2001.

Hübner, R. M., with Markus Vinzent. *Der paradox Eine: Antignostischer Monarchianismus im zweiten Jahrhundert*. VCSup 50. Leiden: Brill, 1999.

Jaeger, Werner. *Two Rediscovered Works of Ancient Christian Literature: Gregory of Nyssa and Macarius*. Leiden: Brill, 1954.

Kannengiesser, C. "Athanasius of Alexandria and the Foundation of Traditional Christology." *Theological Studies* 34.1 (1973): 103–13.

———. "Athanasius of Alexandria, Three Orations against the Arians: A Reappraisal." StPatr 18 (1982): 981–95.

Käsemann, Ernst. *The Testament of Jesus: A Study of the Gospel of John in the Light of Chapter 17*. Translated by Gerhard Krodel. London: SCM, 1968.

Kelly, J. N. D. *Early Christian Doctrines*. London: Black, 1960.

Koestler, Arthur. *The Act of Creation*. London: Hutchinson, 1964.

———. *The Sleepwalkers*. London: Hutchinson, 1959.

Laird, Martin. *Gregory of Nyssa and the Grasp of Faith: Union, Knowledge, and Divine Presence*. OECS. Oxford: Oxford University Press, 2004.

Layton, Richard A. *Didymus the Blind and His Circle in Late-Antique Alexandria*. Urbana: University of Illinois Press, 2004.

———. "*PROPATHEIA*: Origen and Didymus on the Origin of the Passions." *VC* 54 (2000): 262–82.

Louth, Andrew. *Discerning the Mystery: An Essay on the Nature of Theology*. Oxford: Clarendon, 1983.

———. *The Origins of the Christian Mystical Tradition*. 2nd ed. Oxford: Oxford University Press, 2007.

McGilchrist, Iain. *The Master and His Emissary: The Divided Brain and the Making of the Western World*. New Haven: Yale University Press, 2009.

———. *The Matter with Things: Our Brains, Our Delusions, and the Unmaking of the World*. 2 vols. London: Perspectiva, 2021.

McGuckin, John Anthony. *Gregory of Nazianzus: An Intellectual Biography*. Crestwood, NY: St. Vladimir's Seminary Press, 2001.

———. *St. Cyril of Alexandria: The Christological Controversy. Its History, Theology and Texts*. VCSup 23. Leiden: Brill, 1994.

Mendietta, E. Amand de. "The Pair *Kerygma* and *Dogma* in the Thought of Basil of Caesarea." *JTS* 16 (1965): 129–42.

———. *The 'Unwritten' and the 'Secret' Apostolic Traditions in the Theological Thought of St. Basil of Caesarea*. Scottish Journal of Theology Occasional Papers 13. London: Oliver and Boyd, 1965.

Mitchell, Margaret M. *The Heavenly Trumpet: John Chrysostom and the Art of Pauline Interpetation*. HUT 40. Tübingen: Mohr Siebeck, 2000.

Mitchell, Margaret M., and Frances M. Young, eds. *Cambridge History of Christianity*. Vol. 1, *Origins to Constantine*. Cambridge: Cambridge University Press, 2006.

Mühlenberg, E. *Die unendlichkeit Gottes bei Gregor von Nyssa*. Göttingen: Vandenhoeck and Ruprecht, 1966.

Newman, John Henry. *An Essay on the Development of Christian Doctrine: The Edition of 1845*. Harmondsworth: Penguin, 1974.

———. *The Idea of a University*. Edited by M. J. Svaglie. San Francisco: Rinehart, 1960.

Radde-Gallwitz, Andrew. *Basil of Caesarea, Gregory of Nyssa, and the Tranformation of Divine Simplicity*. OECS. Oxford: Oxford University Press, 2009.

Robinson, Marilynne. *Home*. London: Virago, 2008.

Russell, Norman. *The Doctrine of Deification in the Greek Patristic Tradition*. Oxford: Oxford University Press, 2004.

Rylaarsdam, David. *John Chrysostom on Divine Pedagogy: The Coherence of His Theology and Preaching*. OECS. Oxford: Oxford University Press, 2014.

Sellers, R. V. *The Council of Chalcedon: A Historical and Doctrinal Survey*. London: SPCK, 1953.

———. *Two Ancient Christologies: A Study in the Christological Thought of the Schools of Alexandria and Antioch in the Early History of Christian Doctrine*. London: SPCK, 1940.

Simonetti, M., *Studi sull' Arianismo*. Rome: Editrice Studium, 1965.

Sorabji, Richard. *Emotion and Peace of Mind: From Stoic Agitation to Christian Temptation*. Oxford: Oxford University Press, 2000.

Staats, R. *Gregor von Nyssa und die Messalianer: Die Frage der Priorität zweier altkirchlicher Schriften*. PTS 8. Berlin: de Gruyter, 1968.

———. *Makarios-Symeon: Epistola Magna. Eine messalianische Mönchs-regel und ihre Umschrift in Gregors von Nyssa 'De Instituto Christiano'*. Göttingen: Vandenhoeck & Ruprecht, 1984.

Stewart, Columba. *'Working the Earth of the Heart': The Messalian Controversy in History, Texts and Language to AD 431*. Oxford: Clarendon, 1991.

Sullivan, F. A. *The Christology of Theodore of Mopsuestia*. Rome: Analecta Gregoriana, 1956.

Vaggione, Richard Paul. *Eunomius of Cyzicus and the Nicene Revolution*. OECS. Oxford: Oxford University Press, 2000.

Wallace-Hadrill, D. S. *Christian Antioch: A Study of Early Christian Thought in the East*. Cambridge: Cambridge University Press, 1982.

Weinandy, Thomas G. *Athanasius: A Theological Introduction*. Aldershot: Ashgate, 2007.

Wessel, Susan. *Cyril of Alexandria and the Nestorian Controversy: The Making of a Saint and of a Heretic*. OECS. Oxford: Oxford University Press, 2004.

Wiles, M. F. "The Nature of the Early Debate about Christ's Human Soul." *JEH* 16 (1965): 139–51.

———. *The Spiritual Gospel*. Cambridge: Cambridge University Press, 1960.

Williams, Rowan. *Arius: Heresy and Tradition*. London: Darton, Longman and Todd, 1987.

———. "De Trinitate." Pages 845–51 in *Augustine through the Ages*. Edited by Allan D. Fitzgerald, OSA. Grand Rapids: Eerdmans, 1999.

———. *The Edge of Words: God and the Habits of Language*. London: Bloomsbury, 2014.

Young, Frances M. "Adam and Anthropos: A Study of the Interaction of Science and the Bible in Two Anthropological Treatises of the Fourth Century." *VC* 37 (1983): 110–40.

———. *Biblical Exegesis and the Formation of Christian Culture*. Cambridge: Cambridge University Press, 1997.

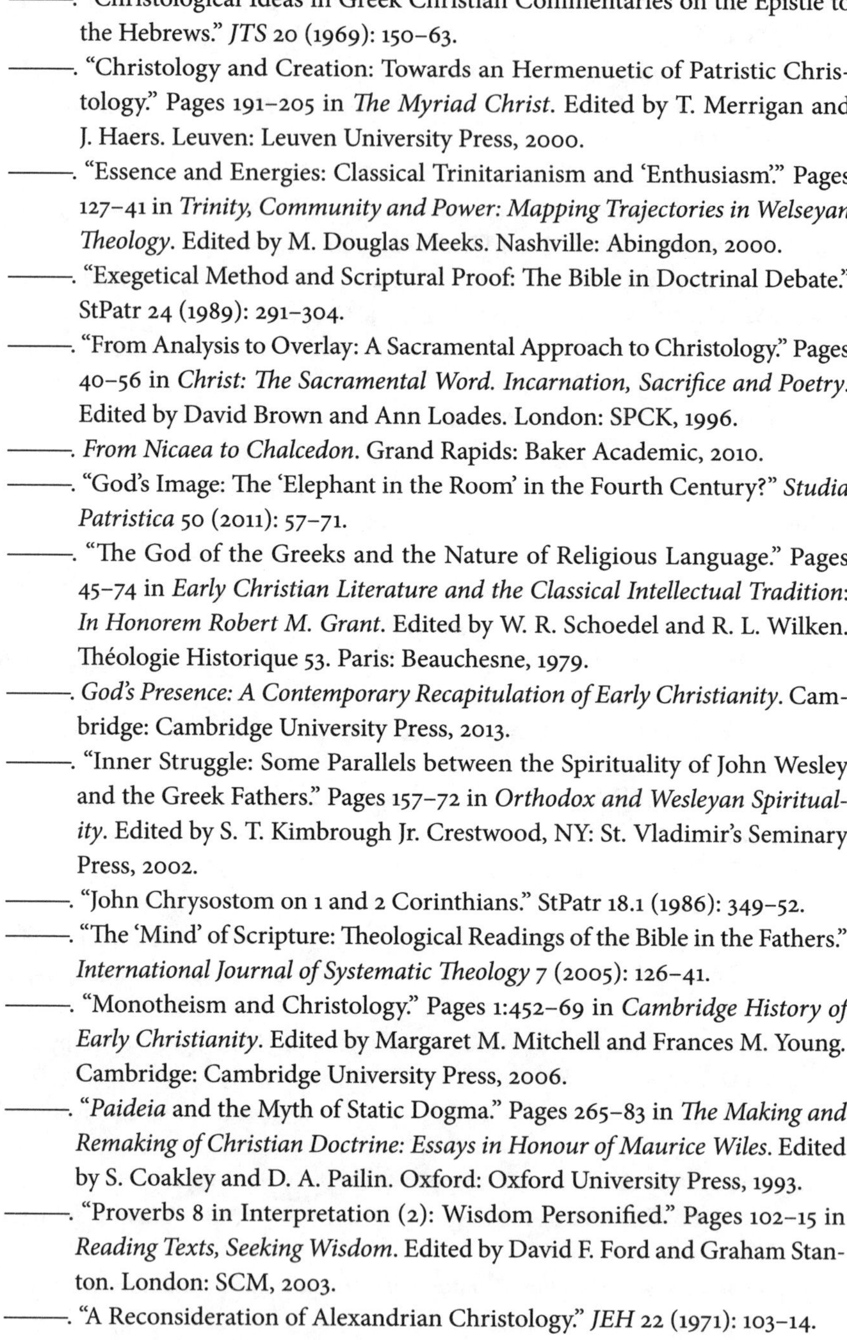

———. "Christological Ideas in Greek Christian Commentaries on the Epistle to the Hebrews." *JTS* 20 (1969): 150–63.

———. "Christology and Creation: Towards an Hermenuetic of Patristic Christology." Pages 191–205 in *The Myriad Christ*. Edited by T. Merrigan and J. Haers. Leuven: Leuven University Press, 2000.

———. "Essence and Energies: Classical Trinitarianism and 'Enthusiasm.'" Pages 127–41 in *Trinity, Community and Power: Mapping Trajectories in Welseyan Theology*. Edited by M. Douglas Meeks. Nashville: Abingdon, 2000.

———. "Exegetical Method and Scriptural Proof: The Bible in Doctrinal Debate." StPatr 24 (1989): 291–304.

———. "From Analysis to Overlay: A Sacramental Approach to Christology." Pages 40–56 in *Christ: The Sacramental Word. Incarnation, Sacrifice and Poetry*. Edited by David Brown and Ann Loades. London: SPCK, 1996.

———. *From Nicaea to Chalcedon*. Grand Rapids: Baker Academic, 2010.

———. "God's Image: The 'Elephant in the Room' in the Fourth Century?" *Studia Patristica* 50 (2011): 57–71.

———. "The God of the Greeks and the Nature of Religious Language." Pages 45–74 in *Early Christian Literature and the Classical Intellectual Tradition: In Honorem Robert M. Grant*. Edited by W. R. Schoedel and R. L. Wilken. Théologie Historique 53. Paris: Beauchesne, 1979.

———. *God's Presence: A Contemporary Recapitulation of Early Christianity*. Cambridge: Cambridge University Press, 2013.

———. "Inner Struggle: Some Parallels between the Spirituality of John Wesley and the Greek Fathers." Pages 157–72 in *Orthodox and Wesleyan Spirituality*. Edited by S. T. Kimbrough Jr. Crestwood, NY: St. Vladimir's Seminary Press, 2002.

———. "John Chrysostom on 1 and 2 Corinthians." StPatr 18.1 (1986): 349–52.

———. "The 'Mind' of Scripture: Theological Readings of the Bible in the Fathers." *International Journal of Systematic Theology* 7 (2005): 126–41.

———. "Monotheism and Christology." Pages 1:452–69 in *Cambridge History of Early Christianity*. Edited by Margaret M. Mitchell and Frances M. Young. Cambridge: Cambridge University Press, 2006.

———. "*Paideia* and the Myth of Static Dogma." Pages 265–83 in *The Making and Remaking of Christian Doctrine: Essays in Honour of Maurice Wiles*. Edited by S. Coakley and D. A. Pailin. Oxford: Oxford University Press, 1993.

———. "Proverbs 8 in Interpretation (2): Wisdom Personified." Pages 102–15 in *Reading Texts, Seeking Wisdom*. Edited by David F. Ford and Graham Stanton. London: SCM, 2003.

———. "A Reconsideration of Alexandrian Christology." *JEH* 22 (1971): 103–14.

———. "Teasing Out Meaning: Some Techniques and Procedures in Early Christian Exegesis." StPatr 100 (2020): 3–18.

———. "Theotokos: Mary and the Pattern of Fall and Redemption in the Theology of Cyril of Alexandria." Pages 55–74 in *The Theology of Cyril of Alexandria: A Critical Appreciation*. Edited by Thomas G. Weinandy and Daniel A. Keating. London: T&T Clark, 2003.

———. *Ways of Reading Scripture*. WUNT 369. Tübingen: Mohr Siebeck, 2018.

Zachhüber, J. *Human Nature in Gregory of Nyssa: Philosophical Background and Theological Significance*. Leiden: Brill, 2000.

Index of Authors

Index of Subjects

Index of Scripture and Other Ancient Sources

Old Testament